SA006770   11·99

THE OPEN SOCIETY
AND ITS ENEMIES
THE SPELL OF PLATO

Other titles by Sir Karl Popper
available from Routledge

THE POVERTY OF HISTORICISM

THE LOGIC OF SCIENTIFIC DISCOVERY

CONJECTURES AND REFUTATIONS

OBJECTIVE KNOWLEDGE

UNENDED QUEST

THE SELF AND ITS BRAIN
(*with J. C. Eccles*)

THE OPEN UNIVERSE

QUANTUM THEORY AND THE SCHISM IN PHYSICS

REALISM AND THE AIM OF SCIENCE

IN SEARCH OF A BETTER WORLD

KNOWLEDGE AND THE BODY-MIND PROBLEM

THE MYTH OF THE FRAMEWORK

THE OPEN SOCIETY AND ITS ENEMIES

by K. R. POPPER

Volume I

THE SPELL OF PLATO

London

First published 1945 by
Routledge & Kegan Paul Ltd
Reprinted 1947
Reprinted 1949
Second edition (revised) 1952
Third edition (revised) 1957
Fourth edition (revised) 1962
Published as a Routledge paperback 1962
Reprinted 1963
Fifth edition (revised) 1966
Reprinted eight times
Reprinted 1991, 1993, 1995 by Routledge
11 New Fetter Lane, London EC4P 4EE

© *Copyright 1962, 1966 by Karl Raimund Popper*

Printed in Great Britain by
T. J. Press (Padstow) Ltd,
Padstow, Cornwall

British Library Cataloguing in Publication Data

A catalogue record for this book is available from the British Library

ISBN 0-415-04031-0

180 POP

It will be seen . . . that the Erewhonians are a meek and long-suffering people, easily led by the nose, and quick to offer up common sense at the shrine of logic, when a philosopher arises among them who carries them away . . . by convincing them that their existing institutions are not based on the strictest principles of morality. SAMUEL BUTLER.

In my course I have known and, according to my measure, have co-operated with great men ; and I have never yet seen any plan which has not been mended by the observations of those who were much inferior in understanding to the person who took the lead in the business.   EDMUND BURKE.

PREFACE TO THE FIRST EDITION

If in this book harsh words are spoken about some of the greatest among the intellectual leaders of mankind, my motive is not, I hope, the wish to belittle them. It springs rather from my conviction that, if our civilization is to survive, we must break with the habit of deference to great men. Great men may make great mistakes ; and as the book tries to show, some of the greatest leaders of the past supported the perennial attack on freedom and reason. Their influence, too rarely challenged, continues to mislead those on whose defence civilization depends, and to divide them. The responsibility for this tragic and possibly fatal division becomes ours if we hesitate to be outspoken in our criticism of what admittedly is a part of our intellectual heritage. By our reluctance to criticize some of it, we may help to destroy it all.

The book is a critical introduction to the philosophy of politics and of history, and an examination of some of the principles of social reconstruction. Its aim and the line of approach are indicated in the *Introduction*. Even where it looks back into the past, its problems are the problems of our own time ; and I have tried hard to state them as simply as I could, in the hope of clarifying matters which concern us all.

Although the book presupposes nothing but open-mindedness in the reader, its object is not so much to popularize the questions treated as to solve them. In an attempt, however, to serve both of these purposes, I have confined all matters of more specialized interest to *Notes* which have been collected at the end of the book.

1943

PREFACE TO THE SECOND EDITION

Although much of what is contained in this book took shape at an earlier date, the final decision to write it was made in March 1938, on the day I received the news of the invasion of Austria. The writing extended into 1943 ; and the fact that most of the book was written during the grave years when the outcome of the war was uncertain may help to explain why some of its criticism strikes me to-day as more emotional and harsher in tone than I could wish. But it was not the time to mince words—or at least, this was what I then felt. Neither the war nor any other contemporary event was explicitly mentioned in the book ; but it was an attempt to understand those events and their background, and some of the issues which were likely to arise after the war was won. The expectation that Marxism would become a major problem was the reason for treating it at some length.

Seen in the darkness of the present world situation, the criticism of Marxism which it attempts is liable to stand out as the main point of the book. This view of it is not wholly wrong and perhaps unavoidable, although the aims of the book are much wider. Marxism is only an episode—one of the many mistakes we have made in the perennial and dangerous struggle for building a better and freer world.

Not unexpectedly, I have been blamed by some for being too severe in my treatment of Marx, while others contrasted my leniency towards him with the violence of my attack upon Plato. But I still feel the need for looking at Plato with highly critical eyes, just because the general adoration of the ' divine philosopher ' has a real foundation in his overwhelming intellectual achievement. Marx, on the other hand, has too often been attacked on personal and moral grounds, so that here the need is, rather, for a severe rational criticism of his theories combined with a sympathetic understanding of their astonishing moral and intellectual appeal. Rightly or wrongly, I felt that my criticism was devastating, and that I could therefore afford to search for Marx's real contributions, and to give his motives the benefit of the doubt. In any case, it is obvious that we must try to appreciate the strength of an opponent if we wish to fight him success-fully. (I have added in 1965 a new note on this subject as *Addendum II* to my second volume.)

No book can ever be finished. While working on it we learn just enough to find it immature the moment we turn away from it. As to my criticism of Plato and Marx, this inevitable experi-ence was not more disturbing than usual. But most of my posi-tive suggestions and, above all, the strong feeling of optimism which pervades the whole book struck me more and more as naïve, as the years after the war went by. My own voice began to sound to me as if it came from the distant past—like the voice of one of the hopeful social reformers of the eighteenth or even the seventeenth century.

But my mood of depression has passed, largely as the result of a visit to the United States ; and I am now glad that, in revising the book, I confined myself to the addition of new material and to the correction of mistakes of matter and style, and that I resisted the temptation to subdue its tenor. For in spite of the present world situation I feel as hopeful as I ever did.

I see now more clearly than ever before that even our greatest troubles spring from something that is as admirable and sound as it is dangerous—from our impatience to better the lot of our fellows. For these troubles are the by-products of what is per-haps the greatest of all moral and spiritual revolutions of history, a movement which began three centuries ago. It is the longing of uncounted unknown men to free themselves and their minds from the tutelage of authority and prejudice. It is their attempt to build up an open society which rejects the absolute authority of the merely established and the merely traditional while trying to preserve, to develop, and to establish traditions, old or new, that measure up to their standards of freedom, of humaneness, and of rational criticism. It is their unwillingness to sit back and leave the entire responsibility for ruling the world to human or superhuman authority, and their readiness to share the burden of responsibility for avoidable suffering, and to work for its avoidance. This revolution has created powers of appalling destructiveness ; but they may yet be conquered.

1950

ACKNOWLEDGEMENTS

I wish to express my gratitude to all my friends who have made it possible for me to write this book. Professor C. G. F. Simkin has not only helped me with an earlier version, but has given me the opportunity of clarifying many problems in detailed discussions over a period of nearly four years. Dr. Margaret Dalziel has assisted me in the preparation of various drafts and of the final manuscript. Her untiring help has been invaluable. Dr. H. Larsen's interest in the problem of historicism was a great encouragement. Professor T. K. Ewer has read the manuscript and has made many suggestions for its improvement.

I am deeply indebted to Professor F. A. von Hayek. Without his interest and support the book would not have been published. Professor E. Gombrich has undertaken to see the book through the press, a burden to which was added the strain of an exacting correspondence between England and New Zealand. He has been so helpful that I can hardly say how much I owe to him.

CHRISTCHURCH, N.Z., *April 1944.*

In preparing the revised edition, I have received great help from detailed critical annotations to the first edition kindly put at my disposal by Professor Jacob Viner and by Mr. J. D. Mabbott.

LONDON, *August 1951.*

In the third edition an Index of Subjects and an Index of Platonic Passages have been added, both prepared by Dr. J. Agassi. He has also drawn my attention to a number of mistakes which I have corrected. I am very grateful for his help. In six places I have tried to improve and correct quotations from Plato, or references to his text, in the light of Mr. Richard Robinson's stimulating and most welcome criticism (*The Philosophical Review*, vol. 60) of the American edition of this book.

STANFORD, CALIFORNIA, *May 1957*

Most of the improvements in the fourth edition I owe to Dr. William W. Bartley and to Mr. Bryan Magee.

PENN, BUCKINGHAMSHIRE, *May 1961*

The fifth edition contains some new historical material (especially on page 312 of volume I and in the *Addenda*) and also a brief new *Addendum* in each volume. Additional material will be found in my *Conjectures and Refutations*, especially in the second edition (1965). Mr. David Miller has discovered, and corrected, many mistakes.

PENN, BUCKINGHAMSHIRE, *July 1965*

K. R. P.

CONTENTS

VOLUME I: THE SPELL OF PLATO

THE OPEN SOCIETY AND ITS ENEMIES

INTRODUCTION

> I do not wish to hide the fact that I can only look with repugnance . . upon the puffed-up pretentiousness of all these volumes filled with wisdom, such as are fashionable nowadays. For I am fully satisfied that . . the accepted methods must endlessly increase these follies and blunders, and that even the complete annihilation of all these fanciful achievements could not possibly be as harmful as this fictitious science with its accursed fertility. KANT.

This book raises issues which may not be apparent from the table of contents.

It sketches some of the difficulties faced by our civilization—a civilization which might be perhaps described as aiming at humaneness and reasonableness, at equality and freedom ; a civilization which is still in its infancy, as it were, and which continues to grow in spite of the fact that it has been so often betrayed by so many of the intellectual leaders of mankind. It attempts to show that this civilization has not yet fully recovered from the shock of its birth—the transition from the tribal or ' closed society ', with its submission to magical forces, to the ' open society ' which sets free the critical powers of man. It attempts to show that the shock of this transition is one of the factors that have made possible the rise of those reactionary movements which have tried, and still try, to overthrow civilization and to return to tribalism. And it suggests that what we call nowadays totalitarianism belongs to a tradition which is just as old or just as young as our civilization itself.

It tries thereby to contribute to our understanding of totalitarianism, and of the significance of the perennial fight against it.

It further tries to examine the application of the critical and rational methods of science to the problems of the open society. It analyses the principles of democratic social reconstruction, the principles of what I may term ' piecemeal social engineering ' in opposition to ' Utopian social engineering ' (as explained in Chapter 9). And it tries to clear away some of the obstacles impeding a rational approach to the problems of social reconstruction.   It does so by criticizing those social philosophies which are responsible for the widespread prejudice against the possibilities of democratic reform.   The most powerful of these philosophies is one which I have called *historicism*.   The story of the rise and influence of some important forms of historicism is one of the main topics of the book, which might even be described as a collection of marginal notes on the development of certain historicist philosophies.   A few remarks on the origin of the book will indicate what is meant by historicism and how it is connected with the other issues mentioned.

Although I am mainly interested in the methods of physics (and consequently in certain technical problems which are far removed from those treated in this book), I have also been interested for many years in the problem of the somewhat unsatisfactory state of some of the social sciences and especially of social philosophy.   This, of course, raises the problem of their methods.   My interest in this problem was greatly stimulated by the rise of totalitarianism, and by the failure of the various social sciences and social philosophies to make sense of it.

In this connection, one point appeared to me particularly urgent.

One hears too often the suggestion that some form or other of totalitarianism is inevitable.   Many who because of their intelligence and training should be held responsible for what they say, announce that there is no escape from it.   They ask us whether we are really naïve enough to believe that democracy can be permanent ; whether we do not see that it is just one of the many forms of government that come and go in the course of history.   They argue that democracy, in order to fight totalitarianism, is forced to copy its methods and thus to become totalitarian itself.   Or they assert that our industrial system cannot continue to function without adopting the methods of collectivist planning, and they infer from the inevitability of a collectivist economic system that the adoption of totalitarian forms of social life is also inevitable.

Such arguments may sound plausible enough.   But plausibility is not a reliable guide in such matters.   In fact, one should not enter into a discussion of these specious arguments before having considered the following question of method : Is it within the power of any social science to make such sweeping historical prophecies ?   Can we expect to get more than the irresponsible reply of the soothsayer if we ask a man what the future has in store for mankind ?

This is a question of the method of the social sciences. It is clearly more fundamental than any criticism of any particular argument offered in support of any historical prophecy.

A careful examination of this question has led me to the conviction that such sweeping historical prophecies are entirely beyond the scope of scientific method. The future depends on ourselves, and we do not depend on any historical necessity. There are, however, influential social philosophies which hold the opposite view. They claim that everybody tries to use his brains to predict impending events ; that it is certainly legitimate for a strategist to try to foresee the outcome of a battle ; and that the boundaries between such a prediction and more sweeping historical prophecies are fluid. They assert that it is the task of science in general to make predictions, or rather, to improve upon our everyday predictions, and to put them upon a more secure basis ; and that it is, in particular, the task of the social sciences to furnish us with long-term historical prophecies. They also believe that they have discovered laws of history which enable them to prophesy the course of historical events. The various social philosophies which raise claims of this kind, I have grouped together under the name *historicism*. Elsewhere, in *The Poverty of Historicism*, I have tried to argue against these claims, and to show that in spite of their plausibility they are based on a gross misunderstanding of the method of science, and especially on the neglect of the distinction between *scientific prediction* and *historical prophecy*. While engaged in the systematic analysis and criticism of the claims of historicism, I also tried to collect some material to illustrate its development. The notes collected for that purpose became the basis of this book.

The systematic analysis of historicism aims at something like scientific status. This book does not. Many of the opinions expressed are personal. What it owes to scientific method is largely the awareness of its limitations : it does not offer proofs where nothing can be proved, nor does it pretend to be scientific where it cannot give more than a personal point of view. It does not try to replace the old systems of philosophy by a new system. It does not try to add to all these volumes filled with wisdom, to the metaphysics of history and destiny, such as are fashionable nowadays. It rather tries to show that this prophetic wisdom is harmful, that the metaphysics of history impede the application of the piecemeal methods of science to the problems of social reform. And it further tries to show that we may become the makers of our fate when we have ceased to pose as its prophets.

In tracing the development of historicism, I found that the dangerous habit of historical prophecy, so widespread among our intellectual leaders, has various functions. It is always flattering to belong to the inner circle of the initiated, and to possess the unusual power of predicting the course of history. Besides, there is a tradition that intellectual leaders are gifted with such powers, and not to possess them may lead to loss of caste. The danger, on the other hand, of their being unmasked as charlatans is very small, since they can always point out that it is certainly permissible to make less sweeping predictions ; and the boundaries between these and augury are fluid.

But there are sometimes further and perhaps deeper motives for holding historicist beliefs. The prophets who prophesy the coming of a millennium may give expression to a deep-seated feeling of dissatisfaction ; and their dreams may indeed give hope and encouragement to some who can hardly do without them. But we must also realize that their influence is liable to prevent us from facing the daily tasks of social life. And those minor prophets who announce that certain events, such as a lapse into totalitarianism (or perhaps into ' managerialism '), are bound to happen may, whether they like it or not, be instrumental in bringing these events about. Their story that democracy is not to last for ever is as true, and as little to the point, as the assertion that human reason is not to last for ever, since only democracy provides an institutional framework that permits reform without violence, and so the use of reason in political matters. But their story tends to discourage those who fight totalitarianism ; its motive is to support the revolt against civilization. A further motive, it seems, can be found if we consider that historicist metaphysics are apt to relieve men from the strain of their responsibilities. If you know that things are bound to happen whatever you do, then you may feel free to give up the fight against them. You may, more especially, give up the attempt to control those things which most people agree to be social evils, such as war ; or, to mention a smaller but nevertheless important thing, the tyranny of the petty official.

I do not wish to suggest that historicism must always have such effects. There are historicists—especially the Marxists— who do not wish to relieve men from the strain of their responsibilities. On the other hand, there are some social philosophies which may or may not be historicistic but which preach the impotence of reason in social life, and which, by this anti-rationalism, propagate the attitude : ' either follow the Leader, the Great Statesman, or become a Leader yourself ' ; an attitude which for most people must mean passive submission to the forces, personal or anonymous, that rule society.

Now it is interesting to see that some of those who denounce reason, and even blame it for the social evils of our time, do so on the one hand because they realize the fact that historical prophecy goes beyond the power of reason, and on the other hand because they cannot conceive of a social science, or of reason in society, having another function but that of historical prophecy. In other words, they are disappointed historicists ; they are men who, in spite of realizing the poverty of historicism, are unaware that they retain the fundamental historicistic preju-dice—the doctrine that the social sciences, if they are to be of any use at all, must be prophetic. It is clear that this attitude must lead to a rejection of the applicability of science or of reason to the problems of social life—and ultimately, to a doctrine of power, of domination and submission.

Why do all these social philosophies support the revolt against civilization ? And what is the secret of their popularity ? Why do they attract and seduce so many intellectuals ? I am inclined to think that the reason is that they give expression to a deep-felt dissatisfaction with a world which does not, and cannot, live up to our moral ideals and to our dreams of perfection. The tendency of historicism (and of related views) to support the revolt against civilization may be due to the fact that historicism itself is, largely, a reaction against the strain of our civilization and its demand for personal responsibility.

These last allusions are somewhat vague, but they must suffice for this introduction. They will later be substantiated by histori-cal material, especially in the chapter ' The Open Society and Its Enemies '. I was tempted to place this chapter at the beginning of the book ; with its topical interest it would certainly have made a more inviting introduction. But I found that the full weight of this historical interpretation cannot be felt unless it is preceded by the material discussed earlier in the book. It seems that one has first to be disturbed by the similarity between the Platonic theory of justice and the theory and practice of modern totalitarianism before one can feel how urgent it is to interpret these matters.

VOL. I

THE SPELL OF PLATO

For the Open Society (about 430 B.C.) :
Although only a few may originate a policy, we are all able to judge it.

PERICLES OF ATHENS.

Against the Open Society (about 80 years later) :
The greatest principle of all is that nobody, whether male or female, should be without a leader. Nor should the mind of anybody be habituated to letting him do anything at all on his own initiative; neither out of zeal, nor even playfully. But in war and in the midst of peace—to his leader he shall direct his eye and follow him faithfully. And even in the smallest matter he should stand under leadership. For example, he should get up, or move, or wash, or take his meals . . only if he has been told to do so. In a word, he should teach his soul, by long habit, never to dream of acting independently, and to become utterly incapable of it.

PLATO OF ATHENS.

THE MYTH OF ORIGIN AND DESTINY

CHAPTER 1 : HISTORICISM AND THE MYTH OF DESTINY

It is widely believed that a truly scientific or philosophical attitude towards politics, and a deeper understanding of social life in general, must be based upon a contemplation and interpretation of human history. While the ordinary man takes the setting of his life and the importance of his personal experiences and petty struggles for granted, it is said that the social scientist or philosopher has to survey things from a higher plane. He sees the individual as a pawn, as a somewhat insignificant instrument in the general development of mankind. And he finds that the really important actors on the Stage of History are either the Great Nations and their Great Leaders, or perhaps the Great Classes, or the Great Ideas. However this may be, he will try to understand the meaning of the play which is performed on the Historical Stage ; he will try to understand the laws of historical development. If he succeeds in this, he will, of course, be able to predict future developments. He might then put politics upon a solid basis, and give us practical advice by telling us which political actions are likely to succeed or likely to fail.

This is a brief description of an attitude which I call *historicism*. It is an old idea, or rather, a loosely connected set of ideas which have become, unfortunately, so much a part of our spiritual atmosphere that they are usually taken for granted, and hardly ever questioned.

I have tried elsewhere to show that the historicist approach to the social sciences gives poor results. I have also tried to outline a method which, I believe, would yield better results.

But if historicism is a faulty method that produces worthless results, then it may be useful to see how it originated, and how it succeeded in entrenching itself so successfully. An historical sketch undertaken with this aim can, at the same time, serve to analyse the variety of ideas which have gradually accumulated around the central historicist doctrine—the doctrine that history is controlled by specific historical or evolutionary laws whose discovery would enable us to prophesy the destiny of man.

Historicism, which I have so far characterized only in a rather abstract way, can be well illustrated by one of the simplest and oldest of its forms, the doctrine of the chosen people. This doctrine is one of the attempts to make history understandable by a theistic interpretation, i.e. by recognizing God as the author of the play performed on the Historical Stage. The theory of the chosen people, more specifically, assumes that God has chosen one people to function as the selected instrument of His will, and that this people will inherit the earth.

In this doctrine, the law of historical development is laid down by the Will of God. This is the specific difference which distinguishes the theistic form from other forms of historicism. A naturalistic historicism, for instance, might treat the developmental law as a law of nature ; a spiritual historicism would treat it as a law of spiritual development ; an economic historicism, again, as a law of economic development. Theistic historicism shares with these other forms the doctrine that there are specific historical laws which can be discovered, and upon which pre-dictions regarding the future of mankind can be based.

There is no doubt that the doctrine of the chosen people grew out of the tribal form of social life. Tribalism, i.e. the emphasis on the supreme importance of the tribe without which the individual is nothing at all, is an element which we shall find in many forms of historicist theories. Other forms which are no longer tribalist may still retain an element of *collectivism* [1] ; they may still emphasize the significance of some group or col-lective—for example, a class—without which the individual is nothing at all. Another aspect of the doctrine of the chosen people is the remoteness of what it proffers as the end of history. For although it may describe this end with some degree of definiteness, we have to go a long way before we reach it. And the way is not only long, but winding, leading up and down, right and left. Accordingly, it will be possible to bring every conceivable historical event well within the scheme of the inter-pretation. No conceivable experience can refute it.[2] But to those who believe in it, it gives *certainty* regarding the ultimate outcome of human history.

A criticism of the theistic interpretation of history will be attempted in the last chapter of this book, where it will also be shown that some of the greatest Christian thinkers have repudiated this theory as idolatry. An attack upon this form of historicism should therefore not be interpreted as an attack upon religion. In the present chapter, the doctrine of the chosen people serves only as an illustration. Its value as such can be seen from the fact that its chief characteristics [3] are shared by the two most important modern versions of historicism, whose analysis will form the major part of this book—the historical philosophy of racialism or fascism on the one (the right) hand and the Marxian historical philosophy on the other (the left). For the chosen people racialism substitutes the chosen race (of Gobineau's choice), selected as the instrument of destiny, ultimately to inherit the earth. Marx's historical philosophy substitutes for it the chosen class, the instrument for the creation of the classless society, and at the same time, the class destined to inherit the earth. Both theories base their historical forecasts on an interpretation of history which leads to the discovery of a law of its development. In the case of racialism, this is thought of as a kind of natural law ; the biological superiority of the blood of the chosen race explains the course of history, past, present, and future ; it is nothing but the struggle of races for mastery. In the case of Marx's philosophy of history, the law is economic ; all history has to be interpreted as a struggle of classes for economic supremacy.

The historicist character of these two movements makes our investigation topical. We shall return to them in later parts of this book. Each of them goes back directly to the philosophy of Hegel. We must, therefore, deal with that philosophy as well. And since Hegel [4] in the main follows certain ancient philosophers, it will be necessary to discuss the theories of Heraclitus, Plato and Aristotle, before returning to the more modern forms of historicism.

CHAPTER 2 : HERACLITUS

It is not until Heraclitus that we find in Greece theories which could be compared in their historicist character with the doctrine of the chosen people. In Homer's theistic or rather polytheistic interpretation, history is the product of divine will. But the Homeric gods do not lay down general laws for its development. What Homer tries to stress and to explain is not the unity of history, but rather its lack of unity. The author of the play on the Stage of History is not one God ; a whole variety of gods dabble in it. What the Homeric interpretation shares with the Jewish is a certain vague feeling of destiny, and the idea of powers behind the scenes. But ultimate destiny, according to Homer, is not disclosed ; unlike its Jewish counterpart, it remains mysterious.

The first Greek to introduce a more markedly historicist doctrine was Hesiod, who was probably influenced by oriental sources. He made use of the idea of a general trend or tendency in historical development. His interpretation of history is pessimistic. He believes that mankind, in their development down from the Golden Age, are destined to *degenerate*, both physically and morally. The culmination of the various historicist ideas proffered by the early Greek philosophers came with Plato, who, in an attempt to interpret the history and social life of the Greek tribes, and especially of the Athenians, painted a grandiose philosophical picture of the world. He was strongly influenced in his historicism by various forerunners, especially by Hesiod ; but the most important influence came from Heraclitus.

Heraclitus was the philosopher who discovered the idea of *change*. Down to this time, the Greek philosophers, influenced by oriental ideas, had viewed the world as a huge edifice of which the material things were the building material.[1] It was the totality of things—the *cosmos* (which originally seems to have been an oriental tent or mantle). The questions which the philosophers asked themselves were, ' What stuff is the world made of ? ' or ' How is it constructed, what is its true ground-plan ? '. They considered philosophy, or physics (the two were indistinguishable for a long time), as the investigation of ' nature ', i.e. of the original material out of which this edifice, the world, had been built. As far as any *processes* were considered, they were thought of either as going on within the edifice, or else as constructing or maintaining it, disturbing and restoring the stability or balance of a structure which was considered to be fundamentally static. They were cyclic processes (apart from the processes connected with the origin of the edifice ; the question ' Who has made it ? ' was discussed by the orientals, by Hesiod, and by others). This very natural approach, natural even to many of us to-day, was superseded by the genius of Heraclitus. The view he introduced was that there was no such edifice, no stable structure, no cosmos. ' The cosmos, at best, is like a rubbish heap scattered at random ', is one of his sayings.[2] He visualized the world not as an edifice, but rather as one colossal process ; not as the sum-total of all *things*, but rather as the totality of all events, or changes, or *facts*. ' Everything is in flux and nothing is at rest ', is the motto of his philosophy.

Heraclitus' discovery influenced the development of Greek philosophy for a long time. The philosophies of Parmenides, Democritus, Plato, and Aristotle can all be appropriately described as attempts to solve the problems of that changing world which Heraclitus had discovered. The greatness of this discovery can hardly be overrated. It has been described as a terrifying one, and its effect has been compared with that of ' an earthquake, in which everything . . seems to sway '[3]. And I do not doubt that this discovery was impressed upon Heraclitus by terrifying personal experiences suffered as a result of the social and political disturbances of his day. Heraclitus, the first philosopher to deal not only with ' nature ' but even more with ethico-political problems, lived in an age of social revolution. It was in his time that the Greek tribal aristocracies were beginning to yield to the new force of democracy.

In order to understand the effect of this revolution, we must remember the stability and rigidity of social life in a tribal aristocracy. Social life is determined by social and religious taboos ; everybody has his assigned place within the whole of the social structure ; everyone feels that his place is the proper, the ' natural ' place, assigned to him by the forces which rule the world ; everyone ' knows his place '.

According to tradition, Heraclitus' own place was that of heir to the royal family of priest kings of Ephesus, but he resigned his claims in favour of his brother. In spite of his proud refusal to take part in the political life of his city, he supported the cause of the aristocrats who tried in vain to stem the rising tide of the new revolutionary forces. These experiences in the social or political field are reflected in the remaining fragments of his work.[4] ' The Ephesians ought to hang themselves man by man, all the adults, and leave the city to be ruled by infants . . .', is one of his outbursts, occasioned by the people's decision to banish Hermodorus, one of Heraclitus's aristocratic friends.   His interpretation of the people's motives is most interesting, for it shows that the stock-in-trade of anti-democratic argument has not changed much since the earliest days of democracy.   ' They said : nobody shall be the best among us ; and if someone is outstanding, then let him be so elsewhere, and among others.'   This hostility towards democracy breaks through everywhere in the fragments : '. . the mob fill their bellies like the beasts. . . They take the bards and popular belief as their guides, unaware that the many are bad and that only the few are good. . .   In Priene lived Bias, son of Teutames, whose word counts more than that of other men. (He said : ' Most men are wicked.') . . The mob does not care, not even about the things they stumble upon ; nor can they grasp a lesson—though they think they do.' In the same vein he says : ' The law can demand, too, that the will of One Man must be obeyed.'   Another expression of Heraclitus' conservative and anti-democratic outlook is, incidentally, quite acceptable to democrats in its wording, though probably not in its intention : ' A people ought to fight for the laws of the city as if they were its walls.'

But Heraclitus' fight for the ancient laws of his city was in vain, and the transitoriness of all things impressed itself strongly upon him.   His theory of change gives expression to this feeling [5] : ' Everything is in flux ', he said ; and ' You cannot step twice into the same river.'   Disillusioned, he argued against the belief that the existing social order would remain for ever : 'We must not act like children reared with the narrow outlook " As it has been handed down to us ".'

This emphasis on change, and especially on change in social life, is an important characteristic not only of Heraclitus' philosophy but of historicism in general.   That things, and even kings, change, is a truth which needs to be impressed especially upon those who take their social environment for granted.   So much is to be admitted.   But in the Heraclitean philosophy one of the less commendable characteristics of historicism manifests itself, namely, an over-emphasis upon change, combined with the complementary belief in an inexorable and immutable *law of destiny*.

In this belief we are confronted with an attitude which, although at first sight contradictory to the historicist's over-emphasis upon change, is characteristic of most, if not all, historicists. We can explain this attitude, perhaps, if we interpret the historicist's over-emphasis on change as a symptom of an effort needed to overcome his unconscious resistance to the idea of change. This would also explain the emotional tension which leads so many historicists (even in our day) to stress the novelty of the unheard-of revelation which they have to make. Such considerations suggest the possibility that these historicists are afraid of change, and that they cannot accept the idea of change without serious inward struggle. It often seems as if they were trying to comfort themselves for the loss of a stable world by clinging to the view that change is ruled by an unchanging law. (In Parmenides and in Plato, we shall even find the theory that the changing world in which we live is an illusion and that there exists a more real world which does not change.)

In the case of Heraclitus, the emphasis upon change leads him to the theory that all material things, whether solid, liquid, or gaseous, are like flames—that they are processes rather than things, and that they are all transformations of fire ; the apparently solid earth (which consists of ashes) is only a fire in a state of transformation, and even liquids (water, the sea) are transformed fire (and may become fuel, perhaps in the form of oil). ' The first transformation of fire is the sea ; but of the sea, half is earth, and half hot air.' [6] Thus all the other ' elements '—earth, water, and air—are transformed fire : ' Everything is an exchange for fire, and fire for everything ; just as gold for wares, and wares for gold.'

But having reduced all things to flames, to processes, like combustion, Heraclitus discerns in the processes a law, a measure, a reason, a wisdom ; and having destroyed the cosmos as an edifice, and declared it to be a rubbish heap, he re-introduces it as the destined order of events in the world-process.

Every process in the world, and especially fire itself, develops according to a definite law, its ' measure '[7]. It is an inexorable and irresistible law, and to this extent it resembles our modern conception of natural law as well as the conception of historical or evolutionary laws of modern historicists. But it differs from these conceptions in so far as it is the decree of reason, enforced by punishment, just as is the law imposed by the state. This failure to distinguish between legal laws or norms on the one hand and natural laws or regularities on the other is characteristic of tribal tabooism : both kinds of law alike are treated as magical, which makes a rational criticism of the man-made taboos as inconceivable as an attempt to improve upon the ultimate wisdom and reason of the laws or regularities of the natural world : ' All events proceed with the necessity of fate. . . The sun will not outstep the measure of his path ; or else the goddesses of Fate, the handmaids of Justice, will know how to find him.' But the sun does not only obey the law ; the Fire, in the shape of the sun and (as we shall see) of Zeus' thunderbolt, watches over the law, and gives judgement according to it. ' The sun is the keeper and guardian of the periods, limiting and judging and heralding and manifesting the changes and seasons which bring forth all things. . . This cosmic order which is the same for all things has not been created, neither by gods nor by men ; it always was, and is, and will be, an ever living Fire, flaring up according to measure, and dying down according to measure. . . In its advance, the Fire will seize, judge, and execute, everything.'

Combined with the historicist idea of a relentless destiny we frequently find an element of mysticism. A critical analysis of mysticism will be given in chapter 24. Here I wish only to show the rôle of anti-rationalism and mysticism in Heraclitus' philosophy [8] : ' Nature loves to hide ', he writes, and ' The Lord whose oracle is at Delphi neither reveals nor conceals, but he indicates his meaning through hints.' Heraclitus' contempt of the more empirically minded scientists is typical of those who adopt this attitude : ' Who knows many things need not have many brains ; for otherwise Hesiod and Pythagoras would have had more, and also Xenophanes. . . Pythagoras is the grandfather of all impostors.' Along with this scorn of scientists goes the mystical theory of an intuitive understanding. Heraclitus' theory of reason takes as its starting point the fact that, if we are awake, we live in a common world. We can communicate, control, and check one another ; and herein lies the assurance that we are not victims of illusion. But this theory is given a second, a symbolic, a mystical meaning. It is the theory of a mystical intuition which is given to the chosen, to those who are awake, who have the power to see, hear, and speak : ' One must not act and talk as if asleep. . . Those who are awake have One common world ; those who are asleep, turn to their private worlds. . . They are incapable both of listening and of talking. . . Even if they do hear they are like the deaf. The saying

applies to them : They are present yet they are not present. . .
One thing alone is wisdom : to understand the thought which
steers everything through everything.' The world whose experience is common to those who are awake is the mystical unity,
the oneness of all things which can be apprehended only by
reason : ' One must follow what is common to all. . . Reason
is common to all. . . All becomes One and One becomes All. . .
The One which alone is wisdom wishes and does not wish to be
called by the name of Zeus. . . It is the thunderbolt which
steers all things.'

So much for the more general features of the Heraclitean
philosophy of universal change and hidden destiny. From this
philosophy springs a theory of the driving force behind all change ;
a theory which exhibits its historicist character by its emphasis
upon the importance of ' social dynamics ' as opposed to ' social
statics '. Heraclitus' dynamics of nature in general and especially
of social life confirms the view that his philosophy was inspired
by the social and political disturbances he had experienced. For
he declares that strife or war is the dynamic as well as the creative
principle of all change, and especially of all differences between
men. And being a typical historicist, he accepts the judgement
of history as a moral one [9] ; for he holds that the outcome of war
is always just [10] : ' War is the father and the king of all things.
It proves some to be gods and others to be mere men, turning
these into slaves and the former into masters. . . One must
know that war is universal, and that justice—the lawsuit—is
strife, and that all things develop through strife and by necessity.'

But if justice is strife or war ; if ' the goddesses of Fate ' are
at the same time ' the handmaids of Justice ' ; if history, or more
precisely, if success, i.e. success in war, is the criterion of merit,
then the standard of merit must itself be ' in flux '. Heraclitus
meets this problem by his relativism, and by his doctrine of the
identity of opposites. This springs from his theory of change
(which remains the basis of Plato's and even more of Aristotle's
theory). A changing thing must give up some property and
acquire the opposite property. It is not so much a thing as a
process of transition from one state to an opposite state, and
thereby a unification of the opposite states [11] : ' Cold things
become warm and warm things become cold ; what is moist
becomes dry and what is dry becomes moist. . . Disease enables
us to appreciate health. . . Life and death, being awake and
being asleep, youth and old age, all this is identical ; for the one

turns into the other and the other turns into the one. . . What struggles with itself becomes committed to itself: there is a link or harmony due to recoil and tension, as in the bow or the lyre . . . The opposites belong to each other, the best harmony results from discord, and everything develops by strife. . . The path that leads up and the path that leads down are identical. . . The straight path and the crooked path are one and the same. . . For gods, all things are beautiful and good and just ; men, however, have adopted some things as just, others as unjust. . . The good and the bad are identical.'

But the relativism of values (it might even be described as an ethical relativism) expressed in the last fragment does not prevent Heraclitus from developing upon the background of his theory of the justice of war and the verdict of history a tribalist and romantic ethic of Fame, Fate, and the superiority of the Great Man, all strangely similar to some very modern ideas [12] : ' Who falls fighting will be glorified by gods and by men. . . The greater the fall the more glorious the fate. . . The best seek one thing above all others : eternal fame. . . One man is worth more than ten thousand, if he is Great.'

It is surprising to find in these early fragments, dating from about 500 B.C., so much that is characteristic of modern historicist and anti-democratic tendencies. But apart from the fact that Heraclitus was a thinker of unsurpassed power and originality, and that, in consequence, many of his ideas have (through the medium of Plato) become part of the main body of philosophic tradition, the similarity of doctrine can perhaps be explained, to some extent, by the similarity of social conditions in the relevant periods. It seems as if historicist ideas easily become prominent in times of great social change. They appeared when Greek tribal life broke up, as well as when that of the Jews was shattered by the impact of the Babylonian conquest [13]. There can be little doubt, I believe, that Heraclitus' philosophy is an expression of a feeling of drift ; a feeling which seems to be a typical reaction to the dissolution of the ancient tribal forms of social life. In modern Europe, historicist ideas were revived during the industrial revolution, and especially through the impact of the political revolutions in America and France [14]. It appears to be more than a mere coincidence that Hegel, who adopted so much of Heraclitus' thought and passed it on to all modern historicist movements, was a mouthpiece of the reaction against the French Revolution.

Chapter 3 : PLATO'S THEORY OF FORMS OR IDEAS

I

Plato lived in a period of wars and of political strife which was, for all we know, even more unsettled than that which had troubled Heraclitus. While he grew up, the breakdown of the tribal life of the Greeks had led in Athens, his native city, to a period of tyranny, and later to the establishment of a democracy which tried jealously to guard itself against any attempts to reintroduce either a tyranny or an oligarchy, i.e. a rule of the leading aristocratic families [1]. During his youth, democratic Athens was involved in a deadly war against Sparta, the leading city-state of the Peloponnese, which had preserved many of the laws and customs of the ancient tribal aristocracy. The Peloponnesian war lasted, with an interruption, for twenty-eight years. (In chapter 10, where the historical background is reviewed in more detail, it will be shown that the war did not end with the fall of Athens in 404 B.C., as is sometimes asserted [2].) Plato was born during the war, and he was about twenty-four when it ended. It brought terrible epidemics, and, in its last year, famine, the fall of the city of Athens, civil war, and a rule of terror, usually called the rule of the Thirty Tyrants ; these were led by two of Plato's uncles, who both lost their lives in the unsuccessful attempt to uphold their régime against the democrats. The re-establishment of the democracy and of peace meant no respite for Plato. His beloved teacher Socrates, whom he later made the main speaker of most of his dialogues, was tried and executed. Plato himself seems to have been in danger ; together with other companions of Socrates he left Athens.

Later, on the occasion of his first visit to Sicily, Plato became entangled in the political intrigues which were spun at the court of the older Dionysius, tyrant of Syracuse, and even after his return to Athens and the foundation of the Academy, Plato continued, along with some of his pupils, to take an active and ultimately fateful part in the conspiracies and revolutions [3] that constituted Syracusan politics.

This brief outline of political events may help to explain why we find in the work of Plato, as in that of Heraclitus, indications that he suffered desperately under the political instability and

insecurity of his time.   Like Heraclitus, Plato was of royal blood ;
at least, the tradition claims that his father's family traced its
descent from Codrus, the last of the tribal kings of Attica [4].
Plato was very proud of his mother's family which, as he explains
in his dialogues (in the *Charmides* and the *Timaeus*), was related
to that of Solon, the lawgiver of Athens.   His uncles, Critias and
Charmides, the leading men of the Thirty Tyrants, also belonged
to his mother's family.   With such a family tradition, Plato could
be expected to take a deep interest in public affairs ; and indeed,
most of his works fulfil this expectation.   He himself relates
(if the *Seventh Letter* is genuine) that he was [5] ' from the beginning
most anxious for political activity ', but that he was deterred by
the stirring experiences of his youth.   ' Seeing that everything
swayed and shifted aimlessly, I felt giddy and desperate.'   From
the feeling that society, and indeed ' everything ', was in flux,
arose, I believe, the fundamental impulse of his philosophy as
well as of the philosophy of Heraclitus ; and Plato summed up
his social experience, exactly as his historicist predecessor had
done, by proffering a law of historical development.   According
to this law, which will be more fully discussed in the next chapter,
all social change is corruption or decay or degeneration.

This fundamental historical law forms, in Plato's view, part
of a cosmic law—of a law which holds for all created or generated
things.   All things in flux, all generated things, are destined to
decay.   Plato, like Heraclitus, felt that the forces which are at
work in history are cosmic forces.

It is nearly certain, however, that Plato believed that this law
of degeneration was not the whole story.   We have found, in
Heraclitus, a tendency to visualize the laws of development as
cyclic laws ; they are conceived after the law which determines
the cyclic succession of the seasons.   Similarly we 'can find, in
some of Plato's works, the suggestion of a Great Year (its length
appears to be 36,000 ordinary years), with a period of improvement or generation, presumably corresponding to Spring and
Summer, and one of degeneration and decay, corresponding to
Autumn and Winter.   According to one of Plato's dialogues (the
Statesman), a Golden Age, the age of Cronos—an age in which
Cronos himself rules the world, and in which men spring from
the earth—is followed by our own age, the age of Zeus, an age
in which the world is abandoned by the gods and left to its own
resources, and which consequently is one of increasing corruption.   And in the story of the *Statesman* there is also a suggestion

that, after the lowest point of complete corruption has been reached, the god will again take the helm of the cosmic ship, and things will start to improve.

It is not certain how far Plato believed in the story of the *Statesman*. He made it quite clear that he did not believe that all of it was literally true. On the other hand, there can be little doubt that he visualized human history in a cosmic setting ; that he believed his own age to be one of deep depravity—possibly of the deepest that can be reached—and the whole preceding historical period to be governed by an inherent tendency toward decay, a tendency shared by both the historical and the cosmic development.[6] Whether or not he also believed that this tendency must *necessarily* come to an end once the point of extreme depravity has been reached seems to me uncertain. But he certainly believed that it is *possible* for us, by a human, or rather by a superhuman effort, to break through the fatal historical trend, and to put an end to the process of decay.

II

Great as the similarities are between Plato and Heraclitus, we have struck here an important difference. Plato believed that the law of historical destiny, the law of decay, can be broken by the moral will of man, supported by the power of human reason.

It is not quite clear how Plato reconciled this view with his belief in a law of destiny. But there are some indications which may explain the matter.

Plato believed that the law of degeneration involved moral degeneration. Political degeneration at any rate depends in his view mainly upon moral degeneration (and lack of knowledge) ; and moral degeneration, in its turn, is due mainly to racial degeneration. This is the way in which the general cosmic law of decay manifests itself in the field of human affairs.

It is therefore understandable that the great cosmic turning-point may coincide with a turning-point in the field of human affairs—the moral and intellectual field—and that it may, therefore, appear to us to be brought about by a moral and intellectual human effort. Plato may well have believed that, just as the general law of decay did manifest itself in moral decay leading to political decay, so the advent of the cosmic turning-point would manifest itself in the coming of a great law-giver whose powers of reasoning and whose moral will are capable of bringing this period of political decay to a close. It seems likely that the prophecy, in the *Statesman*, of the return of the Golden Age, of a new millennium, is the expression of such a belief in the form of a myth.   However this may be, he certainly believed in both —in a general historical tendency towards corruption, and in the possibility that we may stop further corruption in the political field by *arresting all political change*.   This, accordingly, is the aim he strives for.[7]   He tries to realize it by the establishment of a state which is free from the evils of all other states because it does not degenerate, because it does not change.   The state which is free from the evil of change and corruption is the best, the perfect state.   It is the state of the Golden Age which knew no change. It is the *arrested state*.

III

In believing in such an ideal state which does not change, Plato deviates radically from the tenets of historicism which we found in Heraclitus.   But important as this difference is, it gives rise to further points of similarity between Plato and Heraclitus.

Heraclitus, despite the boldness of his reasoning, seems to have shrunk from the idea of replacing the cosmos by chaos. He seems to have comforted himself, we said, for the loss of a stable world by clinging to the view that change is ruled by an unchanging law.   This tendency to shrink back from the last consequences of historicism is characteristic of many historicists.

In Plato, this tendency becomes paramount.   (He was here under the influence of the philosophy of Parmenides, the great critic of Heraclitus.)   Heraclitus had generalized his experience of social flux by extending it to the world of 'all things', and Plato, I have hinted, did the same.   But Plato also extended his belief in a perfect state that does not change to the realm of 'all things'.   He believed that to every kind of ordinary or decaying thing there corresponds also a perfect thing that does not decay. This belief in perfect and unchanging things, usually called the *Theory of Forms or Ideas* [8], became the central doctrine of his philosophy.

Plato's belief that it is possible for us to break the iron law of destiny, and to avoid decay by arresting all change, shows that his historicist tendencies had definite limitations.   An uncompromising and fully developed historicism would hesitate to admit that man, by any effort, can alter the laws of historical destiny even after he has discovered them.   It would hold that he cannot work against them, since all his plans and actions are means by which the inexorable laws of development realize his historical destiny ; just as Oedipus met his fate *because* of the prophecy, and the measures taken by his father for avoiding it, and not in spite of them.   In order to gain a better understanding of this out-and-out historicist attitude, and to analyse the opposite tendency inherent in Plato's belief that he could influence fate, I shall contrast historicism, as we find it in Plato, with a diametrically opposite approach, also to be found in Plato, which may be called the *attitude of social engineering* [9].

IV

The social engineer does not ask any questions about historical tendencies or the destiny of man.   He believes that man is the master of his own destiny and that, in accordance with our aims, we can influence or change the history of man just as we have changed the face of the earth.   He does not believe that these ends are imposed upon us by our historical background or by the trends of history, but rather that they are chosen, or even created, by ourselves, just as we create new thoughts or new works of art or new houses or new machinery.   As opposed to the historicist who believes that intelligent political action is possible only if the future course of history is first determined, the social engineer believes that a scientific basis of politics would be a very different thing ; it would consist of the factual information necessary for the construction or alteration of social institutions, in accordance with our wishes and aims.   Such a science would have to tell us what steps we must take if we wish, for instance, to avoid depressions, or else to produce depressions ; or if we wish to make the distribution of wealth more even, or less even.   In other words, the social engineer conceives as the scientific basis of politics something like a *social technology* (Plato, as we shall see, compares it with the scientific background of medicine), as opposed to the historicist who understands it as a science of immutable historical tendencies.

From what I have said about the attitude of the social engineer, it must not be inferred that there are no important differences within the camp of the social engineers.   On the contrary, the difference between what I call ' piecemeal social engineering ' and ' Utopian social engineering ' is one of the main themes of this book.   (Cp. especially chapter 9, where I shall give my reasons for advocating the former and rejecting the latter.)

But for the time being, I am concerned only with the opposition between historicism and social engineering. This opposition can perhaps be further clarified if we consider the attitudes taken up by the historicist and by the social engineer towards *social institutions*, i.e. such things as an insurance company, or a police force, or a government, or perhaps a grocer's shop.

The historicist is inclined to look upon social institutions mainly from the point of view of their history, i.e. their origin, their development, and their present and future significance. He may perhaps insist that their origin is due to a definite plan or design and to the pursuit of definite ends, either human or divine ; or he may assert that they are not designed to serve any clearly conceived ends, but are rather the immediate expression of certain instincts and passions ; or he may assert that they have once served as means to definite ends, but that they have lost this character. The social engineer and technologist, on the other hand, will hardly take much interest in the origin of institutions, or in the original intentions of their founders (although there is no reason why he should not recognize the fact that ' only a minority of social institutions are consciously designed, while the vast majority have just " grown ", as the undesigned results of human actions ' [10]). Rather, he will put his problem like this. If such and such are our aims, is this institution well designed and organized to serve them ? As an example we may consider the institution of insurance. The social engineer or technologist will not worry much about the question whether insurance originated as a profit-seeking business ; or whether its historical mission is to serve the common weal. But he may offer a criticism of certain institutions of insurances, showing, perhaps, how to increase their profits, or, which is a very different thing, how to increase the benefit they render to the public ; and he will suggest ways in which they could be made more efficient in serving the one end or the other. As another example of a social institution, we may consider a police force. Some historicists may describe it as an instrument for the protection of freedom and security, others as an instrument of class rule and oppression. The social engineer or technologist, however, would perhaps suggest measures that would make it a suitable instrument for the protection of freedom and security, and he might also devise measures by which it could be turned into a powerful weapon of class rule. (In his function as a citizen who pursues certain ends in which he believes, he may demand that these ends, and the appropriate measures, should be adopted. But as a technologist, he would carefully distinguish between the question of the ends and their choice and questions concerning the facts, i.e. the social effects of any measure which might be taken [11].)

Speaking more generally, we can say that the engineer or the technologist approaches institutions rationally as means that serve certain ends, and that as a technologist he judges them wholly according to their appropriateness, efficiency, simplicity, etc. The historicist, on the other hand, would rather attempt to find out the origin and destiny of these institutions in order to assess the ' true rôle ' played by them in the development of history—evaluating them, for instance, as ' willed by God ', or as ' willed by Fate ', or as ' serving important historical trends ', etc. All this does not mean that the social engineer or technologist will be committed to the assertion that institutions *are* means to ends, or instruments ; he may be well aware of the fact that they are, in many important respects, very different from mechanical instruments or machines. He will not forget, for example, that they ' grow ' in a way which is similar (although by no means equal) to the growth of organisms, and that this fact is of great importance for social engineering. He is not committed to an ' instrumentalist ' philosophy of social institutions. (Nobody will say that an orange *is* an instrument, or a means to an end ; but we often *look upon* oranges as means to ends, for example, if we wish to eat them, or, perhaps, to make our living by selling them.)

The two attitudes, historicism and social engineering, occur sometimes in typical combinations. The earliest and probably the most influential example of these is the social and political philosophy of Plato. It combines, as it were, some fairly obvious technological elements in the foreground, with a background dominated by an elaborate display of typically historicist features. The combination is representative of quite a number of social and political philosophers who produced what have been later described as Utopian systems. All these systems recommend some kind of social engineering, since they demand the adoption of certain institutional means, though not always very realistic ones, for the achievement of their ends. But when we proceed to a consideration of these ends, then we frequently find that they are determined by historicism. Plato's political ends, especially, depend to a considerable extent on his historicist doctrines. First, it is his aim to escape the Heraclitean flux, manifested in social revolution and historical decay. Secondly, he believes that this can be done by establishing a state which is so perfect that it does not participate in the general trend of historical development. Thirdly, he believes that the *model or original* of his perfect state can be found in the distant past, in a Golden Age which existed in the dawn of history ; for if the world decays in time, then we must find increasing perfection the further we go back into the past. The perfect state is something like the first ancestor, the primogenitor, of the later states, which are, as it were, the degenerate offspring of this perfect, or best, or 'ideal' state [12] ; an ideal state which is not a mere phantasm, nor a dream, nor an 'idea in our mind', but which is, in view of its stability, more real than all those decaying societies which are in flux, and liable to pass away at any moment.

Thus even Plato's political end, the best state, is largely dependent on his historicism ; and what is true of his philosophy of the state can be extended, as already indicated, to his general philosophy of 'all things', to his *Theory of Forms or Ideas*.

v

The things in flux, the degenerate and decaying things, are (like the state) the offspring, the children, as it were, of perfect things. And like children, they are copies of their original primogenitors. The father or original of a thing in flux is what Plato calls its 'Form' or its 'Pattern' or its 'Idea'. As before, we must insist that the Form or Idea, in spite of its name, is no 'idea in our mind' ; it is not a phantasm, nor a dream, but a real thing. It is, indeed, more real than all the ordinary things which are in flux, and which, in spite of their apparent solidity, are doomed to decay ; for the Form or Idea is a thing that is perfect, and does not perish.

The Forms or Ideas must not be thought to dwell, like perishable things, in space and time. They are outside space, and also outside time (because they are eternal). But they are in contact with space and time ; for since they are the primogenitors or models of the things which are generated, and which develop and decay in space and time, they must have been in contact with space, at the beginning of time. Since they are not with us in our space and time, they cannot be perceived by our senses, as can the ordinary changing things which interact with our senses and are therefore called 'sensible things'. Those sensible things, which are copies or children of the same model or original, resemble not only this original, their Form or Idea, but also one another, as do children of the same family ; and as children are called by the name of their father, so are the sensible things, which bear the name of their Forms or Ideas ; 'They are all called after them', as Aristotle says [13].

As a child may look upon his father, seeing in him an ideal, a unique model, a god-like personification of his own aspiration ; the embodiment of perfection, of wisdom, of stability, glory, and virtue ; the power which created him before his world began ; which now preserves and sustains him ; and in ' virtue ' of which he exists ; so Plato looks upon the Forms or Ideas. The Platonic Idea is the original and the origin of the thing ; it is the rationale of the thing, the reason of its existence—the stable, sustaining principle in ' virtue ' of which it exists. It is the virtue of the thing, its ideal, its perfection.

The comparison between the Form or Idea of a class of sensible things and the father of a family of children is developed by Plato in the *Timaeus*, one of his latest dialogues. It is in close agreement [14] with much of his earlier writing, on which it throws considerable light. But in the *Timaeus*, Plato goes one step beyond his earlier teaching when he represents the contact of the Form or Idea with the world of space and time by an extension of his simile. He describes the abstract ' space ' in which the sensible things move (originally the space or gap between heaven and earth) as a receptacle, and compares it with the mother of things, in which at the beginning of time the sensible things are created by the Forms which stamp or impress themselves upon pure space, and thereby give the offspring their shape. ' We must conceive ', writes Plato, ' three kinds of things : first, those which undergo generation ; secondly, that in which generation takes place ; and thirdly, the model in whose likeness the generated things are born. And we may compare the receiving principle to a mother, and the model to a father, and their product to a child.' And he goes on to describe first more fully the models—the fathers, the unchanging Forms or Ideas : ' There is first the unchanging Form which is uncreated and indestructible, . . invisible and imperceptible by any sense, and which can be contemplated only by pure thought.' To any single one of these Forms or Ideas belongs its offspring or race of sensible things, ' another kind of things, bearing the name of their Form and resembling it, but perceptible to sense, created, always in flux, generated in a place and again vanishing from that place, and apprehended by opinion based upon perception '.

And the abstract space, which is likened to the mother, is described
thus : ' There is a third kind, which is space, and is eternal, and
cannot be destroyed, and which provides a home for all generated
things. . .' [15]

It may contribute to the understanding of Plato's theory of
Forms or Ideas if we compare it with certain Greek religious
beliefs.   As in many primitive religions, some at least of the Greek
gods are nothing but idealized tribal primogenitors and heroes
—personifications of the ' virtue ' or ' perfection ' of the tribe.
Accordingly, certain tribes and families traced their ancestry to
one or other of the gods.   (Plato's own family is reported to have
traced its descent from the god Poseidon [16].)   We have only to
consider that these gods are immortal or eternal, and perfect—or
very nearly so—while ordinary men are involved in the flux of
all things, and subject to decay (which indeed is the ultimate
destiny of every human individual), in order to see that these
gods are related to ordinary men in the same way as Plato's
Forms or Ideas are related to those sensible things which are their
copies [17] (or his perfect state to the various states now existing).
There is, however, an important difference between Greek
mythology and Plato's Theory of Forms or Ideas.   While the
Greeks venerated many gods as the ancestors of various tribes or
families, the Theory of Ideas demands that there should be only
one Form or Idea of man [18] ; for it is one of the central doctrines
of the Theory of Forms that there is only one Form of every
' race ' or ' kind ' of things.   The uniqueness of the Form which
corresponds to the uniqueness of the primogenitor is a necessary
element of the theory if it is to perform one of its most important
functions, namely, to explain the similarity of sensible things, by
proposing that the similar things are copies or imprints of *one*
Form.   Thus if there were two equal or similar Forms, their
similarity would force us to assume that both are copies of a third
original which thereby would turn out to be the only true and
single Form.   Or, as Plato puts it in the *Timaeus* : ' The resemblance would thus be explained, more precisely, not as one between
these two things, but in reference to that superior thing which
is their prototype.' [19]   In the *Republic*, which is earlier than the
Timaeus, Plato had explained his point even more clearly, using
as his example the ' essential bed ', i.e. the Form or Idea of a
bed : ' God . . has made one essential bed, and only one ; two
or more he did not produce, and never will. . .   For . . even
if God were to make two, and no more, then another would be

brought to light, namely the Form exhibited by those two ; this, and not those two, would then be the essential bed.' [20]

This argument shows that the Forms or Ideas provide Plato not only with an origin or starting point for all developments in space and time (and especially for human history) but also with an explanation of the similarities between sensible things of the same kind. If things are similar because of some virtue or property which they share, for instance, whiteness, or hardness, or goodness, then this virtue or property must be one and the same in all of them ; otherwise it would not make them similar. According to Plato, they all participate in the one Form or Idea of whiteness, if they are white ; of hardness, if they are hard. They participate in the sense in which children participate in their father's possessions and gifts ; just as the many particular reproductions of an etching which are all impressions from one and the same plate, and hence similar to one another, may participate in the beauty of the original.

The fact that this theory is designed to explain the similarities in sensible things does not seem at first sight to be in any way connected with historicism. But it is ; and as Aristotle tells us, it was just this connection which induced Plato to develop the Theory of Ideas. I shall attempt to give an outline of this development, using Aristotle's account together with some indications in Plato's own writings.

If all things are in continuous flux, then it is impossible to say anything definite about them. We can have no real knowledge of them, but, at the best, vague and delusive ' opinions '. This point, as we know from Plato and Aristotle [21], worried many followers of Heraclitus. Parmenides, one of Plato's predecessors who influenced him greatly, had taught that the pure knowledge of reason, as opposed to the delusive opinion of experience, could have as its object only a world which did not change, and that the pure knowledge of reason did in fact reveal such a world. But the unchanging and undivided reality which Parmenides thought he had discovered behind the world of perishable things [22] was entirely unrelated to this world in which we live and die. It was therefore incapable of explaining it.

With this, Plato could not be satisfied. Much as he disliked and despised this empirical world of flux, he was, at bottom, most deeply interested in it. He wanted to unveil the secret of its decay, of its violent changes, and of its unhappiness. He hoped to discover the means of its salvation. He was deeply impressed by Parmenides' doctrine of an unchanging, real, solid, and perfect world behind this ghostly world in which he suffered ; but this conception did not solve his problems as long as it remained unrelated to the world of sensible things.   What he was looking for was knowledge, not opinion ; the pure rational knowledge of a world that does not change ; but, at the same time, knowledge that could be used to investigate this changing world, and especially, this changing society ; political change, with its strange historical laws.   Plato aimed at discovering the secret of the royal knowledge of politics, of the art of ruling men.

But an exact science of politics seemed as impossible as any exact knowledge of a world in flux ; there were no fixed objects in the political field.   How could one discuss any political questions when the meaning of words like ' government ' or ' state ' or ' city ' changed with every new phase in the historical development ?   Political theory must have seemed to Plato in his Heraclitean period to be just as elusive, fluctuating, and unfathomable as political practice.

In this situation Plato obtained, as Aristotle tells us, a most important hint from Socrates.   Socrates was interested in ethical matters ; he was an ethical reformer, a moralist who pestered all kinds of people, forcing them to think, to explain, and to account for the principles of their actions.   He used to question them and was not easily satisfied by their answers.   The typical reply which he received—that we act in a certain way because it is ' wise ' to act in this way or perhaps ' efficient ', or ' just ', or ' pious ', etc. —only incited him to continue his questions by asking *what is* wisdom ; or efficiency ; or justice ; or piety.   In other words, he was led to enquire into the ' virtue ' of a thing.   So he discussed, for instance, the wisdom displayed in various trades and professions, in order to find out what is common to all these various and changing ' wise ' ways of behaviour, and so to find out what wisdom really is, or what ' wisdom ' really means, or (using Aristotle's way of putting it) what its *essence* is.   ' It was natural ', says Aristotle, ' that Socrates should search for the essence ' [23], i.e. for the virtue or rationale of a thing and for the real, the unchanging or essential meanings of the terms.   ' In this connection he became the first to raise the problem of universal definitions.'

These attempts of Socrates to discuss ethical terms like ' justice ' or ' modesty ' or ' piety ' have been rightly compared with modern discussions on Liberty (by Mill [24], for instance), or on Authority, or on the Individual and Society (by Catlin, for instance). There is no need to assume that Socrates, in his search for the unchanging or essential meaning of such terms, personified them, or that he treated them like things. Aristotle's report at least suggests that he did not, and that it was Plato who developed Socrates' method of searching for the meaning or essence into a method of determining the real nature, the Form or Idea of a thing. Plato retained ' the Heraclitean doctrines that all sensible things are ever in a state of flux, and that there is no knowledge about them ', but he found in Socrates' method a way out of these difficulties. Though there ' could be no definition of any sensible thing, as they were always changing ', there could be definitions and true knowledge of things of a different kind—of the virtues of the sensible things. ' If knowledge or thought were to have an object, there would have to be some different, some unchanging entities, apart from those which are sensible ', says Aristotle [25], and he reports of Plato that ' things of this other sort, then, he called Forms or Ideas, and the sensible things, he said, were distinct from them, and all called after them. And the many things which have the same name as a certain Form or Idea exist by participating in it '.

This account of Aristotle's corresponds closely to Plato's own arguments proffered in the *Timaeus* [26], and it shows that Plato's fundamental problem was to find a scientific method of dealing with sensible things. He wanted to obtain purely rational knowledge, and not merely opinion ; and since pure knowledge of sensible things could not be obtained, he insisted, as mentioned before, on obtaining at least such pure knowledge as was in some way related, and applicable, to sensible things. Knowledge of the Forms or Ideas fulfilled this demand, since the Form was related to its sensible things like a father to his children who are under age. The Form was the accountable representative of the sensible things, and could therefore be consulted in important questions concerning the world of flux.

According to our analysis, the theory of Forms or Ideas has at least three different functions in Plato's philosophy. (1) It is a most important methodological device, for it makes possible pure scientific knowledge, and even knowledge which could be applied to the world of changing things of which we cannot immediately obtain any knowledge, but only opinion. Thus it becomes possible to enquire into the problems of a changing society, and to build up a political science.   (2) It provides the clue to the urgently needed *theory of change*, and of decay, to a theory of generation and degeneration, and especially, the clue to history. (3) It opens a way, in the social realm, towards some kind of social engineering ; and it makes possible the forging of instruments for arresting social change, since it suggests designing a ' best state ' which so closely resembles the Form or Idea of a state that it cannot decay.

Problem (2), the theory of change and of history, will be dealt with in the next two chapters, 4 and 5, where Plato's descriptive sociology is treated, i.e. his description and explanation of the changing social world in which he lived.   Problem (3), the arresting of social change, will be dealt with in chapters 6 to 9, treating Plato's political programme.   Problem (1), that of Plato's methodology, has with the help of Aristotle's account of the history of Plato's theory been briefly outlined in the present chapter.   To this discussion, I wish to add here a few more remarks.

VI

I use the name *methodological essentialism* to characterize the view, held by Plato and many of his followers, that it is the task of pure knowledge or ' science ' to discover and to describe the true nature of things, i.e. their hidden reality or essence.   It was Plato's peculiar belief that the essence of sensible things can be found in other and more real things—in their primogenitors or Forms.   Many of the later methodological essentialists, for instance Aristotle, did not altogether follow him in this ; but they all agreed with him in determining the task of pure knowledge as the discovery of the hidden nature or Form or essence of things.   All these methodological essentialists also agreed with Plato in holding that these essences may be discovered and discerned with the help of intellectual intuition ; that every essence has a name proper to it, the name after which the sensible things are called ; and that it may be described in words.   And a description of the essence of a thing they all called a ' definition '. According to methodological essentialism, there can be three ways of knowing a thing : ' I mean that we can know its unchanging reality or essence ; and that we can know the definition of the essence ; and that we can know its name.   Accordingly, two questions may be formulated about any real thing. . . : A person may give the name and ask for the definition ; or he may give the definition and ask for the name.' As an example of this method, Plato uses the essence of ' even ' (as opposed to ' odd ') : ' Number . . may be a thing capable of division into equal parts. If it is so divisible, number is named " even ' '; and the definition of the name " even " is " a number divisible into equal parts ". . . And when we are given the name and asked about the definition, or when we are given the definition and asked about the name, we speak, in both cases, of one and the same essence, whether we call it now " even " or " a number divisible into equal parts ".' After this example, Plato proceeds to apply this method to a ' proof' concerning the real nature of the soul, about which we shall hear more later [27].

Methodological essentialism, i.e. the theory that it is the aim of science to reveal essences and to describe them by means of definitions, can be better understood when contrasted with its opposite, *methodological nominalism*. Instead of aiming at finding out what a thing really is, and at defining its true nature, methodological nominalism aims at describing how a thing behaves in various circumstances, and especially, whether there are any regularities in its behaviour. In other words, methodological nominalism sees the aim of science in the description of the things and events of our experience, and in an ' explanation ' of these events, i.e. their description with the help of universal laws [28]. And it sees in our language, and especially in those of its rules which distinguish properly constructed sentences and inferences from a mere heap of words, the great instrument of scientific description [29] ; words it considers rather as subsidiary tools for this task, and not as names of essences. The methodological nominalist will never think that a question like ' *What is* energy ? ' or ' *What is* movement ? ' or ' *What is* an atom ? ' is an important question for physics ; but he will attach importance to a question like : ' How can the energy of the sun be made useful ? ' or ' How does a planet move ? ' or ' Under what condition does an atom radiate light ? ' And to those philosophers who tell him that before having answered the ' what is ' question he cannot hope to give exact answers to any of the ' how ' questions, he will reply, if at all, by pointing out that he much prefers that modest degree of exactness which he can achieve by his methods to the pretentious muddle which they have achieved by theirs.

As indicated by our example, methodological nominalism is nowadays fairly generally accepted in the natural sciences. The problems of the social sciences, on the other hand, are still for the most part treated by essentialist methods. This is, in my opinion, one of the main reasons for their backwardness. But many who have noticed this situation [30] judge it differently. They believe that the difference in method is necessary, and that it reflects an ' essential ' difference between the ' natures ' of these two fields of research.

The arguments usually offered in support of this view emphasize the importance of change in society, and exhibit other aspects of historicism.   The physicist, so runs a typical argument, deals with objects like energy or atoms which, though changing, retain a certain degree of constancy. He can describe the changes encountered by these relatively unchanging entities, and does not have to construct or detect essences or Forms or similar unchanging entities in order to obtain something permanent on which he can make definite pronouncements. The social scientist, however, is in a very different position. His whole field of interest is changing.   There are no permanent entities in the social realm, where everything is under the sway of historical flux.   How, for instance, can we study government ?   How could we identify it in the diversity of governmental institutions, found in different states at different historical periods, without assuming that they have something *essentially* in common ?   We call an institution a government if we think that it is essentially a govern- ment, i.e. if it complies with our intuition of what a government is, an intuition which we can formulate in a definition. The same would hold good for other sociological entities, such as ' civilization '.   We must grasp their essence, so the historicist argument concludes, and lay it down in the form of a definition.

These modern arguments are, I think, very similar to those reported above which, according to Aristotle, led Plato to his doctrine of Forms or Ideas.   The only difference is that Plato (who did not accept the atomic theory and knew nothing about energy) applied his doctrine to the realm of physics also, and thus to the world as a whole.   We have here an indication of the fact that, in the social sciences, a discussion of Plato's methods may be topical even to-day.

Before proceeding to Plato's sociology and to the use he made of his methodological essentialism in that field, I wish to make it quite clear that I am confining my treatment of Plato to his historicism, and to his ' best state '.   I must therefore warn the reader not to expect a representation of the whole of Plato's philosophy, or what may be called a ' fair and just ' treatment of Platonism.   My attitude towards historicism is one of frank hostility, based upon the conviction that historicism is futile, and worse than that.   My survey of the historicist features of Platonism is therefore strongly critical.   Although I admire much in Plato's philosophy, far beyond those parts which I believe to be Socratic, I do not take it as my task to add to the countless tributes to his genius.   I am, rather, bent on destroying what is in my opinion mischievous in this philosophy.   It is the totalitarian tendency of Plato's political philosophy which I shall try to analyse, and to criticize.[31]

CHAPTER 4 : CHANGE AND REST

Plato was one of the first social scientists and undoubtedly by far the most influential. In the sense in which the term 'sociology' was understood by Comte, Mill, and Spencer, he was a sociologist ; that is to say, he successfully applied his idealist method to an analysis of the social life of man, and of the laws of its development as well as the laws and conditions of its stability. In spite of Plato's great influence, this side of his teaching has been little noticed. This seems to be due to two factors. First of all, much of Plato's sociology is presented by him in such close connection with his ethical and political demands that the descriptive elements have been largely overlooked. Secondly, many of his thoughts were taken so much for granted that they were simply absorbed unconsciously and therefore uncritically. It is mainly in this way that his sociological theories became so influential.

Plato's sociology is an ingenious blend of speculation with acute observation of facts. Its speculative setting is, of course, the theory of Forms and of universal flux and decay, of generation and degeneration. But on this idealist foundation Plato constructs an astonishingly realistic theory of society, capable of explaining the main trends in the historical development of the Greek city-states as well as the social and political forces at work in his own day.

I

The speculative or metaphysical setting of Plato's theory of social change has already been sketched. It is the world of unchanging Forms or Ideas, of which the world of changing things in space and time is the offspring. The Forms or Ideas are not only unchanging, indestructible, and incorruptible, but also perfect, true, real, and good ; in fact, ' good ' is once, in the *Republic* [1], explained as ' everything that preserves ', and ' evil ' as ' everything that destroys or corrupts '. The perfect and good Forms or Ideas are prior to the copies, the sensible things, and they are something like primogenitors or starting

35

points [2] of all the changes in the world of flux. This view is used for evaluating the general trend and main direction of all changes in the world of sensible things. For if the starting point of all change is perfect and good, then change can only be a movement that leads away from the perfect and good ; it must be directed towards the imperfect and the evil, towards corruption.

This theory can be developed in detail. The more closely a sensible thing resembles its Form or Idea, the less corruptible it must be, since the Forms themselves are incorruptible. But sensible or generated things are not perfect copies ; indeed, no copy can be perfect, since it is only an imitation of the true reality, only appearance and illusion, not the truth. Accordingly, no sensible things (except perhaps the most excellent ones) resemble their Forms sufficiently closely to be unchangeable. ' Absolute and eternal immutability is assigned only to the most divine of all things, and bodies do not belong to this order ' [3], says Plato. A sensible or generated thing—such as a physical body, or a human soul—if it is a good copy, may change only very little at first ; and the most ancient change or motion—the motion of the soul—is still ' divine ' (as opposed to secondary and tertiary changes). But every change, however small, must make it different, and thus less perfect, by reducing its resemblance to its Form. In this way, the thing becomes more changeable with every change, and more corruptible, since it becomes further removed from its Form which is its ' cause of immobility and of being at rest ', as Aristotle says, who paraphrases Plato's doctrine as follows : ' Things are generated by participating in the Form, and they decay by losing the Form.' This process of degeneration, slow at first and more rapid afterwards—this law of decline and fall—is dramatically described by Plato in the *Laws*, the last of his great dialogues. The passage deals primarily with the destiny of the human soul, but Plato makes it clear that it holds for all things that ' share in soul ', by which he means all living things. ' All things that share in soul change ', he writes, ' . . and while they change, they are carried along by the order and law of destiny. The smaller the change in their character, the less significant is the beginning decline in their level of rank. But when the change increases, and with it the iniquity, then they fall—down into the abyss and what is known as the infernal regions.' (In the continuation of the passage, Plato mentions the possibility that ' a soul gifted with an exceptionally large share of virtue can, by force of its own will . . , if it is in communion with the divine virtue, become supremely virtuous and move to an exalted region '.   The problem of the exceptional soul which can save itself—and perhaps others—from the general law of destiny will be discussed in chapter 8.)   Earlier in the *Laws*, Plato summarizes his doctrine of change : ' Any change whatever, except the change of an evil thing, is the gravest of all the treacherous dangers that can befall a thing—whether it is now a change of season, or of wind, or of the diet of the body, or of the character of the soul.'   And he adds, for the sake of emphasis : ' This statement applies to everything, with the sole exception, as I said just now, of something evil.'   In brief, Plato teaches *that change is evil, and that rest is divine.*

We see now that Plato's theory of Forms or Ideas implies a certain trend in the development of the world in flux.   It leads to the law that the corruptibility of all things in that world must continually increase.   It is not so much a rigid law of universally increasing corruption, but rather a law of increasing corruptibility ; that is to say, the danger or the likelihood of corruption increases, but exceptional developments in the other direction are not excluded.   Thus it is possible, as the last quotations indicate, that a very good soul may defy change and decay, and that a very evil thing, for instance a very evil city, may be improved by changing it.   (In order that such an improvement should be of any value, we would have to try to make it permanent, i.e. to arrest all further change.)

In full accordance with this general theory is Plato's story, in the *Timaeus*, of the origin of species.   According to this story, man, the highest of animals, is generated by the gods ; the other species originate from him by a process of corruption and degeneration.   First, certain men—the cowards and villains— degenerate into women.   Those who are lacking wisdom degenerate step by step into the lower animals.   Birds, we hear, came into being through the transformation of harmless but too easy-going people who would trust their senses too much ; ' land animals came from men who had no interest in philosophy ' ; and fishes, including shell-fish, ' degenerated from the most foolish, stupid, and . . unworthy ' of all men [4].

It is clear that this theory can be applied to human society, and to its history.   It then explains Hesiod's [5] pessimistic law of development, the law of historical decay.   If we are to believe

Aristotle's report (outlined in the last chapter), then the theory of Forms or Ideas was originally introduced in order to meet a methodological demand, the demand for pure or rational knowledge which is impossible in the case of sensible things in flux. We now see that the theory does more than that. Over and above meeting these methodological demands, it provides a *theory of change*. It explains the general direction of the flux of all sensible things, and thereby the historical tendency to degenerate shown by man and human society. (And it does still more ; as we shall see in chapter 6, the theory of Forms determines the trend of Plato's political demands also, and even the means for their realization.) If, as I believe, the philosophies of Plato as well as Heraclitus sprang from their social experience, especially from the experience of class war and from the abject feeling that their social world was going to pieces, then we can understand why the theory of Forms came to play such an important part in Plato's philosophy when he found that it was capable of explaining the trend towards degeneration. He must have welcomed it as the solution of a most mystifying riddle. While Heraclitus had been unable to pass a direct ethical condemnation upon the trend of the political development, Plato found, in his theory of Forms, the theoretical basis for a pessimistic judgement in Hesiod's vein.

But Plato's greatness as a sociologist does not lie in his general and abstract speculations about the law of social decay. It lies rather in the wealth and detail of his observations, and in the amazing acuteness of his sociological intuition. He saw things which had not been seen before him, and which were rediscovered only in our own time. As an example I may mention his theory of the primitive beginnings of society, of tribal patriarchy, and, in general, his attempt to outline the typical periods in the development of social life. Another example is Plato's sociological and economic historicism, his emphasis upon the *economic background* of the political life and the historical development ; a theory revived by Marx under the name ' historical materialism '. A third example is Plato's most interesting law of political revolutions, according to which all revolutions presuppose a disunited ruling class (or ' élite ') ; a law which forms the basis of his analysis of the means of arresting political change and creating a social equilibrium, and which has been recently rediscovered by the theoreticians of totalitarianism, especially by Pareto.

I shall now proceed to a more detailed discussion of these points, especially the third, the theory of revolution and of equilibrium.

II

The dialogues in which Plato discusses these questions are, in chronological order, the *Republic*, a dialogue of much later date called the *Statesman* (or the *Politicus*), and the *Laws*, the latest and longest of his works. In spite of certain minor differences, there is much agreement between these dialogues, which are in some respects parallel, in others complementary, to one another. The *Laws* [6], for instance, present the story of the decline and fall of human society as an account of Greek prehistory merging without any break into history ; while the parallel passages of the *Republic* give, in a more abstract way, a systematic outline of the development of government ; the *Statesman*, still more abstract, gives a logical classification of types of government, with only a few allusions to historical events. Similarly, the *Laws* formulate the historicist aspect of the investigation very clearly. ' What is the archetype or origin of a state ? ' asks Plato there, linking this question with the other : ' Is not the best method of looking for an answer to this question . . that of contemplating the growth of states as they change either towards the good or towards the evil ? ' But within the sociological doctrines, the only major difference appears to be due to a purely speculative difficulty which seems to have worried Plato. Assuming as the starting point of the development a perfect and therefore incorruptible state, he found it difficult to explain the first change, the Fall of Man, as it were, which sets everything going [7]. We shall hear, in the next chapter, of Plato's attempt to solve this problem ; but first I shall give a general survey of his theory of social development.

According to the *Republic*, the original or primitive form of society, and at the same time, the one that resembles the Form or Idea of a state most closely, the ' best state ', is a kingship of the wisest and most godlike of men. This ideal city-state is so near perfection that it is hard to understand how it can ever change. Still, a change does take place ; and with it enters Heraclitus' strife, the driving force of all movement. According to Plato, internal strife, class war, fomented by self-interest and especially material or economic self-interest, is the main force of ' social dynamics '. The Marxian formula ' The history of all hitherto existing societies is a history of class struggle '[8] fits Plato's historicism nearly as well as that of Marx. The four most conspicuous periods or ' landmarks in the history of political degeneration ', and, at the same time, ' the most important . . varieties of existing states '[9], are described by Plato in the following order. First after the perfect state comes ' timarchy ' or ' timocracy ', the rule of the noble who seek honour and fame ; secondly, oligarchy, the rule of the rich families ; ' next in order, democracy is born ', the rule of liberty which means lawlessness ; and last comes ' tyranny . . the fourth and final sickness of the city '[10].

As can be seen from the last remark, Plato looks upon history, which to him is a history of social decay, as if it were the history of an illness : the patient is society ; and, as we shall see later, the statesman ought to be a physician (and vice versa)—a healer, a saviour. Just as the description of the typical course of an illness is not always applicable to every individual patient, so is Plato's historical theory of social decay not intended to apply to the development of every individual city. But it is intended to describe both the original course of development by which the main forms of constitutional decay were first generated, and the typical course of social change [11]. We see that Plato aimed at setting out a system of historical periods, governed by a law of evolution ; in other words, he aimed at a historicist theory of society. This attempt was revived by Rousseau, and was made fashionable by Comte and Mill, and by Hegel and Marx ; but considering the historical evidence then available, Plato's system of historical periods was just as good as that of any of these modern historicists. (The main difference lies in the evaluation of the course taken by history. While the aristocrat Plato condemned the development he described, these modern authors applauded it, believing as they did in a law of historical progress.)

Before discussing Plato's perfect state in any detail, I shall give a brief sketch of his analysis of the rôle played by economic motives and the class struggle in the process of transition between the four decaying forms of the state. The first form into which the perfect state degenerates, timocracy, the rule of the ambitious noblemen, is said to be in nearly all respects similar to the perfect state itself. It is important to note that Plato explicitly identified this best and oldest among the existing states with the Dorian constitution of Sparta and Crete, and that these two tribal aristocracies did in fact represent the oldest existing forms of political life within

Greece. Most of Plato's excellent description of their institutions is given in certain parts of his description of the best or perfect state, to which timocracy is so similar. (Through his doctrine of the similarity between Sparta and the perfect state, Plato became one of the most successful propagators of what I should like to call ' the Great Myth of Sparta '—the perennial and influential myth of the supremacy of the Spartan constitution and way of life.)

The main difference between the best or ideal state and timocracy is that the latter contains an element of instability ; the once united patriarchal ruling class is now disunited, and it is this disunity which leads to the next step, to its degeneration into oligarchy. Disunion is brought about by ambition. ' First ', says Plato, speaking of the young timocrat, ' he hears his mother complaining that her husband is not one of the rulers . .' [12] Thus he becomes ambitious and longs for distinction. But decisive in bringing about the next change are competitive and acquisitive social tendencies. ' We must describe ', says Plato, ' how timocracy changes into oligarchy . . Even a blind man must see how it changes . . It is the treasure house that ruins this constitution. They ' (the timocrats) ' begin by creating opportunities for showing off and spending money, and to this end they twist the laws, and they and their wives disobey them . . ; and they try to outrival one another.' In this way arises the first class conflict : that between virtue and money, or between the old-established ways of feudal simplicity and the new ways of wealth. The transition to oligarchy is completed when the rich establish a law that ' disqualifies from public office all those whose means do not reach the stipulated amount. This change is imposed by force of arms, should threats and blackmail not succeed . .'

With the establishment of the oligarchy, a state of potential civil war between the oligarchs and the poorer classes is reached : ' just as a sick body . . is sometimes at strife with itself . . , so is this sick city. It falls ill and makes war on itself on the slightest pretext, whenever the one party or the other manages to obtain help from outside, the one from an oligarchic city, or the other from a democracy. And does not this sick state break out at times into civil war, even without any such help from outside ? ' [13] This civil war begets democracy : ' Democracy is born . . when the poor win the day, killing some . . , banishing others, and sharing with the rest the rights of citizenship and of public offices, on terms of equality . .'

Plato's description of democracy is a vivid but intensely hostile and unjust parody of the political life of Athens, and of the democratic creed which Pericles had formulated in a manner which has never been surpassed, about three years before Plato was born. (Pericles' programme is discussed in chapter 10, below [14].) Plato's description is a brilliant piece of political propaganda, and we can appreciate what harm it must have done if we consider, for instance, that a man like Adam, an excellent scholar and editor of the *Republic*, is unable to resist the rhetoric of Plato's denunciation of his native city. ' Plato's description of the genesis of the democratic man ', Adam [15] writes, ' is one of the most royal and magnificent pieces of writing in the whole range of literature, whether ancient or modern.' And when the same writer continues : ' the description of the democratic man as the chameleon of the human society *paints him for all time* ', then we see that Plato has succeeded at least in turning this thinker against democracy, and we may wonder how much damage his poisonous writing has done when presented, unopposed, to lesser minds. . .

It seems that often when Plato's style, to use a phrase of Adam's [16], becomes a ' full tide of lofty thoughts and images and words ', he is in urgent need of a cloak to cover up the rags and tatters of his argumentation, or even, as in the present case, the complete absence of rational arguments. In their stead he uses invective, identifying liberty with lawlessness, freedom with licence, and equality before the law with disorder. Democrats are described as profligate and niggardly, as insolent, lawless, and shameless, as fierce and as terrible beasts of prey, as gratifying every whim, as living solely for pleasure, and for unnecessary and unclean desires. (' They fill their bellies like the beasts ', was Heraclitus' way of putting it.) They are accused of calling ' reverence a folly . . ; temperance they call cowardice . . ; moderation and orderly expenditure they call meanness and boorishness ' [17], etc. ' And there are more trifles of this kind ', says Plato, when the flood of his rhetorical abuse begins to abate, ' the schoolmaster fears and flatters his pupils . . , and old men condescend to the young . . in order to avoid the appearance of being sour and despotic.' (It is Plato the Master of the Academy who puts this into the mouth of Socrates, forgetting that the latter had never been a schoolmaster, and that even as an old man he had never appeared to be sour or despotic. He had always loved, not to ' condescend ' to the young, but to treat them, for instance the young Plato, as his companions and friends. Plato himself, we have reason to believe, was less ready to ' condescend ', and to discuss matters with his pupils.) ' But the height of all this abundance of freedom . . is reached ', Plato continues, ' when slaves, male as well as female, who have been bought on the market, are every whit as free as those whose property they are. . . And what is the cumulative effect of all this ? That the citizens' hearts become so very tender that they get irritated at the mere sight of anything like slavery and do not suffer anybody to submit to its presence . . . so that they may have no master over them.' Here, after all, Plato pays homage to his native city, even though he does it unwittingly. It will for ever remain one of the greatest triumphs of Athenian democracy that it treated slaves humanely, and that in spite of the inhuman propaganda of philosophers like Plato himself and Aristotle it came, as he witnesses, very close to abolishing slavery.[18]

Of much greater merit, although it too is inspired by hatred, is Plato's description of tyranny and especially of the transition to it. He insists that he describes things which he has seen himself [19] ; no doubt, the allusion is to his experiences at the court of the older Dionysius, tyrant of Syracuse. The transition from democracy to tyranny, Plato says, is most easily brought about by a popular leader who knows how to exploit the class antagonism between the rich and the poor within the democratic state, and who succeeds in building up a bodyguard or a private army of his own. The people who have hailed him first as the champion of freedom are soon enslaved ; and then they must fight for him, in ' one war after another which he must stir up . . because he must make the people feel the need of a general ' [20]. With tyranny, the most abject state is reached.

A very similar survey of the various forms of government can be found in the *Statesman*, where Plato discusses ' the origin of the tyrant and king, of oligarchies and aristocracies, and of democracies ' [21]. Again we find that the various forms of existing governments are explained as debased copies of the true model or Form of the state, of the perfect state, the standard of all imitations, which is said to have existed in the ancient times of Cronos, father of Zeus. One difference is that Plato here distinguishes six types of debased states ; but this difference is unimportant, especially if we remember that Plato says in the *Republic* [22] that the four types discussed are not exhaustive, and that there are some intermediate stages. The six types are arrived at, in the *Statesman*, by first distinguishing between three forms of government, the rule of one man, of a few, and of the many. Each of these is then subdivided into two types, of which one is comparatively good and the other bad, according to whether or not they imitate ' the only true original ' by copying and preserving its ancient laws [23]. In this way, three conservative or lawful and three utterly depraved or lawless forms are distinguished ; monarchy, aristocracy, and a conservative form of democracy are the lawful imitations, in order of merit. But democracy changes into its lawless form, and deteriorates further, through oligarchy, the lawless rule of the few, into a lawless rule of the one, tyranny, which, just as Plato has said in the *Republic*, is the worst of all.

That tyranny, the most evil state, need not be the end of the development is indicated in a passage in the *Laws* which partly repeats, and partly [24] connects with, the story of the *Statesman*. ' Give me a state governed by a young tyrant ', exclaims Plato there, '. . who has the good fortune to be the contemporary of a great legislator, and to meet him by some happy accident. What more could a god do for a city which he wants to make happy ? ' Tyranny, the most evil state, may be reformed in this way. (This agrees with the remark in the *Laws*, quoted above, that all change is evil, ' except the change of an evil thing '. There is little doubt that Plato, when speaking of the great lawgiver and the young tyrant, must have been thinking of himself and his various experiments with young tyrants, and especially of his attempts at reforming the younger Dionysius' tyranny over Syracuse. These ill-fated experiments will be discussed later.)

One of the main objects of Plato's analysis of political developments is to ascertain the driving force of all historical change. In the *Laws*, the historical survey is explicitly undertaken with this aim in view : ' Have not uncounted thousands of cities been born during this time . . and has not each of them been under all kinds of government ? . . Let us, if we can, get hold of the cause of so much change. I hope that we may thus reveal the secret both of the birth of constitutions, and also of their changes.' [25] As the result of these investigations he discovers the sociological law that internal disunion, class war fomented by the antagonism of economic class interests, is the driving force of all political revolutions. But Plato's formulation of this fundamental law goes even further. He insists that only internal sedition within the ruling class itself can weaken it so much that its rule can be overthrown. ' Changes in any constitution originate, without exception, within the ruling class itself, and only when this class becomes the seat of disunion ' [26], is his formula in the *Republic* ; and in the *Laws* he says (possibly referring to this passage of the *Republic*) : ' How can a kingship, or any other form of government, ever be destroyed by anybody but the rulers themselves ? Have we forgotten what we said a while ago, when dealing with this subject, as we did the other day ? ' This sociological law, together with the observation that economic interests are the most likely causes of disunion, is Plato's clue to history. But it is more. It is also the clue to his analysis of the conditions necessary for the establishment of political equilibrium, i.e. for arresting political change. He assumes that these conditions were realized in the best or perfect state of ancient times.

III

Plato's description of the perfect or best state has usually been interpreted as the Utopian programme of a progressivist. In spite of his repeated assertions, in the *Republic*, *Timaeus*, and *Critias*, that he is describing the distant past, and in spite of the parallel passages in the *Laws* whose historical intention is manifest, it is often assumed that it was his intention to give a veiled description of the future. But I think that Plato meant what he said, and that many characteristics of his best state, especially as described in Books Two to Four of the *Republic*, are intended (like his accounts of primitive society in the *Statesman* and the *Laws*) to be historical [27], or perhaps prehistorical. This may not apply to all characteristics of the best state. Concerning, for example, the kingship of the philosophers (described in Books Five to Seven of the *Republic*), Plato indicates himself that it may be a characteristic only of the timeless world of Forms or Ideas, of the ' City in Heaven '. These intentionally unhistorical elements of his description will be discussed later, together with Plato's ethico-political demands. It must, of course, be admitted that he did not intend, in his description of the primitive or ancient constitutions, to give an exact historical account ; he certainly knew that he did not possess the necessary data for achieving anything like that. I believe, however, that he made a serious attempt to reconstruct the ancient tribal forms of social life as well as he could. There is no reason to doubt this, especially since the attempt was, in a good number of its details, very successful. It could hardly be otherwise, since Plato arrived at his picture by an idealized description of the ancient tribal aristocracies of Crete and Sparta. With his acute sociological intuition he had seen that these forms were not only old, but petrified, arrested ; that they were relics of a still older form. And he concluded that this still older form had been even more stable, more securely arrested. This very ancient and accordingly very good and very stable state he tried to reconstruct in such a way as to make clear how it had been kept free from disunion ; how class war had been avoided, and how the influence of economic interests had been reduced to a minimum, and kept well under control. These are the main problems of Plato's reconstruction of the best state.

How does Plato solve the problem of avoiding class war ? Had he been a progressivist, he might have hit on the idea of a classless, equalitarian society ; for, as we can see for instance from his own parody of Athenian democracy, there were strong equalitarian tendencies at work in Athens. But he was not out to construct a state that might come, but a state that had been—the father of the Spartan state, which was certainly not a classless society. It was a slave state, and accordingly Plato's best state is based on the most rigid class distinctions. It is a caste state. The problem of avoiding class war is solved, not by abolishing classes, but by giving the ruling class a superiority which cannot be challenged. As in Sparta, the ruling class alone is permitted to carry arms, it alone has any political or other rights, and it alone receives education, i.e. a specialized training in the art of keeping down its human sheep or its human cattle (In fact, its overwhelming superiority disturbs Plato a little ; he fears that its members ' may worry the sheep ', instead of merely shearing them, and ' act as wolves rather than dogs ' [28]. This problem is considered later in the chapter.) As long as the ruling class is united, there can be no challenge to their authority, and consequently no class war.

Plato distinguishes three classes in his best state, the guardians, their armed auxiliaries or warriors, and the working class. But actually there are only two castes, the military caste—the armed and educated rulers—and the unarmed and uneducated ruled, the human sheep ; for the guardians are no separate caste, but merely old and wise warriors who have been promoted from the ranks of the auxiliaries. That Plato divides his ruling caste into two classes, the guardians and the auxiliaries, without elaborating similar subdivisions within the working class, is largely due to the fact that he is interested only in the rulers. The workers, tradesmen, etc., do not interest him at all, they are only human cattle whose sole function is to provide for the material needs of the ruling class. Plato even goes so far as to forbid his rulers to legislate for people of this class, and for their petty problems.[29] This is why our information about the lower classes is so scanty. But Plato's silence is not wholly uninterrupted. ' Are there not drudges ', he asks once, ' who do not possess a spark of intelligence and are unworthy to be admitted into the community, but who have strong bodies for hard labour ? ' Since this nasty remark has given rise to the soothing comment that Plato does not admit slaves into his city, I may here point out that this view is mistaken. It is true that Plato discusses nowhere explicitly the status of slaves in his best state, and it is even true that he says that the *name* ' slave ' should better be avoided, and that we should *call* the workers ' supporters ' or even ' employers '. But this is done for propagandist reasons. Nowhere is the slightest suggestion to be found that the institution of slavery is to be abolished, or to be mitigated. On the contrary, Plato has only scorn for those ' tenderhearted ' Athenian democrats who supported the abolitionist movement. And he makes his view quite clear, for example, in his description of timocracy, the second-best state, and the one directly following the best. There he says of the timocratic man : ' He will be inclined to treat slaves cruelly, for he does not despise them as much as a well-educated man would.' But since only in the best city can education be found which is superior to that of timocracy, we are bound to conclude that there are slaves in Plato's best city, and that they are not treated with cruelty, but are properly despised. In his righteous contempt for them, Plato does not elaborate the point. This conclusion is fully corroborated by the fact that a passage in the *Republic* which criticizes the current practice of Greeks enslaving Greeks ends up with the explicit endorsement of the enslaving of barbarians, and even with a recommendation to ' our citizens ' —i.e. those of the best city—to ' do unto barbarians as Greeks now do unto Greeks '. And it is further corroborated by the contents of the *Laws*, and the most inhuman attitude towards slaves adopted there.

Since the ruling class alone has political power, including the power of keeping the number of the human cattle within such limits as to prevent them from becoming a danger, the whole problem of preserving the state is reduced to that of preserving the internal unity of the master class. How is this unity of the rulers preserved ? By training and other psychological influences, but otherwise mainly by the elimination of economic interests which may lead to disunion. This economic abstinence is achieved and controlled by the introduction of communism, i.e. by the abolition of private property, especially of precious metals. (The possession of precious metals was forbidden in Sparta.) This communism is confined to the ruling class, which alone must be kept free from disunion ; quarrels among the ruled are not worthy of consideration. Since all property is common property, there must also be a common ownership of women and children. No member of the ruling class must be able to identify his children, or his parents. The family must be destroyed, or rather, extended to cover the whole warrior class. Family loyalties might otherwise become a possible source of disunion ; therefore ' each should look upon all as if belonging to one family ' [30]. (This suggestion was neither so novel nor so revolutionary as it sounds ; we must remember such Spartan restrictions on the privacy of family life as the ban on private meals, constantly referred to by Plato as the institution of ' common meals '.) But even the common ownership of women and children is not quite sufficient to guard the ruling class from all economic dangers. It is important to avoid prosperity as well as poverty. Both are dangers to unity : poverty, because it drives people to adopt desperate means to satisfy their needs ; prosperity, because most change arises from abundance, from an accumulation of wealth which makes dangerous experiments possible. Only a communist system which has room neither for great want nor for great wealth can reduce economic interests to a minimum, and guarantee the unity of the ruling class.

The communism of the ruling caste of his best city can thus be derived from Plato's fundamental sociological law of change ; it is a necessary condition of the political stability which is its fundamental characteristic. But although an important condition, it is not a sufficient one. In order that the ruling class may feel really united, that it should feel like one tribe, i.e. like one big family, pressure from without the class is as necessary as are the ties between the members of the class. This pressure can be secured by emphasizing and widening the gulf between the rulers and the ruled. The stronger the feeling that the ruled are a different and an altogether inferior race, the stronger will be the sense of unity among the rulers. We arrive in this way at the fundamental principle, announced only after some hesitation, that there must be no mingling between the classes [31] : ' Any meddling or changing over from one class to another ', says Plato, ' is a great crime against the city and may rightly be denounced as the basest wickedness.' But such a rigid division of the classes must be justified, and an attempt to justify it can only proceed from the claim that the rulers are superior to the ruled. Accordingly, Plato tries to justify his class division by the threefold claim that the rulers are vastly superior in three respects—in race, in education, and in their scale of values. Plato's moral valuations, which are, of course, identical with those of the rulers of his best state, will be discussed in chapters 6 to 8 ; I may therefore confine myself here to describing some of his ideas concerning the origin, the breeding, and the education of his ruling class. (Before proceeding to this description, I wish to express my belief that personal superiority, whether racial or intellectual or moral or educational, can never establish a claim to political prerogatives, even if such superiority could be ascertained. Most people in civilized countries nowadays admit racial superiority to be a myth ; but even if it were an established fact, it should not create special political rights, though' it might create special moral responsibilities for the superior persons. Analogous demands should be made of those who are intellectually and morally and educationally superior ; and I cannot help feeling that the opposite claims of certain intellectualists and moralists only show how little successful their education has been, since it failed to make them aware of their own limitations, and of their Pharisaism.)

IV

If we want to understand Plato's views about the origin, breeding, and education of his ruling class, we must not lose sight of the two main points of our analysis. We must keep in mind, first of all, that Plato is reconstructing a city of the past, although one connected with the present in such a way that certain of its features are still discernible in existing states, for instance, in Sparta ; and secondly, that he is reconstructing his city with a view to the conditions of its stability, and that he seeks the guarantees for this stability solely within the ruling class itself, and more especially, in its unity and strength.

Regarding the origin of the ruling class, it may be mentioned that Plato speaks in the *Statesman* of a time, prior even to that of his best state, when ' God himself was the shepherd of men, ruling over them exactly as man . . still rules over the beasts. There was . . no ownership of women and children ' [32]. This is not merely the simile of the good shepherd ; in the light of what Plato says in the *Laws*, it must be interpreted more literally than that. For there we are told that this primitive society, which is prior even to the first and best city, is one of nomad hill shepherds under a patriarch : ' Government originated ', says Plato there of the period prior to the first settlement, '. . as the rule of the eldest who inherited his authority from his father or mother ; all the others followed him like a flock of birds, thus forming one single horde ruled by that patriarchal authority and kingship which of all kingships is the most just.' These nomad tribes, we hear, settled in the cities of the Peloponnese, especially in Sparta, under the name of ' Dorians '. How this happened is not very clearly explained, but we understand Plato's reluctance when we get a hint that the ' settlement ' was in fact a violent subjugation. This, for all we know, is the true story of the Dorian settlement in the Peloponnese. We therefore have every reason to believe that Plato intended his story as a serious description of prehistoric events ; as a description not only of the origin of the Dorian master race but also of the origin of their human cattle, i.e. the original inhabitants. In a parallel passage in the *Republic*, Plato gives us a mythological yet very pointed description of the conquest itself, when dealing with the origin of the ' earthborn ', the ruling class of the best city. (The Myth of the Earthborn will be discussed from a different point of view in chapter 8.) Their victorious march into the city, previously founded by the tradesmen and workers, is described as follows : ' After having armed and trained the earthborn, let us now make them advance, under the command of the guardians, till they arrive in the city. Then let them look round to find out the best place for their camp—the spot that is most suitable for keeping down the inhabitants, should anyone show unwillingness to obey the law, and for holding back external enemies who may come down like wolves on the fold.' This short but triumphant tale of the subjugation of a sedentary population by a conquering war horde (who are identified, in the *Statesman*, with the nomad hill shepherds of the period before the settlement) must be kept in mind when we interpret Plato's reiterated insistence that good rulers, whether gods or demigods or guardians, are patriarchal shepherds of men, and that the true political art, the art of ruling, is a kind of herdsmanship, i.e. the art of managing and keeping down the human cattle. And it is in this light that we must consider his description of the breeding and training of ' the auxiliaries who are subject to the rulers like sheep-dogs to the shepherds of the state '.

The breeding and the education of the auxiliaries and thereby of the ruling class of Plato's best state is, like their carrying of arms, a class symbol and therefore a class prerogative [33]. And breeding and education are not empty symbols but, like arms, instruments of class rule, and necessary for ensuring the stability of this rule. They are treated by Plato solely from this point of view, i.e. as powerful political weapons, as means which are useful for herding the human cattle, and for unifying the ruling class.

To this end, it is important that the master class should feel as one superior master race. ' The race of the guardians must be kept pure ' [34], says Plato (in defence of infanticide), when developing the racialist argument that we breed animals with great care while neglecting our own race, an argument which has been repeated ever since. (Infanticide was not an Athenian institution ; Plato, seeing that it was practised at Sparta for eugenic reasons, concluded that it must be ancient and therefore good.) He demands that the same principles be applied to the breeding of the master race as are applied, by an experienced breeder, to dogs, horses, or birds. ' If you did not breed them in this way, don't you think that the race of your birds or dogs would quickly degenerate ? ' Plato argues ; and he draws the conclusion that ' the same principles apply to the race of men '. The racial qualities demanded from a guardian or from an auxiliary are, more specifically, those of a sheep-dog. ' Our warrior-athletes . . must be vigilant like watch-dogs ', demands Plato, and he asks : ' Surely, there is no difference, so far as their natural fitness for keeping guard is concerned, between a gallant youth and a well-bred dog ? ' In his enthusiasm and admiration for the dog, Plato goes so far as to discern in him a ' genuine philosophical nature ' ; for ' is not the love of learning identical with the philosophical attitude ? '

The main difficulty which besets Plato is that guardians and auxiliaries must be endowed with a character that is fierce and gentle at the same time. It is clear that they must be bred to be fierce, since they must ' meet any danger in a fearless and

unconquerable spirit '. Yet 'if their nature is to be like that,
how are they to be kept from being violent against one another,
or against the rest of the citizens?' [35] Indeed, it would be
'simply monstrous if the shepherds should keep dogs . . who
would worry the sheep, behaving like wolves rather than dogs '.
The problem is important from the point of view of the political
equilibrium, or rather, of the stability of the state, for Plato
does not rely on an equilibrium of the forces of the various
classes, since that would be unstable. A control of the master
class, its arbitrary powers, and its fierceness, through the opposing force of the ruled, is out of the question, for the superiority of
the master class must remain unchallenged. The only admissible
control of the master class is therefore self-control. Just as the
ruling class must exercise economic abstinence, i.e. refrain from an
excessive economic exploitation of the ruled, so it must also be able
to refrain from too much fierceness in its dealings with the ruled.
But this can only be achieved if the fierceness of its nature is
balanced by its gentleness. Plato finds this a very serious
problem, since 'the fierce nature is the exact opposite of the
gentle nature '. His speaker, Socrates, reports that he is per-
plexed, until he remembers the dog again. 'Well-bred dogs are
by nature most gentle to their friends and acquaintances, but
the very opposite to strangers ', he says. It is therefore proved
'that the character we try to give our guardians is not contrary
to nature '. The aim of breeding the master race is thus
established, and shown to be attainable. It has been derived
from an analysis of the conditions which are necessary for
keeping the state stable.

Plato's educational aim is exactly the same. It is the purely
political aim of stabilizing the state by blending a fierce and a
gentle element in the character of the rulers. The two disciplines
in which children of the Greek upper class were educated,
gymnastics and music (the latter, in the wider sense of the word,
included all literary studies), are correlated by Plato with the
two elements of character, fierceness and gentleness. 'Have you
not observed ', asks Plato [36], 'how the character is affected by
an exclusive training in gymnastics without music, and how it
is affected by the opposite training? . . Exclusive preoccupation with gymnastics produces men who are fiercer than they
ought to be, while an analogous preoccupation with music makes
them too soft . . But we maintain that our guardians must
combine both of these natures . . This is why I say that some

god must have given man these two arts, music and gymnastics ; and their purpose is not so much to serve soul and body respectively, but rather to tune properly the two main strings ', i.e. to bring into harmony the two elements of the soul, gentleness and fierceness. ' These are the outlines of our system of education and training ', Plato concludes his analysis.

In spite of the fact that Plato identifies the gentle element of the soul with her philosophic disposition, and in spite of the fact that philosophy is going to play such a dominant rôle in the later parts of the *Republic*, he is not at all biased in favour of the gentle element of the soul, or of musical, i.e. literary, education. The impartiality in balancing the two elements is the more remarkable as it leads him to impose the most severe restrictions on literary education, compared with what was, in his time, customary in Athens. This, of course, is only part of his general tendency to prefer Spartan customs to Athenian ones. (Crete, his other model, was even more anti-musical than Sparta [37].) Plato's political principles of literary education are based upon a simple comparison. Sparta, he saw, treated its human cattle just a little too harshly ; this is a symptom or even an admission of a feeling of weakness [38], and therefore a symptom of the incipient degeneration of the master class. Athens, on the other hand, was altogether too liberal and slack in her treatment of slaves. Plato took this as proof that Sparta insisted just a little too much on gymnastics, and Athens, of course, far too much on music. This simple estimate enabled him readily to reconstruct what in his opinion must have been the true measure or the true blend of the two elements in the education of the best state, and to lay down the principles of his educational policy. Judged from the Athenian viewpoint, it is nothing less than the demand that all literary education be strangled [39] by a close adherence to the example of Sparta with its strict state control of all literary matters. Not only poetry but also music in the ordinary sense of the term are to be controlled by a rigid censorship, and both are to be devoted entirely to strengthening the stability of the state by making the young more conscious of class discipline [40], and thus more ready to serve class interests. Plato even forgets that it is the function of music to make the young more gentle, for he demands such forms of music as will make them braver, i.e. fiercer. (Considering that Plato was an Athenian, his arguments concerning music proper appear to me almost incredible in their superstitious

intolerance, especially if compared with a more enlightened contemporary criticism [41].   But even now he has many musicians on
his side, possibly because they are flattered by his high opinion
of the importance of music, i.e. of its political power.   The same
is true of educationists, and even more of philosophers, since
Plato demands that they should rule ;   a demand which will be
discussed in chapter 8.)

The political principle that determines the education of the
soul, namely, the preservation of the stability of the state,
determines also that of the body.   The aim is simply that of
Sparta.   While the Athenian citizen was educated to a general
versatility, Plato demands that the ruling class shall be trained
as a class of professional warriors, ready to strike against enemies
from without or from within the state.   Children of both sexes,
we are told twice, ' must be taken on horseback within the
sight of actual war ;   and provided it can be done safely, they
must be brought into battle, and made to taste blood ;   just as
one does with young hounds ' [42].   The description of a modern
writer, who characterizes contemporary totalitarian education
as ' an intensified and continual form of mobilization ', fits
Plato's whole system of education very well indeed.

This is an outline of Plato's theory of the best or most ancient
state, of the city which treats its human cattle exactly as a wise but
hardened shepherd treats his sheep ;   not too cruelly, but with
the proper contempt. . .   As an analysis both of Spartan social
institutions and of the conditions of their stability and instability,
and as an attempt at reconstructing more rigid and primitive
forms of tribal life, this description is excellent indeed.   (Only
the descriptive aspect is dealt with in this chapter.   The ethical
aspects will be discussed later.)   I believe that much in Plato's
writings that has been usually considered as mere mythological
or Utopian speculation can in this way be interpreted as sociological description and analysis.   If we look, for instance, at his
myth of the triumphant war hordes subjugating a settled population, then we must admit that from the point of view of descriptive
sociology it is most successful.   In fact, it could even claim to be
an anticipation of an interesting (though possibly too sweeping)
modern theory of the origin of the state, according to which
centralized and organized political power generally originates in
such a conquest [43].   There may be more descriptions of this kind
in Plato's writings than we can at present estimate.

V

To sum up.   In an attempt to understand and to interpret
the changing social world as he experienced it, Plato was led
to develop a systematic historicist sociology in great detail.   He
thought of existing states as decaying copies of an unchanging
Form or Idea.   He tried to reconstruct this Form or Idea of
a state, or at least to describe a society which resembled it as
closely as possible.   Along with ancient traditions, he used as
material for his reconstruction the results of his analysis of the
social institutions of Sparta and Crete—the most ancient forms
of social life he could find in Greece—in which he recognized
arrested forms of even older tribal societies.   But in order to
make a proper use of this material, he needed a principle for
distinguishing between the good or original or ancient traits of
the existing institutions and their symptoms of decay.   This
principle he found in his law of political revolutions, according
to which disunion in the ruling class, and their preoccupation
with economic affairs, are the origin of all social change.   His
best state was therefore to be reconstructed in such a way
as to eliminate all the germs and elements of disunion and
decay as radically as this could be done ; that is to say, it
was to be constructed out of the Spartan state with an eye
to the conditions necessary for the unbroken unity of the master
class, guaranteed by its economic abstinence, its breeding, and
its training.

Interpreting existing societies as decadent copies of an ideal
state, Plato furnished Hesiod's somewhat crude views of human
history at once with a theoretical background and with a wealth
of practical application.   He developed a remarkably realistic
historicist theory which found the cause of social change in
Heraclitus' disunion, and in the strife of classes in which he
recognized the driving as well as the corrupting forces of history.
He applied these historicist principles to the story of the Decline
and Fall of the Greek city-states, and especially to a criticism
of democracy, which he described as effeminate and degenerate.
And we may add that later, in the *Laws* [44], he applied them
also to a story of the Decline and Fall of the Persian Empire,
thus making the beginning of a long series of Decline-and-Fall
dramatizations of the histories of empires and civilizations.
(O. Spengler's notorious *Decline of the West* is perhaps the worst
but not the last [45] of them.)   All this, I think, can be interpreted

as an attempt, and a most impressive one, to explain, and to rationalize, his experience of the breakdown of the tribal society ; an experience analogous to that which had led Heraclitus to develop the first philosophy of change.

But our analysis of Plato's descriptive sociology is still incomplete. His stories of the Decline and Fall, and with it nearly all the later stories, exhibit at least two characteristics which we have not discussed so far. He conceived these declining societies as some kind of organism, and the decline as a process similar to ageing. And he believed that the decline is well deserved, in the sense that moral decay, a fall and decline of the soul, goes hand in hand with that of the social body. All this plays an important rôle in Plato's theory of the first change—in the Story of the Number and of the Fall of Man. This theory, and its connection with the doctrine of Forms or Ideas, will be discussed in the next chapter.

Chapter 5 : NATURE AND CONVENTION

Plato was not the first to approach social phenomena in the spirit of scientific investigation. The beginning of social science goes back at least to the generation of Protagoras, the first of the great thinkers who called themselves ' Sophists '. It is marked by the realization of the need to distinguish between two different elements in man's environment—his natural environment and his social environment. This is a distinction which is difficult to make and to grasp, as can be inferred from the fact that even now it is not clearly established in our minds. It has been questioned ever since the time of Protagoras. Most of us, it seems, have a strong inclination to accept the peculiarities of our social environment as if they were ' natural '.

It is one of the characteristics of the magical attitude of a primitive tribal or ' closed ' society that it lives in a charmed circle [1] of unchanging taboos, of laws and customs which are felt to be as inevitable as the rising of the sun, or the cycle of the seasons, or similar obvious regularities of nature. And it is only after this magical ' closed society ' has actually broken down that a theoretical understanding of the difference between ' nature ' and ' society ' can develop.

I

An analysis of this development requires, I believe, a clear grasp of an important distinction. It is the distinction between (a) *natural laws*, or laws of nature, such as the laws describing the movements of the sun, the moon, and the planets, the succession of the seasons, etc., or the law of gravity or, say, the laws of thermodynamics and, on the other hand, (b) *normative laws*, or norms, or prohibitions and commandments, i.e. such rules as forbid or demand certain modes of conduct ; examples are the Ten Commandments or the legal rules regulating the procedure of the election of Members of Parliament, or the laws that constitute the Athenian Constitution.

Since the discussion of these matters is often vitiated by a tendency to blur this distinction, a few more words may be said about it. A law in sense (a)—a natural law—is describing a strict, unvarying regularity which either in fact holds in nature (in this case, the law is a true statement) or does not hold (in this case it is false).   If we do not know whether a law of nature is true or false, and if we wish to draw attention to our uncertainty, we often call it an 'hypothesis'.   A law of nature is unalterable ; there are no exceptions to it.   For if we are satisfied that something has happened which contradicts it, then we do not say that there is an exception, or an alteration to the law, but rather that our hypothesis has been refuted, since it has turned out that the supposed strict regularity did not hold, or in other words, that the supposed law of nature was not a true law of nature, but a false statement.   Since laws of nature are unalterable, they can be neither broken nor enforced.   They are beyond human control, although they may possibly be used by us for technical purposes, and although we may get into trouble by not knowing them, or by ignoring them.

All this is very different if we turn to laws of the kind (b), that is, to normative laws.   A normative law, whether it is now a legal enactment or a moral commandment, can be enforced by men. Also, it is alterable.   It may be perhaps described as good or bad, right or wrong, acceptable or unacceptable ; but only in a metaphorical sense can it be called ' true ' or ' false ', since it does not describe a fact, but lays down directions for our behaviour. If it has any point or significance, then it can be broken ; and if it cannot be broken then it is superfluous and without significance. ' Do not spend more money than you possess ' is a significant normative law ; it may be significant as a moral or legal rule, and the more necessary as it is so often broken.   ' Do not take more money out of your purse than there was in it ' may be said to be, by its wording, also a normative law ; but nobody would consider seriously such a rule as a significant part of a moral or legal system, since it cannot be broken.   If a significant normative law is observed, then this is always due to human control—to human actions and decisions.   Usually it is due to the decision to introduce sanctions—to punish or restrain those who break the law.

I believe, in common with a great number of thinkers, and especially with many social scientists, that the distinction between laws in sense (a), i.e. statements describing regularities of nature, and laws in sense (b), i.e. norms such as prohibitions or commandments, is a fundamental one, and that these two kinds of law have hardly more in common than a name.   But this view is by no means generally accepted ; on the contrary, many thinkers believe that there are norms—prohibitions or commandments—which are ' natural ' in the sense that they are laid down in accordance with natural laws in sense (*a*). They say, for example, that certain legal norms are in accordance with human nature, and therefore with psychological natural laws in sense (*a*), while other legal norms may be contrary to human nature ; and they add that those norms which can be shown to be in accordance with human nature are really not very different from natural laws in sense (*a*). Others say that natural laws in sense (*a*) are really very similar to normative laws since they are laid down by the will or decision of the Creator of the Universe—a view which, undoubtedly, lies behind the use of the originally normative word ' law ' for laws of the kind (*a*). All these views may be worthy of being discussed. But in order to discuss them, it is necessary first to distinguish between laws in the sense óf (*a*) and laws in the sense of (*b*), and not to confuse the issue by a bad terminology. Thus we shall reserve the term ' natural laws ' exclusively for laws of type (*a*), and we shall refuse to apply this term to any norms which are claimed to be, in some sense or other, ' natural '. The confusion is quite unnecessary since it is easy to speak of ' natural rights and obligations ' or of ' natural norms ' if we wish to stress the ' natural ' character of laws of type (*b*).

II

I believe that it is necessary for the understanding of Plato's sociology to consider how the distinction between natural and normative laws may have developed. I shall first discuss what seem to have been the starting point and the last step of the development, and later what seem to have been three intermediate steps, which all play a part in Plato's theory. The starting point can be described as a *naïve monism*. It may be said to be characteristic of the ' closed society '. The last step, which I describe as *critical dualism* (or critical conventionalism), is characteristic of the ' open society '. The fact that there are still many who try to avoid making this step may be taken as an indication that we are still in the midst of the transition from the closed to the open society. (With all this, compare chapter 10.)

The starting point which I have called ' naïve monism ' is the stage at which the distinction between natural and normative laws is not yet made. Unpleasant experiences are the means by which man learns to adjust himself to his environment. No distinction is made between sanctions imposed by other men, if a normative taboo is broken, and unpleasant experiences suffered in the natural environment. Within this stage, we may further distinguish between two possibilities. The one can be described as a *naïve naturalism*. At this stage regularities, whether natural or conventional, are felt to be beyond the possibility of any alteration whatever. But I believe that this stage is only an abstract possibility which probably was never realized. More important is a stage which we can describe as a *naïve conventionalism*—a stage at which both natural and normative regularities are experienced as expressions of, and as dependent upon, the decisions of man-like gods or demons. Thus the cycle of the seasons, or the peculiarities of the movements of the sun, the moon, and the planets, may be interpreted as obeying the ' laws ' or ' decrees ' or ' decisions ' which ' rule heaven and earth ', and which were laid down and ' pronounced by the creator-god in the beginning ' [2]. It is understandable that those who think in this way may believe that even the natural laws are open to modifications, under certain exceptional circumstances ; that with the help of magical practices man may sometimes influence them ; and that natural regularities are upheld by sanctions, as if they were normative. This point is well illustrated by Heraclitus' saying : ' The sun will not outstep the measure of his path ; or else the goddesses of Fate, the handmaids of Justice, will know how to find him.'

The breakdown of magic tribalism is closely connected with the realization that taboos are different in various tribes, that they are imposed and enforced by man, and that they may be broken without unpleasant repercussions if one can only escape the sanctions imposed by one's fellow-men. This realization is quickened when it is observed that laws are altered and made by human lawgivers. I have in mind not only such lawgivers as Solon, but also the laws which were made and enforced by the common people of democratic cities. These experiences may lead to a conscious differentiation between the man-enforced normative laws, based on decisions or conventions, and the natural regularities which are beyond his power. When this differentiation is clearly understood, then we can describe the position reached as a *critical dualism*, or critical conventionalism. In the development of Greek philosophy this dualism of facts and norms announces itself in terms of the opposition between nature and convention. [3]

In spite of the fact that this position was reached a long time ago by the Sophist Protagoras, an older contemporary of Socrates, it is still so little understood that it seems necessary to explain it in some detail. First, we must not think that critical dualism implies a theory of the historical origin of norms. It has nothing to do with the obviously untenable historical assertion that norms in the first place were *consciously* made or introduced by man, instead of having been found by him to be simply there (whenever he was first able to find anything of this kind). It therefore has nothing to do with the assertion that norms originate with man, and not with God, nor does it underrate the importance of normative laws. Least of all has it anything to do with the assertion that norms, since they are conventional, i.e. man-made, are therefore ' merely arbitrary '. Critical dualism merely asserts that norms and normative laws *can* be made and changed by man, more especially by a decision or convention to observe them or to alter them, and that it is therefore man who is morally responsible for them ; not perhaps for the norms which he finds to exist in society when he first begins to reflect upon them, but for the norms which he is prepared to tolerate once he has found out that he can do something to alter them. Norms are man-made in the sense that we must blame nobody but ourselves for them ; neither nature, nor God. It is our business to improve them as much as we can, if we find that they are objectionable. This last remark implies that by describing norms as conventional, I do not mean that they must be arbitrary, or that one set of normative laws will do just as well as another. By saying that some systems of laws can be improved, that some laws may be better than others, I rather imply that we can compare the existing normative laws (or social institutions) with some standard norms which we have decided are worthy of being realized. But even these standards are of our making in the sense that our decision in favour of them is our own decision, and that we alone carry the responsibility for adopting them. The standards are not to be found in nature. Nature consists of facts and of regularities, and is in itself neither moral nor immoral. It is we who impose our standards upon nature, and who in this way introduce morals into the natural world [4], in spite of the fact that we are part of this world. We are products of nature, but nature has made us together with our power of altering the world, of foreseeing and of planning for the future, and of making far-reaching decisions for which we are morally responsible. Yet responsibility, decisions, enter the world of nature only with us.

It is important for the understanding of this attitude to realize that these decisions can never be derived from facts (or from statements of facts), although they pertain to facts. The decision, for instance, to oppose slavery does not depend upon the fact that all men are born free and equal, and that no man is born in chains. For even if all were born free, some men might perhaps try to put others in chains, and they may even believe that they ought to put them in chains. And conversely, even if men were born in chains, many of us might demand the removal of these chains. Or to put this matter more precisely, if we consider a fact as alterable—such as the fact that many people are suffering from diseases—then we can always adopt a number of different attitudes towards this fact : more especially, we can decide to make an attempt to alter it ; or we can decide to resist any such attempt ; or we can decide not to take action at all.

All moral decisions pertain in this way to some fact or other, especially to some fact of social life, and all (alterable) facts of social life can give rise to many different decisions. Which shows that the decisions can never be derivable from these facts, or from a description of these facts.

But they cannot be derived from another class of facts either ; I mean those natural regularities which we describe with the help of natural laws. It is perfectly true that our decisions must be compatible with the natural laws (including those of human physiology and psychology), if they are ever to be carried into effect ; for if they run counter to such laws, then they simply cannot be carried out. The decision that all should work harder and eat less, for example, cannot be carried out beyond a certain point for physiological reasons, i.e. because beyond a certain point it would be incompatible with certain natural laws of physiology. Similarly, the decision that all should work less and eat more also cannot be carried out beyond a certain point, for various reasons, including the natural laws of economics. (As we shall see below, in section iv of this chapter, there are natural laws in the social sciences also ; we shall call them ' sociological laws '.)

Thus certain decisions may be eliminated as incapable of being executed, because they contradict certain natural laws (or ' unalterable facts '). But this does not mean, of course, that any decision can be logically derived from such ' unalterable facts '. Rather, the situation is this. In view of any fact whatsoever, whether it is alterable or unalterable, we can adopt various decisions—such as to alter it ; to protect it from those who wish to alter it ; not to interfere, etc. But if the fact in question is unalterable—either because an alteration is impossible in view of the existing laws of nature, or because an alteration is for other reasons too difficult for those who wish to alter it—then any decision to alter it will be simply impracticable ; in fact, any decision concerning such a fact will be pointless and without significance.

Critical dualism thus emphasizes the impossibility of reducing decisions or norms to facts ; it can therefore be described as a *dualism of facts and decisions*.

But this dualism seems to be open to attack. Decisions *are* facts, it may be said. If we decide to adopt a certain norm, then the making of this decision is itself a psychological or sociological fact, and it would be absurd to say that there is nothing in common between such facts and other facts. Since it cannot be doubted that our decisions about norms, i.e. the norms we adopt, clearly depend upon certain psychological facts, such as the influence of our upbringing, it seems to be absurd to postulate a dualism of facts and decisions, or to say that decisions cannot be derived from facts. This objection can be answered by pointing out that we can speak of a ' decision ' in two different senses. We may speak of a certain decision which has been submitted, or considered, or reached, or been decided upon ; or alternatively, we may speak of an act of deciding and call this a ' decision '. Only in the second sense can we describe a decision as a fact. The situation is analogous with a number of other expressions. In one sense, we may speak of a certain resolution which has been submitted to some council, and in the other sense, the council's act of taking it may be spoken of as the council's resolution. Similarly, we may speak of a proposal or a suggestion before us, and on the other hand of the act of proposing or suggesting something, which may also be called ' proposal ' or ' suggestion '. An analogous ambiguity is well known in the field of descriptive statements. Let us consider the statement : ' Napoleon died on St. Helena.' It will be useful to distinguish this statement from the fact which it describes, and which we may call the primary fact, viz. the fact that Napoleon died at St. Helena. Now a historian, say Mr. A, when writing the biography of Napoleon, may make the statement mentioned. In doing so, he is describing what we called the primary fact. But there is also a secondary fact, which is altogether different from the primary one, namely the fact that he made this statement ; and another historian, Mr. B, when writing the biography of Mr. A, may describe this second fact by saying : ' Mr. A stated that Napoleon died on St. Helena.' The secondary fact described in this way happens to be itself a description. But it is a description in a sense of the word that must be distinguished from the sense in which we called the statement ' Napoleon died on St. Helena ' a description. The making of a description, or of a statement, is a sociological or psychological fact. But *the description made is to be distinguished from the fact that it has been made.* It cannot even be derived from this fact ; for that would mean that we can validly deduce ' Napoleon died on St. Helena ' from ' Mr. A stated that Napoleon died on St. Helena ', which obviously we cannot.

In the field of decisions, the situation is analogous. The making of a decision, the adoption of a norm or of a standard, is a fact. But the norm or standard which has been adopted, is not a fact. That most people agree with the norm ' Thou shalt not steal ' is a sociological fact. But the norm ' Thou shalt not steal ' is not a fact, and can never be inferred from sentences describing facts. This will be seen most clearly when we remember that there are always various and even opposite decisions possible with respect to a certain relevant fact. For instance, in face of the sociological fact that most people adopt the norm ' Thou shalt not steal ', it is still possible to decide either to adopt this norm, or to oppose its adoption ; it is possible to encourage those who have adopted the norm, or to discourage them, and to persuade them to adopt another norm. To sum up, *it is impossible to derive a sentence stating a norm or a decision or, say, a proposal for a policy from a sentence stating a fact* ; this is only another way of saying that it is impossible to derive norms or decisions *or proposals* from facts [5].

The statement that norms are man-made (man-made not in the sense that they were consciously designed, but in the sense that men can judge and alter them—that is to say, in the sense that the responsibility for them is entirely ours) has often been misunderstood. Nearly all misunderstandings can be traced back to one fundamental misapprehension, namely, to the belief that ' convention ' implies ' arbitrariness ' ; that if we are free to choose any system of norms we like, then one system is just as good as any other. It must, of course, be admitted that the view that norms are conventional or artificial indicates that there will be a certain element of arbitrariness involved, i.e. that there may be different systems of norms between which there is not much to choose (a fact that has been duly emphasized by Protagoras). But artificiality by no means implies full arbitrariness. Mathematical calculi, for instance, or symphonies, or plays, are highly artificial, yet it does not follow that one calculus or symphony or play is just as good as any other. Man has created new worlds—of language, of music, of poetry, of science ; and the most important of these is the world of the moral demands, for equality, for freedom, and for helping the weak [6]. When comparing the field of morals with the field of music or of mathematics, I do not wish to imply that these similarities reach very far. There is, more especially, a great difference between moral decisions and decisions in the field of art. Many moral decisions involve the life and death of other men. Decisions in the field of art are much less urgent and important. It is therefore most misleading to say that a man decides for or against slavery as he may decide for or against certain works of music and literature, or that moral decisions are purely matters of taste. Nor are they merely decisions about how to make the world more beautiful, or about other luxuries of this kind ; they are decisions of much greater urgency. (With all this, cp. also chapter 9.) Our comparison is only intended to show that the view that moral decisions rest with us does not imply that they are entirely arbitrary.

The view that norms are man-made is also, strangely enough, contested by some who see in this attitude an attack on religion. It must be admitted, of course, that this view is an attack on certain forms of religion, namely, on the religion of blind authority, on magic and tabooism. But I do not think that it is in any way opposed to a religion built upon the idea of personal responsibility and freedom of conscience. I have in mind, of course, especially Christianity, at least as it is usually interpreted in democratic countries ; that Christianity which, as against all tabooism, preaches, ' Ye have heard that it was said by them of old time. . . But I say unto you . .' ; opposing in every case the voice of conscience to mere formal obedience and the fulfilment of the law.

I would not admit that to think of ethical laws as being man-made in this sense is incompatible with the religious view that they are given to us by God. Historically, all ethics undoubtedly begin with religion ; but I do not now deal with historical questions. I do not ask who was the first ethical lawgiver. I only maintain that it is we, and we alone, who are responsible for adopting or rejecting some suggested moral laws ; it is we who must distinguish between the true prophets and the false prophets. All kinds of norms have been claimed to be God-given. If you accept the ' Christian ' ethics of equality and toleration and freedom of conscience only because of its claim to rest upon divine authority, then you build on a weak basis ; for it has been only too often claimed that inequality is willed by God, and that we must not be tolerant with unbelievers. If, however, you accept the Christian ethics not because you are commanded to do so but because of your conviction that it is the right decision to take, then it is you who have decided. My insistence that we make the decisions and carry the responsibility must not be taken to imply that we cannot, or must not, be helped by faith, and inspired by tradition or by great examples. Nor does it imply that the creation of moral decisions is merely a ' natural ' process, i.e. of the order of physico-chemical processes. In fact, Protagoras, the first critical dualist, taught that nature does not know norms, and that the introduction of norms is due to man, and the most important of human achievements. He thus held that ' institutions and conventions were what raised men above the brutes ', as Burnet [7] puts it. But in spite of his insistence that man creates norms, that it is man who is the measure of all things, he believed that man could achieve the creation of norms only with supernatural help. Norms, he taught, are superimposed upon the original or natural state of affairs by man, but with the help of Zeus. It is at Zeus' bidding that Hermes gives to men an understanding of justice and honour ; and he distributes this gift to all men equally. The way in which the first clear statement of critical dualism makes room for a religious interpretation of our sense of responsibility shows how little critical dualism is opposed to a religious attitude. A similar approach can be discerned, I believe, in the historical Socrates (see chapter 10) who felt compelled, by his conscience as well as by his religious beliefs, to question all authority, and who searched for the norms in whose justice he could trust. The doctrine of the autonomy of ethics is independent of the problem of religion, but compatible with, or perhaps even necessary for, any religion which respects individual conscience.

IV

So much concerning the dualism of facts and decisions, or the doctrine of the autonomy of ethics, first advocated by Protagoras and Socrates [8]. It is, I believe, indispensable for a reasonable understanding of our social environment. But of course this does not mean that all ' social laws ', i.e. all regularities of our social life, are normative and man imposed. On the contrary, there are important natural laws of social life also. For these, the term *sociological laws* seems appropriate. It is ust the fact that in social life we meet with both kinds of laws, natural and normative, which makes it so important to distinguish them clearly.

In speaking of sociological laws or natural laws of social life, I do not think so much of the alleged laws of evolution in which historicists such as Plato are interested, although if there are any such regularities of historical developments, their formulations would certainly fall under the category of sociological laws. Nor do I think so much of the laws of ' human nature ', i.e. of psychological and socio-psychological regularities of human behaviour. I have in mind, rather, such laws as are formulated by modern economic theories, for instance, the theory of international trade, or the theory of the trade cycle. These and other important sociological laws are connected with the functioning of *social institutions*. (Cp. chapters 3 and 9.) These laws play a rôle in our social life corresponding to the rôle played in mechanical engineering by, say, the principle of the lever. For institutions, like levers, are needed if we want to achieve anything which goes beyond the power of our muscles. Like machines, institutions multiply our power for good and evil. Like machines, they need intelligent supervision by someone who understands their way of functioning and, most of all, their purpose, since we cannot build them so that they work entirely automatically. Furthermore, their construction needs some knowledge of social regularities which impose limitations upon what can be achieved by institutions [9]. (These limitations are somewhat analogous, for instance, to the law of conservation of energy, which amounts to the statement that we cannot build a perpetual motion machine.) But fundamentally, institutions are always made by establishing the observance of certain norms, designed with a certain aim in mind. This holds especially for institutions which are consciously created ; but even those—the vast majority—which arise as the undesigned results of human actions (cp. chapter 14) are the indirect results of purposive actions of some kind or other ; and their functioning depends, largely, on the observance of norms. (Even mechanical engines are made, as it were, not only of iron, but by combining iron and norms ; i.e. by transforming physical things, but according to certain normative rules, namely their plan or design.)   In institutions, normative laws and sociological, i.e. natural, laws are closely interwoven, and it is therefore impossible to understand the functioning of institutions without being able to distinguish between these two. (These remarks are intended to suggest certain problems rather than to give solutions.   More especially, the analogy mentioned between institutions and machines must not be interpreted as proposing the theory that institutions *are* machines—in some essentialist sense.   Of course they are not machines.   And although the thesis is here proposed that we may obtain useful and interesting results if we ask ourselves whether an institution does serve any purpose, and what purposes it may serve, it is not asserted that every institution serves some definite purpose—its essential purpose, as it were.)

V

As indicated before, there are many intermediate steps in the development from a naïve or magical monism to a critical dualism which clearly realizes the distinction between norms and natural laws.   Most of these intermediate positions arise from the misapprehension that if a norm is conventional or artificial, it must be wholly arbitrary.   To understand Plato's position, which combines elements of them all, it is necessary to make a survey of the three most important of these intermediate positions.   They are (1) biological naturalism, (2) ethical or juridical positivism, and (3) psychological or spiritual naturalism.   It is interesting that every one of these positions has been used for defending ethical views which are radically opposed to each other ; more especially, for defending the worship of power, and for defending the rights of the weak.

(1) Biological naturalism, or more precisely, the biological form of ethical naturalism, is the theory that in spite of the fact that moral laws and the laws of states are arbitrary, there are some eternal unchanging laws of nature from which we can derive such norms.   Food habits, i.e. the number of meals, and the kind of food taken, are an example of the arbitrariness of conventions,

the biological naturalist may argue ; yet there are undoubtedly certain natural laws in this field.   For instance, a man will die if he takes either insufficient or too much food.   Thus it seems that just as there are realities behind appearances, so behind our arbitrary conventions there are some unchanging natural laws and especially the laws of biology.

Biological naturalism has been used not only to defend equalitarianism, but also to defend the anti-equalitarian doctrine of the rule of the strong.   One of the first to put forward this naturalism was the poet Pindar, who used it to support the theory that the strong should rule.   He claimed [10] that it is a law, valid throughout nature, that the stronger does with the weaker whatever he likes.   Thus laws which protect the weak are not merely arbitrary but artificial distortions of the true natural law that the strong should be free and the weak should be his slave.   The view is discussed a good deal by Plato ; it is attacked in the *Gorgias*, a dialogue which is still much influenced by Socrates ; in the *Republic*, it is put in the mouth of Thrasymachus, and identified with ethical individualism (see the next chapter) ; in the *Laws*, Plato is less antagonistic to Pindar's view ; but he still contrasts it with the rule of the wisest, which, he says, is a better principle, and just as much in accordance with nature (see also the quotation later in this chapter).

The first to put forward a humanitarian or equalitarian version of biological naturalism was the Sophist Antiphon.   To him is due also the identification of nature with truth, and of convention with opinion (or ' delusive opinion ' [11]).   Antiphon is a radical naturalist.   He believes that most norms are not merely arbitrary, but directly contrary to nature.   Norms, he says, are imposed from outside, while the rules of nature are inevitable.   It is disadvantageous and even dangerous to break man-imposed norms if the breach is observed by those who impose them ; but there is no inner necessity attached to them, and nobody needs to be ashamed of breaking them ; shame and punishment are only sanctions arbitrarily imposed from outside. On this criticism of conventional morals, Antiphon bases a utilitarian ethics.   ' Of the actions here mentioned, one would find many to be contrary to nature.   For they involve more suffering where there should be less, and less pleasure where there could be more, and injury where it is unnecessary.' [12]   At the same time, he taught the need for self-control.   His equalitarianism he formulates as follows : ' The nobly born we revere and adore ; but not the lowly born.   These are barbarous habits. For as to our natural gifts, we are all on an equal footing, on all points, whether we now happen to be Greeks or Barbarians. . . We all breathe the air through our mouths and nostrils.'

A similar equalitarianism was voiced by the Sophist Hippias, whom Plato represents as addressing his audience : ' Gentlemen, I believe that we are all kinsmen and friends and fellow-citizens ; if not by conventional law, then by nature.   For by nature, likeness is an expression of kinship ; but conventional law, the tyrant of mankind, compels us to do much that is against nature.' [13] This spirit was bound up with the Athenian movement against slavery (mentioned in chapter 4) to which Euripides gave expression : ' The name alone brings shame upon the slave who can be excellent in every way and truly equal to the free born man.' Elsewhere, he says : ' Man's law of nature is equality.'   And Alcidamas, a disciple of Gorgias and a contemporary of Plato, wrote : ' God has made all men free ; no man is a slave by nature.'   Similar views are also expressed by Lycophron, another member of Gorgias' school : ' The splendour of noble birth is imaginary, and its prerogatives are based upon a mere word.'

Reacting against this great humanitarian movement—the movement of the ' Great Generation ', as I shall call it later (chapter 10)—Plato, and his disciple Aristotle, advanced the theory of the biological and moral inequality of man.   Greeks and barbarians are unequal by nature ; the opposition between them corresponds to that between natural masters and natural slaves.   The natural inequality of men is one of the reasons for their living together, for their natural gifts are complementary. Social life begins with natural inequality, and it must continue upon that foundation.   I shall discuss these doctrines later in more detail.   At present, they may serve to show how biological naturalism can be used to support the most divergent ethical doctrines.   In the light of our previous analysis of the impossibility of basing norms upon facts this result is not unexpected.

Such considerations, however, are perhaps not sufficient to defeat a theory as popular as biological naturalism ; I therefore propose two more direct criticisms.   First, it must be admitted that certain forms of behaviour may be described as more ' natural ' than other forms ; for instance, going naked or eating only raw food ; and some people think that this in itself justifies the choice of these forms.   But in this sense it certainly is not natural to interest oneself in art, or science, or even in arguments in favour of naturalism. The choice of conformity with ' nature ' as a supreme standard leads ultimately to consequences which few will be prepared to face ; it does not lead to a more natural form of civilization, but to beastliness [14]. The second criticism is more important. The biological naturalist assumes that he can derive his norms from the natural laws which determine the conditions of health, etc., if he does not naïvely believe that we need adopt no norms whatever but simply live according to the ' laws of nature '. He overlooks the fact that he makes a choice, a decision ; that it is possible that some other people cherish certain things more than their health (for instance, the many who have consciously risked their lives for medical research). And he is therefore mistaken if he believes that he has not made a decision, or that he has derived his norms from biological laws.

(2) Ethical positivism shares with the biological form of ethical naturalism the belief that we must try to reduce norms to facts. But the facts are this time sociological facts, namely, the actual existing norms. Positivism maintains that there are no other norms but the laws which have actually been set up (or ' posited ') and which have therefore a positive existence. Other standards are considered as unreal imaginations. The existing laws are the only possible standards of goodness : what is, is good. (Might is right.) 'According to some forms of this theory, it is a gross misunderstanding to believe that the individual can judge the norms of society ; rather, it is society which provides the code by which the individual must be judged.

As a matter of historical fact, ethical (or moral, or juridical) positivism has usually been conservative, or even authoritarian ; and it has often invoked the authority of God. Its arguments depend, I believe, upon the alleged arbitrariness of norms. We must believe in existing norms, it claims, because there are no better norms which we may find for ourselves. In reply to this it might be asked : What about this norm ' We must believe etc.' ? If this is only an existing norm, then it does not count as an argument in favour of these norms ; but if it is an appeal to our insight, then it admits that we can, after all, find norms ourselves. And if we are told to accept norms on authority because we cannot judge them, then neither can we judge whether the claims of the authority are justified, or whether we may not follow a false prophet. And if it is held that there are no false prophets because laws are arbitrary anyhow, so that the main thing is to have some laws, then we may ask ourselves why it should be so important to have laws at all ; for if there are no further standards, why then should we not choose to have no laws ? (These remarks may perhaps indicate the reasons for my belief that authoritarian or conservative principles are usually an expression of ethical nihilism ; that is to say, of an extreme moral scepticism, of a distrust of man and of his possibilities.)

While the theory of natural rights has, in the course of history, often been proffered in support of equalitarian and humanitarian ideas, the positivist school was usually in the opposite camp. But this is not much more than an accident. As has been shown, ethical naturalism may be used with very different intentions. (It has recently been used for confusing the whole issue by advertising certain allegedly ' natural ' rights and obligations as ' natural laws '.) Conversely, there are also humanitarian and progressive positivists. For if all norms are arbitrary, why not be tolerant ? This is a typical attempt to justify a humanitarian attitude along positivist lines.

(3) Psychological or spiritual naturalism is in a way a combination of the two previous views, and it can best be explained by means of an argument against the one-sidedness of these views. The ethical positivist is right, this argument runs, if he emphasizes that all norms are conventional, i.e. a product of man, and of human society ; but he overlooks the fact that they are therefore an expression of the psychological or spiritual nature of man, and of the nature of human society. The biological naturalist is right in assuming that there are certain natural aims or ends, from which we can derive natural norms ; but he overlooks the fact that our natural aims are not necessarily such aims as health, pleasure, or food, shelter or propagation. Human nature is such that man, or at least some men, do not want to live by bread alone, that they seek higher aims, spiritual aims. We may thus derive man's true natural aims from his own true nature, which is spiritual, and social. And we may, further, derive the natural norms of life from his natural ends.

This plausible position was, I believe, first formulated by Plato, who was here under the influence of the Socratic doctrine of the soul, i.e. of Socrates' teaching that the spirit matters more than the flesh [15]. Its appeal to our sentiments is undoubtedly very much stronger than that of the other two positions. It can however be combined, like these, with any ethical decision ; with a humanitarian attitude as well as with the worship of power. For we can, for instance, decide to treat all men as participating in this spiritual human nature ; or we can insist like Heraclitus, that the many ' fill their bellies like the beasts ', and are therefore of an inferior nature, and that only a few elect ones are worthy of the spiritual community of men. Accordingly, spiritual naturalism has been much used, and especially by Plato, to justify the natural prerogatives of the ' noble ' or ' elect ' or ' wise ' or of the ' natural leader '. (Plato's attitude is discussed in the following chapters.) On the other hand, it has been used by Christian and other [16] humanitarian forms of ethics, for instance by Paine and by Kant, to demand the recognition of the ' natural rights ' of every human individual. It is clear that spiritual naturalism can be used to defend any ' positive ', i.e. existing, norm. For it can always be argued that these norms would not be in force if they did not express some traits of human nature. In this way, spiritual naturalism can, in practical problems, become one with positivism, in spite of their traditional opposition. In fact, this form of naturalism is so wide and so vague that it may be used to defend anything. There is nothing that has ever occurred to man which could not be claimed to be ' natural ' ; for if it were not in his nature, how could it have occurred to him ?

Looking back at this brief survey, we may perhaps discern two main tendencies which stand in the way of adopting a critical dualism. The first is a general tendency towards monism [17], that is to say, towards the reduction of norms to facts. The second lies deeper, and it possibly forms the background of the first. It is based upon our fear of admitting to ourselves that the responsibility for our ethical decisions is entirely ours and cannot be shifted to anybody else ; neither to God, nor to nature, nor to society, nor to history. All these ethical theories attempt to find somebody, or perhaps some argument, to take the burden from us [18]. But we cannot shirk this responsibility. Whatever authority we may accept, it is we who accept it. We only deceive ourselves if we do not realize this simple point.

VI

We now turn to a more detailed analysis of Plato's naturalism and its relation to his historicism. Plato, of course, does not always use the term 'nature' in the same sense. The most important meaning which he attaches to it is, I believe, practically identical with that which he attaches to the term 'essence'. This way of using the term 'nature' still survives among essentialists even in our day ; they still speak, for instance, of the nature of mathematics, or of the nature of inductive inference, or of the 'nature of happiness and misery' [19]. When used by Plato in this way, 'nature' means nearly the same as 'Form' or 'Idea'; for the Form or Idea of a thing, as shown above, is also its essence. The main difference between natures and Forms or Ideas seems to be this. The Form or Idea of a sensible thing is, as we have seen, not in that thing, but separated from it ; it is its forefather, its primogenitor ; but this Form or father passes something on to the sensible things which are its offspring or race, namely, their nature. This 'nature' is thus the inborn or original quality of a thing, and in so far, its inherent essence ; it is the original power or disposition of a thing, and it determines those of its properties which are the basis of its resemblance to, or of its innate participation in, its Form or Idea.

'Natural' is, accordingly, what is innate or original or divine in a thing, while 'artificial' is that which has been later changed by man or added or imposed by him, through external compulsion. Plato frequently insists that all products of human 'art' at their best are only copies of 'natural' sensible things. But since these in turn are only copies of the divine Forms or Ideas, the products of art are only copies of copies, twice removed from reality, and therefore less good, less real, and less true [20] than even the (natural) things in flux. We see from this that Plato agrees with Antiphon [21] in at least one point, namely in assuming that the opposition between nature and convention or art corresponds to that between truth and falsehood, between reality and appearance, between primary or original and secondary or man-made things, and to that between the objects of rational knowledge and those of delusive opinion. The opposition corresponds also, according to Plato, to that between 'the offspring of divine workmanship' or 'the products of divine art', and 'what man makes out of them, i.e. the products of human art'.[22] All those things whose intrinsic value Plato wishes to emphasize he therefore claims to be natural as opposed to artificial. Thus he insists in the Laws that the soul has to be considered prior to all material things, and that it must therefore be said to exist by nature : 'Nearly everybody . . is ignorant of the power of the soul, and especially of her origin. They do not know that she is among the first of things, and prior to all bodies. . . In using the word " nature " one wants to describe the things that were created first ; but if it turns out that it is the soul which is prior to other things (and not, perhaps, fire or air), . . then the soul, beyond all others, may be asserted to exist by nature, in the truest sense of the word.' [23] (Plato here re-affirms his old theory that the soul is more closely akin to the Forms or Ideas than the body ; a theory which is also the basis of his doctrine of immortality.)

But Plato not only teaches that the soul is prior to other things and therefore exists ' by nature ' ; he uses the term ' nature ', if applied to man, frequently also as a name for spiritual powers or gifts or natural talents, so that we can say that a man's ' nature ' is much the same as his ' soul ' ; it is the divine principle by which he participates in the Form or Idea, in the divine primogenitor of his race. And the term ' race ', again, is frequently used in a very similar sense. Since a ' race ' is united by being the offspring of the same primo- genitor, it must also be united by a common nature. Thus the terms ' nature ' and ' race ' are frequently used by Plato as synonyms, for instance, when he speaks of the ' race of philoso- phers ' and of those who have ' philosophic natures ' ; so that both these terms are closely akin to the terms ' essence ' and ' soul '.

Plato's theory of ' nature ' opens another approach to his historicist methodology. Since it seems to be the task of science in general to examine the true nature of its objects, it is the task of a social or political science to examine the nature of human society, and of the state. But the nature of a thing, according to Plato, is its origin ; or at least it is determined by its origin. Thus the method of any science will be the investigation of the origin of things (of their ' causes '). This principle, when applied to the science of society and of politics, leads to the demand that the origin of society and of the state must be examined. History therefore is not studied for its own sake but serves as *the* method of the social sciences. *This is the historicist methodology.*

What is the nature of human society, of the state ? Accord- ing to historicist methods, this fundamental question of sociology must be reformulated in this way : what is the origin of society and of the state ? The reply given by Plato in the *Republic* as

well as in the *Laws* [24], agrees with the position described above
as spiritual naturalism. The origin of society is a convention,
a *social contract*. But it is not only that ; it is, rather, a natural
convention, i.e. a convention which is based upon human
nature, and more precisely, upon the social nature of man.

This social nature of man has its origin in the *imperfection
of the human individual*. In opposition to Socrates [25], Plato
teaches that the human individual cannot be self-sufficient,
owing to the limitations inherent in human nature. Although
Plato insists that there are very different degrees of human
perfection, it turns out that even the very few comparatively
perfect men still depend upon others (who are less perfect) ;
if for nothing else, then for having the dirty work, the manual
work, done by them [26]. In this way, even the 'rare and
uncommon natures' who approach perfection depend upon
society, upon the state. They can reach perfection only through
the state and in the state ; the perfect state must offer them the
proper 'social habitat', without which they must grow corrupt
and degenerate. The state therefore must be placed higher
than the individual since only the state can be self-sufficient
(' autark '), perfect, and able to make good the necessary imperfection of the individual.

Society and the individual are thus interdependent. The
one owes its existence to the other. Society owes its existence
to human nature, and especially to its lack of self-sufficiency ;
and the individual owes his existence to society, since he is not
self-sufficient. But within this relationship of interdependence,
the superiority of the state over the individual manifests itself
in various ways ; for instance, in the fact that the seed of the
decay and disunion of a perfect state does not spring up in
the state itself, but rather in its individuals ; it is rooted in the
imperfection of the human soul, of human nature ; or more
precisely, in the fact that the race of men is liable to degenerate.
To this point, the origin of political decay, and its dependence
upon the degeneration of human nature, I shall return presently ;
but I wish first to make a few comments on some of the characteristics of Plato's sociology, especially upon his version of the
theory of the social contract, and upon his view of the state
as a super-individual, i.e. his version of the biological or organic
theory of the state.

Whether Protagoras first proposed a theory that laws originate
with a social contract, or whether Lycophron (whose theory

will be discussed in the next chapter) was the first to do so, is not certain. In any case, the idea is closely related to Protagoras' conventionalism. The fact that Plato consciously combined some conventionalist ideas, and even a version of the contract theory, with his naturalism, is in itself an indication that conventionalism in its original form did not maintain that laws are wholly arbitrary ; and Plato's remarks on Protagoras confirm this [27]. How conscious Plato was of a conventionalist element in his version of naturalism can be seen from a passage in the *Laws*. Plato there gives a list of the various principles upon which political authority might be based, mentioning Pindar's biological naturalism (see above), i.e. ' the principle that the stronger shall rule and the weaker be ruled ', which he describes as a principle ' according to nature, as the Theban poet Pindar once stated '. Plato contrasts this principle with another which he recommends by showing that it combines conventionalism with naturalism : ' But there is also a . . claim which is the greatest principle of all, namely, that the wise shall lead and rule, and that the ignorant shall follow ; and this, O Pindar, wisest of poets, is surely not contrary to nature, but according to nature ; for what it demands is not external compulsion but the truly natural sovereignty of a law which is based upon mutual consent.' [28]

In the *Republic* we find elements of the conventionalist contract theory in a similar way combined with elements of naturalism (and utilitarianism). ' The city originates ', we hear there, ' because we are not self-sufficient ; . . or is there another origin of settlement in cities ? . . Men gather into one settlement many . . helpers, since they need many things. . . And when they share their goods with one another, the one giving, the other partaking, does not every one expect in this way to further his own interest ? ' [29] Thus the inhabitants gather in order that each may further his own interest ; which is an element of the contract theory. But behind this stands the fact that they are not self-sufficient, a fact of human nature ; which is an element of naturalism. And this element is developed further. ' By nature, no two of us are exactly alike. Each has his peculiar nature, some being fit for one kind of work and some for another. . . Is it better that a man should work in many crafts or that he should work in one only ? . . Surely, more will be produced and better and more easily if each man works in one occupation only, according to his natural gifts.'

In this way, the economic principle of the division of labour is introduced (reminding us of the affinity between Plato's historicism and the materialist interpretation of history). But this principle is based here upon an element of biological naturalism, namely, upon the natural inequality of men. At first, this idea is introduced inconspicuously and, as it were, innocently. But we shall see in the next chapter that it has far-reaching consequences ; indeed, the only really important division of labour turns out to be that between rulers and ruled, claimed to be based upon the natural inequality of masters and slaves, of wise and ignorant.

We have seen that there is a considerable element of conventionalism as well as of biological naturalism in Plato's position ; an observation which is not surprising when we consider that this position is, on the whole, that of spiritual naturalism which, because of its vagueness, easily allows for all such combinations. This spiritual version of naturalism is perhaps best formulated in the *Laws*. ' Men say ', says Plato, ' that the greatest and most beautiful things are natural . . and the lesser things artificial.' So far he agrees ; but he then attacks the materialists who say ' that fire and water, and earth and air, all exist by nature . . and that all normative laws are altogether unnatural and artificial and based upon superstitions which are not true.' Against this view, he shows first, that it is not bodies nor elements, but the soul which truly ' exists by nature ' [30] (I have quoted this passage above) ; and from this he concludes that order, and law, must also be by nature, since they spring from the soul : ' If the soul is prior to the body, then things dependent upon the soul ' (i.e. spiritual matters) ' are also prior to those dependent upon body. . . And the soul orders and directs all things.' This supplies the theoretical background for the doctrine that ' laws and purposeful institutions exist by nature, and not by anything lower than nature, since they are born of reason and true thought.' This is a clear statement of spiritual naturalism ; and it is combined as well with positivist beliefs of a conservative kind : ' Thoughtful and prudent legislation will find a most powerful help because the laws will remain unchanged once they have been laid down in writing.'

From all this it can be seen that arguments derived from Plato's spiritual naturalism are quite incapable of helping to answer any question which may arise concerning the ' just ' or ' natural ' character of any particular law. Spiritual naturalism is much too vague to be applied to any practical problem. It cannot do much beyond providing some general arguments in favour of conservativism. In practice, everything is left to the wisdom of the great lawgiver (a godlike philosopher, whose picture, especially in the *Laws*, is undoubtedly a self-portrait ; see also chapter 8). As opposed to his spiritual naturalism, however, Plato's theory of the interdependence of society and the individual furnishes more concrete results ; and so does his anti-equalitarian biological naturalism.

VII

It has been indicated above that because of its self-sufficiency, the ideal state appears to Plato as the perfect individual, and the individual citizen, accordingly, as an imperfect copy of the state. This view which makes of the state a kind of super-organism or Leviathan introduces into the occident the so-called organic or biological theory of the state. The principle of this theory will be criticized later [31]. Here I wish first to draw attention to the fact that Plato does not defend the theory, and indeed hardly formulates it explicitly. But it is clearly enough implied ; in fact, the fundamental analogy between the state and the human individual is one of the standard topics of the *Republic*. It is worth mentioning, in this connection, that the analogy serves to further the analysis of the individual rather than that of the state. One could perhaps defend the view that Plato (perhaps under the influence of Alcmaeon) does not offer so much a biological theory of the state as a political theory of the human individual [32]. This view, I think, is fully in accordance with his doctrine that the individual is lower than the state, and a kind of imperfect copy of it. In the very place in which Plato introduces his fundamental analogy, it is used in this way; that is to say, as a method of explaining and elucidating the individual. The city, it is said, is greater than the individual, and therefore easier to examine. Plato gives this as his reason for suggesting that ' we should begin our inquiry ' (namely, into the nature of justice) ' in the city, and continue it afterwards in the individual, always watching for points of similarity. . . May we not expect in this way to discern more easily what we are looking for ? '

From his way of introducing it we can see that Plato (and perhaps his readers) took his fundamental analogy for granted. This may well be a symptom of nostalgia, of a longing for a unified and harmonious, an ' organic ' state : for a society of a more primitive kind. (See chapter 10.) The city state ought to remain small, he says, and should grow only as long as its increase does not endanger its unity. The whole city should, by its nature, be one, and not many.[33] Plato thus emphasizes the ' oneness ' or individuality of his city. But he also emphasizes the ' manyness ' of the human individual. In his analysis of the individual soul, and of its division into three parts, reason, energy, and animal instincts, corresponding to the three classes of his state, the guardians, warriors, and workers (who still continue to ' fill their bellies like the beasts ', as Heraclitus had said), Plato goes so far as to oppose these parts to one another as if they were ' distinct and conflicting persons ' [34]. ' We are thus told ', says Grote, ' that though man is apparently One, he is in reality Many . . though the perfect Commonwealth is apparently Many, it is in reality One.' It is clear that this corresponds to the Ideal character of the state of which the individual is a kind of imperfect copy. Such an emphasis upon oneness and wholeness—especially of the state ; or perhaps of the world —may be described as ' holism '. Plato's holism, I believe, is closely related to the tribal collectivism mentioned in earlier chapters. Plato was longing for the lost unity of tribal life. A life of change, in the midst of a social revolution, appeared to him unreal. Only a stable whole, the permanent collective, has reality, not the passing individuals. It is ' natural ' for the individual to subserve the whole, which is no mere assembly of individuals, but a ' natural ' unit of a higher order.

Plato gives many excellent sociological descriptions of this ' natural ', i.e. tribal and collectivist, mode of social life : ' The law ', he writes in the *Republic*, ' . . is designed to bring about the welfare of the state as a whole, fitting the citizens into one unit, by means of both persuasion and force. It makes them all share in whatever benefit each of them can contribute to the community. And it is actually the law which creates for the state men of the right frame of mind ; not for the purpose of letting them loose, so that everybody can go his own way, but in order to utilize them all for welding the city together.' [35] That there is in this holism an emotional æstheticism, a longing for beauty, can be seen, for instance, from a remark in the *Laws* : ' Every artist . . executes the part for the sake of the whole, and not the whole for the sake of the part.' At the same place, we also find a truly classical formulation of political holism : ' You are created for the sake of the whole, and not the whole for the sake of you.' Within this whole, the different individuals, and groups of individuals, with their natural inequalities, must render their specific and very unequal services.

All this would indicate that Plato's theory was a form of the organic theory of the state, even if he had not sometimes spoken of the state as an organism. But since he did this, there can be no doubt left that he must be described as an exponent, or rather, as one of the originators, of this theory. His version of this theory may be characterized as a personalist or psychological one, since he describes the state not in a general way as similar to some organism or other, but as analogous to the human individual, and more specifically to the human soul. Especially the disease of the state, the dissolution of its unity, corresponds to the disease of the human soul, of human nature. In fact, the disease of the state is not only correlated with, but is directly produced by, the corruption of human nature, more especially of the members of the ruling class. Every single one of the typical stages in the degeneration of the state is brought about by a corresponding stage in the degeneration of the human soul, of human nature, of the human race. And since this moral degeneration is interpreted as based upon racial degeneration, we might say that the biological element in Plato's naturalism turns out, in the end, to have the most important part in the foundation of his historicism. For the history of the downfall of the first or perfect state is nothing but the history of the biological degeneration of the race of men.

VIII

It was mentioned in the last chapter that the problem of the beginning of change and decay is one of the major difficulties of Plato's historicist theory of society. The first, the natural and perfect city-state, cannot be supposed to carry within itself the germ of dissolution, ' for a city which carries within itself the germ of dissolution is for that very reason imperfect ' [36]. Plato tries to get over the difficulty by laying the blame on his universally valid historical, biological, and perhaps even cosmological, evolutionary law of degeneration, rather than on the particular constitution of the first or perfect city [37] : ' Everything that has been generated must decay.' But this general theory does not provide a fully satisfactory solution, for it does not explain why even a sufficiently perfect state cannot escape the law of decay. And indeed, Plato hints that historical decay

might have been avoided [38], had the rulers of the first or natural
state been trained philosophers. But they were not. They were
not trained (as he demands that the rulers of his heavenly city
should be) in mathematics and dialectics ; and in order to
avoid degeneration, they would have needed to be initiated into
the higher mysteries of eugenics, of the science of ' keeping pure
the race of the guardians ', and of avoiding the mixture of the
noble metals in their veins with the base metals of the workers.
But these higher mysteries are difficult to reveal. Plato distinguishes sharply, in the fields of mathematics, acoustics, and
astronomy, between mere (delusive) opinion which is tainted by
experience, and which cannot reach exactness, and is altogether
on a low level, and pure rational knowledge, which is free from
sensual experience and exact. This distinction he applies also
to the field of eugenics. A merely empirical art of breeding
cannot be precise, i.e. it cannot keep the race perfectly pure.
This explains the downfall of the original city which is so good,
i.e. so similar to its Form or Idea, that ' a city thus constituted
can hardly be shaken '. ' But this ', Plato continues, ' is the
way it dissolves ', and he proceeds to outline his theory of
breeding, of the Number, and of the Fall of Man.

All plants and animals, he tells us, must be bred according
to definite periods of time, if barrenness and degeneration are to
be avoided. Some knowledge of these periods, which are connected with the length of the life of the race, will be available to
the rulers of the best state, and they will apply it to the breeding
of the master race. It will not, however, be rational, but only
empirical knowledge ; it will be ' *calculation aided by (or based on)
perception* ' (cp. the next quotation). But as we have just seen,
perception and experience can never be exact and reliable, since
its objects are not the pure Forms or Ideas, but the world of things
in flux ; and since the guardians have no better kind of knowledge at their disposal, the breed cannot be kept pure, and racial
degeneration must creep in. This is how Plato explains the
matter : ' Concerning your own race ' (i.e. the race of men, as
opposed to animals), ' the rulers of the city whom you have
trained may be wise enough ; but since they are using calculation aided by perception, they will not hit, accidentally, upon the
way of getting either good offspring, or none at all.' Lacking a
purely rational method,[39] ' they will blunder, and some day they
will beget children in the wrong way '. In what follows next,
Plato hints, rather mysteriously, that there is now a way to avoid

this through the discovery of a purely rational and mathematical science which possesses in the ' Platonic Number ' (a number determining the True Period of the human race) the key to the master law of higher eugenics. But since the guardians of old times were ignorant of Pythagorean number-mysticism, and with it, of this key to the higher knowledge of breeding, the otherwise perfect natural state could not escape decay. After partially revealing the secret of his mysterious Number, Plato continues : ' This . . number is master over better or worse births ; and whenever these guardians of yours—who are ignorant of these matters—unite bride and bridegroom in the wrong manner [40], the children will have neither good natures nor good luck. Even the best of them . . will prove unworthy when succeeding to the power of their fathers ; and as soon as they are guardians, they will not listen to us any more '—that is, in matters of musical and gymnastic education, and, as Plato especially emphasizes, in the supervision of breeding. ' Hence rulers will be appointed who are not altogether fit for their task as guardians ; namely to watch, and to test, the metals in the races (which are Hesiod's races as well as yours), gold and silver and bronze and iron. So iron will mingle with silver and bronze with gold and from this mixture, Variation will be born and absurd Irregularity ; and whenever these are born they will beget Strife and Hostility. And this is how we must describe the ancestry and birth of Dissension, wherever she arises.'

This is Plato's story of the Number and of the Fall of Man. It is the basis of his historicist sociology, especially of his fundamental law of social revolutions discussed in the last chapter [41]. For racial degeneration explains the origin of disunion in the ruling class, and with it, the origin of all historical development. The internal disunion of human nature, the schism of the soul, leads to the schism of the ruling class. And as with Heraclitus, war, class war, is the father and promoter of all change, and of the history of man, which is nothing but the history of the breakdown of society. We see that Plato's idealist historicism ultimately rests not upon a spiritual, but upon a biological basis ; it rests upon a kind of meta-biology [42] of the race of men. Plato was not only a naturalist who proffered a biological theory of the state, he was also the first to proffer a biological and racial theory of social dynamics, of political history. ' The Platonic Number ', says Adam [43], ' is thus the setting in which Plato's " Philosophy of History " is framed.'

It is, I think, appropriate to conclude this sketch of Plato's descriptive sociology with a summary and an evaluation.

Plato succeeded in giving an astonishingly true, though of course somewhat idealized, reconstruction of an early Greek tribal and collectivist society similar to that of Sparta. An analysis of the forces, especially the economic forces, which threaten the stability of such a society, enables him to describe the general policy as well as the social institutions which are necessary for arresting it. And he gives, furthermore, a rational reconstruction of the economic and historical development of the Greek city-states.

These achievements are impaired by his hatred of the society in which he was living, and by his romantic love for the old tribal form of social life. It is this attitude which led him to formulate an untenable law of historical development, namely, the law of universal degeneration or decay. And the same attitude is also responsible for the irrational, fantastic, and romantic elements of his otherwise excellent analysis. On the other hand, it was just his personal interest and his partiality which sharpened his eye and so made his achievements possible. He derived his historicist theory from the fantastic philosophical doctrine that the changing visible world is only a decaying copy of an unchanging invisible world. But this ingenious attempt to combine a historicist pessimism with an ontological optimism leads, when elaborated, to difficulties. These difficulties forced upon him the adoption of a biological naturalism, leading (together with ' psychologism ' [44], i.e. the theory that society depends on the ' human nature ' of its members) to mysticism and superstition, culminating in a pseudo-rational mathematical theory of breeding. They even endangered the impressive unity of his theoretical edifice.

IX

Looking back at this edifice, we may briefly consider its ground-plan [45]. This ground-plan, conceived by a great architect, exhibits a fundamental metaphysical dualism in Plato's thought. In the field of logic, this dualism presents itself as the opposition between the universal and the particular. In the field of mathematical speculation, it presents itself as the opposition between the One and the Many. In the field of epistemology, it is the opposition between rational knowledge based on pure thought, and opinion based on particular experiences. In the field of ontology, it is the opposition between the one, original, invariable, and true, reality, and the many, varying, and delusive, appearances ; between pure being and becoming, or more precisely, changing.   In the field of cosmology, it is the opposition between that which generates and that which is generated, and which must decay.   In ethics, it is the opposition between the good, i.e. that which preserves, and the evil, i.e. that which corrupts.   In politics, it is the opposition between the one collective, the state, which may attain perfection and autarchy, and the great mass of the people—the many individuals, the particular men who must remain imperfect and dependent, and· whose particularity is to be suppressed for the sake of the unity of the state (see the next chapter).   And this whole dualist philosophy, I believe, originated from the urgent wish to explain the contrast between the vision of an ideal society, and the hateful actual state of affairs in the social field—the contrast between a stable society, and a society in the process of revolution.

CHAPTER 6 : TOTALITARIAN JUSTICE

The analysis of Plato's sociology makes it easy to present his political programme. His fundamental demands can be expressed in either of two formulæ, the first corresponding to his idealist theory of change and rest, the second to his naturalism. The idealist formula is : *Arrest all political change!* Change is evil, rest divine [1]. All change can be arrested if the state is made an exact copy of its original, i.e. of the Form or Idea of the city. Should it be asked how this is practicable, we can reply with the naturalistic formula : *Back to nature!* Back to the original state of our forefathers, the primitive state founded in accordance with human nature, and therefore stable ; back to the tribal patriarchy of the time before the Fall, to the natural class rule of the wise few over the ignorant many.

I believe that practically all the elements of Plato's political programme can be derived from these demands. They are, in turn, based upon his historicism ; and they have to be combined with his sociological doctrines concerning the conditions for the stability of class rule. The principal elements I have in mind are :

(*A*) The strict division of the classes ; i.e. the ruling class consisting of herdsmen and watch-dogs must be strictly separated from the human cattle.

(*B*) The identification of the fate of the state with that of the ruling class ; the exclusive interest in this class, and in its unity ; and subservient to this unity, the rigid rules for breeding and educating this class, and the strict supervision and collectivization of the interests of its members.

From these principal elements, others can be derived, for instance the following :

(*C*) The ruling class has a monopoly of things like military virtues and training, and of the right to carry arms and to receive education of any kind ; but it is excluded from any participation in economic activities, and especially from earning money.

(*D*) There must be a censorship of all intellectual activities of the ruling class, and a continual propaganda aiming at mould-

ing and unifying their minds.   All innovation in education, legislation, and religion must be prevented or suppressed.

(*E*) The state must be self-sufficient.   It must aim at economic
autarchy ;   for otherwise the rulers would either be dependent
upon traders, or become traders themselves.   The first of these
alternatives would undermine their power, the second their unity
and the stability of the state.

This programme can, I think, be fairly described as totalitarian.   And it is certainly founded upon a historicist sociology.

But is that all ?   Are there no other features of Plato's
programme, elements which are neither totalitarian nor founded
upon historicism ?   What about Plato's ardent desire for Goodness
and Beauty, or his love of Wisdom and of Truth ?   What about
his demand that the wise, the philosophers, should rule ?   What
about his hopes of making the citizens of his state virtuous as
well as happy ?   And what about his demand that the state
should be founded upon Justice ?   Even writers who criticize
Plato believe that his political doctrine, in spite of certain
similarities, is clearly distinguished from modern totalitarianism
by these aims of his, the happiness of the citizens, and the rule
of justice.   Crossman, for instance, whose critical attitude can
be gauged from his remark that ' Plato's philosophy is the most
savage and most profound attack upon liberal ideas which history
can show ' [2], seems still to believe that Plato's plan is ' the building
of a perfect state in which every citizen is really happy '.   Another
example is Joad who discusses the similarities between Plato's
programme and that of fascism at some length, but who asserts
that there are fundamental differences, since in Plato's best
state ' the ordinary man . . achieves such happiness as appertains
to his nature ', and since this state is built upon the ideas of
' an absolute good and an absolute justice '.

In spite of such arguments I believe that Plato's political
programme, far from being morally superior to totalitarianism,
is fundamentally identical with it.   I believe that the objections
against this view are based upon an ancient and deep-rooted
prejudice in favour of idealizing Plato.   That Crossman has
done much to point out and to destroy this inclination may be
seen from this statement : ' Before the Great War . . Plato . .
was rarely condemned outright as a reactionary, resolutely
opposed to every principle of the liberal creed.   Instead he was
elevated to a higher rank, . . removed from practical life,
dreaming of a transcendent City of God.' [3]   Crossman himself,

however, is not free from that tendency which he so clearly exposes. It is interesting that this tendency could persist for such a long time in spite of the fact that Grote and Gomperz had pointed out the reactionary character of some doctrines of the *Republic* and the *Laws*. But even they did not see all the implications of these doctrines ; they never doubted that Plato was, fundamentally, a humanitarian. And their adverse criticism was ignored, or interpreted as a failure to understand and to appreciate Plato who was by Christians considered a ' Christian before Christ ', and by revolutionaries a revolutionary. This kind of complete faith in Plato is undoubtedly still dominant, and Field, for instance, finds it necessary to warn his readers that ' we shall misunderstand Plato entirely if we think of him as a revolutionary thinker '. This is, of course, very true ; and it would clearly be pointless if the tendency to make of Plato a revolutionary thinker, or at least a progressivist, were not fairly widespread. But Field himself has the same kind of faith in Plato ; for when he goes on to say that Plato was ' in strong opposition to the new and subversive tendencies ' of his time, then surely he accepts too readily Plato's testimony for the subversiveness of these new tendencies. The enemies of freedom have always charged its defenders with subversion. And nearly always they have succeeded in persuading the guileless and well-meaning.

The idealization of the great idealist permeates not only the interpretations of Plato's writings, but also the translations. Drastic remarks of Plato's which do not fit the translator's views of what a humanitarian should say are frequently either toned down or misunderstood. This tendency begins with the translation of the very title of Plato's so-called ' Republic '. What comes first to our mind when hearing this title is that the author must be a liberal, if not a revolutionary. But the title ' Republic ' is, quite simply, the English form of the Latin rendering of a Greek word that had no associations of this kind, and whose proper English translation would be ' The Constitution ' or ' The City State ' or ' The State '. The traditional translation ' The Republic ' has undoubtedly contributed to the general conviction that Plato could not have been a reactionary.

In view of all that Plato says about Goodness and Justice and the other Ideas mentioned, my thesis that his political demands are purely totalitarian and anti-humanitarian needs to be defended. In order to undertake this defence, I shall, for the next four chapters, break off the analysis of historicism, and concentrate upon a critical examination of the ethical Ideas mentioned, and of their part in Plato's political demands. In the present chapter, I shall examine the Idea of Justice ; in the three following chapters, the doctrine that the wisest and best should rule, and the Ideas of Truth, Wisdom, Goodness, and Beauty.

I

What do we really mean when we speak of ' Justice ' ? I do not think that verbal questions of this kind are particularly important, or that it is possible to make a definite answer to them, since such terms are always used in various senses. However, I think that most of us, especially those whose general outlook is humanitarian, mean something like this : (a) an equal distribution of the burden of citizenship, i.e. of those limitations of freedom which are necessary in social life [4] ; (b) equal treatment of the citizens before the law, provided, of course, that (c) the laws show neither favour nor disfavour towards individual citizens or groups or classes ; (d) impartiality of the courts of justice ; and (e) an equal share in the advantages (and not only in the burden) which membership of the state may offer to its citizens. If Plato had meant by ' justice ' anything of this kind, then my claim that his programme is purely totalitarian would certainly be wrong and all those would be right who believe that Plato's politics rested upon an acceptable humanitarian basis. But the fact is that he meant by ' justice ' something entirely different.

What did Plato mean by ' justice ' ? I assert that in the *Republic* he used the term ' just ' as a synonym for ' that which is in.the interest of the best state '. And what is in the interest of this best state ? To arrest all change, by the maintenance of a rigid class division and class rule. If I am right in this interpretation, then we should have to say that Plato's demand for justice leaves his political programme at the level of totalitarianism ; and we should have to conclude that we must guard against the danger of being impressed by mere words.

Justice is the central topic of the *Republic* ; in fact, ' On Justice ' is its traditional sub-title. In his enquiry into the nature of justice, Plato makes use of the method mentioned [5] in the last chapter ; he first tries to search for this Idea in the state, and then attempts to apply the result to the individual. One cannot say that Plato's question ' What is justice ? ' quickly finds an answer, for it is only given in the Fourth Book. The considerations which lead up to it will be analysed more fully later in this chapter. Briefly, they are these.

The city is founded upon human nature, its needs, and its limitations [6]. 'We have stated, and, you will remember, repeated over and over again that each man in our city should do one work only ; namely, that work for which his nature is naturally best fitted.' From this Plato concludes that everyone should mind his own business ; that the carpenter should confine himself to carpentering, the shoemaker to making shoes. Not much harm is done, however, if two workers change their natural places. 'But should anyone who is by nature a worker (or else a member of the money-earning class) . . manage to get into the warrior class ; or should a warrior get into the class of the guardians, without being worthy of it ; . . then this kind of change and of underhand plotting would mean the downfall of the city.' From this argument which is closely related to the principle that the carrying of arms should be a class prerogative, Plato draws his final conclusion that any changing or intermingling within the three classes must be injustice, and that the opposite, therefore, is justice : 'When each class in the city minds its own business, the money-earning class as well as the auxiliaries and the guardians, then this will be justice.' This conclusion is reaffirmed and summed up a little later : 'The city is just . . if each of its three classes attends to its own work.' But this statement means that Plato identifies justice with the principle of class rule and of class privilege. For the principle that every class should attend to its own business means, briefly and bluntly, that *the state is just if the ruler rules, if the worker works, and* [7] *if the slave slaves.*

It will be seen that Plato's concept of justice is fundamentally different from our ordinary view as analysed above. Plato calls class privilege 'just', while we usually mean by justice rather the absence of such privilege. But the difference goes further than that. We mean by justice some kind of equality in the treatment of *individuals*, while Plato considers justice not as a relationship between individuals, but as a property of the *whole state*, based upon a relationship between its classes. The state is just if it is healthy, strong, united—stable.

II

But was Plato perhaps right ? Does 'justice' perhaps mean what he says ? I do not intend to discuss such a question. If anyone should hold that 'justice' means the unchallenged rule of one class, then I should simply reply that I am all for injustice. In other words, I believe that nothing depends upon words, and everything upon our practical demands or upon the proposals for framing our policy which we decide to adopt. Behind Plato's definition of justice stands, fundamentally, his demand for a totalitarian class rule, and his decision to bring it about.

But was he not right in a different sense? Did his idea of justice perhaps correspond to the Greek way of using this word? Did the Greeks perhaps mean by 'justice', something holistic, like the 'health of the state', and is it not utterly unfair and unhistorical to expect from Plato an anticipation of our modern idea of justice as equality of the citizens before the law? This question, indeed, has been answered in the affirmative, and the claim has been made that Plato's holistic idea of 'social justice' is characteristic of the traditional Greek outlook, of the 'Greek genius' which 'was not, like the Roman, specifically legal', but rather 'specifically metaphysical' [8]. But this claim is untenable. As a matter of fact, the Greek way of using the word 'justice' was indeed surprisingly similar to our own individualistic and equalitarian usage.

In order to show this, I may first refer to Plato himself who, in the dialogue *Gorgias* (which is earlier than the *Republic*), speaks of the view that 'justice is equality' as one held by the great mass of the people, and as one which agrees not only with 'convention', but with 'nature itself'. I may further quote Aristotle, another opponent of equalitarianism, who, under the influence of Plato's naturalism, elaborated among other things the theory that some men are by nature born to slave [9]. Nobody could be less interested in spreading an equalitarian and individualistic interpretation of the term 'justice'. But when speaking of the judge, whom he describes as 'a personification of that which is just', Aristotle says that it is the task of the judge to 'restore equality'. He tells us that 'all men think justice to be a kind of equality', an equality, namely, which 'pertains to persons'. He even thinks (but here he is wrong) that the Greek word for 'justice' is to be derived from a root that means 'equal division'. (The view that 'justice' means a kind of 'equality in the division of spoils and honours to the citizens' agrees with Plato's views in the *Laws*, where two kinds of equality in the distribution of spoils and honours are distinguished—'numerical' or 'arithmetical' equality and ' proportionate ' equality ; the second of which takes account of the degree in which the persons in question possess virtue, breeding, and wealth—and where this proportionate equality is said to constitute ' political justice '.) And when Aristotle discusses the principles of democracy, he says that ' democratic justice is the application of the principle of arithmetical equality (as distinct from proportionate equality) '. All this is certainly not merely his personal impression of the meaning of justice, nor is it perhaps only a description of the way in which the word was used, after Plato, under the influence of the *Gorgias* and the *Laws* ; it is, rather, the expression of a universal and ancient as well as popular use of the word ' justice '.[10]

In view of this evidence, we must say, I think, that the holistic and anti-equalitarian interpretation of justice in the *Republic* was an innovation, and that Plato attempted to present his totalitarian class rule as ' just ' while people generally meant by ' justice ' the exact opposite.

This result is startling, and opens up a number of questions. Why did Plato claim, in the *Republic*, that justice meant inequality if in general usage, it meant equality ? To me the only likely reply seems to be that he wanted to make propaganda for his totalitarian state by persuading the people that it was the ' just ' state. But was such an attempt worth his while, considering that it is not words but what we mean by them that matters ? Of course it was worth while ; this can be seen from the fact that he fully succeeded in persuading his readers, down to our own day, that he was candidly advocating justice, i.e. that justice they were striving for. And it is a fact that he thereby spread doubt and confusion among equalitarians and individualists who, under the influence of his authority, began to ask themselves whether his idea of justice was not truer and better than theirs. Since the word ' justice ' symbolizes to us an aim of such importance, and since so many are prepared to endure anything for it, and to do all in their power for its realization, the enlistment of these humanitarian forces, or at least, the paralysing of equalitarianism, was certainly an aim worthy of being pursued by a believer in totalitarianism. But was Plato aware that justice meant so much to men ? He was ; for he writes in the *Republic* : ' When a man has committed an injustice, . . is it not true that his courage refuses to be stirred ? . . But when he believes that he has suffered injustice, does not his vigour and his wrath flare up at once ? And is it not equally true that when fighting on the side of what he believes to be just, he can endure hunger and cold, and any kind of hardship? And does he not hold on until he conquers, persisting in his exalted state until he has either achieved his aim, or perished?' [11]

Reading this, we cannot doubt that Plato knew the power of faith, and, above all, of a faith in justice. Nor can we doubt that the *Republic* must tend to pervert this faith, and to replace it by a directly opposite faith. And in the light of the available evidence, it seems to me most probable that Plato knew very well what he was doing. Equalitarianism was his arch-enemy, and he was out to destroy it; no doubt in the sincere belief that it was a great evil and a great danger. But his attack upon equalitarianism was not an honest attack. Plato did not dare to face the enemy openly.

I proceed to present the evidence in support of this contention.

III

The *Republic* is probably the most elaborate monograph on justice ever written. It examines a variety of views about justice, and it does this in a way which leads us to believe that Plato omitted none of the more important theories known to him. In fact, Plato clearly implies [12] that because of his vain attempts to track it down among the current views, a new search for justice is necessary. Yet in his survey and discussion of the current theories, the view that justice is equality before the law (' *isonomy* ') is never mentioned. This omission can be explained only in two ways. Either he overlooked the equalitarian theory [13], or he purposely avoided it. The first possibility seems very unlikely if we consider the care with which the *Republic* is composed, and the necessity for Plato to analyse the theories of his opponents if he was to make a forceful presentation of his own. But this possibility appears even more improbable if we consider the wide popularity of the equalitarian theory. We need not, however, rely upon merely probable arguments since it can be easily shown that Plato was not only acquainted with the equalitarian theory but well aware of its importance when he wrote the *Republic*. As already mentioned in this chapter (in section II), and as will be shown in detail later (in section VIII), equalitarianism played a considerable rôle in the earlier *Gorgias* where it is even defended; and in spite of the fact that the merits or demerits of equalitarianism are nowhere seriously discussed in the *Republic*, Plato did not change his mind regarding its influence, for the *Republic* itself testifies to its popularity. It is there alluded to as a very popular democratic belief; but it is treated only with scorn, and all we hear about it consists of a few sneers and pin-pricks [14], well matched with the abusive attack upon Athenian democracy, and made at a place where justice is not the topic of the discussion. The possibility that the equalitarian theory of justice was overlooked by Plato is therefore ruled out, and so is the possibility that he did not see that a discussion of an influential theory diametrically opposed to his own was requisite. The fact that his silence in the *Republic* is broken only by a few jocular remarks (apparently he thought them too good to be suppressed [15]) can be explained only as a conscious refusal to discuss it. In view of all that, I do not see how Plato's method of impressing upon his readers the belief that all important theories have been examined can be reconciled with the standards of intellectual honesty; though we must add that his failure is undoubtedly due to his complete devotion to a cause in whose goodness he firmly believed.

In order to appreciate fully the implications of Plato's practically unbroken silence on this issue, we must first see clearly that the equalitarian movement as Plato knew it represented all he hated, and that his own theory, in the *Republic* and in all later works, was largely a reply to the powerful challenge of the new equalitarianism and humanitarianism. To show this, I shall discuss the main principles of the humanitarian movement, and contrast them with the corresponding principles of Platonic totalitarianism.

The humanitarian theory of justice makes three main demands or proposals, namely (*a*) the equalitarian principle proper, i.e. the proposal to eliminate ' natural ' privileges, (*b*) the general principle of individualism, and (*c*) the principle that it should be the task and the purpose of the state to protect the freedom of its citizens. To each of these political demands or proposals there corresponds a directly opposite principle of Platonism, namely (a^1) the principle of natural privilege, (b^1) the general principle of holism or collectivism, and (c^1) the principle that it should be the task and the purpose of the individual to maintain, and to strengthen, the stability of the state.—I shall discuss these three points in order, devoting to each of them one of the sections IV, V, and VI of this chapter.

IV

Equalitarianism proper is the demand that the citizens of the state should be treated impartially. It is the demand that birth, family connection, or wealth must not influence those who administer the law to the citizens. In other words, it does not recognize any ' natural ' privileges, although certain privileges may be conferred by the citizens upon those they trust.

This equalitarian principle had been admirably formulated by Pericles a few years before Plato's birth, in an oration which has been preserved by Thucydides [16]. It will be quoted more fully in chapter 10, but two of its sentences may be given here : ' Our laws ', said Pericles, ' afford equal justice to all alike in their private disputes, but we do not ignore the claims of excellence. When a citizen distinguishes himself, then he is preferred to the public service, not as a matter of privilege, but as a reward for merit ; and poverty is not a bar. . .' These sentences express some of the fundamental aims of the great equalitarian movement which, as we have seen, did not even shrink from attacking slavery. In Pericles' own generation, this movement was represented by Euripides, Antiphon, and Hippias, who·have all been quoted in the last chapter, and also by Herodotus [17]. In Plato's generation, it was represented by Alcidamas and Lycophron, both quoted above ; another supporter was Antisthenes, who had been one of Socrates' closest friends.

Plato's principle of justice was, of course, diametrically opposed to all this. He demanded natural privileges for the natural leaders. But how did he contest the equalitarian principle ? And how did he establish his own demands ?

It will be remembered from the last chapter that some of the best-known formulations of the equalitarian demands were couched in the impressive but questionable language of ' natural rights ', and that some of their representatives argued in favour of these demands by pointing out the ' natural ', i.e. biological, equality of men. We have seen that the argument is irrelevant ; that men are equal in some important respects, and unequal in others ; and that normative demands cannot be derived from this fact, or from any other fact. It is therefore interesting to note that the naturalist argument was not used by all equalitarians, and that Pericles, for one, did not even allude to it [18].

Plato quickly found that naturalism was a weak spot within the equalitarian doctrine, and he took the fullest advantage of this weakness. To tell men that they are equal has a certain sentimental appeal. But this appeal is small compared with that made by a propaganda that tells them that they are superior to others, and that others are inferior to them. Are you naturally equal to your servants, to your slaves, to the manual worker who is no better than an animal? The very question is ridiculous! Plato seems to have been the first to appreciate the possibilities of this reaction, and to oppose contempt, scorn, and ridicule to the claim to natural equality. This explains why he was anxious to impute the naturalistic argument even to those of his opponents who did not use it; in the *Menexenus*, a parody of Pericles' oration, he therefore insists on linking together the claims to equal laws and to natural equality: ' The basis of our constitution is equality of birth ', he says ironically. ' We are all brethren, and are all children of one mother; . . and the natural equality of birth induces us to strive for equality before the law.' [19]

Later, in the *Laws*, Plato summarizes his reply to equalitarianism in the formula: ' Equal treatment of unequals must beget inequity ' [20]; and this was developed by Aristotle into the formula ' Equality for equals, inequality for unequals '. This formula indicates what may be termed the standard objection to equalitarianism; the objection that equality would be excellent if only men were equal, but that it is manifestly impossible since they are not equal, and since they cannot be made equal. This apparently very realistic objection is, in fact, most unrealistic, for political privileges have never been founded upon natural differences of character. And, indeed, Plato does not seem to have had much confidence in this objection when writing the *Republic*, for it is used there only in one of his sneers at democracy when he says that it ' distributes equality to equals and unequals alike.' [21] Apart from this remark, he prefers not to argue against equalitarianism, but to forget it.

Summing up, it can be said that Plato never underrated the significance of the equalitarian theory, supported as it was by a man like Pericles, but that, in the *Republic*, he did not treat it at all; he attacked it, but not squarely and openly.

But how did he try to establish his own anti-equalitarianism, his principle of natural privilege? In the *Republic*, he proffered three different arguments, though two of them hardly deserve the name. The first [22] is the surprising remark that, since all the other three virtues of the state have been examined, the remaining fourth, that of ' minding one's own business ', must be ' justice '. I am reluctant to believe that this was meant as an argument ; but it must be, for Plato's leading speaker, ' Socrates ', introduces it by asking : ' Do you know how I arrive at this conclusion ? ' The second argument is more interesting, for it is an attempt to show that his anti-equalitarianism can be derived from the ordinary (i.e. equalitarian) view that justice is impartiality. I quote the passage in full. Remarking that the rulers of the city will also be its judges, ' Socrates ' says [23] : ' And will it not be the aim of their jurisdiction that no man shall take what belongs to another, and shall be deprived of what is his own ? '—' Yes ', is the reply of ' Glaucon ', the interlocutor, ' that will be their intention.'— ' Because that would be just ? '—' Yes.'—' Accordingly, to keep and to practise what belongs to us and is our own will be generally agreed upon to be justice.' Thus it is established that ' to keep and to practise what is one's own ' is the principle of just jurisdiction, according to our ordinary ideas of justice. Here the second argument ends, giving way to the third (to be analysed below) which leads to the conclusion that it is justice to keep one's own station (or to do one's own business), which is the station (or the business) *of one's own class or caste.*

The sole purpose of this second argument is to impress upon the reader that ' justice ', in the ordinary sense of the word, requires us to keep our own station, since we should always keep what belongs to us. That is to say, Plato wishes his readers to draw the inference : ' It is just to keep and to practise what is one's own. My place (or my business) is my own. Thus it is just for me to keep to my place (or to practise my business).' This is about as sound as the argument : ' It is just to keep and to practise what is one's own. This plan of stealing your money is my own. Thus it is just for me to keep to my plan, and to put it into practice, i.e. to steal your money.' It is clear that the inference which Plato wishes us to draw is nothing but a crude juggle with the meaning of the term ' one's own '. (For the problem is whether justice demands that everything which is in some sense ' our own ', e.g. ' our own ' class, should therefore be treated, not only as our possession, but as our inalienable possession. But in such a principle Plato himself does not believe ; for it would clearly make a transition to communism impossible. And what about keeping our own children ?) This crude juggle is Plato's way of establishing what Adam calls ' a point of contact between his own view of Justice and the popular . . meaning of the word '. This is how the greatest philosopher of all time tries to convince us that he has discovered the true nature of justice.

The third and last argument which Plato offers is much more serious. It is an appeal to the principle of holism or collectivism, and is connected with the principle that it is the purpose of the individual to maintain the stability of the state. It will therefore be discussed, in this analysis, below, in sections v and vi.

But before proceeding to these points, I wish to draw attention to the ' preface ' which Plato places before his description of the ' discovery ' which we are here examining. It must be considered in the light of the observations we have made so far. Viewed in this light, the ' lengthy preface '—this is how Plato himself describes it—appears as an ingenious attempt to prepare the reader for the ' discovery of justice ' by making him believe that there is an argument going on when in reality he is only faced with a display of dramatic devices, designed to soothe his critical faculties.

Having discovered wisdom as the virtue proper to the guardians and courage as that proper to the auxiliaries, ' Socrates ' announces his intention of making a final effort to discover justice. ' Two things are left ' [24], he says, ' which we shall have to discover in the city : temperance, and finally that other thing which is the main object of all our investigations, namely justice.' —' Exactly ', says Glaucon. Socrates now suggests that temperance shall be dropped. But Glaucon protests and Socrates gives in, saying that ' it would be wrong ' (or ' crooked ') to refuse. This little dispute prepares the reader for the re-introduction of justice, suggests to him that Socrates possesses the means for its ' discovery ', and reassures him that Glaucon is carefully watching Plato's intellectual honesty in conducting the argument which he, the reader himself, need not therefore watch at all [25].

Socrates next proceeds to discuss temperance, which he discovers to be the only virtue proper to the workers. (By the way, the much debated question whether Plato's ' justice ' is distinguishable from his ' temperance ' can be easily answered. Justice means *to keep one's place* ; temperance means *to know one's place*—that is to say, more precisely, to be satisfied with it. What other virtue could be proper to the workers who fill their bellies like the beasts ?) When temperance has been discovered, Socrates asks : ' And what about the last principle ? Obviously it will be justice.'—' Obviously ', replies Glaucon.

' Now, my dear Glaucon ', says Socrates, ' we must, like

hunters, surround her cover and keep a close watch, and we must not allow her to escape, and to get away ; for surely, justice must be somewhere near this spot. You had better look out and search the place. And if you are the first to see her, then give me a shout ! ' Glaucon, like the reader, is of course unable to do anything of the sort, and implores Socrates to take the lead. ' Then offer your prayers with me ', says Socrates, ' and follow me.' But even Socrates finds the ground ' hard to traverse, since it is covered with underwood ; it is dark, and difficult to explore . . But ' , he says, ' we must go on with it '. And instead of protesting ' Go on with what ? With our exploration, i.e. with our argument ? But we have not even started. There has not been a glimmer of sense in what you have said so far ', Glaucon, and the naïve reader with him replies meekly : ' Yes, we must go on.' Now Socrates reports that he has ' got a glimpse ' (we have not), and gets excited. ' Hurray ! Hurray ! ' he cries, ' Glaucon ! There seems to be a track ! I think now that the quarry will not escape us ! '—' That is good news ', replies Glaucon. ' Upon my word ', says Socrates, ' we have made utter fools of ourselves. What we were looking for at a distance, has been lying at our very feet all the time ! . And we never saw it ! ' With exclamations and repeated assertions of this kind, Socrates continues for a good while, interrupted by Glaucon, who gives expression to the reader's feelings and asks Socrates what he has found. But when Socrates says only ' We have been talking of it all the time, without realizing that we were actually describing it ', Glaucon expresses the reader's impatience and says : ' This preface gets a bit lengthy ; remember that I want to hear what it is all about.' And only then does Plato proceed to proffer the two ' arguments ' which I have outlined.

Glaucon's last remark may be taken as an indication that Plato was conscious of what he was doing in this ' lengthy preface '. I cannot interpret it as anything but an attempt—it proved to be highly successful—to lull the reader's critical faculties, and, by means of a dramatic display of verbal fireworks, to divert his attention from the intellectual poverty of this masterly piece of dialogue. One is tempted to think that Plato knew its weakness, and how to hide it.

v

The problem of individualism and collectivism is closely related to that of equality and inequality. Before going on to discuss it, a few terminological remarks seem to be necessary.

The term 'individualism' can be used (according to the *Oxford Dictionary*) in two different ways : (*a*) in opposition to collectivism, and (*b*) in opposition to altruism. There is no other word to express the former meaning, but several synonyms for the latter, for example 'egoism' or 'selfishness'. This is why in what follows I shall use the term 'individualism' *exclusively* in sense (*a*), using terms like 'egoism' or 'selfishness' if sense (*b*) is intended. A little table may be useful :

(*a*) *Individualism*   is opposed to   (*a'*) *Collectivism.*
(*b*) *Egoism*   is opposed to   (*b'*) *Altruism*

Now these four terms describe certain attitudes, or demands, or decisions, or proposals, for codes of normative laws. Though necessarily vague, they can, I believe, be easily illustrated by examples and so be used with a precision sufficient for our present purpose. Let us begin with collectivism [26], since this attitude is already familiar to us from our discussion of Plato's holism. His demand that the individual should subserve the interests of the whole, whether this be the universe, the city, the tribe, the race, or any other collective body, was illustrated in the last chapter by a few passages. To quote one of these again, but more fully [27] : ' The part exists for the sake of the whole, but the whole does not exist for the sake of the part. . . You are created for the sake of the whole and not the whole for the sake of you.' This quotation not only illustrates holism and collectivism, but also conveys its strong emotional appeal of which Plato was conscious (as can be seen from the preamble to the passage.) The appeal is to various feelings, e.g. the longing to belong to a group or a tribe ; and one factor in it is the moral appeal for altruism and against selfishness, or egoism. Plato suggests that if you cannot sacrifice your interests for the sake of the whole, then you are selfish.

Now a glance at our little table will show that this is not so. Collectivism is not opposed to egoism, nor is it identical with altruism or unselfishness. Collective or group egoism, for instance class egoism, is a very common thing (Plato knew [28] this very well), and this shows clearly enough that collectivism as such is not opposed to selfishness. On the other hand, an anti-collectivist, i.e. an individualist, can, at the same time, be an altruist ; he can be ready to make sacrifices in order to help other individuals. One of the best examples of this attitude is perhaps Dickens. It would be difficult to say which is the stronger, his passionate hatred of selfishness or his passionate interest in individuals with all their human weaknesses ; and this attitude is combined with a dislike, not only of what we now call collective bodies or collectives [29], but even of a genuinely devoted altruism, if directed towards anonymous groups rather than concrete individuals. (I remind the reader of Mrs. Jellyby in *Bleak House*, ' a lady devoted to public duties '.) These illustrations, I think, explain sufficiently clearly the meaning of our four terms ; and they show that any of the terms in our table can be combined with either of the two terms that stand in the other line (which gives four possible combinations).

Now it is nteresting that for Plato, and for most Platonists, an altruistic individualism (as for instance that of Dickens) cannot exist. According to Plato, the only alternative to collectivism is egoism ; he simply identifies all altruism with collectivism, and all individualism with egoism. This is not a mattef of terminology, of mere words, for instead of four possibilities, Plato recognized only two. This has created considerable confusion in speculation on ethical matters, even down to our own day.

Plato's identification of individualism with egoism furnishes him with a powerful weapon for his defence of collectivism as well as for his attack upon individualism. In defending collectivism, he can appeal to our humanitarian feeling of unselfishness ; in his attack, he can brand all individualists as selfish, as incapable of devotion to anything but themselves. This attack, although aimed by Plato against individualism in our sense, i.e, against the rights of human individuals, reaches of course only a very different target, egoism. But this difference is constantly ignored by Plato and by most Platonists.

Why did Plato try to attack individualism ? I think he knew very well what he was doing when he trained his guns upon this position, for individualism, perhaps even more than equalitarianism, was a stronghold in the defences of the new humanitarian creed. The emancipation of the individual was indeed the great spiritual revolution which had led to the breakdown of tribalism and to the rise of democracy. Plato's uncanny sociological intuition shows itself in the way in which he invariably discerned the enemy wherever he met him.

Individualism was part of the old intuitive idea of justice. That justice is not, as Plato would have it, the health and harmony of the state, but rather a certain way of treating individuals, is

emphasized by Aristotle, it will be remembered, when he says
'justice is something that pertains to persons' [30]. This individualistic element had been emphasized by the generation of
Pericles. Pericles himself made it clear that the laws must
guarantee equal justice ' to all alike in their private disputes ' ;
but he went further. ' We do not feel called upon ', he said,
' to nag at our neighbour if he chooses to go his own way.' (Compare this with Plato's remark [31] that the state does not produce
men ' for the purpose of letting them loose, each to go his own
way . .'.) Pericles insists that this individualism must be linked
with altruism : ' We are taught . . never to forget that we must
protect the injured ' ; and his speech culminates in a description
of the young Athenian who grows up ' to a happy versatility, and
to self-reliance.'

This individualism, united with altruism, has become the
basis of our western civilization. It is the central doctrine of
Christianity ('love your neighbour ', say the Scriptures, not ' love
your tribe ') ; and it is the core of all ethical doctrines which
have grown from our civilization and stimulated it. It is also,
for instance, Kant's central practical doctrine (' always recognize
that human individuals are ends, and do not use them as mere
means to your ends '). There is no other thought which has
been so powerful in the moral development of man.

Plato was right when he saw in this doctrine the enemy of
his caste state ; and he hated it more than any other of the
' subversive ' doctrines of his time. In order to show this even
more clearly, I shall quote two passages from the *Laws* [32] whose
truly astonishing hostility towards the individual is, I think, too
little appreciated. The first of them is famous as a reference to
the *Republic*, whose ' community of women and children and
property ' it discusses. Plato describes here the constitution of
the *Republic* as ' the highest form of the state '. In this highest
state, he tells us, ' there is common property of wives, of children,
and of all chattels. And everything possible has been done to
eradicate from our life everywhere and in every way all that is
private and individual. So far as it can be done, even those
things which nature herself has made private and individual have
somehow become the common property of all. Our very eyes
and ears and hands seem to see, to hear, and to act, as if they
belonged not to individuals but to the community. All men are
moulded to be unanimous in the utmost degree in bestowing
praise and blame, and they even rejoice and grieve about the

same things, and at the same time.   And all the laws are perfected for unifying the city to the utmost.' Plato goes on to
say that ' no man can find a better criterion of the highest
excellence of a state than the principles just expounded ' ; and he
describes such a state as ' divine ', and as the ' model ' or ' pattern '
or ' original ' of the state, i.e. as its Form or Idea.   This is Plato's
own view of the *Republic*, expressed at a time when he had given
up hope of realizing his political ideal in all its glory.

The second passage, also from the *Laws*, is, if possible, even
more outspoken. It should be emphasized that the passage deals
primarily with military expeditions and with military discipline,
but Plato leaves no doubt that these same militarist principles
should be adhered to not only in war, but also ' in peace, and from
the earliest childhood on '.   Like other totalitarian militarists and
admirers of Sparta, Plato urges that the all-important requirements of military discipline must be paramount, even in peace,
and that they must determine the whole life of all citizens ; for
not only the full citizens (who are all soldiers) and the children,
but also the very beasts must spend their whole life in a state of
permanent and total mobilization[33].   ' The greatest principle of
all ', he writes, ' is that nobody, whether male or female, should
ever be without a leader.   Nor should the mind of anybody be
habituated to letting him do anything at all on his own initiative,
neither out of zeal, nor even playfully.   But in war and in the
midst of peace—to his leader he shall direct his eye, and follow
him faithfully.   And even in the smallest matters he should stand
under leadership.   For example, he should get up, or move, or
wash, or take his meals [34] . . only if he has been told to do so. . .
In a word, he should teach his soul, by long habit, never to dream
of acting independently, and to become utterly incapable of it.
In this way the life of all will be spent in total community.   There
is no law, nor will there ever be one, which is superior to this, or
better and more effective in ensuring salvation and victory in war.
And in times of peace, and from the earliest childhood on should it be
fostered—this habit of ruling others, and of being ruled by others.
And every trace of anarchy should be utterly eradicated from *all
the life of all the men*, and even of the wild beasts which are subject
to men.'

These are strong words.   Never was a man more in earnest
in his hostility towards the individual.   And this hatred is deeply
rooted in the fundamental dualism of Plato's philosophy ; he
hated the individual and his freedom just as he hated the varying

particular experiences, the variety of the changing world of sensible things. In the field of politics, the individual is to Plato the Evil One himself.

This attitude, anti-humanitarian and anti-Christian as it is, has been consistently idealized. It has been interpreted as humane, as unselfish, as altruistic, and as Christian. E. B. England, for instance, calls [35] the first of these two passages from the *Laws* ' a vigorous denunciation of selfishness '. Similar words are used by Barker, when discussing Plato's theory of justice. He says that Plato's aim was ' to replace selfishness and civil discord by harmony ', and that ' the old harmony of the interests of the State and the individual . . is thus restored in the teachings of Plato ; but restored on a new and higher level, because it has been elevated into a conscious sense of harmony '. Such statements and countless similar ones can be easily explained if we remember Plato's identification of individualism with egoism ; for all these Platonists believe that anti-individualism is the same as selflessness. This illustrates my contention that this identification had the effect of a successful piece of anti-humanitarian propaganda, and that it has confused speculation on ethical matters down to our own time. But we must also realize that those who, deceived by this identification and by high-sounding words, exalt Plato's reputation as a teacher of morals and announce to the world that his ethics is the nearest approach to Christianity before Christ, are preparing the way for totalitarianism and especially for a totalitarian, anti-Christian interpretation of Christianity. And this is a dangerous thing, for there have been times when Christianity was dominated by totalitarian ideas. There was an Inquisition ; and, in another form, it may come again.

It may therefore be worth while to mention some further reasons why guileless people have persuaded themselves of the humaneness of Plato's intentions. One is that when preparing the ground for his collectivist doctrines, Plato usually begins by quoting a maxim or proverb (which seems to be of Pythagorean origin) : ' Friends have in common all things they possess.' [36] This is, undoubtedly, an unselfish, high-minded and excellent sentiment. Who could suspect that an argument starting from such a commendable assumption would arrive at a wholly anti-humanitarian conclusion ? Another and important point is that there are many genuinely humanitarian sentiments expressed in Plato's dialogues, particularly in those written before the *Republic* when he was still under the influence of Socrates. I mention especially Socrates' doctrine, in the *Gorgias*, that it is worse to do injustice than to suffer it.   Clearly, this doctrine is not only altruistic, but also individualistic ; for in a collectivist theory of justice like that of the *Republic*, injustice is an act against the state, not against a particular man, and though a man may commit an act of injustice, only the collective can suffer from it. But in the *Gorgias* we find nothing of the kind.   The theory of justice is a perfectly normal one, and the examples of injustice given by ' Socrates ' (who has here probably a good deal of the real Socrates in him) are such as boxing a man's ears, injuring, or killing him.   Socrates' teaching that it is better to suffer such acts than to do them is indeed very similar to Christian teaching, and his doctrine of justice fits in excellently with the spirit of Pericles.   (An attempt to interpret this will be made in chapter 10.)

Now the *Republic* develops a new doctrine of justice which is not merely incompatible with such an individualism, but utterly hostile towards it.   But a reader may easily believe that Plato is still holding fast to the doctrine of the *Gorgias*.   For in the *Republic*, Plato frequently alludes to the doctrine that it is better to suffer than to commit injustice, in spite of the fact that this is simply nonsense from the point of view of the collectivist theory of justice proffered in this work.   Furthermore, we hear in the *Republic* the opponents of ' Socrates ' giving voice to the opposite theory, that it is good and pleasant to inflict injustice, and bad to suffer it.   Of course, every humanitarian is repelled by such cynicism, and when Plato formulates his aims through the mouth of Socrates : ' I fear to commit a sin if I permit such evil talk about Justice in my presence, without doing my utmost to defend her ' [37], then the trusting reader is convinced of Plato's good intentions, and ready to follow him wherever he goes.

The effect of this assurance of Plato's is much enhanced by the fact that it follows, and is contrasted with, the cynical and selfish speeches [38] of Thrasymachus, who is depicted as a political desperado of the worst kind.   At the same time, the reader is led to identify individualism with the views of Thrasymachus, and to think that Plato, in his fight against it, is fighting against all the subversive and nihilistic tendencies of his time.   But we should not allow ourselves to be frightened by an individualist bogy such as Thrasymachus (there is a great similarity between his portrait and the modern collectivist bogy of ' bolshevism ') into accepting another more real and more dangerous because less

obvious form of barbarism.   For Plato replaces Thrasymachus'
doctrine that the individual's might is right by the equally bar-
baric doctrine that right is everything that furthers the stability
and the might of the state.

To sum up.   Because of his radical collectivism, Plato is not
even interested in those problems which men usually call the
problems of justice, that is to say, in the impartial weighing of the
contesting claims of individuals.   Nor is he interested in adjusting
the individual's claims to those of the state.   For the individual
is altogether inferior.   ' I legislate with a view to what is best for
the whole state ', says Plato, ' . . for I justly place the interests of
the individual on an inferior level of value.' [39]   He is concerned
solely with the collective whole as such, and justice, to him, is
nothing but the health, unity, and stability of the collective
body.

VI

So far, we have seen that humanitarian ethics demands an
equalitarian and individualistic interpretation of justice ; but we
have not yet outlined the humanitarian view of the state as such.
On the other hand, we have seen that Plato's theory of the state
is totalitarian ; but we have not yet explained the application
of this theory to the ethics of the individual.   Both these tasks
will be undertaken now, the second first ; and I shall begin by
analysing the third of Plato's arguments in his ' discovery ' of
justice, an argument which has so far been sketched only very
roughly.   Here is Plato's third argument [40] :

' Now see whether you agree with me ', says Socrates.   ' Do
you think it would do much harm to the city if a carpenter
started making shoes and a shoemaker carpentering ? '—' Not
very much.'—' But should one who is by nature a worker, or a
member of the money-earning class . . manage to get into the
warrior class ; or should a warrior get into the guardians' class
without being worthy of it ; then this kind of change and of
underhand plotting would mean the downfall of the city ? '—
' Most definitely it would.'—' We have three classes in our city,
and I take it that any such plotting or changing from one class
to another is a great crime against the city, and may rightly be
denounced as the utmost wickedness ? '—' Assuredly.'—' But you
will certainly declare that utmost wickedness towards one's own
city is injustice ? '—' Certainly.'—' Then this is injustice.   And
conversely, we shall say that when each class in the city attends to

its own business, the money-earning class as well as the auxiliaries and the guardians, then this will be justice.'

Now if we look at this argument, we find (a) the sociological assumption that any relaxing of the rigid caste system must lead to the downfall of the city ; (b) the constant reiteration of the one argument that what harms the city is injustice ; and (c) the inference that the opposite is justice. Now we may grant here the sociological assumption (a) since it is Plato's ideal to arrest social change, and since he means by ' harm ' anything that may lead to change ; and it is probably quite true that social change can be arrested only by a rigid caste system. And we may further grant the inference (c) that the opposite of injustice is justice. Of greater interest, however, is (b) ; a glance at Plato's argument will show that his whole trend of thought is dominated by the question : does this thing harm the city? Does it do much harm or little harm? He constantly reiterates that what threatens to harm the city is morally wicked and unjust.

We see here that Plato recognizes only one ultimate standard, the interest of the state. Everything that furthers it is good and virtuous and just ; everything that threatens it is bad and wicked and unjust. Actions that serve it are moral ; actions that endanger it, immoral. In other words, Plato's moral code is strictly utilitarian ; it is a code of collectivist or political utilitarianism. *The criterion of morality is the interest of the state.* Morality is nothing but political hygiene.

This is the collectivist, the tribal, the totalitarian theory of morality : ' Good is what is in the interest of my group ; or my tribe ; or my state.' It is easy to see what this morality implied for international relations : that the state itself can never be wrong in any of its actions, as long as it is strong ; that the state has the right, not only to do violence to its citizens, should that lead to an increase of strength, but also to attack other states, provided it does so without weakening itself. (This inference, the explicit recognition of the amorality of the state, and consequently the defence of moral nihilism in international relations, was drawn by Hegel.)

From the point of view of totalitarian ethics, from the point of view of collective utility, Plato's theory of justice is perfectly correct. To keep one's place *is* a virtue. It is that civil virtue which corresponds exactly to the military virtue of discipline. And this virtue plays exactly that rôle which ' justice ' plays in Plato's system of virtues. For the cogs in the great clockwork

of the state can show ' virtue ' in two ways.   First, they must be
fit for their task, by virtue of their size, shape, strength, etc. ;   and
secondly, they must be fitted each into its right place and must
retain that place.   The first type of virtues, fitness for a specific
task, will lead to a differentiation, in accordance with the specific
task of the cog.   Certain cogs will be virtuous, i.e. fit, only if they
are (' by their nature ') large ;   others if they are strong ;   and
others if they are smooth.   But the virtue of keeping to one's
place will be common to all of them ;   and it will at the same
time be a virtue of the whole :   that of being properly fitted
together—of being in harmony.   To this universal virtue Plato
gives the name ' justice '.   This procedure is perfectly consistent
and it is fully justified from the point of view of totalitarian
morality.   If the individual is nothing but a cog, then ethics is
nothing but the study of how to fit him into the whole.

I wish to make it clear that I believe in the sincerity of Plato's
totalitarianism.   His demand for the unchallenged domination of
one class over the rest was uncompromising, but his ideal was not
the maximum exploitation of the working classes by the upper
class ;   it was the stability of the whole.   The reason, however,
which he gives for the need to keep the exploitation within limits,
is again purely utilitarian.   It is the interest of stabilizing the
class rule.   Should the guardians try to get too much, he argues,
then they will in the end have nothing at all.   ' If they are not
satisfied with a life of stability and security, . . and are tempted,
by their power, to appropriate for themselves all the wealth of
the city, then surely they are bound to find out how wise Hesiod
was when he said, " the half is more than the whole ".' [41]   But
we must realize that even this tendency to restrict the exploitation of class privileges is a fairly common ingredient of totalitarianism.   Totalitarianism is not simply amoral.   It is the
morality of the closed society—of the group, or of the tribe ;   it
is not individual selfishness, but it is collective selfishness.

Considering that Plato's third argument is straightforward
and consistent, the question may be asked why he needed the
' lengthy preface ' as well as the   two preceding arguments ?
Why all this uneasiness ?   (Platonists will of course reply that this
uneasiness exists only in my imagination.   That may be so.   But
the irrational character of the passages can hardly be explained
away.)   The answer to this question is, I believe, that Plato's
collective clockwork would hardly have appealed to his readers
if it had been presented to them in all its barrenness and meaning-

lessness. Plato was uneasy because he knew and feared the strength and the moral appeal of the forces he tried to break. He did not dare to challenge them, but tried to win them over for his own purposes. Whether we witness in Plato's writings a cynical and conscious attempt to employ the moral sentiments of the new humanitarianism for his own purposes, or whether we witness rather a tragic attempt to persuade his own better conscience of the evils of individualism, we shall never know. My personal impression is that the latter is the case, and that this inner conflict is the main secret of Plato's fascination. I think that Plato was moved to the depths of his soul by the new ideas, and especially by the great individualist Socrates and his martyrdom. And I think that he fought against this influence upon himself as well as upon others with all the might of his unequalled intelligence, though not always openly. This explains also why from time to time, amid all his totalitarianism, we find some humanitarian ideas. And it explains why it was possible for philosophers to represent Plato as a humanitarian.

A strong argument in support of this interpretation is the way in which Plato treated, or rather, maltreated, the humanitarian and rational theory of the state, a theory which had been developed for the first time in his generation.

In a clear presentation of this theory, the *language of political demands or of political proposals* (cp. chapter 5, III) should be used ; that is to say, we should not try to answer the essentialist question : What is the state, what is its true nature, its real meaning ? Nor should we try to answer the historicist question : How did the state originate, and what is the origin of political obligation ? We should rather put our question in this way : What do we demand from a state ? What do we propose to consider as the legitimate aim of state activity ? And in order to find out what our fundamental political demands are, we may ask : Why do we prefer living in a well-ordered state to living without a state, i.e. in anarchy ? This way of asking our question is a rational one. It is a question which a technologist must try to answer before he can proceed to the construction or reconstruction of any political institution. For only if he knows what he wants can he decide whether a certain institution is or is not well adapted to its function.

Now if we ask our question in this way, the reply of the humanitarian will be : What I demand from the state is protection ; not only for myself, but for others too. I demand protection for my own freedom and for other people's. I do not wish to live at the mercy of anybody who has the larger fists or the bigger guns. In other words, I wish to be protected against aggression from other men. I want the difference between aggression and defence to be recognized, and defence to be supported by the organized power of the state. (The defence is one of a *status quo*, and the principle proposed amounts to this —that the *status quo* should not be changed by violent means, but only according to law, by compromise or arbitration, except where there is no legal procedure for its revision.) I am perfectly ready to see my own freedom of action somewhat curtailed by the state, provided I can obtain protection of that freedom which remains, since I know that some limitations of my freedom are necessary ; for instance, I must give up my ' freedom ' to attack, if I want the state to support defence against any attack. But I demand that the fundamental purpose of the state should not be lost sight of ; I mean, the protection of that freedom which does not harm other citizens. Thus I demand that the state must limit the freedom of the citizens as equally as possible, and not beyond what is necessary for achieving an equal limitation of freedom.

Something like this will be the demand of the humanitarian, of the equalitarian, of the individualist. It is a demand which permits the social technologist to approach political problems rationally, i.e. from the point of view of a fairly clear and definite aim.

Against the claim that an aim like this can be formulated sufficiently clearly and definitely, many objections have been raised. It has been said that once it is recognized that freedom must be limited, the whole principle of freedom breaks down, and the question what limitations are necessary and what are wanton cannot be decided rationally, but only by authority. But this objection is due to a muddle. It mixes up the fundamental question of what we want from a state with certain important technological difficulties in the way of the realization of our aims. It is certainly difficult to determine exactly the degree of freedom that can be left to the citizens without endangering that freedom whose protection is the task of the state. But that something like an approximate determination of that degree is possible is proved by experience, i.e. by the existence of democratic states. In fact, this process of approximate determination is one of the main tasks of legislation in democracies. It

is a difficult process, but its difficulties are certainly not such as to
force upon us a change in our fundamental demands.   These are,
stated very briefly, that the state should be considered as a society
for the prevention of crime, i.e. of aggression.   And the whole
objection that it is hard to know where freedom ends and crime
begins is answered, in principle, by the famous story of the
hooligan who protested that, being a free citizen, he could move
his fist in any direction he liked ; whereupon the judge wisely
replied : ' The freedom of the movement of your fists is limited
by the position of your neighbour's nose.'

The view of the state which I have sketched here may be
called ' protectionism '.   The term ' protectionism ' has often
been used to describe tendencies which are opposed to freedom.
Thus the economist means by protectionism the policy of protecting certain industrial interests against competition ; and the
moralist means by it the demand that officers of the state shall
establish a moral tutelage over the population.   Although the
political theory which I call protectionism is not connected with
any of these tendencies, and although it is fundamentally a
liberal theory, I think that the name may be used to indicate
that, though liberal, it has nothing to do with the *policy of strict
non-intervention* (often, but not quite correctly, called ' *laissez faire* ').
Liberalism and state-interference are not opposed to each other.
On the contrary, any kind of freedom is clearly impossible unless
it is guaranteed by the state [42].   A certain amount of state control
in education, for instance, is necessary, if the young are to be
protected from a neglect which would make them unable to
defend their freedom, and the state should see that all educational
facilities are available to everybody.   But too much state control
in educational matters is a fatal danger to freedom, since it must
lead to indoctrination.   As already indicated, the important
and difficult question of the limitations of freedom cannot be
solved by a cut and dried formula.   And the fact that there will
always be borderline cases must be welcomed, for without the
stimulus of political problems and political struggles of this
kind, the citizens' readiness to fight for their freedom would soon
disappear, and with it, their freedom.   (Viewed in this light, the
alleged clash between freedom and security, that is, a security
guaranteed by the state, turns out to be a chimera.   For there is
no freedom if it is not secured by the state ; and conversely,
only a state which is controlled by free citizens can offer them
any reasonable security at all.)

Stated in this way, the protectionist theory of the state is free from any elements of historicism or essentialism. It does not say that the state originated as an association of individuals with a protectionist aim, or that any actual state in history was ever consciously ruled in accordance with this aim. And it says nothing about the essential nature of the state, or about a natural right to freedom. Nor does it say anything about the way in which states actually function. It formulates a political *demand*, or more precisely, a *proposal* for the adoption of a certain policy. I suspect, however, that many conventionalists who have described the state as originating from an association for the protection of its members, intended to express this very demand, though they did it in a clumsy and misleading language—the language of historicism. A similar misleading way of expressing this demand is to assert that it is essentially the function of the state to protect its members ; or to assert that the state is to be defined as an association for mutual protection. All these theories must be translated, as it were, into the language of demands or proposals for political actions before they can be seriously discussed. Otherwise, endless discussions of a merely verbal character are unavoidable.

An example of such a translation may be given. A criticism of what I call protectionism has been proffered by Aristotle [43], and repeated by Burke, and by many modern Platonists. This criticism asserts that protectionism takes too mean a view of the tasks of the state which is (using Burke's words) ' to be looked upon with other reverence, because it is not a partnership in things subservient only to the gross animal existence of a temporary and perishable nature '. In other words, the state is said to be something higher or nobler than an association with rational ends ; it is an object of worship. It has higher tasks than the protection of human beings and their rights. It has moral tasks. ' To take care of virtue is the business of a state which truly deserves this name ', says Aristotle. If we try to translate this criticism into the language of political demands, then we find that these critics of protectionism want two things. First, they wish to make the state an object of worship. From our point of view, there is nothing to say against this wish. It is a religious problem ; and the state-worshippers must solve for themselves how to reconcile their creed with their other religious beliefs, for example, with the First Commandment. The second demand is political. In practice, this demand would simply mean that officers of the state should be concerned with the morality of the citizens, and that they should use their power not so much for the protection of the citizens' freedom as for the control of their moral life.   In other words, it is the demand that the realm of legality, i.e. of state-enforced norms, should be increased at the expense of the realm of morality proper, i.e. of norms enforced not by the state but by our own moral decisions—by our conscience.   Such a demand or proposal can be rationally discussed ; and it can be said against it that those who raise such demands apparently do not see that this would be the end of the individual's moral responsibility, and that it would not improve but destroy morality.   It would replace personal responsibility by tribalistic taboos and by the totalitarian irresponsibility of the individual. Against this whole attitude, the individualist must maintain that the morality of states (if there is any such thing) tends to be considerably lower than that of the average citizen, so that it is much more desirable that the morality of the state should be controlled by the citizens than the opposite.   What we need and what we want is to moralize politics, and not to politicize morals.

It should be mentioned that, from the protectionist point of view, the existing democratic states, though far from perfect, represent a very considerable achievement in social engineering of the right kind.   Many forms of crime, of attack on the rights of human individuals by other individuals, have been practically suppressed or very considerably reduced, and courts of law administer justice fairly successfully in difficult conflicts of interest. There are many who think that the extension of these methods [44] to international crime and international conflict is only a Utopian dream ; but it is not so long since the institution of an effective executive for upholding civil peace appeared Utopian to those who suffered under the threats of criminals, in countries where at present civil peace is quite successfully maintained.   And I think that the engineering problems of the control of international crime are really not so difficult, once they are squarely and rationally faced.   If the matter is presented clearly, it will not be hard to get people to agree that protective institutions are necessary, both on a regional and on a world-wide scale.   Let the state-worshippers continue to worship the state, but demand that the institutional technologists be allowed not only to improve its internal machinery, but also to build up an organization for the prevention of international crime.

VII

Returning now to the history of these movements, it seems that the protectionist theory of the state was first proffered by the Sophist Lycophron, a pupil of Gorgias. It has already been mentioned that he was (like Alcidamas, also a pupil of Gorgias) one of the first to attack the theory of natural privilege. That he held the theory which I have called ' protectionism ' is recorded by Aristotle, who speaks about him in a manner which makes it very likely that he originated it. From the same source we learn that he formulated it with a clarity which has hardly been attained by any of his successors.

Aristotle tells us that Lycophron considered the law of the state as a ' covenant by which men assure one another of justice ' (and that it has not the power to make citizens good or just). He tells us furthermore [45] that Lycophron looked upon the state as an instrument for the protection of its citizens against acts of injustice (and for permitting them peaceful intercourse, especially exchange), demanding that the state should be a ' co-operative association for the prevention of crime '. It is interesting that there is no indication in Aristotle's account that Lycophron expressed his theory in a historicist form, i.e. as a theory concerning the historical origin of the state in a social contract. On the contrary, it emerges clearly from Aristotle's context that Lycophron's theory was solely concerned with the end of the state ; for Aristotle argues that Lycophron has not seen that the essential end of the state is to make its citizens virtuous. This indicates that Lycophron interpreted this end rationally, from a technological point of view, adopting the demands of equalitarianism, individualism, and protectionism.

In this form, Lycophron's theory is completely secure from the objections to which the traditional historicist theory of the social contract is exposed. It is often said, for instance by Barker [46], that the contract theory ' has been met by modern thinkers point by point '. That may be so ; but a survey of Barker's points will show that they certainly do not meet the theory of Lycophron, in whom Barker sees (and in this point I am inclined to agree with him) the probable founder of the earliest form of a theory which has later been called the contract theory. Barker's points can be set down as follows : (a) There was, historically, never a contract ; (b) the state was, historically, never instituted ; (c) laws are not conventional, but arise out of tradition, superior force, perhaps instinct, etc. ; they are customs before they become codes ; (d) the strength of the laws does not lie in the sanctions, in the protective power of the state which enforces them, but in the individual's readiness to obey them, i.e. in the individual's moral will.

It will be seen at once that objections (a), (b), and (c), which in themselves are admittedly fairly correct (although there have been some contracts) concern the theory only in its historicist form and are irrelevant to Lycophron's version. We therefore need not consider them at all. Objection (d), however, deserves closer consideration. What can be meant by it ? The theory attacked stresses the ' will ', or better the decision of the individual, more than any other theory ; in fact, the word ' contract ' suggests an agreement by ' free will ' ; it suggests, perhaps more than any other theory, that the strength of the laws lies in the individual's readiness to accept and to obey them. How, then, can (d) be an objection against the contract theory ? The only explanation seems to be that Barker does not think the contract to spring from the ' moral will ' of the individual, but rather from a selfish will ; and this interpretation is the more likely as it is in keeping with Plato's criticism. But one need not be selfish in order to be a protectionist. Protection need not mean self-protection ; many people insure their lives with the aim of protecting others and not themselves, and in the same way they may demand state protection mainly for others, and to a lesser degree (or not at all) for themselves. The fundamental idea of protectionism is : protect the weak from being bullied by the strong. This demand has been raised not only by the weak, but often by the strong also. It is, to say the least of it, misleading to suggest that it is a selfish or an immoral demand.

Lycophron's protectionism is, I think, free of all these objections. It is the most fitting expression of the humanitarian and equalitarian movement of the Periclean age. And yet, we have been robbed of it. It has been handed down to later generations only in a distorted form ; as the historicist theory of the origin of the state in a social contract ; or as an essentialist theory claiming that the true nature of the state is that of a convention ; and as a theory of selfishness, based on the assumption of the fundamentally immoral nature of man. All this is due to the overwhelming influence of Plato's authority.

VIII

There can be little doubt that Plato knew Lycophron's theory well, for he was (in all likelihood) Lycophron's younger contemporary. And, indeed, this theory can be easily identified with one which is mentioned first in the *Gorgias* and later in the *Republic*. (In neither place does Plato mention its author ; a procedure often adopted by him when his opponent was alive.) In the *Gorgias*, the theory is expounded by Callicles, an ethical nihilist like the Thrasymachus of the *Republic*. In the *Republic*, it is expounded by Glaucon. In neither case does the speaker identify himself with the theory he presents.

The two passages are in many respects parallel. Both present the theory in a historicist form, i.e. as a theory of the origin of 'justice'. Both present it as if its logical premises were necessarily selfish and even nihilistic ; i.e. as if the protectionist view of the state was upheld only by those who would *like* to inflict injustice, but are too weak to do so, and who *therefore* demand that the strong should not do so either ; a presentation which is certainly not fair, since the only necessary premise of the theory is the demand that crime, or injustice, should be suppressed.

So far, the two passages in the *Gorgias* and in the *Republic* run parallel, a parallelism which has often been commented upon. But there is a tremendous difference between them which has, so far as I know, been overlooked by commentators. It is this. In the *Gorgias*, the theory is presented by Callicles as one which he opposes ; and since he also opposes Socrates, the protectionist theory is, by implication, not attacked but rather defended by Plato. And, indeed, a closer view shows that Socrates upholds several of its features against the nihilist Callicles. But in the *Republic*, the same theory is presented by Glaucon as an elaboration and development of the views of Thrasymachus, i.e. of the nihilist who takes here the place of Callicles ; in other words, the theory is presented as nihilist, and Socrates as the hero who victoriously destroys this devilish doctrine of selfishness.

Thus the passages in which most commentators find a similarity between the tendencies of the *Gorgias* and the *Republic* reveal, in fact, a complete change of front. In spite of Callicles' hostile presentation, the tendency of the *Gorgias* is favourable to protectionism ; but the *Republic* is violently against it.

Here is an extract from Calli es' speech in the *Gorgias* [47] : ' The laws are made by the great mass of the people which

consists mainly of the weak men. And they make the laws . .
in order to protect themselves and their interests. Thus they
deter the stronger men . . and all others who might get the
better of them, from doing so ; . . and they mean by the word
" injustice " the attempt of a man to get the better of his neighbours ; and being aware of their inferiority, they are, I should
say, only too glad if they can obtain equality.' If we look at
this account and eliminate what is due to Callicles' open scorn
and hostility, then we find all the elements of Lycophron's
theory : equalitarianism, individualism, and protection against
injustice. Even the reference to the ' strong ' and to the ' weak '
who are aware of their inferiority fits the protectionist view very
well indeed, provided the element of caricature is allowed for.
It is not at all unlikely that Lycophron's doctrine explicitly
raised the demand that the state should protect the weak, a
demand which is, of course, anything but ignoble. (The hope
that this demand will one day be fulfilled is expressed by the
Christian teaching : ' The meek shall inherit the earth.')

Callicles himself does not like protectionism ; he is in favour
of the ' natural ' rights of the stronger. It is very significant that
Socrates, in his argument against Callicles, comes to the rescue
of protectionism; for he connects it with his own central thesis—
that it is better to suffer injustice than to inflict it. He says, for
instance [48] : ' Are not the many of the opinion, as you were
lately saying, that justice is equality ? And also that it is more
disgraceful to inflict injustice than to suffer it ? ' And later :
' . . nature itself, and not only convention, affirms that to
inflict injustice is more disgraceful than to suffer it, and that
justice is equality.' (In spite of its individualistic and equalitarian and protectionist tendencies, the *Gorgias* also exhibits some
leanings which are strongly anti-democratic. The explanation
may be that Plato when writing the *Gorgias* had not yet developed
his totalitarian theories ; although his sympathies were already
anti-democratic, he was still under Socrates' influence. How anybody can think that the *Gorgias* and the *Republic* can be both at the
same time true accounts of Socrates' opinions, I fail to understand).

Let us now turn to the *Republic*, where Glaucon presents
protectionism as a logically more stringent but ethically unchanged version of Thrasymachus' nihilism. ' My theme ', says
Glaucon [49], ' is the origin of justice, and what sort of thing it
really is. According to some it is by nature an excellent thing
to inflict injustice upon others, and a bad thing to suffer it. But

they hold that the badness of suffering injustice much exceeds the desirability of inflicting it. For a time, then, men will inflict injustice on one another, and of course suffer it, and they will get a good taste of both. But ultimately, those who are not strong enough to repel it, or to enjoy inflicting it, decide that it is more profitable for them to join in a contract, mutually assuring one another that no one should inflict injustice, or suffer it. This is the way in which laws were established. . . And this is the nature and the origin of justice, according to that theory.'

As far as its rational content goes, this is clearly the same theory ; and the way in which it is represented also resembles in detail [50] Callicles' speech in the *Gorgias*. And yet, Plato has made a complete change of front. The protectionist theory is now no longer defended against the allegation that it is based on cynical egoism ; on the contrary. Our humanitarian sentiments, our moral indignation, already aroused by Thrasymachus' nihilism, are utilized for turning us into enemies of protectionism. This theory, whose humanitarian character has been indicated in the *Gorgias*, is now made by Plato to appear as anti-humanitarian, and indeed, as the outcome of the repulsive and most unconvincing doctrine that injustice is a very good thing—for those who can get away with it. And he does not hesitate to rub this point in. In an extensive continuation of the passage quoted, Glaucon elaborates in much detail the allegedly necessary assumptions or premises of protectionism. Among these he mentions, for instance, the view that the inflicting of injustice is ' the best of all things ' [51] ; that justice is established only because many men are too weak to commit crimes ; and that to the individual citizen, a life of crime would be most profitable. And ' Socrates ', i.e. Plato, vouches explicitly [52] for the authenticity of Glaucon's interpretation of the theory presented. By this method, Plato seems to have succeeded in persuading most of his readers, and at any rate all Platonists, that the protectionist theory here developed is identical with the ruthless and cynical selfishness of Thrasymachus [53] ; and, what is more important, that all forms of individualism amount to the same, namely, selfishness. But it was not only his admirers he persuaded ; he even succeeded in persuading his opponents, and especially the adherents of the contract theory. From Carneades [54] to Hobbes, they not only adopted his fatal historicist presentation, but also Plato's assurances that the basis of their theory was an ethical nihilism.

Now it must be realized that the elaboration of its allegedly selfish basis is the whole of Plato's argument against protectionism ; and considering the space taken up by this elaboration, we may safely assume that it was not his reticence which made him proffer no better argument, but the fact that he had none. Thus protectionism had to be dismissed by an appeal to our moral sentiments—as an affront against the idea of justice, and against our feelings of decency.

This is Plato's method of dealing with a theory which was not only a dangerous rival of his own doctrine, but also representative of the new humanitarian and individualistic creed, i.e. the arch-enemy of everything that was dear to Plato. The method is clever ; its astonishing success proves it. But I should not be fair if I did not frankly admit that Plato's method appears to me dishonest. For the theory attacked does not need any assumption more immoral than that injustice is evil, i.e. that it should be avoided, and brought under control. And Plato knew quite well that the theory was not based on selfishness, for in the *Gorgias* he had presented it not as identical with the nihilistic theory from which it is ' derived ' in the *Republic*, but as opposed to it.

Summing up, we can say that Plato's theory of justice, as presented in the *Republic* and later works, is a conscious attempt to get the better of the equalitarian, individualistic, and pro-tectionist tendencies of his time, and to re-establish the claims of tribalism by developing a totalitarian moral theory. At the same time, he was strongly impressed by the new humanitarian morality ; but instead of combating equalitarianism with argu-ments, he avoided even discussing it. And he successfully enlisted the humanitarian sentiments, whose strength he knew so well, in the cause of the totalitarian class rule of a naturally superior master race.

These class prerogatives, he claimed, are necessary for uphold-ing the stability of the state. They constitute therefore the essence of justice. Ultimately, this claim is based upon the argument that justice is useful to the might, health, and stability of the state ; an argument which is only too similar to the modern totalitarian definition : right is whatever is useful to the might of my nation, or my class, or my party.

But this is not yet the whole story. By its emphasis on class prerogative, Plato's theory of justice puts the problem ' Who should rule ? ' in the centre of political theory. His reply to this question was that the wisest, and the best, should rule. Does not this excellent reply modify the character of his theory ?

CHAPTER 7: THE PRINCIPLE OF LEADERSHIP

> The wise shall lead and rule, and the ignorant shall follow.
>
> PLATO.

Certain objections [1] to our interpretation of Plato's political programme have forced us into an investigation of the part played, within this programme, by such moral ideas as Justice, Goodness, Beauty, Wisdom, Truth, and Happiness. The present and the two following chapters are to continue this analysis, and the part played by the idea of Wisdom in Plato's political philosophy will occupy us next.

We have seen that Plato's idea of justice demands, fundamentally, that the natural rulers should rule and the natural slaves should slave. It is part of the historicist demand that the state, in order to arrest all change, should be a copy of its Idea, or of its true 'nature'. This theory of justice indicates very clearly that Plato saw the fundamental problem of politics in the question : *Who shall rule the state?*

I

It is my conviction that by expressing the problem of politics in the form 'Who should rule?' or 'Whose will should be supreme?', etc., Plato created a lasting confusion in political philosophy. It is indeed analogous to the confusion he created in the field of moral philosophy by his identification, discussed in the last chapter, of collectivism and altruism. It is clear that once the question 'Who should rule?' is asked, it is hard to avoid some such reply as 'the best' or 'the wisest' or 'the born ruler' or 'he who masters the art of ruling' (or, perhaps, 'The General Will' or 'The Master Race' or 'The Industrial Workers' or 'The People'). But such a reply, convincing as it may sound—for who would advocate the rule of 'the worst' or 'the greatest fool' or 'the born slave'?—is, as I shall try to show, quite useless.

First of all, such a reply is liable to persuade us that some fundamental problem of political theory has been solved. But if we approach political theory from a different angle, then we find that far from solving any fundamental problems, we have merely skipped over them, by assuming that the question ' Who should rule ? ' is fundamental. For even those who share this assumption of Plato's admit that political rulers are not always sufficiently ' good ' or ' wise ' (we need not worry about the precise meaning of these terms), and that it is not at all easy to get a government on whose goodness and wisdom one can implicitly rely. If that is granted, then we must ask whether political thought should not face from the beginning the possibility of bad government ; whether we should not prepare for the worst leaders, and hope for the best. But this leads to a new approach to the problem of politics, for it forces us to replace the question : *Who should rule ?* by the new ² question : *How can we so organize political institutions that bad or incompetent rulers can be prevented from doing too much damage ?*

Those who believe that the older question is fundamental, tacitly assume that political power is ' essentially ' unchecked. They assume that someone has the power—either an individual or a collective body, such as a class. And they assume that he who has the power can, very nearly, do what he wills, and especially that he can strengthen his power, and thereby approximate it further to an unlimited or unchecked power. They assume that political power is, essentially, sovereign. If this assumption is made, then, indeed, the question ' Who is to be the sovereign ? ' is the only important question left.

I shall call this assumption the *theory of (unchecked) sovereignty*, using this expression not for any particular one of the various theories of sovereignty, proffered more especially by such writers as Bodin, Rousseau, or Hegel, but for the more general assumption that political power is practically unchecked, or for the demand that it ought to be so ; together with the implication that the main question left is to get this power into the best hands. This theory of sovereignty is tacitly assumed in Plato's approach, and has played its rôle ever since. It is also implicitly assumed, for instance, by those modern writers who believe that the main problem is : Who should dictate ? The capitalists or the workers ?

Without entering into a detailed criticism, I wish to point out that there are serious objections against a rash and implicit acceptance of this theory. Whatever its speculative merits may appear to be, it is certainly a very unrealistic assumption. No political power has ever been unchecked, and as long as men remain human (as long as the ' Brave New World ' has not materialized), there can be no absolute and unrestrained political power. So long as one man cannot accumulate enough physical power in his hands to dominate all others, just so long must he depend upon his helpers. Even the most powerful tyrant depends upon his secret police, his henchmen and his hangmen. This dependence means that his power, great as it may be, is not unchecked, and that he has to make concessions, playing one group off against another. It means that there are other political forces, other powers besides his own, and that he can exert his rule only by utilizing and pacifying them. This shows that even the extreme cases of sovereignty are never cases of pure sovereignty. They are never cases in which the will or the interest of one man (or, if there were such a thing, the will or the interest of one group) can achieve his aim directly, without giving up some of it in order to enlist powers which he cannot conquer. And in an overwhelming number of cases, the limitations of political power go much further than this.

I have stressed these empirical points, not because I wish to use them as an argument, but merely in order to avoid objections. My claim is that every theory of sovereignty omits to face a more fundamental question—the question, namely, whether we should not strive towards institutional control of the rulers by balancing their powers against other powers. This *theory of checks and balances* can at least claim careful consideration. The only objections to this claim, as far as I can see, are (*a*) that such a control is *practically* impossible, or (*b*) that it is *essentially* inconceivable since political power is essentially sovereign [3]. Both of these dogmatic objections are, I believe, refuted by the facts ; and with them fall a number of other influential views (for instance, the theory that the only alternative to the dictatorship of one class is that of another class).

In order to raise the question of institutional control of the rulers, we need not assume more than that governments are not always good or wise. But since I have said something about historical facts, I think I should confess that I feel inclined to go a little beyond this assumption. I am inclined to think that rulers have rarely been above the average, either morally or intellectually, and often below it. And I think that it is reasonable to adopt, in politics, the principle of preparing for the worst, as well as we can, though we should, of course, at the same time try to obtain the best. It appears to me madness to base all our political efforts upon the faint hope that we shall be successful in obtaining excellent, or even competent, rulers.   Strongly as I feel in these matters, I must insist, however, that my criticism of the theory of sovereignty does not depend on these more personal opinions.

Apart from these personal opinions, and apart from the above mentioned empirical arguments against the general theory of sovereignty, there is also a kind of logical argument which can be used to show the inconsistency of any of the particular forms of the theory of sovereignty ; more precisely, the logical argument can be given different but analogous forms to combat the theory that the wisest should rule, or else the theories that the best, or the law, or the majority, etc., should rule.   One particular form of this logical argument is directed against a too naïve version of liberalism, of democracy, and of the principle that the majority should rule ; and it is somewhat similar to the well-known ' *paradox of freedom* ' which has been used first, and with success, by Plato.   In his criticism of democracy, and in his story of the rise of the tyrant, Plato raises implicitly the following question :   What if it is the will of the people that they should not rule, but a tyrant instead ?   The free man, Plato suggests, may exercise his absolute freedom, first by defying the laws and ultimately by defying freedom itself and by clamouring for a tyrant [4].   This is not just a far-fetched possibility ; it has happened a number of times ; and every time it has happened, it has put in a hopeless intellectual position all those democrats who adopt, as the ultimate basis of their political creed, the principle of the majority rule or a similar form of the principle of sovereignty.   On the one hand, the principle they have adopted demands from them that they should oppose any but the majority rule, and therefore the new tyranny ; on the other hand, the same principle demands from them that they should accept any decision reached by the majority, and thus the rule of the new tyrant.   The inconsistency of their theory must, of course, paralyse their actions [5].   Those of us democrats who demand the institutional control of the rulers by the ruled, and especially the right of dismissing the government by a majority vote, must therefore base these demands upon better grounds than a self-contradictory theory of sovereignty.   (That this is possible will be briefly shown in the next section of this chapter.)

Plato, we have seen, came near to discovering the paradoxes of freedom and of democracy.   But what Plato and his followers overlooked is that all the other forms of the theory of sovereignty give rise to analogous inconsistencies. *All theories of sovereignty are paradoxical.* For instance, we may have selected 'the wisest' or 'the best' as a ruler. But 'the wisest' in his wisdom may find that not he but 'the best' should rule, and 'the best' in his goodness may perhaps decide that 'the majority' should rule. It is important to notice that even that form of the theory of sovereignty which demands the 'Kingship of the Law' is open to the same objection. This, in fact, has been seen very early, as Heraclitus' remark[6] shows : 'The law can demand, too, that the will of One Man must be obeyed.'

In summing up this brief criticism, one can, I believe, assert that the theory of sovereignty is in a weak position, both empirically and logically. The least that can be demanded is that it must not be adopted without careful consideration of other possibilities.

II

And indeed, it is not difficult to show that a theory of democratic control can be developed which is free of the paradox of sovereignty. The theory I have in mind is one which does not proceed, as it were, from a doctrine of the intrinsic goodness or righteousness of a majority rule, but rather from the baseness of tyranny ; or more precisely, it rests upon the decision, or upon the adoption of the proposal, to avoid and to resist tyranny.

For we may distinguish two main types of government. The first type consists of governments of which we can get rid without bloodshed—for example, by way of general elections ; that is to say, the social institutions provide means by which the rulers may be dismissed by the ruled, and the social traditions [7] ensure that these institutions will not easily be destroyed by those who are in power. The second type consists of governments which the ruled cannot get rid of except by way of a successful revolution—that is to say, in most cases, not at all. I suggest the term 'democracy' as a short-hand label for a government of the first type, and the term 'tyranny' or 'dictatorship' for the second. This, I believe, corresponds closely to traditional usage. But I wish to make clear that no part of my argument depends on the choice of these labels ; and should anybody reverse this usage (as is frequently done nowadays), then I should simply say that I am in favour of what he calls 'tyranny', and object to what he calls 'democracy' ; and I should reject as irrelevant any attempt to discover what 'democracy' 'really' or 'essentially' means, for example, by translating the term into 'the

rule of the people '.   (For although ' the people ' may influence
the actions of their rulers by the threat of dismissal, they never
rule themselves in any concrete, practical sense.)

If we make use of the two labels as suggested, then we can
now describe, as the principle of a democratic policy, the proposal to create, develop, and protect, political institutions for the
avoidance of tyranny.   This principle does not imply that we
can ever develop institutions of this kind which are faultless or
foolproof, or which ensure that the policies adopted by a democratic government will be right or good or wise—or even necessarily better or wiser than the policies adopted by a benevolent
tyrant.   (Since no such assertions are made, the paradox of
democracy is avoided.)   What may be said, however, to be
implied in the adoption of the democratic principle is the conviction that the acceptance of even a bad policy in a democracy
(as long as we can work for a peaceful change) is preferable to
the submission to a tyranny, however wise or benevolent.   Seen
in this light, the theory of democracy is not based upon the
principle that the majority should rule ; rather, the various
equalitarian methods of democratic control, such as general elections and representative government, are to be considered as no
more than well-tried and, in the presence of a widespread traditional distrust of tyranny, reasonably effective institutional safe-
guards against tyranny, always open to improvement, and even
providing methods for their own improvement.

He who accepts the principle of democracy in this sense is
therefore not bound to look upon the result of a democratic vote
as an authoritative expression of what is right.   Although he
will accept a decision of the majority, for the sake of making
the democratic institutions work, he will feel free to combat it
by democratic means, and to work for its revision.   And should
he live to see the day when the majority vote destroys the democratic institutions, then this sad experience will tell him only that
there does not exist a foolproof method of avoiding tyranny.
But it need not weaken his decision to fight tyranny, nor will
it expose his theory as inconsistent.

III

Returning to Plato, we find that by his emphasis upon the
problem ' who should rule ', he implicitly assumed the general
theory of sovereignty.   The question of an institutional control
of the rulers, and of an institutional balancing of their powers,

is thereby eliminated without ever having been raised. The interest is shifted from institutions to questions of personnel, and the most urgent problem now becomes that of selecting the natural leaders, and that of training them for leadership.

In view of this fact some people think that in Plato's theory, the welfare of the state is ultimately an ethical and spiritual matter, depending on persons and personal responsibility rather than on the construction of impersonal institutions. I believe that this view of Platonism is superficial. *All long-term politics are institutional.* There is no escape from that, not even for Plato. The principle of leadership does not replace institutional problems by problems of personnel, it only creates new institutional problems. As we shall see, it even burdens the institutions with a task which goes beyond what can be reasonably demanded from a mere institution, namely, with *the task of selecting the future leaders.* It would be therefore a mistake to think that the opposition between the theory of balances and the theory of sovereignty corresponds to that between institutionalism and personalism. Plato's principle of leadership is far removed from a pure personalism since it involves the working of institutions ; and indeed it may be said that a pure personalism is impossible. But it must be said that a pure institutionalism is impossible also. Not only·does the construction of institutions involve important personal decisions, but the functioning of even the best institutions (such as democratic checks and balances) will always depend, to a considerable degree, on the persons involved. Institutions are like fortresses. They must be well designed *and* manned.

This distinction between the personal and the institutional element in a social situation is a point which is often missed by the critics of democracy. Most of them are dissatisfied with democratic institutions because they find that these do not necessarily prevent a state or a policy from falling short of some moral standards or of some political demands which may be urgent as well as admirable. But these critics misdirect their attacks ; they do not understand what democratic institutions may be expected to do, and what the alternative to democratic institutions would be. Democracy (using this label in the sense suggested above) provides the institutional framework for the reform of political institutions. It makes possible the reform of institutions without using violence, and thereby the use of reason in the designing of new institutions and the adjusting of old ones. It cannot provide reason. The question of the intellectual and moral standard of its citizens is to a large degree a personal problem. (The idea that this problem can be tackled, in turn, by an institutional eugenic and educational control is, I believe, mistaken ; some reasons for my belief will be given below.) It is quite wrong to blame democracy for the political shortcomings of a democratic state. We should rather blame ourselves, that is to say, the citizens of the democratic state. In a non-democratic state, the only way to achieve reasonable reforms is by the violent over-throw of the government, and the introduction of a democratic framework. Those who criticize democracy on any ' moral ' grounds fail to distinguish between personal and institutional problems. It rests with us to improve matters. The democratic institutions cannot improve themselves. The problem of im-proving them is always a problem for *persons* rather than for institutions. But if we want improvements, we must make clear which *institutions* we want to improve.

There is another distinction within the field of political problems corresponding to that between persons and institutions. It is the one between the problems of the day and the problems of the future. While the problems of the day are largely personal, the building of the future must necessarily be institutional. If the political problem is approached by asking ' Who should rule ', and if Plato's principle of leadership is adopted—that is to say, the principle that the best should rule—then the problem of the future must take the form of designing institutions for the selection of future leaders.

This is one of the most important problems in Plato's theory of education. In approaching it I do not hesitate to say that Plato utterly corrupted and confused the theory and practice of education by linking it up with his theory of leadership. The damage done is, if possible, even greater than that inflicted upon ethics by the identification of collectivism with altruism, and upon political theory by the introduction of the principle of sovereignty. Plato's assumption that it should be the task of education (or more precisely, of the educational institutions) to select the future leaders, and to train them for leadership, is still largely taken for granted. By burdening these institutions with a task which must go beyond the scope of any institution, Plato is partly responsible for their deplorable state. But before entering into a general discussion of his view of the task of education, I wish to develop, in more detail, his theory of leadership, the leadership of the wise.

IV

I think it most likely that this theory of Plato's owes a number of its elements to the influence of Socrates. One of the fundamental tenets of Socrates was, I believe, his moral intellectualism. By this I understand (a) his identification of goodness and wisdom, his theory that nobody acts against his better knowledge, and that lack of knowledge is responsible for all moral mistakes ; (b) his theory that moral excellence can be taught, and that it does not require any particular moral faculties, apart from the universal human intelligence.

Socrates was a moralist and an enthusiast. He was the type of man who would criticize any form of government for its shortcomings (and indeed, such criticism would be necessary and useful for any government, although it is possible only under a democracy) but he recognized the importance of being loyal to the laws of the state. As it happened, he spent his life largely under a democratic form of government, and as a good democrat he found it his duty to expose the incompetence and windbaggery of some of the democratic leaders of his time. At the same time, he opposed any form of tyranny ; and if we consider his courageous behaviour under the Thirty Tyrants then we have no reason to assume that his criticism of the democratic leaders was inspired by anything like anti-democratic leanings[8]. It is not unlikely that he demanded (like Plato) that the best should rule, which would have meant, in his view, the wisest, or those who knew something about justice. But we must remember that by ' justice ' he meant equalitarian justice (as indicated by the passages from the *Gorgias* quoted in the last chapter), and that he was not only an equalitarian but also an individualist—perhaps the greatest apostle of an individualistic ethics of all time. And we should realize that, if he demanded that the wisest men should rule, he clearly stressed that he did not mean the learned men ; in fact, he was sceptical of all professional learnedness, whether it was that of the philosophers of the past or of the learned men of his own generation, the Sophists. The wisdom he meant was of a different kind. It was simply the realization : how little do I know ! Those who did not know this, he taught, knew nothing at all. (This is the true scientific spirit. Some people still think, as Plato did when he had established himself as a learned Pythagorean sage[9], that Socrates' agnostic attitude must be explained by the lack of success of the science of his day. But this only shows that they do not understand this spirit, and that they are still possessed by the pre-Socratic magical attitude towards science, and towards the scientist, whom they consider as a somewhat glorified shaman, as wise, learned, initiated. They judge him by the amount of knowledge in his possession, instead of taking, with Socrates, his awareness of what he does not know as a measure of his scientific level as well as of his intellectual honesty.)

It is important to see that this Socratic intellectualism is decidedly equalitarian. Socrates believed that everyone can be taught ; in the *Meno*, we see him teaching a young slave a version [10] of the now so-called theorem of Pythagoras, in an attempt to prove that any uneducated slave has the capacity to grasp even abstract matters. And his intellectualism is also anti-authoritarian. A technique, for instance rhetoric, may perhaps be dogmatically taught by an expert, according to Socrates ; but real knowledge, wisdom, and also virtue, can be taught only by a method which he describes as a form of midwifery. Those eager to learn may be helped to free themselves from their prejudice ; thus they may learn self-criticism, and that truth is not easily attained. But they may also learn to make up their minds, and to rely, critically, on their decisions, and on their insight. In view of such teaching, it is clear how much the Socratic demand (if he ever raised this demand) that the best, i.e. the intellectually honest, should rule, differs from the authoritarian demand that the most learned, or from the aristocratic demand that the best, i.e. the most noble, should rule. (Socrates' belief that even courage is wisdom can, I think, be interpreted as a direct criticism of the aristocratic doctrine of the nobly born hero.)

But this moral intellectualism of Socrates is a two-edged sword. It has its equalitarian and democratic aspect, which was later developed by Antisthenes. But it has also an aspect which may give rise to strongly anti-democratic tendencies. Its stress upon the need for enlightenment, for education, might easily be misinterpreted as a demand for *authoritarianism*. This is connected with a question which seems to have puzzled Socrates a great deal : that those who are not sufficiently educated, and thus not wise enough to know their deficiencies, are just those who are in the greatest need of education. Readiness to learn in itself proves the possession of wisdom, in fact all the wisdom claimed by Socrates for himself ; for he who is ready to learn knows how little he knows. The uneducated seems thus to be in need of an authority to wake him up, since he cannot be expected to be self-critical. But this one element of authoritarianism was wonderfully balanced in Socrates' teaching by the emphasis that the authority must not claim more than that. The true teacher can prove himself only by exhibiting that self-criticism which the uneducated lacks. 'Whatever authority I may have rests solely upon my knowing how little I know': this is the way in which Socrates might have justified his mission to stir up the people from their dogmatic slumber. This educational mission he believed to be also a political mission. He felt that the way to improve the political life of the city was to educate the citizens to self-criticism. In this sense he claimed to be 'the only politician of his day' [11], in opposition to those others who flatter the people instead of furthering their true interests.

This Socratic identification of his educational and political activity could easily be distorted into the Platonic and Aristotelian demand that the state should look after the moral life of its citizens. And it can easily be used for a dangerously convincing proof that all democratic control is vicious. For how can those whose task it is to educate be judged by the uneducated? How can the better be controlled by the less good? But this argument is, of course, entirely un-Socratic. It assumes an authority of the wise and learned man, and goes far beyond Socrates' modest idea of the teacher's authority as founded solely on his consciousness of his own limitations. State-authority in these matters is liable to achieve, in fact, the exact opposite of Socrates' aim. It is liable to produce dogmatic self-satisfaction and massive intellectual complacency, instead of critical dissatisfaction and eagerness for improvement. I do not think that it is unnecessary to stress this danger which is seldom clearly realized. Even an author like Crossman, who, I believe, understood the true Socratic spirit, agrees [12] with Plato in what he calls Plato's third criticism of Athens : '*Education, which should be the major responsibility of the State*, had been left to individual caprice . . Here again was a task which should be entrusted only to the man of proven probity. The future of any State depends on the younger generation, and it is therefore madness to allow the minds of children to be moulded by individual taste and force of circumstances. Equally disastrous had been the State's *laissez faire* policy with regard to teachers and schoolmasters and sophist-lecturers.' [13] But the Athenian state's *laissez faire* policy, criticized by Crossman and Plato, had the invaluable result of enabling certain sophist-lecturers to teach, and especially the greatest of them all, Socrates. And when this policy was later dropped, the result was Socrates' death. This should be a warning that state control in such matters is dangerous, and that the cry for the ' man of proven probity ' may easily lead to the suppression of the best. (Bertrand Russell's recent suppression is a case in point.) But as far as basic principles are concerned, we have here an instance of the deeply rooted prejudice that the only alternative to *laissez faire* is full state responsibility. I certainly believe that it is the responsibility of the state to see that its citizens are given an education enabling them to participate in the life of the community, and to make use of any opportunity to develop their special interests and gifts ; and the state should certainly also see (as Crossman rightly stresses) that the lack of ' the individual's capacity to pay ' should not debar him from higher studies. This, I believe, belongs to the state's protective functions. To say, however, that ' the future of the state depends on the younger generation, and that it is therefore madness to allow the minds of children to be moulded by individual taste ', appears to me to open wide the door to totalitarianism. State interest must not be lightly invoked to defend measures which may endanger the most precious of all forms of freedom, namely, intellectual freedom. And although I do not advocate ' *laissez faire* with regard to teachers and schoolmasters ', I believe that this policy is infinitely superior to an authoritative policy that gives officers of the state full powers to mould minds, and to control the teaching of science, thereby backing the dubious authority of the expert by that of the state, ruining science by the customary practice of teaching it as an authoritative doctrine, and destroying the scientific spirit of inquiry—the spirit of the search for truth, as opposed to the belief in its possession.

I have tried to show that Socrates' intellectualism was fundamentally equalitarian and individualistic, and that the element of authoritarianism which it involved was reduced to a minimum by Socrates' intellectual modesty and his scientific attitude. The intellectualism of Plato is very different from this. The Platonic ' Socrates ' of the *Republic* [14] is the embodiment of an unmitigated authoritarianism. (Even his self-deprecating remarks are not based upon awareness of his limitations, but are rather an ironical way of asserting his superiority.) His educational aim is not the awakening of self-criticism and of critical thought in general.

It is, rather, indoctrination—the moulding of minds and of souls which (to repeat a quotation from the *Laws* [15]) are ' to become, by long habit, utterly incapable of doing anything at all independently '. And Socrates' great equalitarian and liberating idea that it is possible to reason with a slave, and that there is an intellectual link between man and man, a medium of universal understanding, namely, ' reason ', this idea is replaced by a demand for an educational monopoly of the ruling class, coupled with the strictest censorship, even of oral debates.

Socrates had stressed that he was not wise ; that he was not in the possession of truth, but that he was a searcher, an inquirer, a lover of truth. This, he explained, is expressed by the word ' philosopher ', i.e. the lover of wisdom, and the seeker for it, as opposed to ' Sophist ', i.e. the professionally wise man. If ever he claimed that statesmen should be philosophers, he could only have meant that, burdened with an excessive responsibility, they should be searchers for truth, and conscious of their limitations.

How did Plato convert this doctrine ? At first sight, it might appear that he did not alter it at all, when demanding that the sovereignty of the state should be invested in the philosophers ; especially since, like Socrates, he defined philosophers as lovers of truth. But the change made by Plato is indeed tremendous. His lover is no longer the modest seeker, he is the proud possessor of truth. A trained dialectician, he is capable of intellectual intuition, i.e. of seeing, and of communicating with, the eternal, the heavenly Forms or Ideas. Placed high above all ordinary men, he is ' god-like, if not . . divine ' [16], both in his wisdom and in his power. Plato's ideal philosopher approaches both to omniscience and to omnipotence. He is the Philosopher-King. It is hard, I think, to conceive a greater contrast than that between the Socratic and the Platonic ideal of a philosopher. It is the contrast between two worlds—the world of a modest, rational individualist and that of a totalitarian demi-god.

Plato's demand that the wise man should rule—the possessor of truth, the ' fully qualified philosopher ' [17]—raises, of course, the problem of selecting and educating the rulers. In a purely personalist (as opposed to an institutional) theory, this problem might be solved simply by declaring that the wise ruler will in his wisdom be wise enough to choose the best man for his successor. This is not, however, a very satisfactory approach to the problem. Too much would depend on uncontrolled circumstances ; an accident may destroy the future stability of the state.

But the attempt to control circumstances, to foresee what might happen and to provide for it, must lead here, as everywhere, to the abandonment of a purely personalist solution, and to its replacement by an institutional one. As already stated, the attempt to plan for the future must always lead to institutionalism.

V

The institution which according to Plato has to look after the future leaders can be described as the educational department of the state. It is, from a purely political point of view, by far the most important institution within Plato's society. It holds the keys to power. For this reason alone it should be clear that at least the higher grades of education are to be directly controlled by the rulers. But there are some additional reasons for this. The most important is that only ' the expert and . . the man of proven probity ', as Crossman puts it, which in Plato's view means only the very wisest adepts, that is to say, the rulers themselves, can be entrusted with the final initiation of the future sages into the higher mysteries of wisdom. This holds, above all, for dialectics, i.e. the art of intellectual intuition, of visualizing the divine originals, the Forms or Ideas, of unveiling the Great Mystery behind the common man's everyday world of appearances.

What are Plato's institutional demands regarding this highest form of education ? They are remarkable. He demands that only those who are past their prime of life should be admitted. ' When their bodily strength begins to fail, and when they are past the age of public and military duties, then, and only then, should they be permitted to enter at will the sacred field. . .' [18] namely, the field of the highest dialectical studies. Plato's reason for this amazing rule is clear enough. He is afraid of the power of thought. ' All great things are dangerous ' [19] is the remark by which he introduces the confession that he is afraid of the effect which philosophic thought may have upon brains which are not yet on the verge of old age. (All this he puts into the mouth of Socrates, who died in defence of his right of free discussion with the young.) But this is exactly what we should expect if we remember that Plato's fundamental aim was to arrest political change. In their youth, the members of the upper class shall fight. When they are too old to think independently, they shall become dogmatic students to be imbued with wisdom and authority in order to become sages themselves and to hand on their wisdom, the doctrine of collectivism and authoritarianism, to future generations.

It is interesting that in a later and more elaborate passage which attempts to paint the rulers in the brightest colours, Plato modifies his suggestion. Now [20] he allows the future sages to begin their preparatory dialectical studies at the age of thirty, stressing, of course, ' the need for great caution ' and the dangers of ' insubordination . . which corrupts so many dialecticians ' ; and he demands that ' those to whom the use of arguments may be permitted must possess disciplined and well-balanced natures '. This alteration certainly helps to brighten the picture. But the fundamental tendency is the same. For, in the continuation of this passage, we hear that the future leaders must not be initiated into the higher philosophical studies—into the dialectic vision of the essence of the Good—before they reach, having passed through many tests and temptations, the age of fifty.

This is the teaching of the *Republic*. It seems that the dialogue *Parmenides* [21] contains a similar message, for here Socrates is depicted as a brilliant young man who, having dabbled successfully in pure philosophy, gets into serious trouble when asked to give an account of the more subtle problems of the theory of ideas. He is dismissed by the old Parmenides with the admonition that he should train himself more thoroughly in the art of abstract thought before venturing again into the higher field of philosophical studies. It looks as if we had here (among other things) Plato's answer—' Even a Socrates was once too young for dialectics '—to his pupils who pestered him for an initiation which he considered premature.

Why is it that Plato does not wish his leaders to have originality or initiative ? The answer, I think, is clear. He hates change and does not want to see that re-adjustments may become necessary. But this explanation of Plato's attitude does not go deep enough. In fact, we are faced here with a fundamental difficulty of the leader principle. The very idea of selecting or educating future leaders is self-contradictory. You may solve the problem, perhaps, to some degree in the field of bodily excellence. Physical initiative and bodily courage are perhaps not so hard to ascertain. But the secret of intellectual excellence is the spirit of criticism ; it is intellectual independence. And this leads to difficulties which must prove insurmountable for any kind of authoritarianism. The authoritarian will in general select those who obey, who believe, who respond to his influence. But in doing so, he is bound to select mediocrities.   For he excludes those who revolt, who doubt, who dare to resist his influence.   Never can an authority admit that the intellectually courageous, i.e. those who dare to defy his authority, may be the most valuable type.   Of course, the authorities will always remain convinced of their ability to detect initiative.   But what they mean by this is only a quick grasp of their intentions, and they will remain for ever incapable of seeing the difference.   (Here we may perhaps penetrate the secret of the particular difficulty of selecting capable military leaders.   The demands of military discipline enhance the difficulties discussed, and the methods of military advancement are such that those who do dare to think for themselves are usually eliminated.   Nothing is less true, as far as intellectual initiative is concerned, than the idea that those who are good in obeying will also be good in commanding[22].   Very similar difficulties arise in political parties : the ' Man Friday ' of the party leader is seldom a capable successor.)

We are led here, I believe, to a result of some importance, and to one which can be generalized.   Institutions for the selection of the outstanding can hardly be devised.   Institutional selection may work quite well for such purposes as Plato had in mind, namely for arresting change.   But it will never work well if we demand more than that, for it will always tend to eliminate initiative and originality, and, more generally, qualities which are unusual and unexpected.   This is not a criticism of political institutionalism.   It only re-affirms what has been said before, that we should always prepare for the worst leaders, although we should try, of course, to get the best.   But it *is* a criticism of the tendency to burden institutions, especially educational institutions, with the impossible task of selecting the best.   This should never be made their task.   This tendency transforms our educational system into a race-course, and turns a course of studies into a hurdle-race.   Instead of encouraging the student to devote himself to his studies for the sake of studying, instead of encouraging in him a real love for his subject and for inquiry [23], he is encouraged to study for the sake of his personal career ; he is led to acquire only such knowledge as is serviceable in getting him over the hurdles which he must clear for the sake of his advancement.   In other words, even in the field of science, our methods of selection are based upon an appeal to personal ambition of a somewhat crude form.   (It is a natural reaction to this appeal if the eager student is looked upon with suspicion by his colleagues.)

The impossible demand for an institutional selection of intellectual leaders endangers the very life not only of science, but of intelligence.

It has been said, only too truly, that Plato was the inventor of both our secondary schools and our universities. I do not know a better argument for an optimistic view of mankind, no better proof of their indestructible love for truth and decency, of their originality and stubbornness and health, than the fact that this devastating system of education has not utterly ruined them. In spite of the treachery of so many of their leaders, there are quite a number, old as well as young, who are decent, and intelligent, and devoted to their task. ' I sometimes wonder how it was that the mischief done was not more clearly perceptible,' says Samuel Butler [24], ' and that the young men and women grew up as sensible and goodly as they did, in spite of the attempts almost deliberately made to warp and stunt their growth. Some doubtless received damage, from which they suffered to their life's end ; but many seemed little or none the worse, and some almost the better. The reason would seem to be that the natural instinct of the lads in most cases so absolutely rebelled against their training, that do what the teachers might they could never get them to pay serious heed to it.'

It may be mentioned here that, in practice, Plato did not prove too successful as a selector of political leaders. I have in mind not so much the disappointing outcome of his experiment with Dionysius the Younger, tyrant of Syracuse, but rather the participation of Plato's Academy in Dio's successful expedition against Dionysius. Plato's famous friend Dio was supported in this adventure by a number of members of Plato's Academy. One of them was Callippus, who became Dio's most trusted comrade. After Dio had made himself tyrant of Syracuse he ordered Heraclides, his ally (and perhaps his rival), to be murdered. Shortly afterwards he was himself murdered by Callippus who usurped the tyranny, which he lost after thirteen months. (He was, in turn, murdered by the Pythagorean philosopher Leptines.) But this event was not the only one of its kind in Plato's career as a teacher. Clearchus, one of Plato's (and of Isocrates') disciples, made himself tyrant of Heraclea after having posed as a democratic leader. He was murdered by his relation, Chion, another member of Plato's Academy. (We cannot know how Chion, whom some represent as an idealist, would have developed, since he was soon killed.) These and a few similar experiences of Plato's [25]—who could boast a total of at least nine tyrants among his one-time pupils and associates—throw light on the peculiar difficulties connected with the selection of men who are to be invested with absolute power. It is hard to find a man whose character will not be corrupted by it. As Lord Acton says—all power corrupts, and absolute power corrupts absolutely.

To sum up. Plato's political programme was much more institutional than personalist ; he hoped to arrest political change by the institutional control of succession in leadership. The control was to be educational, based upon an authoritarian view of learning—upon the authority of the learned expert, and ' the man of proven probity '. This is what Plato made of Socrates' demand that a responsible politician should be a lover of truth and of wisdom rather than an expert, and that he was wise only [26] if he knew his limitations.

Chapter 8 : THE PHILOSOPHER KING

> And the state will erect monuments . . . to com-
> memorate them. And sacrifices will be offered to
> them as demigods, . . . as men who are blessed
> by grace, and godlike.
>
> PLATO.

The contrast between the Platonic and the Socratic creed is
even greater than I have shown so far. Plato, I have said,
followed Socrates in his definition of the philosopher. 'Whom
do you call true philosophers ?—Those who love truth ', we read
in the *Republic* [1]. But he himself is not quite truthful when he
makes this statement. He does not really believe in it, for he
bluntly declares in other places that it is one of the royal privileges
of the sovereign to make full use of lies and deceit : ' It is the
business of the rulers of the city, if it is anybody's, to tell lies,
deceiving both its enemies and its own citizens for the benefit
of the city ; and no one else must touch this privilege.' [2]

' For the benefit of the city ', says Plato. Again we find that
the appeal to the principle of collective utility is the ultimate
ethical consideration. Totalitarian morality overrules everything, even the definition, the Idea, of the philosopher. It need
hardly be mentioned that, by the same principle of political
expediency, the ruled are to be forced to tell the truth. ' If the
ruler catches *anyone else* in a lie . . then he will punish him for
introducing a practice which injures and endangers the city. . .' [3]
Only in this slightly unexpected sense are the Platonic rulers—
the philosopher kings—lovers of truth.

I

Plato illustrates this application of his principle of collective
utility to the problem of truthfulness by the example of the
physician. The example is well chosen, since Plato likes to
visualize his political mission as one of the healer or saviour of
the sick body of society. Apart from this, the rôle which he
assigns to medicine throws light upon the totalitarian character
of Plato's city where state interest dominates the life of the citizen
from the mating of his parents to his grave. Plato interprets
medicine as a form of politics, or as he puts it himself, he ' regards
Aesculapius, the god of medicine, as a politician ' [4]. Medical

art, he explains, must not consider the prolongation of life as its aim, but only the interest of the state. ' In all properly ruled communities, each man has his particular work assigned to him in the state. This he must do, and no one has time to spend his life in falling ill and getting cured.' Accordingly, the physician has ' no right to attend to a man who cannot carry out his ordinary duties ; for such a man is useless to himself and to the state '. To this is added the consideration that such a man might have ' children who would probably be equally sick ', and who also would become a burden to the state. (In his old age, Plato mentions medicine, in spite of his increased hatred of individualism, in a more personal vein. He complains of the doctor who treats even free citizens as if they were slaves, ' issuing his orders like a tyrant whose will is law, and then rushing off to the next slave-patient ' [5], and he pleads for more gentleness and patience in medical treatment, at least for those who are not slaves.) Concerning the use of lies and deceit, Plato urges that these are ' useful only as a medicine ' [6] ; but the ruler of the state, Plato insists, must not behave like some of those ' ordinary doctors ' who have not the courage to administer strong medicines. The philosopher king, a lover of truth as a philosopher, must, as a king, be ' a more courageous man ', since he must be determined ' to administer a great many lies and deceptions '—for the benefit of the ruled, Plato hastens to add. Which means, as we already know, and as we learn here again from Plato's reference to medicine, ' for the benefit of the state '. (Kant remarked once in a very different spirit that the sentence ' Truthfulness is the best policy ' might indeed be questionable, whilst the sentence ' Truthfulness is better than policy ' is beyond dispute [7].)

What kind of lies has Plato in mind when he exhorts his rulers to use strong medicine ? Crossman rightly emphasizes that Plato means ' propaganda, the technique of controlling the behaviour of . . the bulk of the ruled majority ' [8]. Certainly, Plato had these first in his mind ; but when Crossman suggests that the propaganda lies were only intended for the consumption of the ruled, while the rulers should be a fully enlightened intelligentsia, then I cannot agree. I think, rather, that Plato's complete break with anything resembling Socrates' intellectualism is nowhere more obvious than in the place where he twice expresses his hope that even *the rulers themselves*, at least after a few generations, might be induced to believe his greatest propaganda lie ; I mean his racialism, his Myth of Blood and Soil, known as the

Myth of the Metals in Man and of the Earthborn. Here we see that Plato's utilitarian and totalitarian principles overrule everything, even the ruler's privilege of knowing, and of demanding to be told, the truth. The motive of Plato's wish that the rulers themselves should believe in the propaganda lie is his hope of increasing its wholesome effect, i.e. of strengthening the rule of the master race, and ultimately, of arresting all political change.

II

Plato introduces his Myth of Blood and Soil with the blunt admission that it is a fraud. ' Well then ', says the Socrates of the *Republic*, ' could we perhaps fabricate one of those very handy lies which indeed we mentioned just recently ? With the help of one single lordly lie we may, if we are lucky, persuade even the rulers themselves—but at any rate the rest of the city.' [9] It is interesting to note the use of the term ' persuade '. To persuade somebody to believe a lie means, more precisely, to mislead or to hoax him ; and it would be more in tune with the frank cynicism of the passage to translate ' we may, if we are lucky, hoax even the rulers themselves '. But Plato uses the term ' persuasion ' very frequently, and its occurrence here throws some light on other passages.· It may be taken as a warning that in similar passages he may have propaganda lies in his mind ; more especially where he advocates that the statesman should rule ' by means of both persuasion and force ' [10].

After announcing his ' lordly lie ', Plato, instead of proceeding directly to the narration of his Myth, first develops a lengthy preface, somewhat similar to the lengthy preface which precedes his discovery of justice ; an indication, I think, of his uneasiness. It seems that he did not expect the proposal which follows to find much favour with his readers. The Myth itself introduces two ideas. The first is to strengthen the defence of the mother country ; it is the idea that the warriors of his city are autochthonous, ' born of the earth of their country ', and ready to defend their country which is their mother. This old and well-known idea is certainly not the reason for Plato's hesitation (although the wording of the dialogue cleverly suggests it). The second idea, however, ' the rest of the story ', is the myth of racialism : ' God . . has put gold into those who are capable of ruling, silver into the auxiliaries, and iron and copper into the peasants and the other producing classes.' [11] These metals are hereditary, they are racial characteristics. In this passage, in which Plato, hesitatingly, first introduces his racialism, he allows for the possibility that children may be born with an admixture of another metal than those of their parents ; and it must be admitted that he here announces the following rule : if in one of the lower classes ' children are born with an admixture of gold and silver, they shall . . be appointed guardians, and . . auxiliaries '. But this concession is rescinded in later passages of the *Republic* (and also in the *Laws*), especially in the story of the Fall of Man and of the Number [12], partially quoted in chapter 5 above. From this passage we learn that *any* admixture of one of the base metals must be excluded from the higher classes. The possibility of admixtures and corresponding changes in status therefore only means that nobly born but degenerate children may be pushed down, and not that any of the base born may be lifted up. The way in which any mixing of metals must lead to destruction is described in the concluding passage of the story of the Fall of Man : ' Iron will mingle with silver and bronze with gold, and from this mixture variation will be born and absurd irregularity ; and whenever these are born they will beget struggle and hostility. And this is how we must describe the ancestry and birth of Dissension, wherever she arises ' [13]. It is in this light that we must consider that the Myth of the Earthborn concludes with the cynical fabrication of a prophecy by a fictitious oracle ' that the city must perish when guarded by iron and copper ' [14]. Plato's reluctance to proffer his racialism at once in its more radical form indicates, I suppose, that he knew how much it was opposed to the democratic and humanitarian tendencies of his time.

If we consider Plato's blunt admission that his Myth of Blood and Soil is a propaganda lie, then the attitude of the commentators towards the Myth is somewhat puzzling. Adam, for instance, writes : ' Without it, the present sketch of a state would be incomplete. We require some guarantee for the permanence of the city . . ; and nothing could be more in keeping with the *prevailing moral and religious spirit* of Plato's . . education than that he should find that guarantee in *faith rather than in reason.*' [15] I agree (though this is not quite what Adam meant) that nothing is more in keeping with Plato's totalitarian morality than his advocacy of propaganda lies. But I do not quite understand how the religious and idealistic commentator can declare, by implication, that religion and faith are on the level of an opportunist lie. As a matter of fact, Adam's comment is reminiscent of Hobbes' conventionalism, of the view that the tenets of religion, although not true, are a most expedient and indispensable political device.   And this consideration shows us that Plato, after all, was more of a conventionalist than one might think.   He does not even stop short of establishing a religious faith ' by convention ' (we must credit him with the frankness of his admission that it is only a fabrication), while the reputed conventionalist Protagoras at least believed that the laws, which are our making, are made with the help of divine inspiration.   It is hard to understand why those of Plato's commentators [16] who praise him for fighting against the subversive conventionalism of the Sophists, and for establishing a spiritual naturalism ultimately based on religion, fail to censure him for making a convention, or rather an invention, the ultimate basis of religion.   In fact, Plato's attitude towards religion as revealed by his ' inspired lie ' is practically identical with that of Critias, his beloved uncle, the brilliant leader of the Thirty Tyrants who established an inglorious blood-régime in Athens after the Peloponnesian war.   Critias, a poet, was the first to glorify propaganda lies, whose invention he described in forceful verses eulogizing the wise and cunning man who fabricated religion, in order to ' persuade ' the people, i.e. to threaten them into submission.[17]

' Then came, it seems, that wise and cunning man,
The first inventor of the fear of gods. . .
He framed a tale, a most alluring doctrine,
Concealing truth by veils of lying lore.
He told of the abode of awful gods,
Up in revolving vaults, whence thunder roars
And lightning's fearful flashes blind the eye. . .
He thus encircled men by bonds of fear ;
Surrounding them by gods in fair abodes,
He charmed them by his spells, and daunted them—
And lawlessness turned into law and order.'

In Critias' view, religion is nothing but the lordly lie of a great and clever statesman.   Plato's views are strikingly similar, both in the introduction of the Myth in the *Republic* (where he bluntly admits that the Myth is a lie) and in the *Laws* where he says that the installation of rites and of gods is ' a matter for a great thinker ' [18].—But is this the whole truth about Plato's religious attitude ?   Was he nothing but an opportunist in this field, and was the very different spirit of his earlier works merely Socratic ?

There is of course no way of deciding this question with certainty, though I feel, intuitively, that there may sometimes be a more genuine religious feeling expressed even in the later works. But I believe that wherever Plato considers religious matters in their relation to politics, his political opportunism sweeps all other feelings aside. Thus Plato demands, in the *Laws*, the severest punishment even for honest and honourable people [19] if their opinions concerning the gods deviate from those held by the state. Their souls are to be treated by a Nocturnal Council of inquisitors [20], and if they do not recant or if they repeat the offence, the charge of impiety means death. Has he forgotten that Socrates had fallen a victim to that very charge?

That it is mainly state interest which inspires these demands, rather than interest in the religious faith as such, is indicated by Plato's central religious doctrine. The gods, he teaches in the *Laws*, punish severely all those on the wrong side in the conflict between good and evil, a conflict which is explained as that between collectivism and individualism [21]. And the gods, he insists, take an active interest in men, they are not merely spectators. It is impossible to appease them. Neither through prayers nor through sacrifices can they be moved to abstain from punishment [22]. The political interest behind this teaching is clear, and it is made even clearer by Plato's demand that the state must suppress all doubt about any part of this politico-religious dogma, and especially about the doctrine that the gods never abstain from punishment.

Plato's opportunism and his theory of lies makes it, of course, difficult to interpret what he says. How far did he believe in his theory of justice? How far did he believe in the truth of the religious doctrines he preached? Was he perhaps himself an atheist, in spite of his demand for the punishment of other (lesser) atheists? Although we cannot hope to answer any of these questions definitely, it is, I believe, difficult, and methodologically unsound, not to give Plato at least the benefit of the doubt. And especially the fundamental sincerity of his belief that there is an urgent need to arrest all change can, I think, hardly be questioned. (I shall return to this in chapter 10.) On the other hand, we cannot doubt that Plato subjects the Socratic love of truth to the more fundamental principle that the rule of the master class must be strengthened.

It is interesting, however, to note that Plato's theory of truth is slightly less radical than his theory of justice. Justice, we have seen, is defined, practically, as that which serves the interest of his totalitarian state. It would have been possible, of course, to define the concept of truth in the same utilitarian or pragmatist fashion. The Myth is true, Plato could have said, since anything that serves the interest of my state must be believed and therefore must be called ' true ' ; and there must be no other criterion of truth. In theory, an analogous step has actually been taken by the pragmatist successors of Hegel ; in practice, it has been taken by Hegel himself and his racialist successors. But Plato retained enough of the Socratic spirit to admit candidly that he was lying. The step taken by the school of Hegel was one that could never have occurred, I think, to any companion of Socrates [23].

III

So much for the rôle played by the Idea of Truth in Plato's best state. But apart from Justice and Truth, we have still to consider some further Ideas, such as Goodness, Beauty, and Happiness, if we wish to remove the objections, raised in chapter 6, against our interpretation of Plato's political programme as purely totalitarian, and as based on historicism. An approach to the discussion of these Ideas, and also to that of Wisdom, which has been partly discussed in the last chapter, can be made by considering the somewhat negative result reached by our discussion of the Idea of Truth. For this result raises a new problem : Why does Plato demand that the philosophers should be kings or the kings philosophers, if he defines the philosopher as a lover of truth, insisting, on the other hand, that the king must be ' more courageous ', and use lies ?

The only reply to this question is, of course, that Plato has, in fact, something very different in mind 'when he uses the term ' philosopher '. And indeed, we have seen in the last chapter that his philosopher is not the devoted seeker for wisdom, but its proud possessor. He is a learned man, a sage. What Plato demands, therefore, is the rule of learnedness—*sophocracy*, if I may so call it. In order to understand this demand, we must try to find what kind of functions make it desirable that the ruler of Plato's state should be a possessor of knowledge, a ' fully qualified philosopher ', as Plato says. The functions to be considered can be divided into two main groups, namely those connected with the *foundation* of the state, and those connected with its *preservation*.

IV

The first and the most important function of the philosopher king is that of the city's founder and lawgiver. It is clear why Plato needs a philosopher for this task. If the state is to be stable, then it must be a true copy of the divine Form or Idea of the State. But only a philosopher who is fully proficient in the highest of sciences, in dialectics, is able to see, and to copy, the heavenly Original. This point receives much emphasis in the part of the *Republic* in which Plato develops his arguments for the sovereignty of the philosophers [24]. Philosophers ' love to see the truth ', and a real lover always loves to see the whole, not merely the parts. Thus he does not love, as ordinary people do, sensible things and their ' beautiful sounds and colours and shapes ', but he wants ' to see, and to admire the real nature of beauty '—the Form or Idea of Beauty. *In this way, Plato gives the term philosopher a new meaning*, that of a lover and a seer of the divine world of Forms or Ideas. As such, the philosopher is the man who may become the founder of a virtuous city [25] : ' The philosopher who has communion with the divine ' may be ' overwhelmed by the urge to realize . . his heavenly vision ', of the ideal city and of its ideal citizens. He is like a draughtsman or a painter who has ' the divine as his model '. Only true philosophers can ' sketch the ground-plan of the city ', for they alone can see the original, and can copy it, by ' letting their eyes wander to and fro, from the model to the picture, and back from the picture to the model '.

As ' a painter of constitutions ' [26], the philosopher must be helped by the light of goodness and of wisdom. A few remarks will be added concerning these two ideas, and their significance for the philosopher in his function as a founder of the city.

Plato's *Idea of the Good* is the highest in the hierarchy of Forms. It is the sun of the divine world of Forms or Ideas, which not only sheds light on all the other members, but is the source of their existence [27]. It is also the source or cause of all knowledge and all truth [28]. The power of seeing, of appreciating, of knowing the Good is thus indispensable [29] to the dialectician. Since it is the sun and the source of light in the world of Forms, it enables the philosopher-painter to discern his objects. Its functio is therefore of the greatest importance for the founder of the city. But this purely formal information is all we get. Plato's Idea of the Good nowhere plays a more direct ethical or political rôle ; never do we hear which deeds are good, or produce good, apart from the well-known collectivist moral code whose precepts are introduced without recourse to the Idea of Good. Remarks that the Good is the aim, that it is desired by every man [30], do not enrich our information. This empty formalism is still more marked in the *Philebus*, where the Good is identified [31] with the Idea of 'measure' or 'mean'. And when I read the report that Plato, in his famous lecture 'On the Good', disappointed an uneducated audience by defining the Good as 'the class of the determinate conceived as a unity', then my sympathy is with the audience. In the *Republic*, Plato says frankly [32] that he cannot explain what he means by 'the Good'. The only practical suggestion we ever get is the one mentioned at the beginning of chapter 4—that good is everything that preserves, and evil everything that leads to corruption or degeneration. ('Good' does not, however, seem to be here the Idea of Good, but rather a property of things which makes them resemble the ideas.) Good is, accordingly, an unchanging, an arrested state of things ; it is the state of things at rest.

This does not seem to carry us very far beyond Plato's political totalitarianism ; and the analysis of Plato's *Idea of Wisdom* leads to equally disappointing results. Wisdom, as we have seen, does not mean to Plato the Socratic insight into one's own limitations ; nor does it mean what most of us would expect, a warm interest in, and a helpful understanding of, humanity and human affairs. Plato's wise men, highly preoccupied with the problems of a superior world, 'have no time to look down at the affairs of men . . ; they look upon, and hold fast to, the ordered and the measured'. It is the right kind of learning that makes a man wise : 'Philosophic natures are lovers of that kind of learning which reveals to them a reality that exists for ever and is not harassed by generation and degeneration.' It does not seem that Plato's treatment of wisdom can carry us beyond the ideal of arresting change.

v

Although the analysis of the functions of the city's founder has not revealed any new ethical elements in Plato's doctrine, it has shown that there is a definite reason why the founder of the city must be a philosopher. But this does not fully justify the demand for the permanent sovereignty of the philosopher. It only explains why the philosopher must be the first lawgiver, but not why he is needed as the permanent ruler, especially since none of the later rulers must introduce any change. For a full justification of the demand that the philosophers should rule, we must therefore proceed to analyse the tasks connected with the city's preservation.

We know from Plato's sociological theories that the state, once established, will continue to be stable as long as there is no split in the unity of the master class. The bringing up of that class is, therefore, the great preserving function of the sovereign, and a function which must continue as long as the state exists. How far does it justify the demand that a philosopher must rule ? To answer this question, we distinguish again, within this function, between two different activities : the supervision of education, and the supervision of eugenic breeding.

Why should the director of education be a philosopher ? Why is it not sufficient, once the state and its educational system are established, to put an experienced general, a soldier-king, in charge of it ? The answer that the educational system must provide not only soldiers but philosophers, and therefore needs philosophers as well as soldiers as supervisors, is obviously unsatisfactory ; for if no philosophers were needed as directors of education and as permanent rulers, then there would be no need for the educational system to produce new ones. The requirements of the educational system cannot as such justify the need for philosophers in Plato's state, or the postulate that the rulers must be philosophers. This would be different, of course, if Plato's education had an individualistic aim, apart from its aim to serve the interest of the state ; for example, the aim to develop philosophical faculties for their own sake. But when we see, as we did in the preceding chapter, how frightened Plato was of permitting anything like independent thought [33] ; and when we now see that the ultimate theoretical aim of this philosophic education was merely a ' Knowledge of the Idea of the Good ' which is incapable of giving an articulate account of this Idea, then we begin to realize that this cannot be the explanation. And this impression is strengthened if we remember chapter 4, where we have seen that Plato also demanded restrictions in the Athenian ' musical ' education. The great importance which Plato attaches to a philosophical education of the rulers must be explained by other reasons—by reasons which must be purely political.

The main reason I can see is the need for increasing to the utmost the authority of the rulers. If the education of the auxiliaries functions properly, there will be plenty of good soldiers. Outstanding military faculties may therefore be insufficient to establish an unchallenged and unchallengeable authority. This must be based on higher claims. Plato bases it upon the claims of supernatural, mystical powers which he develops in his leaders. They are not like other men. They belong to another world, they communicate with the divine. Thus the philosopher king seems to be, partly, a copy of a tribal priest-king, an institution which we have mentioned in connection with Heraclitus. (The institution of tribal priest-kings or medicine-men or shamans seems also to have influenced the old Pythagorean sect, with their surprisingly naïve tribal taboos. Apparently, most of these were dropped even before Plato. But the claim of the Pythagoreans to a supernatural basis of their authority remained.) Thus Plato's philosophical education has a definite political function. *It puts a mark on the rulers, and it establishes a barrier between the rulers and the ruled.* (This has remained a major function of ' higher ' education down to our own time.) Platonic wisdom is acquired largely for the sake of establishing a permanent political class rule. It can be described as political ' medicine ', giving mystic powers to its possessors, the medicine-men.[34]

But this cannot be the full answer to our question of the functions of the philosopher in the state. It means, rather, that the question why a philosopher is needed has only been shifted, and that we would have now to raise the analogous question of the practical political functions of the shaman or the medicine-man. Plato must have had some definite aim when he devised his specialized philosophic training. We must look for a permanent function of the ruler, analogous to the temporary function of the lawgiver. The only hope of discovering such a function seems to be in the field of breeding the master race.

VI

The best way to find out why a philosopher is needed as a permanent ruler is to ask the question : What happens, according to Plato, to a state which is not permanently ruled by a philosopher ? Plato has given a clear answer to this question. If the guardians of the state, even of a very perfect one, are unaware of Pythagorean lore and of the Platonic Number, then the race of the guardians, and with it the state, must degenerate.

Racialism thus takes up a more central part in Plato's political programme than one would expect at first sight. Just as the

Platonic racial or nuptial Number provides the setting for his descriptive sociology, ' the setting in which Plato's Philosophy of History is framed ' (as Adam puts it), so it also provides the setting of Plato's political demand for the sovereignty of the philosophers.   After what has been said in chapter 4 about the graziers' or cattle breeders' background of Plato's state, we are perhaps not quite unprepared to find that his *king* is a breeder king.   But it may still surprise some that his *philosopher* turns out to be a philosophic breeder.   The need for scientific, for mathematico-dialectical and philosophical breeding is not the least of the arguments behind the claim for the sovereignty of the philosophers.

It has been shown in chapter 4 how the problem of obtaining a pure breed of human watch-dogs is emphasized and elaborated in the earlier parts of the *Republic*.   But so far we have not met with any plausible reason why only a genuine and fully qualified philosopher should be a proficient and successful political breeder. And yet, as every breeder of dogs or horses or birds knows, rational breeding is impossible without a pattern, an aim to guide him in his efforts, an ideal which he may try to approach by the methods of mating and of selecting.   Without such a standard, he could never decide which offspring is ' good enough ' ; he could never speak of the difference between ' good offspring ' and ' bad offspring '.   But this standard corresponds exactly to a Platonic Idea of the race which he intends to breed.

Just as only the true philosopher, the dialectician, can see, according to Plato, the divine original of the city, so it is only the dialectician who can see that other divine original—the Form or Idea of Man.   Only he is capable of copying this model, of calling it down from Heaven to Earth [35], and of realizing it here. It is a kingly Idea, this Idea of Man.   It does not, as some have thought, represent what is common to all men ; it is not the universal concept ' man '.   It is, rather, the godlike original of man, an unchanging superman ; it is a super-Greek, and a super-master.   The philosopher must try to realize on earth what Plato describes as the race of ' the most constant, the most virile, and, within the limits of possibilities, the most beautifully formed men . . : nobly born, and of awe-inspiring character ' [36]. It is to be a race of men and women who are ' godlike if not divine . . sculptured in perfect beauty ' [37]—a lordly race, destined by nature to kingship and mastery.

We see that the two fundamental functions of the philosopher

king are analogous : he has to copy the divine original of the city,
and he has to copy the divine original of man. He is the only
one who is able, and who has the urge, ' to realize, in the individual
as well as in the city, his heavenly vision ' [38].

Now we can understand why Plato drops his first hint that a
more than ordinary excellence is needed in his rulers in the same
place where he first claims that the principles of animal breeding
must be applied to the race of men. We are, he says, most
careful in breeding animals. ' If you did not breed them in this
way, don't you think that the race of your birds or your dogs
would quickly degenerate ? ' When inferring from this that man
must be bred in the same careful way, ' Socrates ' exclaims :
' Good heavens ! . . What surpassing excellence we shall have
to demand from our rulers, if the same principles apply to the
race of men ! ' [39] This exclamation is significant ; it is one of
the first hints that the rulers may constitute a class of ' surpassing
excellence ' with status and training of their own ; and it thus
prepares us for the demand that they ought to be philosophers.
But the passage is even more significant in so far as it directly
leads to Plato's demand that it must be the duty of the rulers,
as doctors of the race of men, to administer lies and deception.
Lies are necessary, Plato asserts, ' if your herd is to reach
highest perfection ' ; for this needs ' arrangements that must
be kept secret from all but the rulers, if we wish to keep the herd
of guardians really free from disunion '. Indeed, the appeal
(quoted above) to the rulers for more courage in administering
lies as a medicine is made in this connection ; it prepares the
reader for the next demand, considered by Plato as particularly
important. He decrees [40] that the rulers should fabricate, for
the purpose of mating the young auxiliaries, ' an ingenious system
of balloting, so that the persons who have been disappointed . .
may blame their bad luck, and not the rulers ', who are, secretly,
to engineer the ballot. And immediately after this despicable
advice for dodging the admission of responsibility (by putting
it into the mouth of Socrates, Plato libels his great teacher),
' Socrates ' makes a suggestion [41] which is soon taken up and
elaborated by Glaucon and which we may therefore call the
Glauconic Edict. I mean the brutal law [42] which imposes on everybody of either sex the duty of submitting, for the duration of a
war, to the wishes of the brave : ' As long as the war lasts, . .
nobody may say " No " to him. Accordingly, if a soldier wishes
to make love to anybody, whether male or female, this law will

make him more eager to carry off the price of valour.' The state, it is carefully pointed out, will thereby obtain two distinct benefits—more heroes, owing to the incitement, and again more heroes, owing to the increased numbers of children from heroes. (The latter benefit, as the most important one from the point of view of a long-term racial policy, is put into the mouth of ' Socrates '.)

VII

No special philosophical training is required for this kind of breeding. Philosophical breeding, however, plays its main part in counteracting the dangers of degeneration. In order to fight these dangers, a fully qualified philosopher is needed, i.e. one who is trained in pure mathematics (including solid geometry), pure astronomy, pure harmonics, and, the crowning achievement of all, in dialectics. Only he who knows the secrets of mathematical eugenics, of the Platonic Number, can bring back to man, and preserve for him, the happiness enjoyed before the Fall [43]. All this should be borne in mind when, after the announcement of the Glauconic Edict (and after an interlude dealing with the natural distinction between Greeks and Barbarians, corresponding, according to Plato, to that between masters and slaves), the doctrine is enunciated which Plato carefully marks as his central and most sensational political demand—the sovereignty of the philosopher king. This demand alone, he teaches, can put an end to the evils of social life ; to the evil rampant in states, i.e. *political instability*, as well as to its more hidden cause, the evil rampant in the members of the race of men, i.e. *racial degeneration*. This is the passage.[44]

' Well,' says Socrates, ' I am now about to dive into that topic which I compared before to the greatest wave of all. Yet I must speak, even though I foresee that this will bring upon me a deluge of laughter. Indeed, I can see it now, this very wave, breaking over my head into an uproar of laughter and defamation . .' —' Out with the story ! ' says Glaucon. ' Unless,' says Socrates, ' unless, in their cities, philosophers are vested with the might of kings, or those now called kings and oligarchs become genuine and fully qualified philosophers ; and unless these two, political might and philosophy, are fused (while the many who nowadays follow their natural inclination for only one of these two are suppressed by force), unless this happens, my dear Glaucon, there can be no rest ; and the evil will not cease to be rampant in the cities—nor, I believe, in the race of men.' (To which Kant wisely replied : 'That kings should become philosophers, or philosophers kings, is not likely to happen ; nor would it be desirable, since the possession of power invariably debases the free judgement of reason. It is, however, indispensable that a king—or a kingly, i.e. self-ruling, people—should *not suppress* philosophers but leave them the right of public utterance.' [45])

This important Platonic passage has been quite appropriately described as the key to the whole work. Its last words, ' nor, I believe, in the race of men ', are, I think, an afterthought of comparatively minor importance in this place. It is, however, necessary to comment upon them, since the habit of idealizing Plato has led to the interpretation [46] that Plato speaks here about ' humanity ', extending his promise of salvation from the scope of the cities to that of ' mankind as a whole '. It must be said, in this connection, that the ethical category of ' humanity ' as something that transcends the distinction of nations, raçes, and classes, is entirely foreign to Plato. In fact, we have sufficient evidence of Plato's hostility towards the equalitarian creed, a hostility which is seen in his attitude towards Antisthenes [47], an old disciple and friend of Socrates. Antisthenes also belonged to the school of Gorgias, like Alcidamas and Lycophron, whose equalitarian theories he seems to have extended into the doctrine of the brotherhood of all men, and of the universal empire of men [48]. This creed is attacked in the *Republic* by correlating the natural inequality of Greeks and Barbarians to that of masters and slaves ; and it so happens that this attack is launched [49] immediately before the key passage we are here considering. For these and other reasons [50], it seems safe to assume that Plato, when speaking of the evil rampant in the race of men, alluded to a theory with which his readers would be sufficiently acquainted at this place, namely, to his theory that the welfare of the state depends, ultimately, upon the ' nature ' of the individual members of the ruling class ; and that their nature, and the nature of their race, or offspring, is threatened, in turn, by the evils of an individualistic education, and, more important still, by racial degeneration. Plato's remark, with its clear allusion to the opposition between divine rest and the evil of change and decay, foreshadows the story of the Number and the Fall of Man [51].

It is very appropriate that Plato should allude to his racialism in this key passage in which he enunciates his most important political demand. For without the ' genuine and fully qualified philosopher ', trained in all those sciences which are prerequisite to eugenics, the state is lost. In his story of the Number and the Fall of Man, Plato tells us that one of the first and fatal sins of omission committed by the degenerate guardians will be their loss of interest in eugenics, in watching and testing the purity of the race : ' Hence rulers will be ordained who are altogether unfit for their task as guardians ; namely, to watch, and to test, the metals in the races (which are Hesiod's races as well as yours), gold and silver and bronze and iron.' [52]

It is ignorance of the mysterious nuptial Number which leads to all that. But the Number was undoubtedly Plato's own invention. (It presupposes pure harmonics, which in turn presupposes solid geometry, a new science at the time when the *Republic* was written.) Thus we see that nobody but Plato himself knew the secret of, and held the key to, true guardianship. But this can mean only one thing. The philosopher king is Plato himself, and the *Republic* is Plato's own claim for kingly power— to the power which he thought his due, uniting in himself, as he did, both the claims of the philosopher and of the descendant and legitimate heir of Codrus the martyr, the last of Athens' kings, who, according to Plato, had sacrificed himself ' in order to preserve the kingdom for his children '.

VIII

Once this conclusion has been reached, many things which otherwise would remain unrelated become connected and clear. It can hardly be doubted, for instance, that Plato's work, full of allusions as it is to contemporary problems and characters, was meant by its author not so much as a theoretical treatise, but as a topical political manifesto. ' We do Plato the gravest of wrongs ', says A. E. Taylor, ' if we forget that the *Republic* is no mere collection of theoretical discussions about government . . but a serious project of practical reform put forward by an Athenian . . , set on fire, like Shelley, with a " passion for reforming the world ".' [53] This is undoubtedly true, and we could have concluded from this consideration alone that, in describing his philosopher kings, Plato must have thought of some of the contemporary philosophers. But in the days when the *Republic* was written, there were in Athens only three outstanding men who might have claimed to be philosophers : Antisthenes, Isocrates, and Plato himself. If we approach the *Republic* with this in mind, we find at once that, in the discussion of the characteristics of the philosopher kings, there is a lengthy passage which is clearly marked out by Plato as containing personal allusions. It begins [54] with an unmistakable allusion to a popular character, namely Alcibiades, and ends by openly mentioning a name (that of Theages), and with a reference of 'Socrates' to himself [55]. Its upshot is that only very few can be described as true philosophers, eligible for the post of philosopher king. The nobly born Alcibiades, who was of the right type, deserted philosophy, in spite of Socrates' attempts to save him. Deserted and defenceless, philosophy was claimed by unworthy suitors. Ultimately, 'there is left only a handful of men who are worthy of being associated with philosophy'. From the point of view we have reached, we would have to expect that the 'unworthy suitors' are Antisthenes and Isocrates and their school (and that they are the same people whom Plato demands to have 'suppressed by force', as he says in the key-passage of the philosopher king). And, indeed, there is some independent evidence corroborating this expectation [56]. Similarly, we should expect that the 'handful of men who are worthy' includes Plato and, perhaps, some of his friends (possibly Dio) ; and, indeed, a continuation of this passage leaves little doubt that Plato speaks here of himself : ' He who belongs to this small band . . can see the madness of the many, and the general corruption of all public affairs. The philosopher . . is like a man in a cage of wild beasts. He will not share the injustice of the many, but his power does not suffice for continuing his fight alone, surrounded as he is by a world of savages. He would be killed before he could do any good, to his city or to his friends. . . Having duly considered all these points, he will hold his peace, and confine his efforts to his own work . .' [57]. The strong resentment expressed in these sour and most un-Socratic [58] words marks them clearly as Plato's own. For a full apprecia- tion, however, of this personal confession, it must be compared with the following : ' It is not in accordance with nature that the skilled navigator should beg the unskilled sailors to accept his command ; nor that the wise man should wait at the doors of the rich. . . But the true and natural procedure is that the sick, whether rich or poor, should hasten to the doctor's door. Likewise should those who need to be ruled besiege the door of him who can rule ; and never should a ruler beg them to accept his rule, if he is any good at all.' Who can miss the sound of an immense personal pride in this passage ? Here am I, says Plato, your natural ruler, the philosopher king who knows how to rule. If you want me, you must come to me, and if you insist, I may become your ruler. But I shall not come begging to you.

Did he believe that they would come? Like many great works of literature, the *Republic* shows traces that its author experienced exhilarating and extravagant hopes of success [59], alternating with periods of despair. Sometimes, at least, Plato hoped that they would come; that the success of his work, the fame of his wisdom, would bring them along. Then again, he felt that they would only be incited to furious attacks; that all he would bring upon himself was ' an uproar of laughter and defamation '—perhaps even death.

Was he ambitious? He was reaching for the stars—for god-likeness. I sometimes wonder whether part of the enthusiasm for Plato is not due to the fact that he gave expression to many secret dreams [60]. Even where he argues against ambition, we cannot but feel that he is inspired by it. The philosopher, he assures us [61], is not ambitious; although ' destined to rule, he is the least eager for it '. But the reason given is—that his status is too high. He who has had communion with the divine may descend from his heights to the mortals below, sacrificing himself for the sake of the interest of the state. He is not eager; but as a natural ruler and saviour, he is ready to come. The poor mortals need him. Without him the state must perish, for he alone knows the secret of how to preserve it—the secret of arresting degeneration. . .

I think we must face the fact that behind the sovereignty of the philosopher king stands the quest for power. The beautiful portrait of the sovereign is a self-portrait. When we have recovered from the shock of this finding, we may look anew at the awe-inspiring portrait; and if we can fortify ourselves with a small dose of Socrates' irony then we may cease to find it so terrifying. We may begin to discern its human, indeed, its only too human features. We may even begin to feel a little sorry for Plato, who had to be satisfied with establishing the first professorship, instead of the first kingship, of philosophy; who could never realize his dream, the kingly Idea which he had formed after his own image. Fortified by our dose of irony, we may even find, in Plato's story, a melancholy resemblance to that innocent and unconscious little satire on Platonism, the story of the *Ugly Dachshund*, of Tono, the Great Dane, who forms his kingly Idea of ' Great Dog ' after his own image (but who happily finds in the end that he is Great Dog himself) [62].

What a monument of human smallness is this idea of the philosopher king. What a contrast between it and the simplicity and humaneness of Socrates, who warned the statesman against the danger of being dazzled by his own power, excellence, and wisdom, and who tried to teach him what matters most—that we are all frail human beings. What a decline from this world of irony and reason and truthfulness down to Plato's kingdom of the sage whose magical powers raise him high above ordinary men ; although not quite high enough to forgo the use of lies, or to neglect the sorry trade of every shaman—the selling of spells, of breeding spells, in exchange for power over his fellow-men.

CHAPTER 9 : AESTHETICISM, PERFECTIONISM, UTOPIANISM

'Everything has got to be smashed to start with.
Our whole damned civilization has got to go, before
we can bring any decency into the world.'
'Mourlan', in Du Gard's *Les Thibaults.*

Inherent in Plato's programme there is a certain approach towards politics which, I believe, is most dangerous. Its analysis is of great practical importance from the point of view of rational social engineering. The Platonic approach I have in mind can be described as that of *Utopian engineering*, as opposed to another kind of social engineering which I consider as the only rational one, and which may be described by the name of *piecemeal engineering*. The Utopian approach is the more dangerous as it may seem to be the obvious alternative to an out-and-out historicism—to a radically historicist approach which implies that we cannot alter the course of history ; at the same time, it appears to be a necessary complement to a less radical historicism, like that of Plato, which permits human interference.

The Utopian approach may be described as follows. Any rational action must have a certain aim. It is rational in the same degree as it pursues its aim consciously and consistently, and as it determines its means according to this end. To choose the end is therefore the first thing we have to do if we wish to act rationally ; and we must be careful to determine our real or ultimate ends, from which we must distinguish clearly those intermediate or partial ends which actually are only means, or steps on the way, to the ultimate end. If we neglect this distinction, then we must also neglect to ask whether these partial ends are likely to promote the ultimate end, and accordingly, we must fail to act rationally. These principles, if applied to the realm of political activity, demand that we must determine our ultimate political aim, or the Ideal State, before taking any practical action. Only when this ultimate aim is determined, in rough outline at least, only when we are in possession of something like a blueprint of the society at which we aim, only then can we begin to consider the best ways and means for its realization, and to draw up a plan for practical action. These

are the necessary preliminaries of any practical political move
that can be called rational, and especially of social engineering.

This, in brief, is the methodological approach which I call
Utopian engineering [1]. It is convincing and attractive. In fact,
it is just the kind of methodological approach to attract all those
who are either unaffected by historicist prejudices or reacting
against them. This makes it only the more dangerous, and its
criticism the more imperative.

Before proceeding to criticize Utopian engineering in detail, I
wish to outline another approach to social engineering, namely,
that of piecemeal engineering. It is an approach which I think
to be methodologically sound. The politician who adopts this
method may or may not have a blueprint of society before his
mind, he may or may not hope that mankind will one day
realize an ideal state, and achieve happiness and perfection on
earth. But he will be aware that perfection, if at all attainable,
is far distant, and that every generation of men, and therefore
also the living, have a claim ; perhaps not so much a claim to be
made happy, for there are no institutional means of making a
man happy, but a claim not to be made unhappy, where it can
be avoided. They have a claim to be given all possible help, if
they suffer. The piecemeal engineer will, accordingly, adopt
the method of searching for, and fighting against, the greatest
and most urgent evils of society, rather than searching for, and
fighting for, its greatest ultimate good [2]. This difference is far
from being merely verbal. In fact, it is most important. It is
the difference between a reasonable method of improving the
lot of man, and a method which, if really tried, may easily lead to
an intolerable increase in human suffering. It is the difference
between a method which can be applied at any moment, and a
method whose advocacy may easily become a means of continually
postponing action until a later date, when conditions are more
favourable. And it is also the difference between the only
method of improving matters which has so far been really successful, at any time, and in any place (Russia included, as will be
seen), and a method which, wherever it has been tried, has led
only to the use of violence in place of reason, and if not to its
own abandonment, at any rate to that of its original blueprint.

In favour of his method, the piecemeal engineer can claim that
a systematic fight against suffering and injustice and war is more
likely to be supported by the approval and agreement of a great
number of people than the fight for the establishment of some

ideal. The existence of social evils, that is to say, of social conditions under which many men are suffering, can be comparatively well established. Those who suffer can judge for themselves, and the others can hardly deny that they would not like to change places. It is infinitely more difficult to reason about an ideal society. Social life is so complicated that few men, or none at all, could judge a blueprint for social engineering on the grand scale ; whether it be practicable ; whether it would result in a real improvement ; what kind of suffering it may involve ; and what may be the means for its realization. As opposed to this, blueprints for piecemeal engineering are comparatively simple. They are blueprints for single institutions, for health and unemployed insurance, for instance, or arbitration courts, or anti-depression budgeting [3], or educational reform. If they go wrong, the damage is not very great, and a re-adjustment not very difficult. They are less risky, and for this very reason less controversial. But if it is easier to reach a reasonable agreement about existing evils and the means of combating them than it is about an ideal good and the means of its realization, then there is also more hope that by using the piecemeal method we may get over the very greatest practical difficulty of all reasonable political reform, namely, the use of reason, instead of passion and violence, in executing the programme. There will be a possibility of reaching a reasonable compromise and therefore of achieving the improvement by democratic methods. (' Compromise ' is an ugly word, but it is important for us to learn its proper use. *Institutions* are inevitably the result of a compromise with circumstances, interests, etc., though as *persons* we should resist influences of this kind.)

As opposed to that, the Utopian attempt to realize an ideal state, using a blueprint of society as a whole, is one which demands a strong centralized rule of a few, and which therefore is likely to lead to a dictatorship [4]. This I consider a criticism of the Utopian approach ; for I have tried to show, in the chapter on the Principle of Leadership, that an authoritarian rule is a most objectionable form of government. Some points not touched upon in that chapter furnish us with even more direct arguments against the Utopian approach. One of the difficulties faced by a benevolent dictator is to find whether the effects of his measures agree with his good intentions (as de Tocqueville saw clearly more than a hundred years ago [5]). The difficulty arises out of the fact that authoritarianism must discourage criticism ; accordingly, the benevolent dictator will not easily hear of complaints concerning the measures he has taken. But without some such check, he can hardly find out whether his measures achieve the desired benevolent aim. The situation must become even worse for the Utopian engineer. The reconstruction of society is a big undertaking which must cause considerable inconvenience to many, and for a considerable span of time. Accordingly, the Utopian engineer will have to be deaf to many complaints ; in fact, it will be part of his business to suppress unreasonable objections. (He will say, like Lenin, ' You can't make an omelette without breaking eggs.') But with it, he must invariably suppress reasonable criticism also. Another difficulty of Utopian engineering is related to the *problem of the dictator's successor*. In chapter 7 I have mentioned certain aspects of this problem. Utopian engineering raises a difficulty analogous to but even more serious than the one which faces the benevolent tyrant who tries to find an equally benevolent successor (see note 25 to chapter 7). The very sweep of such a Utopian undertaking makes it improbable that it will realize its ends during the lifetime of one social engineer, or group of engineers. And if the successors do not pursue the same ideal, then all the sufferings of the people for the sake of the ideal may have been in vain.

A generalization of this argument leads to a further criticism of the Utopian approach. This approach, it is clear, can be of practical value only if we assume that the original blueprint, perhaps with certain adjustments, remains the basis of the work until it is completed. But that will take some time. It will be a time of revolutions, both political and spiritual, and of new experiments and experience in the political field. It is therefore to be expected that ideas and ideals will change. What had appeared the ideal state to the people who made the original blueprint, may not appear so to their successors. If that is granted, then the whole approach breaks down. The method of first establishing an ultimate political aim and then beginning to move towards it is futile if we admit that the aim may be considerably changed during the process of its realization. It may at any moment turn out that the steps so far taken actually lead away from the realization of the new aim. And if we change our direction according to the new aim, then we expose ourselves to the same risk again. In spite of all the sacrifices made, we may never get anywhere at all. Those who prefer one step towards a distant ideal to the realization of a piecemeal compromise should always remember that if the ideal is very distant, it may even become difficult to say whether the step taken was towards or away from it. This is especially so if the course should proceed by zigzag steps, or, in Hegel's jargon, ' dialectically ', or if it is not clearly planned at all. (This bears upon the old and somewhat childish question of how far the end can justify the means. Apart from claiming that no end could ever justify all means, I think that a fairly concrete and realizable end may justify temporary measures which a more distant ideal never could [6].)

We see now that the Utopian approach can be saved only by the Platonic belief in one absolute and unchanging ideal, together with two further assumptions, namely (a) that there are rational methods to determine once and for all what this ideal is, and (b) what the best means of its realization are. Only such far-reaching assumptions could prevent us from declaring the Utopian methodology to be utterly futile. But even Plato himself and the most ardent Platonists would admit that (a) is certainly not true ; that there is no rational method for determining the ultimate aim, but, if anything, only some kind of intuition. Any difference of opinion between Utopian engineers must therefore lead, in the absence of rational methods, to the use of power instead of reason, i.e. to violence. If any progress in any definite direction is made at all, then it is made in spite of the method adopted, not because of it. The success may be due, for instance, to the excellence of the leaders ; but we must never forget that excellent leaders cannot be produced by rational methods, but only by luck.

It is important to understand this criticism properly ; I do not criticize the ideal by claiming that an ideal can never be realized, that it must always remain a Utopia. This would not be a valid criticism, for many things have been realized which have once been dogmatically declared to be unrealizable, for instance, the establishment of institutions for securing civil peace, i.e. for the prevention of crime *within* the state ; and I think that, for instance, the establishment of corresponding institutions for the prevention of international crime, i.e. armed aggression or blackmail, though often branded as Utopian, is not even a very difficult problem [7]. What I criticize under the name Utopian engineering recommends the reconstruction of society as a whole, i.e. very sweeping changes whose practical consequences are hard to calculate, owing to our limited experiences. It claims to plan rationally for the whole of society, although we do not possess anything like the factual knowledge which would be necessary to make good such an ambitious claim. We cannot possess such knowledge since we have insufficient practical experience in this kind of planning, and knowledge of facts must be based upon experience. At present, the sociological knowledge necessary for large-scale engineering is simply non-existent.

In view of this criticism, the Utopian engineer is likely to grant the need for practical experience, and for a social technology based upon practical experiences. But he will argue that we shall never know more about these matters if we recoil from making social experiments which alone can furnish us with the practical experience needed. And he might add that Utopian engineering is nothing but the application of the experimental method to society. Experiments cannot be carried out without involving sweeping changes. They must be on a large scale, owing to the peculiar character of modern society with its great masses of people. An experiment in socialism, for instance, if confined to a factory, or to a village, or even to a district, would never give us the kind of realistic information which we need so urgently.

Such arguments in favour of Utopian engineering exhibit a prejudice which is as widely held as it is untenable, namely, the prejudice that social experiments must be on a ' large scale ', that they must involve the whole of society if they are to be carried out under realistic conditions. But piecemeal social experiments can be carried out under realistic conditions, in the midst of society, in spite of being on a ' small scale ', that is to say, without revolutionizing the whole of society. In fact, we are making such experiments all the time. The introduction of a new kind of life-insurance, of a new kind of taxation, of a new penal reform, are all social experiments which have their repercussions through the whole of society without remodelling society as a whole. Even a man who opens a new shop, or who reserves a ticket for the theatre, is carrying out a kind of social experiment on a small scale ; and all our knowledge of social conditions is based on experience gained by making experiments of this kind. The Utopian engineer we are opposing is right when he stresses that an experiment in socialism would be of little value if carried out under laboratory conditions, for instance, in an isolated village, since what we want to know is how things work out in society under normal social conditions. But this very example shows where the prejudice of the Utopian engineer lies. He is convinced that we must recast the whole structure of society, when we experiment with it ; and he can therefore conceive a more *modest* experiment only as one that recasts the whole structure of a *small* society. But the kind of experiment from which we can learn most is the alteration of one social institution at a time. For only in this way can we learn how to fit institutions into the framework of other institutions, and how to adjust them so that they work according to our intentions. And only in this way can we make mistakes, and learn from our mistakes, without risking repercussions of a gravity that must endanger the will to future reforms. Furthermore, the Utopian method must lead to a dangerous dogmatic attachment to a blueprint for which countless sacrifices have been made. Powerful interests must become linked up with the success of the experiment. All this does not contribute to the rationality, or to the scientific value, of the experiment. But the piecemeal method permits repeated experiments and continuous readjustments. In fact, it might lead to the happy situation where politicians begin to look out for their own mistakes instead of trying to explain them away and to prove that they have always been right. This—and nôt Utopian planning or historical prophecy—would mean the introduction of scientific method into politics, since the whole secret of scientific method is a readiness to learn from mistakes [8].

These views can be corroborated, I believe, by comparing social and, for instance, mechanical engineering. The Utopian engineer will of course claim that mechanical engineers sometimes plan even very complicated machinery as a whole, and that their blueprints may cover, and plan in advance, not only a certain kind of machinery, but even the whole factory which produces this machinery. My reply would be that the mechanical engineer can do all this because he has sufficient experience at his disposal, i.e. theories developed by trial and error. But this means that he can plan because he has made all kinds of mistakes already ; or in other words, because he relies on experience which he has gained by applying piecemeal methods. His new machinery is the result of a great many small improvements. He usually has a model first, and only after a great number of piecemeal adjustments to its various parts does he proceed to a stage where he could draw up his final plans for the production. Similarly, his plan for the production of his machine incorporates a great number of experiences, namely, of piecemeal improvements made in older factories. The wholesale or large-scale method works only where the piecemeal method has furnished us first with a great number of detailed experiences, and even then only within the realm of these experiences. Few manufacturers would be prepared to proceed to the production of a new engine on the basis of a blueprint alone, even if it were drawn up by the greatest expert, without first making a model and ' developing ' it by little adjustments as far as possible.

It is perhaps useful to contrast this criticism of Platonic Idealism in politics with Marx's criticism of what he calls ' Utopianism '. What is common to Marx's criticism and mine is that both demand more realism. We both believe that Utopian plans will never be realized in the way they were conceived, because hardly any social action ever produces precisely the result expected. (This does not, in my opinion, invalidate the piecemeal approach, because here we may learn—or rather, we ought to learn—and change our views, while we act.) But there are many differences. In arguing against Utopianism, Marx condemns in fact *all* social engineering—a point which is rarely understood. He denounces the faith in a rational planning of social institutions as altogether unrealistic, since society must grow according to the laws of history and not according to our rational plans. All we can do, he asserts, is to lessen the birthpangs of the historical processes. In other words, he adopts a radically historicist attitude, opposed to all social engineering. But there is one element within Utopianism which is particularly characteristic of Plato's approach and which Marx does not oppose, although it is perhaps the most important of those elements which I have attacked as unrealistic. It is the sweep of Utopianism, its attempt to deal with society as a whole, leaving no stone unturned. It is the conviction that one has to go to the very root of the social evil, that nothing short of a complete eradication of the offending social system will do if we wish to ' bring any decency into the world ' (as Du Gard says). It is, in short, its uncompromising *radicalism*. (The reader will notice that I am using this term in its original and literal sense—not in the now customary sense of a ' liberal progressivism ', but in order to characterize an attitude of ' going to the root of the matter '.) Both Plato and Marx are dreaming of the apocalyptic revolution which will radically transfigure the whole social world.

This sweep, this extreme radicalism of the Platonic approach (and of the Marxian as well) is, I believe, connected with its æstheticism, i.e. with the desire to build a world which is not only a little better and more rational than ours, but which is free from all its ugliness : not a crazy quilt, an old garment badly patched, but an entirely new gown, a really beautiful new world [9]. This æstheticism is a very understandable attitude ; in fact, I believe most of us suffer a little from such dreams of perfection. (Some reasons why we do so will, I hope, emerge from the next chapter.) But this æsthetic enthusiasm becomes valuable only if it is bridled by reason, by a feeling of responsibility, and by a humanitarian urge to help. Otherwise it is a dangerous enthusiasm, liable to develop into a form of neurosis or hysteria.

Nowhere do we find this æstheticism more strongly expressed than in Plato. Plato was an artist ; and like many of the best artists, he tried to visualize a model, the ' divine original ' of his work, and to ' copy ' it faithfully. A good number of the quotations given in the last chapter illustrate this point. What Plato describes as dialectics is, in the main, the intellectual intuition of the world of pure beauty. His trained philosophers are men who ' have seen the truth of what is beautiful and just, and good ' [10], and can bring it down from heaven to earth. Politics, to Plato, is the Royal Art. It is an art—not in a metaphorical sense in which we may speak about the art of handling men, or the art of getting things done, but in a more literal sense of the word. It is an art of composition, like music, painting, or architecture. The Platonic politician composes cities, for beauty's sake.

But here I must protest. I do not believe that human lives may be made the means for satisfying an artist's desire for self-expression. We must demand, rather, that every man should be given, if he wishes, the right to model his life himself, as far as this does not interfere too much with others. Much as I may sympathize with the æsthetic impulse, I suggest that the artist might seek expression in another material. Politics, I demand, must uphold equalitarian and individualistic principles ; dreams of beauty have to submit to the necessity of helping men in distress, and men who suffer injustice ; and to the necessity of constructing institutions to serve such purposes [11].

It is interesting to observe the close relationship between Plato's utter radicalism, the demand for sweeping measures, and his æstheticism. The following passages are most characteristic. Plato, speaking about ' the philosopher who has communion with the divine ', mentions first that he will be ' overwhelmed by the

urge . . to realize his heavenly vision in individuals as well as
in the city ',—a city which ' will never know happiness unless its
draughtsmen are artists who have the divine as their model '.
Asked about the details of their draughtsmanship, Plato's
' Socrates ' gives the following striking reply : ' They will take as
their canvas a city and the characters of men, and they will, first
of all, *make their canvas clean*—by no means an easy matter. But
this is just the point, you know, where they will differ from all
others. They will not start work on a city nor on an individual
(nor will they draw up laws) unless they are given a clean canvas,
or have cleaned it themselves.' [12]

The kind of thing Plato has in mind when he speaks of canvas-
cleaning is explained a little later. ' How can that be done ? '
asks Glaucon. ' All citizens above the age of ten ', Socrates
answers, ' must be expelled from the city and deported somewhere into the country ; and the children who are now free from
the influence of the manners and habits of their parents must be
taken over. They must be educated in the ways [of true philo-
sophy], and according to the laws, which we have described.'
(The philosophers are not, of course, among the citizens to be
expelled : they remain as educators, and so do, presumably, those
non-citizens who must keep them going.) In the same spirit,
Plato says in the *Statesman* of the royal rulers who rule in accordance with the Royal Science of Statesmanship : ' Whether they
happen to rule by law or without law, over willing or unwilling
subjects ; . . . and whether they purge the state for its good,
by killing or by deporting [or ' banishing '] some of its citizens
. . .—so long as they proceed according to science and justice,
and preserve . . . the state and make it better than it was, this
form of government must be declared the only one that is right.'

This is the way in which the artist-politician must proceed.
This is what canvas-cleaning means. He must eradicate the
existing institutions and traditions. He must purify, purge,
expel, banish, and kill. (' Liquidate ' is the terrible modern
term for it.) Plato's statement is indeed a true description of
the uncompromising attitude of all forms of out-and-out radicalism—of the æstheticist's refusal to compromise. The view that
society should be beautiful like a work of art leads only too easily
to violent measures. But all this radicalism and violence is both
unrealistic and futile. (This has been shown by the example of
Russia's development. After the economic breakdown to which
the canvas-cleaning of the so-called ' war communism ' had led,

Lenin introduced his ' New Economic Policy ', in fact a kind of piecemeal engineering, though without the conscious formulation of its principles or of a technology.   He started by restoring most of the features of the picture which had been eradicated with so much human suffering.   Money, markets, differentiation of income, and private property—for a time even private enterprise in production—were reintroduced, and only after this basis was re-established began a new period of reform [13].)

In order to criticize the foundations of Plato's æsthetic radicalism, we may distinguish two different points.

The first is this.   What some people have in mind who speak of our ' social system ', and of the need to replace it by another ' system ', is very similar to a picture painted on a canvas which has to be wiped clean before one can paint a new one.   But there are some great differences.   One of them is that the painter and those who co-operate with him as well as the institutions which make their life possible, his dreams and plans for a better world, and his standards of decency and morality, are all part of the social system, i.e. of the picture to be wiped out.   If they were really to clean the canvas, they would have to destroy themselves, and their Utopian plans.   (And what follows then would probably not be a beautiful copy of a Platonic ideal but chaos.)   The political artist clamours, like Archimedes, for a place outside the social world on which he can take his stand, in order to lever it off its hinges.   But such a place does not exist ; and the social world must continue to function during any reconstruction.   This is the simple reason why we must reform its institutions little by little, until we have more experience in social engineering.

This leads us to the more important second point, to the irrationalism which is inherent in radicalism.   In all matters, we can only learn by trial and error, by making mistakes and improvements ; we can never rely on inspiration, although inspirations may be most valuable as long as they can be checked by experience.   Accordingly, *it is not reasonable to assume that a complete reconstruction of our social world would lead at once to a workable system.* Rather we should expect that, owing to lack of experience, many mistakes would be made which could be eliminated only by a long and laborious process of small adjustments ; in other words, by that rational method of piecemeal engineering whose application we advocate.   But those who dislike this method as insufficiently radical would have again to wipe out their freshly constructed society, in order to start anew with a clean canvas ;

and since the new start, for the same reasons, would not lead to perfection either, they would have to repeat this process without ever getting anywhere.   Those who admit this and are prepared to adopt our more modest method of piecemeal improvements, but only after the first radical canvas-cleaning, can hardly escape the criticism that their first sweeping and violent measures were quite unnecessary.

Aestheticism and radicalism must lead us to jettison reason, and to replace it by a desperate hope for political miracles.   This irrational attitude which springs from an intoxication with dreams of a beautiful world is what I call Romanticism [14].   It may seek its heavenly city in the past or in the future ; it may preach ' back to nature ' or ' forward to a world of love and beauty ' ; but its appeal is always to our emotions rather than to reason.   Even with the best intentions of making heaven on earth it only succeeds in making it a hell—that hell which man alone prepares for his fellow-men.

CHAPTER 10 : THE OPEN SOCIETY AND ITS ENEMIES

> He will restore us to our original nature, and heal
> us, and make us happy and blessed.
>   PLATO.

There is still something missing from our analysis. The contention that Plato's political programme is purely totalitarian, and the objections to this contention which were raised in chapter 6, have led us to examine the part played, within this programme, by such moral ideas as Justice, Wisdom, Truth, and Beauty. The result of this examination was always the same. We found that the rôle of these ideas is important, but that they do not lead Plato beyond totalitarianism and racialism. But one of these ideas we have still to examine : that of Happiness. It may be remembered that we quoted Crossman in connection with the belief that Plato's political programme is fundamentally a ' plan for the building of a perfect state in which every citizen is really happy ', and that I described this belief as a relic of the tendency to idealize Plato. If called upon to justify my opinion, I should not have much difficulty in pointing out that Plato's treatment of happiness is exactly analogous to his treatment of justice ; and especially, that it is based upon the same belief that society is ' by nature ' divided into classes or castes. True happiness [1], Plato insists, is achieved only by justice, i.e. by keeping one's place. The ruler must find happiness in ruling, the warrior in warring ; and, we may infer, the slave in slaving. Apart from that, Plato says frequently that what he is aiming at is neither the happiness of individuals nor that of any particular class in the state, but only the happiness of the whole, and this, he argues, is nothing but the outcome of that rule of justice which I have shown to be totalitarian in character. That only this justice can lead to any true happiness is one of the main theses of the *Republic*.

In view of all this, it seems to be a consistent and hardly refutable interpretation of the material to present Plato as a totalitarian party-politician, unsuccessful in his immediate and practical undertakings, but in the long run only too successful [2] in his propaganda for the arrest and overthrow of a civilization which he hated.   But one only has to put the matter in this blunt fashion in order to feel that there is something seriously amiss with this interpretation.   At any rate, so I felt, when I had formulated it.   I felt perhaps not so much that it was untrue, but that it was defective.   I therefore began to search for evidence which would refute this interpretation [3].   However, in every point but one, this attempt to refute my interpretation was quite unsuccessful.   The new material made the identity between Platonism and totalitarianism only the more manifest.

The one point in which I felt that my search for a refutation had succeeded concerned Plato's hatred of tyranny.   Of course, there was always the possibility of explaining this away.   It would have been easy to say that his indictment of tyranny was mere propaganda.   Totalitarianism often professes a love for ' true ' freedom, and Plato's praise of freedom as opposed to tyranny sounds exactly like this professed love.   In spite of this, I felt that certain of his observations on tyranny [4], which will be mentioned later in this chapter, were sincere.   The fact, of course, that ' tyranny ' usually meant in Plato's day a form of rule based on the support of the masses made it possible to claim that Plato's hatred of tyranny was consistent with my original interpretation.   But I felt that this did not remove the need for modifying my interpretation.   I also felt that the mere emphasis on Plato's fundamental sincerity was quite insufficient to accomplish this modification.   No amount of emphasis could offset the general impression of the picture.   A new picture was needed which would have to include Plato's sincere belief in his mission as healer of the sick social body, as well as the fact that he had seen more clearly than anybody else before or after him what was happening to Greek society.   Since the attempt to reject the identity of Platonism and totalitarianism had not improved the picture, I was ultimately forced to modify my interpretation of totalitarianism itself.   In other words, my attempt to understand Plato by analogy with modern totalitarianism led me, to my own surprise, to modify my view of totalitarianism.   It did not modify my hostility, but it ultimately led me to see that the strength of both the old and the new totalitarian movements rested on the fact that they attempted to answer a very real need, however badly conceived this attempt may have been.

In the light of my new interpretation, it appears to me that Plato's declaration of his wish to make the state and its citizens happy is not merely propaganda. I am ready to grant his fundamental benevolence [5]. I also grant that he was right, to a limited extent, in the sociological analysis on which he based his promise of happiness. To put this point more precisely : I believe that Plato, with deep sociological insight, found that his contemporaries were suffering under a severe strain, and that this strain was due to the social revolution which had begun with the rise of democracy and individualism. He succeeded in discovering the main causes of their deeply rooted unhappiness—social change, and social dissension—and he did his utmost to fight them. There is no reason to doubt that one of his most powerful motives was to win back happiness for the citizens. For reasons discussed later in this chapter, I believe that the medico-political treatment which he recommended, the arrest of change and the return to tribalism, was hopelessly wrong. But the recommendation, though not practicable as a therapy, testifies to Plato's power of diagnosis. It shows that he knew what was amiss, that he understood the strain, the unhappiness, under which the people were labouring, even though he erred in his fundamental claim that by leading them back to tribalism he could lessen the strain, and restore their happiness.

It is my intention to give in this chapter a very brief survey of the historical material which induced me to hold such opinions. A few critical remarks on the method adopted, that of historical interpretation, will be found in the last chapter of the book. It will therefore suffice here if I say that I do not claim scientific status for this method, since the tests of an historical interpretation can never be as rigorous as those of an ordinary hypothesis. The interpretation is mainly a *point of view*, whose value lies in its fertility, in its power to throw light upon the historical material, to lead us to find new material, and to help us to rationalize and to unify it. What I am going to say here is therefore not meant as a dogmatic assertion, however boldly I may perhaps sometimes express my opinions.

I

Our Western civilization originated with the Greeks. They were, it seems, the first to make the step from tribalism to humanitarianism. Let us consider what that means.

The early Greek tribal society resembles in many respects that of peoples like the Polynesians, the Maoris for instance. Small bands of warriors, usually living in fortified settlements, ruled by tribal chiefs or kings, or by aristocratic families, were waging war against one another on sea as well as on land. There were, of course, many differences between the Greek and the Polynesian ways of life, for there is, admittedly, no uniformity in tribalism. There is no standardized ' tribal way of life '. It seems to me, however, that there are some characteristics that can be found in most, if not all, of these tribal societies. I mean their magical or irrational attitude towards the customs of social life, and the corresponding rigidity of these customs.

The magical attitude towards social custom has been discussed before. Its main element is the lack of distinction between the customary or conventional regularities of social life and the regularities found in ' nature ' ; and this often goes together with the belief that both are enforced by a supernatural will. The rigidity of the social customs is probably in most cases only another aspect of the same attitude. (There are some reasons to believe that this aspect is even more primitive, and that the supernatural belief is a kind of rationalization of the fear of changing a routine —a fear which we can find in very young children.) When I speak of the rigidity of tribalism I do not mean that no changes can occur in the tribal ways of life. I mean rather that the comparatively infrequent changes have the character of religious conversions or revulsions, or of the introduction of new magical taboos. They are not based upon a rational attempt to improve social conditions. Apart from such changes—which are rare— taboos rigidly regulate and dominate all aspects of life. They do not leave many loop-holes. There are few problems in this form of life, and nothing really equivalent to moral problems. I do not mean to say that a member of a tribe does not sometimes need much heroism and endurance in order to act in accordance with the taboos. What I mean is that he will rarely find himself in the position of doubting how he ought to act. The right way is always determined, though difficulties must be overcome in fol- lowing it. It is determined by taboos, by magical tribal institu- tions which can never become objects of critical consideration. Not even a Heraclitus distinguishes clearly between the institu- tional laws of tribal life and the laws of nature ; both are taken to be of the same magical character. Based upon the collective tribal tradition, the institutions leave no room for personal res- ponsibility. The taboos that establish some form of group- responsibility may be the forerunner of what we call personal responsibility, but they are fundamentally different from it. They are not based upon a principle of reasonable accountability, but rather upon magical ideas, such as the idea of appeasing the powers of fate.

It is well known how much of this still survives. Our own ways of life are still beset with taboos; food taboos, taboos of politeness, and many others. And yet, there are some important differences. In our own way of life there is, between the laws of the state on the one hand and the taboos we habitually observe on the other, an ever-widening field of personal decisions, with its problems and responsibilities ; and we know the importance of this field. Personal decisions may lead to the alteration of taboos, and even of political laws which are no longer taboos. The great difference is the possibility of rational reflection upon these matters. Rational reflection begins, in a way, with Heraclitus [6]. With Alcmaeon, Phaleas and Hippodamus, with Herodotus and the Sophists, the quest for the ' best constitution ' assumes, by degrees, the character of a problem which can be rationally discussed. And in our own time, many of us make rational decisions concerning the desirability or otherwise of new legislation, and of other institutional changes ; that is to say, decisions based upon an estimate of possible consequences, and upon a conscious preference for some of them. We recognize rational personal responsibility.

In what follows, the magical or tribal or collectivist society will also be called the *closed society*, and the society in which individuals are confronted with personal decisions, the *open society*.

A closed society at its best can be justly compared to an organism. The so-called organic or biological theory of the state can be applied to it to a considerable extent. A closed society resembles a herd or a tribe in being a semi-organic unit whose members are held together by semi-biological ties— kinship, living together, sharing common efforts, common dangers, common joys and common distress. It is still a concrete group of concrete individuals, related to one another not merely by such abstract social relationships as division of labour and exchange of commodities, but by concrete physical relationships such as touch, smell, and sight. And although such a society may be based on slavery, the presence of slaves need not create a fundamentally different problem from that of domesticated animals. Thus those aspects are lacking which make it impossible to apply the organic theory successfully to an open society.

The aspects I have in mind are connected with the fact that, in an open society, many members strive to rise socially, and to take the places of other members. This may lead, for example, to such an important social phenomenon as class struggle. We cannot find anything like class struggle in an organism. The cells or tissues of an organism, which are sometimes said to correspond to the members of a state, may perhaps compete for food ; but there is no inherent tendency on the part of the legs to become the brain, or of other members of the body to become the belly. Since there is nothing in the organism to correspond to one of the most important characteristics of the open society, competition for status among its members, the so-called organic theory of the state is based on a false analogy. The closed society, on the other hand, does not know much of such tendencies. Its institutions, including its castes, are sacrosanct —taboo. The organic theory does not fit so badly here. It is therefore not surprising to find that most attempts to apply the organic theory to our society are veiled forms of propaganda for a return to tribalism [7].

As a consequence of its loss of organic character, an open society may become, by degrees, what I should like to term an ' abstract society '. It may, to a considerable extent, lose the character of a concrete or real group of men, or of a system of such real groups. This point which has been rarely understood may be explained by way of an exaggeration. We could conceive of a society in which men practically never meet face to face—in which all business is conducted by individuals in isolation who communicate by typed letters or by telegrams, and who go about in closed motor-cars. (Artificial insemination would allow even propagation without a personal element.) Such a fictitious society might be called a ' completely abstract or depersonalized society '. Now the interesting point is that our modern society resembles in many of its aspects such a completely abstract society. Although we do not always drive alone in closed motor cars (but meet face to face thousands of men walking past us in the street) the result is very nearly the same as if we did—we do not establish as a rule any personal relation with our fellow-pedestrians. Similarly, membership of a trade union may mean no more than the possession of a membership card and the payment of a contribution to an unknown secretary. There are many people living in a modern society who have no, or extremely few, intimate personal contacts, who live in anonymity and isolation, and consequently in unhappiness.   For although society has become abstract, the biological make-up of man has not changed much ; men have social needs which they cannot satisfy in an abstract society.

Of course, our picture is even in this form highly exaggerated. There never will be or can be a completely abstract or even a predominantly abstract society—no more than a completely rational or even a predominantly rational society.   Men still form real groups and enter into real social contacts of all kinds, and try to satisfy their emotional social needs as well as they can.   But most of the social groups of a modern open society (with the exception of some lucky family groups) are poor substitutes, since they do not provide for a common life.   And many of them do not have any function in the life of the society at large.

Another way in which the picture is exaggerated is that it does not, so far, contain any of the gains made—only the losses. But there are gains.   Personal relationships of a new kind can arise where they can be freely entered into, instead of being determined by the accidents of birth ; and with this, a new individualism arises.   Similarly, spiritual bonds can play a major rôle where the biological or physical bonds are weakened ; etc. However this may be, our example, I hope, will have made plain what is meant by a more abstract society in contradistinction to a more concrete or real social group ; and it will have made it clear that our modern open societies function largely by way of abstract relations, such as exchange or co-operation.   (It is the analysis of these abstract relations with which modern social theory, such as economic theory, is mainly concerned.   This point has not been understood by many sociologists, such as Durkheim, who never gave up the dogmatic belief that society must be analysed in terms of real social groups.)

In the light of what has been said, it will be clear that the transition from the closed to the open society can be described as one of the deepest revolutions through which mankind has passed. Owing to what we have described as the biological character of the closed society, this transition must be felt deeply indeed. Thus when we say that our Western civilization derives from the Greeks, we ought to realize what it means.   It means that the Greeks started for us that great revolution which, it seems, is still in its beginning—the transition from the closed to the open society.

II

Of course, this revolution was not made consciously. The breakdown of tribalism, of the closed societies of Greece, may be traced back to the time when population growth began to make itself felt among the ruling class of landed proprietors. This meant the end of 'organic' tribalism. For it created social tension within the closed society of the ruling class. At first, there appeared to be something like an 'organic' solution of this problem, the creation of daughter cities. (The 'organic' character of this solution was underlined by the magical procedures followed in the sending out of colonists.) But this ritual of colonization only postponed the breakdown. It even created new danger spots wherever it led to cultural contacts ; and these, in turn, created what was perhaps the worst danger to the closed society—commerce, and a new class engaged in trade and seafaring. By the sixth century B.C., this development had led to the partial dissolution of the old ways of life, and even to a series of political revolutions and reactions. And it had led not only to attempts to retain and to arrest tribalism by force, as in Sparta, but also to that great spiritual revolution, the invention of critical discussion, and, in consequence, of thought that was free from magical obsessions. At the same time we find the first symptoms of a new uneasiness. *The strain of civilization was beginning to be felt.*

This strain, this uneasiness, is a consequence of the breakdown of the closed society. It is still felt even in our day, especially in times of social change. It is the strain created by the effort which life in an open and partially abstract society continually demands from us—by the endeavour to be rational, to forgo at least some of our emotional social needs, to look after ourselves, and to accept responsibilities. We must, I believe, bear this strain as the price to be paid for every increase in knowledge, in reasonableness, in co-operation and in mutual help, and consequently in our chances of survival, and in the size of the population. It is the price we have to pay for being human.

The strain is most closely related to the problem of the tension between the classes which is raised for the first time by the breakdown of the closed society. The closed society itself does not know this problem. At least to its ruling members, slavery, caste, and class rule are 'natural' in the sense of being unquestionable. But with the breakdown of the closed society, this certainty disappears, and with it all feeling of security.   The tribal community (and later the ' city ') is the place of security for the member of the tribe.   Surrounded by enemies and by dangerous or even hostile magical forces, he experiences the tribal community as a child experiences his family and his home, in which he plays his definite part ; a part he knows well, and plays well.   The breakdown of the closed society, raising as it does the problems of class and other problems of social status, must have had the same effect upon the citizens as a serious family quarrel and the breaking up of the family home is liable to have on children [8].   Of course, this kind of strain was felt by the privileged classes, now that they were threatened, more strongly than by those who had formerly been suppressed ; but even the latter felt uneasy.   They also were frightened by the breakdown of their ' natural ' world.   And though they continued to fight their struggle, they were often reluctant to exploit their victories over their class enemies who were supported by tradition, the *status quo*, a higher level of education, and a feeling of natural authority.

In this light we must try to understand the history of Sparta, which successfully tried to arrest these developments, and of Athens, the leading democracy.

Perhaps the most powerful cause of the breakdown of the closed society was the development of sea-communications and commerce.   Close contact with other tribes is liable to undermine the feeling of necessity with which tribal institutions are viewed ; and trade, commercial initiative, appears to be one of the few forms in which individual initiative [9] and independence can assert itself, even in a society in which tribalism still prevails. These two, seafaring and commerce, became the main characteristics of Athenian imperialism, as it developed in the fifth century B.C.   And indeed they were recognized as the most dangerous developments by the oligarchs, the members of the privileged, or of the formerly privileged, classes of Athens.   It became clear to them that the trade of Athens, its monetary commercialism, its naval policy, and its democratic tendencies were parts of one single movement, and that it was impossible to defeat democracy without going to the roots of the evil and destroying both the naval policy and the empire.   But the naval policy of Athens was based upon its harbours, especially the Piraeus, the centre of commerce and the stronghold of the democratic party ; and strategically, upon the walls which fortified Athens, and later, upon the Long Walls which linked it to the harbours of the Piraeus and Phalerum. Accordingly, we find that for more than a century the empire, the fleet, the harbour, and the walls were hated by the oligarchic parties of Athens as the symbols of the democracy and as the sources of its strength which they hoped one day to destroy.

Much evidence of this development can be found in Thucydides' *History of the Peloponnesian War*, or rather, of the two great wars of 431–421 and 419–403 B.C., between Athenian democracy and the arrested oligarchic tribalism of Sparta. When reading Thucydides we must never forget that his heart was not with Athens, his native city. Although he apparently did not belong to the extreme wing of the Athenian oligarchic clubs who conspired throughout the war with the enemy, he was certainly a member of the oligarchic party, and a friend neither of the Athenian people, the demos, who had exiled him, nor of its imperialist policy. (I do not intend to belittle Thucydides, the greatest historian, perhaps, who ever lived. But however successful he was in making sure of the facts he records, and however sincere his efforts to be impartial, his comments and moral judgements represent an interpretation, a point of view ; and in this we need not agree with him.) I quote first from a passage describing Themistocles' policy in 482 B.C., half a century before the Peloponnesian war : ' Themistocles also persuaded the Athenians to finish the Piraeus. . . Since the Athenians had now taken to the sea, he thought that they had a great opportunity for building an empire. He was the first who dared to say that they should make the sea their domain. . .' [10] Twenty-five years later, ' the Athenians began to build their Long Walls to the sea, one to the harbour of Bhalerum, the other to the Piraeus ' [11]. But this time, twenty-six years before the outbreak of the Peloponnesian war, the oligarchic party was fully aware of the meaning of these developments. We hear from Thucydides that they did not shrink even from the most blatant treachery. As sometimes happens with oligarchs, class interest superseded their patriotism. An opportunity offered itself in the form of a hostile Spartan expeditionary force operating in the north of Athens, and they determined to conspire with Sparta against their own country. Thucydides writes : ' Certain Athenians were privately making overtures to them ' (i.e. to the Spartans) ' *in the hope that they would put an end to the democracy*, and to the building of the Long Walls. But the other Athenians . . suspected their design against democracy.' The loyal Athenian citizens therefore went out to meet the Spartans, but were defeated. It appears, however, that they had weakened the enemy sufficiently to prevent him from joining forces with the fifth columnists within their own city. Some months later, the Long Walls were completed, which meant that the democracy could enjoy security as long as it upheld its naval supremacy.

This incident throws light on the tenseness of the class situation in Athens, even twenty-six years before the outbreak of the Peloponnesian war, during which the situation became much worse. It also throws light on the methods employed by the subversive and pro-Spartan oligarchic party. Thucydides, one must note, mentions their treachery only in passing, and he does not censure them, although in other places he speaks most strongly against class struggle and party spirit. The next passages quoted, written as a general reflection on the Corcyraean Revolution of 427 B.C., are interesting, first as an excellent picture of the class situation ; secondly, as an illustration of the strong words Thucydides could find when he wanted to describe analogous tendencies on the side of the democrats of Corcyral (In order to judge his lack of impartiality we must remember that in the beginning of the war Corcyra had been one of Athens' democratic allies, and that the revolt had been started by the oligarchs.) Moreover, the passage is an excellent expression of the feeling of a general social breakdown : ' Nearly the whole Hellenic world ', writes Thucydides, ' was in commotion. In every city, the leaders of the democratic and of the oligarchic parties were trying hard, the one to bring in the Athenians, the other the Lacedaemonians. . . The tie of party was stronger than the tie of blood. . . The leaders on either side used specious names, the one party professing to uphold the constitutional equality of the many, the other the wisdom of the nobility ; in reality they made the public interest their price, professing, of course, their devotion to it. They used any conceivable means for getting the better of one another, and committed the most monstrous crimes. . . This revolution gave birth to every form of wickedness in Hellas. . . Everywhere prevailed an attitude of perfidious antagonism. There was no word binding enough, no oath terrible enough, to reconcile enemies. Each man was strong only in the conviction that nothing was secure.' [12]

The full significance of the attempt of the Athenian oligarchs to accept the help of Sparta and stop the building of the Long Walls can be gauged when we realize that this treacherous attitude had not changed when Aristotle wrote his *Politics*, more than a century later. We hear there about an oligarchic oath, which, Aristotle said, ' is now in vogue '. This is how it runs : ' I promise to be an enemy of the people, and to do my best to give them bad advice ! ' [13] It is clear that we cannot understand the period without remembering this attitude.

I mentioned above that Thucydides himself was an anti-democrat. This becomes clear when we consider his description of the Athenian empire, and the way it was hated by the various Greek states. Athens' rule over its empire, he tells us, was felt to be no better than a tyranny, and all the Greek tribes were afraid of her. In describing public opinion at the outbreak of the Peloponnesian war, he is mildly critical of Sparta and very critical of Athenian imperialism. ' The general feeling of the peoples was strongly on the side of the Lacedaemonians ; for they maintained that they were the liberators of Hellas. Cities and individuals were eager to assist them . . , and the general indignation against the Athenians was intense. Some were longing to be liberated from Athens, others fearful of falling under its sway.' [14] It is most interesting that this judgement of the Athenian empire has become, more or less, the official judgement of ' History ', i.e. of most of the historians. Just as the philo-sophers find it hard to free themselves from Plato's point of view, so are the historians bound to that of Thucydides. As an example I may quote Meyer (the best German authority on this period), who simply repeats Thucydides when he says : ' The sympathies of the educated world of Greece were . . turned away from Athens.' [15]

But such statements are only expressions of the anti-democratic point of view. Many facts recorded by Thucydides—for instance, the passage quoted which describes the attitude of the democratic and oligarchic party leaders—show that Sparta was ' popular ' not among the peoples of Greece but only among the oligarchs ; among the ' educated ', as Meyer puts it so nicely. Even Meyer admits that ' the democratically minded masses hoped in many places for her victory ' [16], i.e. for the victory of Athens ; and Thucydides' narrative contains many instances which prove Athens' popularity among the democrats and the suppressed. But who cares for the opinion of the uneducated masses ? If Thucydides and the ' educated ' assert that Athens was a tyrant, then she was a tyrant.

It is most interesting that the same historians who hail Rome for her achievement, the foundation of a universal empire, condemn Athens for her attempt to achieve something better. The fact that Rome succeeded where Athens failed is not a sufficient explanation of this attitude. They do not really censure Athens for her failure, since they loathe the very idea that her attempt might have been successful. Athens, they believe, was a ruthless democracy, a place ruled by the uneducated, who hated and suppressed the educated, and were hated by them in turn. But this view—the myth of the cultural intolerance of democratic Athens—makes nonsense of the known facts, and above all of the astonishing spiritual productivity of Athens in this particular period. Even Meyer must admit this productivity. ' What Athens produced in this decade ', he says with characteristic modesty, ' ranks equal with one of the mightiest decades of German literature.' [17] Pericles, who was the democratic leader of Athens at this time, was more than justified when he called her ' The School of Hellas '.

I am far from defending everything that Athens did in building up her empire, and I certainly do not wish to defend wanton attacks (if such have occurred), or acts of brutality ; nor do I forget that Athenian democracy was still based on slavery [18]. But it is necessary, I believe, to see that tribalist exclusiveness and self-sufficiency could be superseded only by some form of imperialism. And it must be said that certain of the imperialist measures introduced by Athens were rather liberal. One very interesting instance is the fact that Athens offered, in 405 B.C., to her ally, the Ionian island Samos, ' that the Samians should be Athenians from now on ; and that both cities should be one state ; and that the Samians should order their internal affairs as they chose, and retain their laws.' [19] Another instance is Athens' method of taxing her empire. Much has been said about these taxes, or tributes, which have been described—very unjustly, I believe—as a shameless and tyrannical way of exploiting the smaller cities. In an attempt to evaluate the significance of these taxes, we must, of course, compare them with the volume of the trade which, in return, was protected by the Athenian fleet. The necessary information is given by Thucydides, from whom we learn that the Athenians imposed upon their allies, in 413 B.C., ' in place of the tribute, a duty of 5 per cent. on all things imported and exported by sea ; and they thought that this would yield more ' [20]. This measure, adopted under severe strain of war, compares favourably, I believe, with the Roman methods of centralization. The Athenians, by this method of taxation, became interested in the development of allied trade, and so in the initiative and independence of the various members of their empire. Originally, the Athenian empire had developed out of a league of equals. In spite of the temporary predominance of Athens, publicly criticized by some of her citizens (cp. Aristophanes' *Lysistrata*), it seems probable that her interest in the development of trade would have led, in time, to some kind of federal constitution. At least, we know in her case of nothing like the Roman method of ' transferring ' the cultural possessions from the empire to the dominant city, i.e. of looting. And whatever one might say against plutocracy, it is preferable to a rule of looters [21].

This favourable view of Athenian imperialism can be supported by comparing it with the Spartan methods of handling foreign affairs. They were determined by the ultimate aim that dominated Sparta's policy, by its attempt to arrest all change and to return to tribalism. (This is impossible, as I shall contend later on. Innocence once lost cannot be regained, and an artificially arrested closed society, or a cultivated tribalism, cannot equal the genuine article.) The principles of Spartan policy were these. (1) Protection of its arrested tribalism : shut out all foreign influences which might endanger the rigidity of tribal taboos.—(2) Anti-humanitarianism : shut out, more especially, all equalitarian, democratic, and individualistic ideologies.—(3) Autarky : be independent of trade.—(4) Anti-universalism or particularism : uphold the differentiation between your tribe and all others ; do not mix with inferiors.—(5) Mastery : dominate and enslave your neighbours.—(6) But do not become too large : ' The city should grow only as long as it can do so without impairing its unity ' [22], and especially, without risking the introduction of universalistic tendencies.—If we compare these six principal tendencies with those of modern totalitarianism, then we see that they agree fundamentally, with the sole exception of the last. The difference can be described by saying that modern totalitarianism appears to have imperialist tendencies. But this imperialism has no element of a tolerant universalism, and the world-wide ambitions of the modern totalitarians are imposed upon them, as it were, against their will. Two factors are responsible for this. The first is the general tendency of all tyrannies to justify their existence by saving the state (or the people) from its enemies—a tendency

which must lead, whenever the old enemies have been successfully subdued, to the creation or invention of new ones. The
second factor is the attempt to carry into effect the closely related
points (2) and (5) of the totalitarian programme. Humanitarianism, which, according to point (2), must be kept out, has
become so universal that, in order to combat it effectively at
home, it must be destroyed all over the world. But our world
has become so small that everybody is now a neighbour, so that,
to carry out point (5), everybody must be dominated and enslaved.
But in ancient times, nothing could have appeared more dangerous to those who adopted a particularism like Sparta's, than
Athenian imperialism, with its inherent tendency to develop into
a commonwealth of Greek cities, and perhaps even into a universal empire of man.

Summing up our analysis so far, we can say that the political
and spiritual revolution which had begun with the breakdown
of Greek tribalism reached its climax in the fifth century, with
the outbreak of the Peloponnesian war. It had developed into
a violent class war, and, at the same time, into a war between the
two leading cities of Greece.

III

But how can we explain the fact that outstanding Athenians
like Thucydides stood on the side of reaction against these new
developments ? Class interest is, I believe, an insufficient explanation ; for what we have to explain is the fact that, while many
of the ambitious young nobles became active, although not always
reliable, members of the democratic party, some of the most
thoughtful and gifted resisted its attraction. The main point
seems to be that although the open society was already in existence, although it had, in practice, begun to develop new values,
new equalitarian standards of life, there was still something missing, especially for the ' educated '. The new faith of the open
society, its only possible faith, humanitarianism, was beginning
to assert itself, but was not yet formulated. For the time being,
one could not see much more than class war, the democrats' fear
of the oligarchic reaction, and the threat of further revolutionary
developments. The reaction against these developments had
therefore much on its side—tradition, the call for defending old
virtues, and the old religion. These tendencies appealed to the
feelings of most men, and their popularity gave rise to a movement
to which, although it was led and used for their own ends by the

Spartans and their oligarchic friends, many upright men must have belonged, even at Athens. From the slogan of the movement, ' Back to the state of our forefathers ', or ' Back to the old paternal state ', derives the term ' patriot '. It is hardly necessary to insist that the beliefs popular among those who supported this ' patriotic ' movement were grossly perverted by those oligarchs who did not shrink from handing over their own city to the enemy, in the hope of gaining support against the democrats. Thucydides was one of the representative leaders of this movement for the ' paternal state ' [23], and though he probably did not support the treacherous acts of the extreme anti-democrats, he could not disguise his sympathies with their fundamental aim—to arrest social change, and to fight the universalistic imperialism of the Athenian democracy and the instruments and symbols of its power, the navy, the walls, and commerce. (In view of Plato's doctrines concerning commerce, it may be interesting to note how great the fear of commercialism was. When after his victory over Athens in 404 B.C. the Spartan king, Lysander, returned with great booty, the Spartan ' patriots ', i.e. the members of the movement for the ' paternal state ', tried to prevent the import of gold ; and though it was ultimately admitted, its possession was limited to the state, and capital punishment was imposed on any citizen found in possession of precious metals. In Plato's *Laws*, very similar procedures are advocated [24]).

Although the ' patriotic ' movement was partly the expression of the longing to return to more stable forms of life, to religion, decency, law and order, it was itself morally rotten. Its ancient faith was lost, and was largely replaced by a hypocritical and even cynical exploitation of religious sentiments. [25] Nihilism, as painted by Plato in the portraits of Callicles and Thrasymachus, could be found if anywhere among the young ' patriotic ' aristocrats who, if given the opportunity, became leaders of the democratic party. The clearest exponent of this nihilism was perhaps the oligarchic leader who helped to deal the death-blow at Athens, Plato's uncle Critias, the leader of the Thirty Tyrants. [26]

But at this time, in the same generation to which Thucydides belonged, there rose a new faith in reason, freedom and the brotherhood of all men—the new faith, and, as I believe, the only possible faith, of the open society.

IV

This generation which marks a turning point in the history of mankind, I should like to call the Great Generation ; it is the generation which lived in Athens just before, and during, the Peloponnesian war.[27]   There were great conservatives among them, like Sophocles, or Thucydides.   There were men among them who represent the period of transition ; who were wavering, like Euripides, or sceptical, like Aristophanes.   But there was also the great leader of democracy, Pericles, who formulated the principle of equality before the law and of political individualism, and Herodotus, who was welcomed and hailed in Pericles' city as the author of a work that glorified these principles.   Protagoras, a native of Abdera who became influential in Athens, and his countryman Democritus must also be counted among the Great Generation.   They formulated the doctrine that human institutions of language, custom, and law are not of the magical character of taboos but man-made, not natural but conventional, insisting, at the same time, that we are responsible for them. Then there was the school of Gorgias—Alcidamas, Lycophron and Antisthenes, who developed the fundamental tenets of anti-slavery, of a rational protectionism, and of anti-nationalism, i.e. the creed of the universal empire of men.   And there was, perhaps the greatest of all, Socrates, who taught the lesson that we must have faith in human reason, but at the same time beware of dogmatism ; that we must keep away both from misology [28], the distrust of theory and of reason, and from the magical attitude of those who make an idol of wisdom ; who taught, in other words, that the spirit of science is criticism.

Since I have not so far said much about Pericles, and nothing at all about Democritus, I may use some of their own words in order to illustrate the new faith.   First Democritus : ' Not out of fear but out of a feeling of what is right should we abstain from doing wrong. . .   Virtue is based, most of all, upon respecting the other man. . .   Every man is a little world of his own. . .   We ought to do our utmost to help those who have suffered injustice. . .   To be good means to do no wrong ; and also, not to want to do wrong. . .   It is good deeds, not words, that count. . .   The poverty of a democracy is better than the prosperity which allegedly goes with aristocracy or monarchy, just as liberty is better than slavery. . .   The wise man belongs to all countries, for the home of a great soul is the whole world.'

To him is due also that remark of a true scientist : ' I would rather find a single causal law than be the king of Persia ! ' [29]

In their humanitarian and universalistic emphasis some of these fragments of Democritus sound, although they are of earlier date, as if they were directed against Plato. The same impression is conveyed, only much more strongly, by Pericles' famous funeral oration, delivered at least half a century before the *Republic* was written. I have quoted two sentences from this oration in chapter 6, when discussing equalitarianism [30], but a few passages may be quoted here more fully in order to give a clearer impression of its spirit. ' Our political system does not compete with institutions which are elsewhere in force. We do not copy our neighbours, but try to be an example. Our administration favours the many instead of the few : this is why it is called a democracy. The laws afford equal justice to all alike in their private disputes, but we do not ignore the claims of excellence. When a citizen distinguishes himself, then he will be called to serve the state, in preference to others, not as a matter of privilege, but as a reward of merit ; and poverty is no bar. . . The freedom we enjoy extends also to ordinary life ; we are not suspicious of one another, and do not nag our neighbour if he chooses to go his own way. . . But this freedom does not make us lawless. We are taught to respect the magistrates and the laws, and never to forget that we must protect the injured. And we are also taught to observe those unwritten laws whose sanction lies only in the universal feeling of what is right. . .

' Our city is thrown open to the world ; we never expel a foreigner. . . We are free to live exactly as we please, and yet we are always ready to face any danger. . . We love beauty without indulging in fancies, and although we try to improve our intellect, this does not weaken our will. . . To admit one's poverty is no disgrace with us ; but we consider it disgraceful not to make an effort to avoid it. An Athenian citizen does not neglect public affairs when attending to his private business. . . We consider a man who takes no interest in the state not as harmless, but as useless ; and *although only a few may originate a policy, we are all able to judge it.* We do not look upon discussion as a stumbling-block in the way of political action, but as an indispensable preliminary to acting wisely. . . We believe that happiness is the fruit of freedom and freedom that of valour, and we do not shrink from the dangers of war. . . To sum up, I claim that Athens is the School of Hellas, and that the individual

Athenian grows up to develop a happy versatility, a readiness for emergencies, and self-reliance.' [31]

These words are not merely an eulogy on Athens ; they express the true spirit of the Great Generation. They formulate the political programme of a great equalitarian individualist, of a democrat who well understands that democracy cannot be exhausted by the meaningless principle that ' the people should rule ', but that it must be based on faith in reason, and on humanitarianism. At the same time, they are an expression of true patriotism, of just pride in a city which had made it its task to set an example ; which became the school, not only of Hellas, but, as we know, of mankind, for millennia past and yet to come.

Pericles' speech is not only a programme. It is also a defence, and perhaps even an attack. It reads, as I have already hinted, like a direct attack on Plato. I do not doubt that it was directed, not only against the arrested tribalism of Sparta, but also against the totalitarian ring or ' link ' at home ; against the movement for the paternal state, the Athenian ' Society of the Friends of Laconia ' (as Th. Gomperz called them in 1902 [32]). The speech is the earliest [33] and at the same time perhaps the strongest statement ever made in opposition to this kind of movement. Its importance was felt by Plato, who caricatured Pericles' oration half a century later in the passages of the *Republic* [34] in which he attacks democracy, as well as in that undisguised parody, the dialogue called *Menexenus or the Funeral Oration* [35]. But the friends of Laconia whom Pericles attacked retaliated long before Plato. Only five or six years after Pericles' oration, a pamphlet on the *Constitution of Athens* [36] was published by an unknown author (possibly Critias), now usually called the ' Old Oligarch '. This ingenious pamphlet, the oldest extant treatise on political theory, is, at the same time, perhaps the oldest monument of the desertion of mankind by its intellectual leaders. It is a ruthless attack upon Athens, written no doubt by one of her best brains. Its central idea, an idea which became an article of faith with Thucydides and Plato, is the close connection between naval imperialism and democracy. And it tries to show that there can be no compromise in a conflict between two worlds [37], the worlds of democracy and of oligarchy ; that only the use of ruthless violence, of total measures, including the intervention of allies from outside (the Spartans), can put an end to the unholy rule of freedom. This remarkable pamphlet was to become the first of a practically infinite sequence of works on political philosophy which were to repeat more or less, openly or covertly, the same theme down to our own day.   Unwilling and unable to help mankind along their difficult path into an unknown future which they have to create for themselves, some of the ' educated ' tried to make them turn back into the past.   Incapable of leading a new way, they could only make themselves leaders of the *perennial revolt against freedom*.   It became the more necessary for them to assert their superiority by fighting against equality as they were (using Socratic language) misanthropists and misologists—incapable of that simple and ordinary generosity which inspires faith in men, and faith in human reason and freedom.   Harsh as this judgement may sound, it is just, I fear, if it is applied to those intellectual leaders of the revolt against freedom who came after the Great Generation, and especially after Socrates.   We can now try to see them against the background of our historical interpretation.

The rise of philosophy itself can be interpreted, I think, as a response to the breakdown of the closed society and its magical beliefs.   It is an attempt to replace the lost magical faith by a rational faith ; it modifies the tradition of passing on a theory or a myth by founding a new tradition—the tradition of challenging theories and myths and of critically discussing them [38].   (A significant point is that this attempt coincides with the spread of the so-called Orphic sects whose members tried to replace the lost feeling of unity by a new mystical religion.)   The earliest philosophers, the three great Ionians and Pythagoras, were probably quite unaware of the stimulus to which they were reacting. They were the representatives as well as the unconscious antagonists of a social revolution.   The very fact that they founded schools or sects or orders, i.e. new social institutions or rather concrete groups with a common life and common functions, and modelled largely after those of an idealized tribe, proves that they were reformers in the social field, and therefore, that they were reacting to certain social needs.   That they reacted to these needs and to their own sense of drift, not by imitating Hesiod in inventing a historicist myth of destiny and decay [39], but by inventing the tradition of criticism and discussion, and with it the art of thinking rationally, is one of the inexplicable facts which stand at the beginning of our civilization.   But even these rationalists reacted to the loss of the unity of tribalism in a largely emotional way.   Their reasoning gives expression to their feeling of drift, to the strain of a development which was about to create our individualistic civilization. One of the oldest expressions of this strain goes back to Anaximander [40], the second of the Ionian philosophers. Individual existence appeared to him as *hubris*, as an impious act of injustice, as a wrongful act of usurpation, for which individuals must suffer, and do penance. The first to become conscious of the social revolution and the struggle of classes was Heraclitus. How he rationalized his feeling of drift by developing the first anti-democratic ideology and the first historicist philosophy of change and destiny, has been described in the second chapter of this book. Heraclitus was the first conscious enemy of the open society.

Nearly all these early thinkers were labouring under a tragic and desperate strain [41]. The only exception is perhaps the monotheist Xenophanes [42], who carried his burden courageously. We cannot blame them for their hostility towards the new developments in the way in which we may, to some extent, blame their successors. The new faith of the open society, the faith in man, in equalitarian justice, and in human reason, was perhaps beginning to take shape, but it was not yet formulated.

v

The greatest contribution to this faith was to be made by Socrates, who died for it. Socrates was not a leader of Athenian democracy, like Pericles, or a theorist of the open society, like Protagoras. He was, rather, a critic of Athens and of her democratic institutions, and in this he may have borne a superficial resemblance to some of the leaders of the reaction against the open society. But there is no need for a man who criticizes democracy and democratic institutions to be their enemy, although both the democrats he criticizes, and the totalitarians who hope to profit from any disunion in the democratic camp, are likely to brand him as such. There is a fundamental difference between a democratic and a totalitarian criticism of democracy. Socrates' criticism was a democratic one, and indeed of the kind that is the very life of democracy. (Democrats who do not see the difference between a friendly and a hostile criticism of democracy are themselves imbued with the totalitarian spirit. Totalitarianism, of course, cannot consider any criticism as friendly, since every criticism of such an authority must challenge the principle of authority itself.)

I have already mentioned some aspects of Socrates' teaching : his intellectualism, i.e. his equalitarian theory of human reason as a universal medium of communication ; his stress on intellectual honesty and self-criticism ; his equalitarian theory of justice, and his doctrine that it is better to be a victim of injustice than to inflict it upon others.   I think it is this last doctrine which can help us best to understand the core of his teaching, his creed of individualism, his belief in the human individual as an end in himself.

The closed society, and with it its creed that the tribe is everything and the individual nothing, had broken down. Individual initiative and self-assertion had become a fact. Interest in the human individual as individual, and not only as tribal hero and saviour, had been aroused [43].   But a philosophy which makes man the centre of its interest began only with Protagoras.   And the belief that there is nothing more important in our life than other individual men, the appeal to men to respect one another and themselves, appears to be due to Socrates.

Burnet has stressed [44] that it was Socrates who created the conception of the *soul*, a conception which had such an immense influence upon our civilization.   I believe that there is much in this view, although I feel that its formulation may be misleading, especially the use of the term ' soul ' ; for Socrates seems to have kept away from metaphysical theories as much as he could.   His appeal was a moral appeal, and his theory of individuality (or of the ' soul ', if this word is preferred) is, I think, a moral and not a metaphysical doctrine.   He was fighting, with the help of this doctrine, as always, against self-satisfaction and complacency. He demanded that individualism should not be merely the dissolution of tribalism, but that the individual should prove worthy of his liberation.   This is why he insisted that man is not merely a piece of flesh—a body.   There is more in man, a divine spark, reason ; and a love of truth, of kindness, humaneness, a love of beauty and of goodness.   It is these that make a man's life worth while.   But if I am not merely a ' body ', what am I, then ? You are, first of all, intelligence, was Socrates' reply.   It is your reason that makes you human ; that enables you to be more than a mere bundle of desires and wishes ; that makes you a self-sufficient individual and entitles you to claim that you are an end in yourself.   Socrates' saying ' care for your souls ' is largely an appeal for *intellectual* honesty, just as the saying ' know thyself ' is used by him to remind us of our intellectual limitations.

These, Socrates insisted, are the things that matter.   And

what he criticized in democracy and democratic statesmen was their inadequate realization of these things. He criticized them rightly for their lack of intellectual honesty, and for their obsession with power-politics [45]. With his emphasis upon the human side of the political problem, he could not take much interest in institutional reform. It was the immediate, the personal aspect of the open society in which he was interested. He was mistaken when he considered himself a politician ; he was a teacher.

But if Socrates was, fundamentally, the champion of the open society, and a friend of democracy, why, it may be asked, did he mix with anti-democrats ? For we know that among his companions were not only Alcibiades, who for a time went over to the side of Sparta, but also two of Plato's uncles, Critias who later became the ruthless leader of the Thirty Tyrants, and Charmides who became his lieutenant.

There is more than one reply to this question. First we are told by Plato that Socrates' attack upon the democratic politicians of his time was carried out partly with the purpose of exposing the selfishness and lust for power of the hypocritical flatterers of the people, more particularly, of the young aristocrats who posed as democrats, but who looked upon the people as mere instruments of their lust for power [46]. This activity made him, on the one hand, attractive to some at least of the enemies of democracy ; on the other hand it brought him into contact with ambitious aristocrats of that very type. And here enters a second consideration. Socrates, the moralist and individualist, would never merely attack these men. He would, rather, take a real interest in them, and he would hardly give them up without making a serious attempt to convert them. There are many allusions to such attempts in Plato's dialogues. We have reason, and this is a third consideration, to believe that Socrates, the teacher-politician, even went out of his way to attract young men and to gain influence over them, especially when he considered them open to conversion, and thought that some day they might possibly hold offices of responsibility in their city. The outstanding example is, of course, Alcibiades, singled out from his very childhood as the great future leader of the Athenian empire. And Critias' brilliancy, ambition and courage made him one of the few likely competitors of Alcibiades. (He co-operated with Alcibiades for a time, but later turned against him. It is not at all improbable that the temporary co-operation was due to Socrates' influence.) From all we know about Plato's own

early and later political aspirations, it is more than likely that
his relations with Socrates were of a similar kind [47]. Socrates,
though one of the leading spirits of the open society, was not a
party man. He would have worked in any circle where his work
might have benefited his city. If he took interest in a promising
youth he was not to be deterred by oligarchic family connections.

But these connections were to cause his death. When the
great war was lost, Socrates was accused of having educated the
men who had betrayed democracy and conspired with the enemy
to bring about the downfall of Athens.

The history of the Peloponnesian war and the fall of Athens is
still often told, under the influence of Thucydides' authority, in
such a way that the defeat of Athens appears as the ultimate
proof of the moral weaknesses of the democratic system. But
this view is merely a tendentious distortion, and the well-known
facts tell a very different story. The main responsibility for the
lost war rests with the treacherous oligarchs who continuously
conspired with Sparta. Prominent among these were three
former disciples of Socrates, Alcibiades, Critias, and Charmides.
After the fall of Athens in 404 B.C. the two latter became the
leaders of the Thirty Tyrants, who were no more than a puppet
government under Spartan protection. The fall of Athens, and
the destruction of the walls, are often presented as the final
results of the great war which had started in 431 B.C. But in
this presentation lies a major distortion ; for the democrats fought
on. At first only seventy strong, they prepared under the leadership of Thrasybulus and Anytus the liberation of Athens, where
Critias was meanwhile killing scores of citizens ; during the
eight months of his reign of terror the death-roll contained
' rather a greater number of Athenians than the Peloponnesians
had killed during the last ten years of war ' [48]. But after eight
months (in 403 B.C.) Critias and the Spartan garrison were
attacked and defeated by the democrats, who established themselves in the Piraeus, and both of Plato's uncles lost their lives
in the battle. Their oligarchic followers continued for a time
the reign of terror in the city of Athens itself, but their forces
were in a state of confusion and dissolution. Having proved
themselves incapable of ruling, they were ultimately abandoned
by their Spartan protectors, who concluded a treaty with the
democrats. The peace re-established democracy in Athens.
Thus the democratic form of government had proved its
superior strength under the most severe trials, and even its enemies

began to think it invincible. (Nine years later, after the battle of Cnidus, the Athenians could re-erect their walls. The defeat of democracy had turned into victory.)

As soon as the restored democracy had re-established normal legal conditions [49], a case was brought against Socrates. Its meaning was clear enough ; he was accused of having had his hand in the education of the most pernicious enemies of the state, Alcibiades, Critias, and Charmides. Certain difficulties for the prosecution were created by an amnesty for all political crimes committed before the re-establishment of the democracy. The charge could not therefore openly refer to these notorious cases. And the prosecutors probably sought not so much to punish Socrates for the unfortunate political events of the past which, as they knew well, had happened against his intentions ; their aim was, rather, to prevent him from continuing his teaching, which, in view of its effects, they could hardly regard otherwise than as dangerous to the state. For all these reasons, the charge was given the vague and rather meaningless form that Socrates was corrupting the youth, that he was impious, and that he had attempted to introduce novel religious practices into the state. (The latter two charges undoubtedly expressed, however clumsily, the correct feeling that in the ethico-religious field he was a revolutionary.) Because of the amnesty, the ' corrupted youth ' could not be more precisely named, but everybody knew, of course, who was meant [50]. In his defence, Socrates insisted that he had no sympathy with the policy of the Thirty, and that he had actually risked his life by defying their attempt to implicate him in one of their crimes. And he reminded the jury that among his closest associates and most enthusiastic disciples there was at least one ardent democrat, Chaerephon, who fought against the Thirty (and who was, it appears, killed in battle) [51].

It is now usually recognized that Anytus, the democratic leader who backed the prosecution, did not intend to make a martyr of Socrates. The aim was to exile him. But this plan was defeated by Socrates' refusal to compromise his principles. That he wanted to die, or that he enjoyed the rôle of martyr, I do not believe [52]. He simply fought for what he believed to be right, and for his life's work. He had never intended to undermine democracy. In fact, he had tried to give it the faith it needed. This had been the work of his life. It was, he felt, seriously threatened. The betrayal of his former companions let his work and himself appear in a light which must have disturbed him deeply. He may even have welcomed the trial as an opportunity to prove that his loyalty to his city was unbounded.

Socrates explained this attitude most carefully when he was given an opportunity to escape. Had he seized it, and become an exile, everybody would have thought him an opponent of democracy. So he stayed, and stated his reasons. This explanation, his last will, can be found in Plato's *Crito* [53]. It is simple. If I go, said Socrates, I violate the laws of the state. Such an act would put me in opposition to the laws, and prove my disloyalty. It would do harm to the state. Only if I stay can I put beyond doubt my loyalty to the state, with its democratic laws, and prove that I have never been its enemy. There can be no better proof of my loyalty than my willingness to die for it.

Socrates' death is the ultimate proof of his sincerity. His fearlessness, his simplicity, his modesty, his sense of proportion, his humour never deserted him. ' I am the gadfly that God has attached to this city ', he said in his *Apology*, ' and all day long and in all places I am always fastening upon you, arousing and persuading and reproaching you. You would not readily find another like me, and therefore I should advise you to spare me . . If you strike at me, as Anytus advises you, and rashly put me to death, then you will remain asleep for the rest of your lives, unless God in his care sends you another gadfly ' [54]. He showed that a man could die, not only for fate and fame and other grand things of this kind, but also for the freedom of critical thought, and for a self-respect which has nothing to do with self-importance or sentimentality.

VI

Socrates had only *one* worthy successor, his old friend Antisthenes, the last of the Great Generation. Plato, his most gifted disciple, was soon to prove the least faithful. He betrayed Socrates, just as his uncles had done. These, besides betraying Socrates, had also tried to implicate him in their terrorist acts, but they did not succeed, since he resisted. Plato tried to implicate Socrates in his grandiose attempt to construct the theory of the arrested society ; and he had no difficulty in succeeding, for Socrates was dead.

I know of course that this judgement will seem outrageously harsh, even to those who are critical of Plato [55]. But if we look upon the *Apology* and the *Crito* as Socrates' last will, and if we compare these testaments of his old age with Plato's testament, the *Laws*, then it is difficult to judge otherwise. Socrates had been condemned, but his death was not intended by the initiators of the trial. Plato's *Laws* remedy this lack of intention. Here he elaborates coolly and carefully the theory of inquisition. Free thought, criticism of political institutions, teaching new ideas to the young, attempts to introduce new religious practices or even opinions, are all pronounced capital crimes. In Plato's state, Socrates might have never been given the opportunity of defending himself publicly ; and he certainly would have been handed over to the secret Nocturnal Council for the purpose of ' attending ' to his diseased soul, and finally for punishing it.

I cannot doubt the fact of Plato's betrayal, nor that his use of Socrates as the main speaker of the *Republic* was the most successful attempt to implicate him. But it is another question whether this attempt was conscious.

In order to understand Plato we must visualize the whole contemporary situation. After the Peloponnesian war, the strain of civilization was felt as strongly as ever. The old oligarchic hopes were still alive, and the defeat of Athens had even tended to encourage them. The class struggle continued. Yet Critias' attempt to destroy democracy by carrying out the programme of the Old Oligarch had failed. It had not failed through lack of determination ; the most ruthless use of violence had been unsuccessful, in spite of favourable circumstances in the shape of powerful support from victorious Sparta. Plato felt that a complete reconstruction of the programme was needed. The Thirty had been beaten in the realm of power politics largely because they had offended the citizens' sense of justice. The defeat had been largely a moral defeat. The faith of the Great Generation had proved its strength. The Thirty had nothing of this kind to offer ; they were moral nihilists. The programme of the Old Oligarch, Plato felt, could not be revived without basing it upon another faith, upon a persuasion which re-affirmed the old values of tribalism, opposing them to the faith of the open society. *Men must be taught that justice is inequality*, and that the tribe, the collective, stands higher than the individual [56]. But since Socrates' faith was too strong to be challenged openly, Plato was driven to re-interpret it as a faith in the closed society. This was difficult ; but it was not impossible. For had not Socrates been killed by the democracy ? Had not democracy lost any right to claim him ? And had not Socrates always criticized

the anonymous multitude as well as its leaders for their lack of
wisdom? It was not so very difficult, moreover, to re-interpret
Socrates as having recommended the rule of the ' educated ',
the learned philosophers. In this interpretation, Plato was much
encouraged when he discovered that it was also part of the
ancient Pythagorean creed ; and most of all, when he found, in
Archytas of Tarentum, a Pythagorean sage as well as a great
and successful statesman. Here, he felt, was the solution of the
riddle. Had not Socrates himself encouraged his disciples to
participate in politics? Did this not mean that he wanted the
enlightened, the wise, to rule? What a difference between the
crudity of the ruling mob of Athens and the dignity of an
Archytas ! Surely Socrates, who had never stated his solution of
the constitutional problem, must have had Pythagoreanism in
mind.

In this way Plato may have found that it was possible to give
by degrees a new meaning to the teaching of the most influential
member of the Great Generation, and to persuade himself that
an opponent whose overwhelming strength he would never have
dared to attack directly, was an ally. This, I believe, is the
simplest interpretation of the fact that Plato retained Socrates
as his main speaker even after he had departed so widely from
his teaching that he could no longer deceive himself about this
deviation [57]. But it is not the whole story. He felt, I believe,
in the depth of his soul, that Socrates' teaching was very different
indeed from this presentation, and that he was betraying Socrates.
And I think that Plato's continuous efforts to make Socrates
re-interpret himself are at the same time Plato's efforts to quiet
his own bad conscience. By trying again and again to prove that
his teaching was only the logical development of the true Socratic
doctrine, he tried to persuade himself that he was not a traitor.

In reading Plato we are, I feel, witnesses of an inner conflict,
of a truly titanic struggle in Plato's mind. Even his famous
' fastidious reserve, the suppression of his own personality ' [58], or
rather, the attempted suppression—for it is not at all difficult to
read between the lines—is an expression of this struggle. And
I believe that Plato's influence can partly be explained by the
fascination of this conflict between two worlds in one soul, a
struggle whose powerful repercussions upon Plato can be felt
under that surface of fastidious reserve. This struggle touches
our feelings, for it is still going on within ourselves. Plato was
the child of a time which is still our own. (We must not forget

that it is, after all, only a century since the abolition of slavery in the United States, and even less since the abolition of serfdom in Central Europe.) Nowhere does this inner struggle reveal itself more clearly than in Plato's theory of the soul. That Plato, with his longing for unity and harmony, visualized the structure of the human soul as analogous to that of a class-divided society [59] shows how deeply he must have suffered.

Plato's greatest conflict arises from the deep impression made upon him by the example of Socrates, but his own oligarchic inclinations strive only too successfully against it. In the field of rational argument, the struggle is conducted by using the argument of Socrates' humanitarianism against itself. What appears to be the earliest example of this kind can be found in the *Euthyphro* [60]. I am not going to be like Euthyphro, Plato assures himself ; I shall never take it upon myself to accuse my own father, my own venerated ancestors, of having sinned against a law and a humanitarian morality which is on the level of vulgar piety. Even if they took human life, it was, after all, only the lives of their own serfs, who are no better than criminals ; and it is not my task to judge them. Did not Socrates show how hard it is to know what is right and wrong, pious and impious ? And was he not himself prosecuted for impiety by these so-called humanitarians ? Other traces of Plato's struggle can, I believe, be found in nearly every place where he turns against humanitarian ideas, especially in the *Republic*. His evasiveness and his resort to scorn in combating the equalitarian theory of justice, his hesitant preface to his defence of lying, to his introduction of racialism, and to his definition of justice, have all been mentioned in previous chapters. But perhaps the clearest expression of the conflict can be found in the *Menexenus*, that sneering reply to Pericles' funeral oration. Here, I feel, Plato gives himself away. In spite of his attempt to hide his feelings behind irony and scorn, he cannot but show how deeply he was impressed by Pericles' sentiments. This is how Plato makes his ' Socrates ' maliciously describe the impression made upon him by Pericles' oration : ' A feeling of exultation stays with me for more than three days ; not until the fourth or fifth day, and not without an effort, do I come to my senses and realize where I am.' [61] Who can doubt that Plato reveals here how seriously he was impressed by the creed of the open society, and how hard he had to struggle to come to his senses and to realize where he was—namely, in the camp of its enemies.

VII

Plato's strongest argument in this struggle was, I believe, sincere : According to the humanitarian creed, he argued, we should be ready to help our neighbours. The people need help badly, they are unhappy, they labour under a severe strain, a sense of drift. There is no certainty, no security [62] in life, when everything is in flux. I am ready to help them. But I cannot make them happy without going to the root of the evil.

And he found the root of the evil. It is the ' Fall of Man ', the breakdown of the closed society. This discovery convinced him that the Old Oligarch and his followers had been fundamentally right in favouring Sparta against Athens, and in aping the Spartan programme of arresting change. But they had not gone far enough ; their analysis had not been carried sufficiently deep. They had not been aware of the fact, or had not cared for it, that even Sparta showed signs of decay, in spite of its heroic effort to arrest all change ; that even Sparta had been half-hearted in her attempts at controlling breeding in order to eliminate the causes of the Fall, the ' variations ' and ' irregularities ' in the number as well as the quality of the ruling race [63]. (Plato realized that population increase was one of the causes of the Fall.) Also, the Old Oligarch and his followers had thought, in their superficiality, that with the help of a tyranny, such as that of the Thirty, they would be able to restore the good old days. Plato knew better. The great sociologist saw clearly that these tyrannies were supported by, and that they were kindling in their turn, the modern revolutionary spirit ; that they were forced to make concessions to the equalitarian cravings of the people ; and that they had indeed played an important part in the breakdown of tribalism. Plato hated tyranny. Only hatred can see as sharply as he did in his famous description of the tyrant. Only a genuine enemy of tyranny could say that tyrants must ' stir up one war after another in order to make the people feel the need of a general ', of a saviour from extreme danger. Tyranny, Plato insisted, was not the solution, nor any of the current oligarchies. Although it is imperative to keep the people in their place, their suppression is not an end in itself. The end must be the complete return to nature, a complete cleaning of the canvas.

The difference between Plato's theory on the one hand, and that of the Old Oligarch and the Thirty on the other, is due to the influence of the Great Generation. Individualism, equalitarianism, faith in reason and love of freedom were new, powerful, and, from the point of view of the enemies of the open society, dangerous sentiments that had to be fought. Plato had himself felt their influence, and, within himself, he had fought them. His answer to the Great Generation was a truly great effort. It was an effort to close the door which had been opened, and to arrest society by casting upon it the spell of an alluring philosophy, unequalled in depth and richness. In the political field he added but little to the old oligarchic programme against which Pericles had once argued [64]. But he discovered, perhaps unconsciously, the great secret of the revolt against freedom, formulated in our own day by Pareto [65] : ' *To take advantage of sentiments, not wasting one's energies in futile efforts to destroy them.*' Instead of showing his hostility to reason, he charmed all intellectuals with his brilliance, flattering and thrilling them by his demand that the learned should rule. Although arguing against justice he convinced all righteous men that he was its advocate. Not even to himself did he fully admit that he was combating the freedom of thought for which Socrates had died ; and by making Socrates his champion he persuaded all others that he was fighting for it. Plato thus became, unconsciously, the pioneer of the many propagandists who, often in good faith, developed the technique of appealing to moral, humanitarian sentiments, for anti-humanitarian, immoral purposes. And he achieved the somewhat surprising effect of convincing even great humanitarians of the immorality and selfishness of their creed [66]. I do not doubt that he succeeded in persuading himself. He transfigured his hatred of individual initiative, and his wish to arrest all change, into a love of justice and temperance, of a heavenly state in which everybody is satisfied and happy and in which the crudity of money-grabbing [67] is replaced by laws of generosity and friendship. This dream of unity and beauty and perfection, this æstheticism and holism and collectivism, is the product as well as the symptom of the lost group spirit of tribalism [68]. It is the expression of, and an ardent appeal to, the sentiments of those who suffer from the strain of civilization. (It is part of the strain that we are becoming more and more painfully aware of the gross imperfections in our life, of personal as well as of institutional imperfection ; of avoidable suffering, of waste and of unnecessary ugliness ; and at the same time of the fact that it it not impossible for us to do something about all this, but that such improvements would be just as hard to achieve as they are important. This awareness increases the strain of personal responsibility, of carrying the cross of being human.)

VIII

Socrates had refused to compromise his personal integrity. Plato, with all his uncompromising canvas-cleaning, was led along a path on which he compromised his integrity with every step he took. He was forced to combat free thought, and the pursuit of truth. He was led to defend lying, political miracles, tabooistic superstition, the suppression of truth, and ultimately, brutal violence. In spite of Socrates' warning against misanthropy and misology, he was led to distrust man and to fear argument. In spite of his own hatred of tyranny, he was led to look to a tyrant for help, and to defend the most tyrannical measures. By the internal logic of his anti-humanitarian aim, the internal logic of power, he was led unawares to the same point to which once the Thirty had been led, and at which, later, his friend Dio arrived, and others among his numerous tyrant-disciples [69]. He did not succeed in arresting social change. (Only much later, in the dark ages, was it arrested by the magic spell of the Platonic-Aristotelian essentialism.) Instead, he succeeded in binding himself, by his own spell, to powers which once he had hated.

The lesson which we thus should learn from Plato is the exact opposite of what he tries to teach us. It is a lesson which must not be forgotten. Excellent as Plato's sociological diagnosis was, his own development proves that the therapy he recommended is worse than the evil he tried to combat. Arresting political change is not the remedy ; it cannot bring happiness. We can never return to the alleged innocence and beauty of the closed society [70]. Our dream of heaven cannot be realized on earth. Once we begin to rely upon our reason, and to use our powers of criticism, once we feel the call of personal responsibilities, and with it, the responsibility of helping to advance knowledge, we cannot return to a state of implicit submission to tribal magic. For those who have eaten of the tree of knowledge, paradise is lost. The more we try to return to the heroic age of tribalism, the more surely do we arrive at the Inquisition, at the Secret Police, and at a romanticized gangsterism. Beginning with the suppression of reason and truth, we must end with the most brutal and violent destruction of all that is human [71]. *There is no return to a harmonious state of nature.   If we turn back, then we must go the whole way—we must return to the beasts.*

It is an issue which we must face squarely, hard though it may be for us to do so.   If we dream of a return to our childhood, if we are tempted to rely on others and so be happy, if we shrink from the task of carrying our cross, the cross of humaneness, of reason, of responsibility, if we lose courage and flinch from the strain, then we must try to fortify ourselves with a clear understanding of the simple decision before us.   We can return to the beasts.   But if we wish to remain human, then there is only one way, the way into the open society.   We must go on into the unknown, the uncertain and insecure, using what reason we may have to plan as well as we can for both security *and* freedom.

NOTES

GENERAL REMARKS. The text of the book is self-contained and may be read without these Notes. However, a considerable amount of material which is likely to interest all readers of the book will be found here, as well as some references and controversies which may not be of general interest. Readers who wish to consult the notes for the sake of this material may find it convenient first to read without interruption through the text of a chapter, and then to turn to the Notes.

I wish to apologize for the perhaps excessive number of cross references which have been included for the benefit of those readers who take a special interest in one or other of the side issues touched upon (such as Plato's preoccupation with racialism, or the Socratic Problem). Knowing that war conditions would make it impossible for me to read the proofs, I decided to refer not to pages but to note numbers. Accordingly, references to the text have been indicated by notes such as : ' cp. text to note 24 to chapter 3 ', etc. War conditions also restricted library facilities, making it impossible for me to obtain a number of books, some recent and some not, which would have been consulted in normal circumstances.

* Notes which make use of material which was not available to me when writing the manuscript for the first edition of this book (and other notes which I wish to characterize as having been added to the book since 1943) are enclosed by asterisks ; not all new additions to the notes have, however, been so marked.*

NOTE TO THE INTRODUCTION

For Kant's motto, see note 41 to chapter 24, and text.

The terms ' *open society* ' and ' *closed society* ' were first used, to my knowledge, by Henri Bergson, in *Two Sources of Morality and Religion* (Engl. ed., 1935). In spite of a considerable difference (due to a fundamentally different approach to nearly every problem of philosophy) between Bergson's way of using these terms and mine, there is a certain similarity also, which I wish to acknowledge. (Cp. Bergson's characterization of the closed society, *op. cit.*, p. 229, as ' human society fresh from the hands of nature '.) The main difference, however, is this. My terms indicate, as it were, a *rationalist distinction* ; the closed society is characterized by the belief in magical taboos, while the open society is one in which men have learned to be to some extent critical of taboos, and to base decisions on the authority of their own intelligence (after discussion). Bergson, on the other hand, has a kind of *religious distinction* in mind. This explains why he can look upon his open society as the product of a mystical intuition, while I suggest (in chapters 10 and 24) that mysticism may be interpreted as an expression of the longing for the lost unity of the closed society, and therefore as a reaction against the rationalism of the open society. From the way my term ' The Open Society ' is used in chapter 10, it may be seen that there is some resemblance to Graham Wallas' term 'The Great Society'; but my term may cover a 'small society' too, as it were, like that of Periclean Athens, while it is perhaps conceivable that a 'Great Society' may be arrested and thereby closed. There is also, perhaps, a similarity between my 'open society' and the term used by Walter Lippmann as the title of his most admirable book, *The Good Society* (1937). See also notes 59 (2) to chapter 10 and notes 29, 32, and 58 to chapter 24, and text.

NOTES TO CHAPTER 1

For Pericles' motto, see note 31 to chapter 10, and text. Plato's motto is discussed in some detail in notes 33 and 34 to chapter 6, and text.

[1] I use the term 'collectivism' only for a doctrine which emphasizes the significance of some collective or group, for instance, 'the state' (or a certain state; or a nation; or a class) as against that of the individual. The problem of collectivism versus individualism is explained more fully in chapter 6, below; see especially notes 26 to 28 to that chapter, and text.—Concerning 'tribalism', cp. chapter 10, and especially note 38 to that chapter (list of Pythagorean tribal taboos).

[2] This means that the interpretation does not convey any empirical information, as shown in my *The Logic of Scientific Discovery*.

[3] One of the features which the doctrines of the chosen people, the chosen race, and the chosen class have in common is that they originated, and became important, as reactions against some kind of oppression. The doctrine of the chosen people became important at the time of the foundation of the Jewish church, i.e. during the Babylonian captivity; Count Gobineau's theory of the Aryan master race was a reaction of the aristocratic emigrant to the claim that the French Revolution had successfully expelled the Teutonic masters. Marx's prophecy of the victory of the proletariat is his reply to one of the most sinister periods of oppression and exploitation in modern history. Compare with these matters chapter 10, especially note 39, and chapter 17, especially notes 13–15, and text.

[*] One of the briefest and best summaries of the historicist creed can be found in the radically historicist pamphlet which is quoted more fully at the end of note 12 to chapter 9, entitled *Christians in the Class Struggle*, by Gilbert Cope, Foreword by the Bishop of Bradford. ('Magnificat' Publication No. 1, Published by the Council of Clergy and Ministers for Common Ownership, 1942, 28, Maypole Lane, Birmingham 14.) Here we read, on pp. 5–6: 'Common to all these views is a certain quality of "inevitability plus freedom". Biological evolution, the class conflict succession, the action of the Holy Spirit —all three are characterized by a definite motion towards an end. That motion may be hindered or deflected for a time by deliberate human action, but its gathering momentum cannot be dissipated, and though the final stage is but dimly apprehended, . .' it is 'possible to know enough about the process to help forward or to delay the inevitable flow. In other words, the natural laws of what we observe to be "progress" are sufficiently . . understood by men so that they can . . either . . make efforts to arrest or divert the main stream—efforts which may seem to be successful for a time, but which are in fact foredoomed to failure.' [*]

[4] Hegel said that, in his Logic, he had preserved the whole of Heraclitus' teaching. He also said that he owed everything to Plato. [*] It may be worth mentioning that Ferdinand von Lassalle, one of the founders of the German social democratic movement (and, like Marx, a Hegelian), wrote two volumes on Heraclitus. [*]

NOTES TO CHAPTER 2

[1] The question ' What is the world made of? ' is more or less generally accepted as the fundamental problem of the early Ionian philosophers. I we assume that they viewed the world as an edifice, the question of the ground-plan of the world would be complementary to that of its building material. And indeed, we hear that Thales was not only interested in the stuff the world is made of, but also in descriptive astronomy and geography, and that Anaximander was the first to draw up a ground-plan, i.e. a map of the earth. Some further remarks on the Ionian school (and especially on Anaximander as predecessor of Heraclitus) will be found in chapter 10 ; cp. notes 38–40 to that chapter, especially note 39.

* According to R. Eisler, *Weltenmantel und Himmelszelt*, p. 693, Homer's feeling of destiny (' moira ') can be traced back to oriental astral mysticism which deifies time, space, and fate. According to the same author (*Revue de Synthèse Historique*, 41, app., p. 16 f.), Hesiod's father was a native of Asia Minor, and the sources of his idea of the Golden Age, and the metals in man, are oriental. (Cp. on this question Eisler's forthcoming posthumous study of Plato, Oxford 1950.) Eisler also shows (*Jesus Basileus*, vol. II, 618 f.) that the idea of the world as a totality of things (' cosmos ') goes back to Babylonian political theory. The idea of the world as an edifice (a house or tent) is treated in his *Weltenmantel*.*

[2] See Diels, *Die Vorsokratiker*, 5th edition, 1934 (abbreviated here as ' D^5 '), fragment 124 ; cp. also D^5, vol. II, p. 423, lines 21 f. (The interpolated negation seems to me methodologically as unsound as the attempt of certain authors to discredit the fragment altogether ; apart from this, I follow Rüstow's emendation.) For the two other quotations in this paragraph, see Plato, *Cratylus*, 401d, 402a/b.

My interpretation of the teaching of Heraclitus is perhaps different from that commonly assumed at present, for instance from that of Burnet. Those who may feel doubtful whether it is at all tenable are referred to my notes, especially the present note and notes 6, 7, and 11, in which I am dealing with Heraclitus' natural philosophy, having confined my text to a presentation of the historicist aspect of Heraclitus' teaching and to his social philosophy. I further refer them to the evidence of chapters 4 to 9, and especially of chapter 10, in whose light Heraclitus' philosophy, as I see it, appears as a somewhat typical reaction to the social revolution which he witnessed. Cp. also the notes 39 and 59 to that chapter (and text), and the general criticism of Burnet's and Taylor's methods in note 56.

As indicated in the text, I hold (with many others, for instance, with Zeller and Grote) that the doctrine of universal flux is the central doctrine of Heraclitus. As opposed to this, Burnet holds that this ' is hardly the central point in the system ' of Heraclitus (cp. *Early Greek Philosophy*, 2nd ed., 163). But a close inspection of his arguments (158 f.) leaves me quite unconvinced that Heraclitus' fundamental discovery was the abstract metaphysical doctrine ' that wisdom is not the knowledge of many things, but the perception of the underlying unity of warring opposites ', as Burnet puts it. The unity of opposites is certainly an important part of Heraclitus' teaching, but it can be derived (as far as such things can be derived ; cp. note 11 to this chapter, and the corresponding text) from the more concrete and intuitively understandable theory of flux ; and the same can be said of Heraclitus' doctrine of the fire (cp. note 7 to this chapter).

Those who suggest, with Burnet, that the doctrine of universal flux was not new, but anticipated by the earlier Ionians, are, I feel, unconscious witnesses to Heraclitus' originality ; for they fail now, after 2,400 years, to grasp his main point. They do not see the difference between a flux or circulation *within* a vessel or an edifice or a cosmic framework, i.e. *within a totality of things* (part of the Heraclitean theory can indeed be understood in this way, but only that part of it which is not very original ; see below), and a universal flux which embraces everything, even the vessel, the framework itself (cp. Lucian in D⁵ I, p. 190) and which is described by Heraclitus' denial of the existence of any fixed thing whatever. (In a way, Anaximander had made a beginning by dissolving the framework, but there was still a long way from this to the theory of universal flux. Cp. also note 15 (4) to chapter 3.)

The doctrine of universal flux forces Heraclitus to attempt an explanation of the *apparent stability* of the things in this world, and of other typical regularities. This attempt leads him to the development of subsidiary theories, especially to his doctrine of fire (cp. note 7 to this chapter) and of natural laws (cp. note 6). It is in this explanation of the apparent stability of the world that he makes much use of the theories of his predecessors by developing their theory of rarefaction and condensation, together with their doctrine of the revolution of the heavens, into a general theory of the circulation of matter, and of periodicity. But this part of his teaching, I hold, is not central to it, but subsidiary. It is, so to speak, apologetic, for it attempts to reconcile the new and revolutionary doctrine of flux with common experience as well as with the teaching of his predecessors. I believe, therefore, that he is not a mechanical materialist who teaches something like the conservation and circulation of matter and of energy ; this view seems to me to be excluded by his magical attitude towards laws as well as by his theory of the unity of opposites which emphasizes his mysticism.

My contention that the universal flux is the central theory of Heraclitus is, I believe, corroborated by Plato. The overwhelming majority of his explicit references to Heraclitus (*Crat.*, 401d, 402a/b, 411, 437 ff., 440 ; *Theaet.*, 153c/d, 160d, 177c, 179d f., 182a ff., 183a ff., cp. also *Symp.*, 207d, *Phil.*, 43a ; cp. also Aristotle's *Metaphysics*, 987a33, 1010a13, 1078b13) witness to the tremendous impression made by this central doctrine upon the thinkers of that period. These straightforward and clear testimonies are much stronger than the admittedly interesting passage which does not mention Heraclitus' name (*Soph.*, 242d f., quoted already, in connection with Heraclitus, by Ueberweg and Zeller), on which Burnet attempts to base his interpretation. (His other witness, Philo Judaeus, cannot count much as against the evidence of Plato and Aristotle.) But even this passage agrees completely with our interpretation. (With regard to Burnet's somewhat wavering judgement concerning the value of this passage, cp. note 56 (7) to chapter 10.) Heraclitus' discovery that the world is not the totality of *things* but of events or *facts* is not at all trivial ; this can be perhaps gauged by the fact that Wittgenstein has found it necessary to reaffirm it quite recently : ' The world is the totality of facts, *not of things*.' (Cp. *Tractatus Logico-Philosophicus*, 1921/22, sentence 1.1 ; italics mine.)

To sum up. I consider the doctrine of universal flux as fundamental, and as emerging from the realm of Heraclitus' social experiences. All other doctrines of his are in a way subsidiary to it. The doctrine of fire (cp. Aristotle's *Metaphysics*, 984a7, 1067a2 ; also 989a2, 996a9, 1001a15 ; *Physics*, 205a3) I consider to be his central doctrine in the field of natural philosophy ; it is an attempt to reconcile the doctrine of flux with our experience of stable things, a link with the older theories of circulation, and it leads to a theory of laws. And the doctrine of the unity of opposites I consider as something less central and more abstract, as a forerunner of a kind of logical or methodological theory (as such it inspired Aristotle to formulate his law of contradiction), and as linked to his mysticism.

³ W. Nestle, *Die Vorsokratiker* (1905). 35.

⁴ In order to facilitate the identification of the fragments quoted, I give the numbers of Bywater's edition (adopted, in his English translation of the fragments, by Burnet, *Early Greek Philosophy*), and also the numbers of Diels' 5th edition.

Of the eight passages quoted in the present paragraph, (1) and (2) are from the fragments B 114 (= Bywater, and Burnet), D⁵ 121 (= Diels, 5th edition). The others are from the fragments : (3) B 111, D⁵ 29 ; cp. Plato's *Republic*, 586a/b . . . (4) : B 111, D⁵ 104 . . . (5) : B 112, D⁵ 39 (cp. D⁵, vol. I, p. 65, Bias, 1) . . . (6) : B 5, D⁵ 17 . . . (7) : B 110, D⁵ 33 . . . (8) : B 100, D⁵ 44.

⁵ The three passages quoted in this paragraph are from the fragments : (1) and (2) : cp. B 41, D⁵ 91 ; for (1) cp. also note 2 to this chapter. (3) : D⁵ 74.

⁶ The two passages are B 21, D⁵ 31 ; and B 22, D⁵ 90.

⁷ For Heraclitus' ' measures ' (or laws, or periods), see B 20, 21, 23, 29 ; D⁵ 30, 31, 94. (D 31 brings ' measure ' and ' law ' (*logos*) together.)

The five passages quoted later in this paragraph are from the fragments : (1) : D⁵, vol. I, p. 141, line 10. (Cp. *Diog. Laert.*, IX, 7.) . . . (2) : B 29, D⁵ 94 (cp. note 2 to chapter 5) . . . (3) : B 34, D⁵ 100 . . . (4) : B 20, D⁵ 30 . . . (5) : B 26, D⁵ 66.

(1) The idea of law is *correlative* to that of change or flux, since only laws or regularities within the flux can explain the apparent stability of the world. The most typical regularities within the changing world known to man are the natural periods : the day, the moon-month, and the year (the seasons). Heraclitus' theory of law is, I believe, logically intermediate between the comparatively modern views of ' causal laws ' (held by Leucippus and especially by Democritus) and Anaximander's dark powers of fate. Heraclitus' laws are still ' magical ', i.e. he has not yet distinguished between abstract causal regularities and laws enforced, like taboos, by sanctions (with this, cp. chapter 5, note 2). It appears that his theory of fate was connected with a theory of a ' Great Year ' or ' Great Cycle ' of 18,000 or 36,000 ordinary years. (Cp. for instance J. Adam's edition of *The Republic of Plato*, vol. II, 303.) I certainly do not think that this theory is an indication that Heraclitus did not really believe in a universal flux, but only in various circulations which always re-established the stability of the framework ; but I think it possible that he had difficulties in conceiving a law of change, and even of fate, other than one involving a certain amount of periodicity. (Cp. also note 6 to chapter 3.)

(2) Fire plays a central rôle in Heraclitus' philosophy of nature. (There may be some Persian influence here.) The flame is the obvious symbol of a flux or *process which appears in many respects as a thing*. It thus explains the experience of stable things, and reconciles this experience with the doctrine of flux. This idea can easily be extended to living bodies which are like flames, only burning more slowly. Heraclitus teaches that *all* things are in flux, *all* are like fire ; their flux has only different ' measures ' or laws of motion. The ' bowl ' or ' trough ' in which the fire burns will be in a much slower flux than the fire, but it will be in flux nevertheless. It changes, it has its fate and its laws, it must be burned into by the fire, and consumed, even if it takes a longer time before its fate is fulfilled. Thus, ' in its advance, the fire will judge and convict everything ' (B 26, D⁵ 66).

Accordingly, the fire is the symbol and the explanation of the apparent rest of things in spite of their real state of flux. But it is also a symbol of the transmutation of matter from one stage (fuel) into another. It thus provides the link between Heraclitus' intuitive theory of nature and the theories of rarefaction and condensation. etc., of his predecessors. But its flaring up and dying down, in accordance with the measure of fuel provided, is also an instance of a law. If this is combined with some form of periodicity, then it can be used to explain the regularities of natural periods, such as days or years. (This trend of thought renders it unlikely that Burnet is right in disbelieving the traditional reports of Heraclitus' belief in a periodical conflagration, which was probably connected with his Great Year ; cp. Aristotle, *Physics*, 205a3 with D⁵ 66.)

⁸ The thirteen passages quoted in this paragraph are from the fragments. (1) : B 10, D⁵ 123 . . . (2) : B 11, D⁵ 93 . . . (3) : B 16, D⁵ 40 . . . (4) : B 94, D⁵ 73 . . . (5) : B 95, D⁵ 89 . . . with (4) and (5), cp. Plato's *Republic*, 476c f., and 520c . . . (6) : B 6, D⁵ 19 . . . (7) : B 3, D⁵ 34 . . . (8) : B 19, D⁵ 41 . . . (9) : B 92, D⁵ 2 . . . (10) : B 91a, D⁵ 113 . . . (11) : B 59, D⁵ 10 . . . (12) : B 65, D⁵ 32 . . . (13) : B 28, D⁵ 64.

⁹ More consistent than most moral historicists, Heraclitus is also an ethical and juridical positivist (for this term, cp. chapter 5) : ' All things are, to the gods, fair and good and right ; men, however, have taken up some things as wrong, and some as right.' (D⁵ 102, B 61 ; see passage (8) in note 11.) That he was the first juridical positivist is attested by Plato (*Theaet.*, 177c/d). On moral and juridical positivism in general, cp. chapter 5 (text to notes 14–18) and chapter 22.

¹⁰ The two passages quoted in this paragraph are : (1) : B 44, D⁵ 53 . . . (2) : B 62, D⁵ 80.

¹¹ The nine passages quoted in this paragraph are : (1) : B 39, D⁵ 126 . . . (2) : B 104, D⁵ 111 . . . (3) : B 78, D⁵ 88 . . . (4) : B 45, D⁵ 51 . . . (5) : D⁵ 8 . . . (6) : B 69, D⁵ 60 . . . (7) : B 50, D⁵ 59 . . . (8) : B 61, D⁵ 102 (cp. note 9) . . . (9) : B 57, D⁵ 58. (Cp. Aristotle, *Physics*, 185b20.)

Flux or change must be the transition from one stage or property or position to another. In so far as flux presupposes something that changes, this something must remain identically the same, even though it assumes an opposite stage or property or position. This links the theory of flux to that of the unity of opposites (cp. Aristotle, *Metaphysics*, 1005b25, 1024a24 and 34, 1062a32, 1063a25) as well as the doctrine of the oneness of all things ; they are all only different phases or appearances of the one changing something (of fire).

Whether ' the path that leads up ' and ' the path that leads down ' were originally conceived as an ordinary path leading first up a mountain, and later down again (or perhaps : leading up from the point of view of the man who is down, and down from that of the man who is up), and whether this metaphor was only later applied to the processes of circulation, to the path that leads up from earth through water (perhaps liquid fuel in a bowl ?) to the fire, and down again from the fire through the water (rain ?) to earth ; or whether Heraclitus' path up and down was originally applied by him to this process of circulation of matter ; all this can of course not be decided. (But I think that the first alternative is more likely in view of the great number of similar ideas in Heraclitus' fragments : cp. the text.)

¹² The four passages are : (1) : B 102, D⁵ 24 . . . (2) : B 101, D⁵ 25 (a closer version which more or less preserves Heraclitus' pun is : ' Greater death wins greater destiny.' Cp. also Plato's *Laws*, 903 d/e ; contrast with *Rep.* 617 d/e) . . . (3) : B 111, D⁵ 29 (part of the continuation is quoted above ; see passage (3) in note 4) . . . (4) : B 113, D⁵ 49.

¹³ It seems very probable (cp. Meyer's *Gesch. d. Altertums*, esp. vol. I) that such characteristic teachings as that of the chosen people originated in this period, which produced several other religions of salvation besides the Jewish.

¹⁴ Comte, who in France developed a historicist philosophy not very dissimilar from Hegel's Prussian version, tried, like Hegel, to stem the revolutionary tide. (Cp. F. A. von Hayek, *The Counter-Revolution of Science, Economica*,

N.S. vol. VIII, 1941, pp. 119 ff, 281 ff.)   For Lassalle's interest in Heraclitus, see
note 4 to chapter 1.—It is interesting to note, in this connection, the parallelism between the history of historicist and of evolutionary ideas.   They
originated in Greece with the semi-Heraclitean Empedocles (for Plato's
version, see note 1 to chapter 11), and they were revived, in England as
well as in France, in the time of the French Revolution.

NOTES TO CHAPTER 3

[1] With this explanation of the term oligarchy, cp. also the end of notes
44 and 57 to chapter 8.

[2] Cp. especially note 48 to chapter 10.

[3] Cp. the end of chapter 7, esp. note 25, and chapter 10, esp. note 69.

[4] Cp. *Diogenes Laert.*, III, 1.—Concerning Plato's family connections, and
especially the alleged descent of his father's family from Codrus, ' and even
from the God Poseidon ', see G. Grote, *Plato and other Companions of Socrates*
(ed. 1875), vol. I, 114.   (See, however, the similar remark on Critias' family,
i.e. on that of Plato's mother, in E. Meyer, *Geschichte des Altertums*, vol. V,
1922, p. 66.)   Plato says of Codrus in the *Symposium* (208d) : ' Do you suppose
that Alcestis, . . . or Achilles, . . . or that your own Codrus would have
sought death—*in order to save the kingship for his children*—had they not expected
to win that immortal memory of their virtue in which indeed we keep them ? '
Plato praises Critias' (i.e. his mother's) family in the early *Charmides* (157e ff.)
and in the late *Timaeus* (20e), where the family is traced back to the Athenian
ruler (*archōn*) Dropides, the friend of Solon.

[5] The two autobiographical quotations which follow in this paragraph are
from the *Seventh Letter* (325).   Plato's authorship of the *Letters* has been questioned by some eminent scholars (perhaps without sufficient foundation ;
I think Field's treatment of this problem very convincing ; cp. note 57 to
chapter 10 ; on the other hand, even the *Seventh Letter* looks to me a little
suspicious—it repeats too much what we know from the *Apology*, and says
too much what the occasion requires).   I have therefore taken care to base
my interpretation of Platonism mainly on some of the most famous dialogues ;
it is, however, in general agreement with the *Letters*.   For the reader's con-
venience, a list of those Platonic dialogues which are frequently mentioned
in the text may be given here, in what is their probable historical order ;
cp. note 56 (8) to chapter 10.   *Crito—Apology—Eutyphro* ; *Protagoras—Meno
—Gorgias* ; *Cratylus—Menexenus—Phaedo* ; *Republic* ; *Parmenides—Theaetetus* ;
Sophist—Statesman (or *Politicus*)—*Philebus* ; *Timaeus—Critias* ; *Laws*.

[6] (1) That *historical* developments may have a *cyclic* character is nowhere
very clearly stated by Plato.   It is, however, alluded to in at least four
dialogues, namely in the *Phaedo*, in the *Republic*, in the *Statesman* (or *Politicus*),
and in the *Laws*.   In all these places, Plato's theory may possibly allude to
Heraclitus' Great Year (cp. note 6 to chapter 2).   It may be, however, that
the allusion is not to Heraclitus directly, but rather to Empedocles, whose
theory (cp. also Aristotle, *Met.*, 1000a25 f.) Plato considered as merely a
' milder ' version of the Heraclitean theory of the unity of all flux.   He
expresses this in a famous passage of the *Sophist* (242e f.).   According to this
passage, and to Aristotle (*De Gen. Corr.*, B, 6., 334a6), there is a historical cycle
embracing a period in which love rules, and a period in which Heraclitus'
strife rules ; and Aristotle tells us that, according to Empedocles, the present
period is ' now a period of the reign of Strife, as it was formerly one of Love '.
This insistence that the flux of our own cosmic period is a kind of strife, and
therefore bad, is in close accordance both with Plato's theories and with
his experiences.

The length of the Great Year is, probably, the period of time after which *all* heavenly bodies return to the same positions relative to each other as were held by them at the moment from which the period is reckoned. (This would make it the smallest common multiple of the periods of the ' seven planets '.)

(2) The passage in the *Phaedo* mentioned under (1) alludes first to the Heraclitean theory of change leading from one state to its opposite state, or from one opposite to the other : ' that which becomes less must once have been greater . . ' (70e/71a). It then proceeds to indicate a cyclic law of development : ' Are there not two processes which are ever going on, from one extreme to its opposite, and back again . . ? ' (*loc. cit.*). And a little later (72a/b) the argument is put like this : ' If the development were in a straight line only, and there were no compensation or cycle in nature, . . then, in the end, all things would take on the same properties . . and there would be no further development.' It appears that the general tendency of the *Phaedo* is more optimistic (and shows more faith in man and in human reason) than that of the later dialogues, but there are no direct references to human historical development.

(3) Such references are, however, made in the *Republic* where, in Books VIII and IX, we find an elaborate description of historical decay treated here in chapter 4. This description is introduced by Plato's Story of the Fall of Man and of the Number, which will here be discussed more fully in chapters 5 and 8. J. Adam, in his edition of *The Republic of Plato* (1902, 1921), rightly calls this story ' the setting in which Plato's " Philosophy of History " is framed ' (vol. II, 210). This story does not contain any explicit statement on the cyclic character of history, but it contains a few rather mysterious hints which, according to Aristotle's (and Adam's) interesting but uncertain interpretation, are possibly allusions to the Heraclitean Great Year, i.e. to the cyclic development. (Cp. note 6 to chapter 2, and Adam, *op. cit.*, vol. II, 303 ; the remark on Empedocles made there, 303 f., needs correction ; see (1) in this note, above.)

(4) There is, furthermore, the myth in the *Statesman* (268e–274e). According to this myth, God himself steers the world for half a cycle of the great world period. When he lets go, then the world, which so far has moved forward, begins to roll back again. Thus we have two half-periods or half-cycles in the full cycle, a forward movement led by God constituting the good period without war or strife, and a backward movement when God abandons the world, which is a period of increasing disorganization and strife. It is, of course, the period in which we live. Ultimately, things will become so bad that God will take the wheel again, and reverse the motion, in order to save the world from utter destruction.

This myth shows great resemblances to Empedocles' myth mentioned in (1) above, and probably also to Heraclitus' Great Year.—Adam (*op. cit.*, vol. II, 296 f.) also points out the similarities with Hesiod's story. * One of the points which allude to Hesiod is the reference to a Golden Age of Cronos ; and it is important to note that the men of this age are earth-born. This establishes a point of contact with the Myth of the Earth-born, and of the metals in man, which plays a rôle in the *Republic* (414b ff. and 546e f.) ; this rôle is discussed below in chapter 8. The Myth of the Earth-born is also alluded to in the *Symposium* (191b) ; possibly the allusion is to the popular claim that the Athenians are ' like grasshoppers '—autochthonous (cp. notes 32 (1)e to chapter 4 and 11 (2) to chapter 8).*

When, however, later in the *Statesman* (302b ff.) the six forms of imperfect government are ordered according to their degree of imperfection, there is no indication any longer to be found of a cyclic theory of history. Rather, the six forms, which are all degenerate copies of the perfect or best state (*Statesman*, 293d/e ; 297c ; 303b), appear all as steps in the process of degeneration ;

i.e. both here and in the *Republic* Plato confines himself, when it comes to more concrete historical problems, to that part of the cycle which leads to decay.

* (5) Analogous remarks hold for the *Laws*. Something like a cyclic theory is sketched in Book III, 676b/c–677b, where Plato turns to a more detailed analysis of the beginning of one of the cycles ; and in 678e and 679c, this beginning turns out to be a Golden Age, so that the further story again becomes one of deterioration.—It may be mentioned that Plato's doctrine, that the planets are gods, together with the doctrine that the gods influence human lives (and with his belief that cosmic forces are at work in history), played an important part in the astrological speculations of the neo-Platonists. All three doctrines can be found in the *Laws* (see, for example, 821b–d and 899b ; 899d–905d ; 677a ff.). Astrology, it should be realized, shares with historicism the belief in a determinate destiny which can be predicted ; and it shares with some important versions of historicism (especially with Platonism and Marxism) the belief that, notwithstanding the possibility of predicting the future, we have some influence upon it, especially if we actually know what is coming.*

(6) Apart from these scanty allusions, there is hardly anything to indicate that Plato took the upward or forward part of the cycle seriously. But there are many remarks, apart from the elaborate description in the *Republic* and that quoted in (5), which show that he believed very seriously in the downward movement, in the decay of history. We must consider, especially, the *Timaeus*, and the *Laws*.

(7) In the *Timaeus* (42b f., 90e ff., and especially 91d f. ; cp. also the *Phaedrus*, 248d f.), Plato describes what may be called the origin of species by degeneration (cp. text to note 4 to chapter 4, and note 11 to chapter 11) : Men degenerate into women, and later into lower animals.

(8) In Book III of the *Laws* (cp. also Book IV, 713a ff. ; see however the short allusion to a cycle mentioned above) we have a rather elaborate theory of historical decay, largely analogous to that in the *Republic*. See also the next chapter, especially notes 3, 6, 7, 27, 31, and 44.

⁷ A similar opinion of Plato's political aims is expressed by G. C. Field, *Plato and His Contemporaries* (1930), p. 91 : ' The chief aim of Plato's philosophy may be regarded as the attempt to re-establish standards of thought and conduct for a civilization that seemed on the verge of dissolution.' See also note 3 to chapter 6, and text.

⁸ I follow the majority of the older and a good number of contemporary authorities (e.g. G. C. Field, F. M. Cornford, A. K. Rogers) in believing, against John Burnet and A. E. Taylor, that the theory of Forms or Ideas is nearly entirely Plato's, and not Socrates', in spite of the fact that Plato puts it into the mouth of Socrates as his main speaker. Though Plato's dialogues are our only first-rate source for Socrates' teaching, it is, I believe, possible to distinguish in them between ' Socratic ', i.e. historically true, and ' Platonic ' features of Plato's speaker ' Socrates '. The so-called *Socratic Problem* is discussed in chapters 6, 7, 8, and 10 ; cp. especially note 56 to chapter 10.

⁹ The term ' social engineering ' seems to have been used first by Roscoe Pound, in his *Introduction to the Philosophy of Law* (1922, p. 99 ;* Bryan Magee tells me now that the Webbs used it almost certainly before 1922.*) He uses the term in the ' piecemeal ' sense. In another sense it is used by M. Eastman, *Marxism : is it Science?* (1940). I read Eastman's book after the text of my own book was written ; my term ' social engineering ' is, accordingly, used without any intention of alluding to Eastman's terminology. As far as I can see, he advocates the approach which I criticize in chapter 9 under the name ' Utopian social engineering ' ; cp. note 1 to that chapter.—See also note 18 (3) to chapter 5. As the first social engineer one might describe the

town-planner Hippodamus of Miletus.   (Cp. Aristotle's *Politics* 1276b22, and R. Eisler, *Jesus Basileus*, II, p. 754.)

The term 'social technology' has been suggested to me by C. G. F. Simkin.—I wish to make it clear that in discussing problems of method, my main emphasis is upon gaining practical institutional experience. Cp. chapter 9, especially text to note 8 to that chapter. For a more detailed analysis of the problems of method connected with social engineering and social technology, see my *The Poverty of Historicism* (2nd edition, 1960), part III.

[10] The quoted passage is from my *The Poverty of Historicism*, p. 65.   The 'undesigned results of human actions' are more fully discussed below, in chapter 14, see especially note 11 and text.

[11] I believe in a dualism of facts and decisions or demands (or of 'is' and 'ought') ; in other words, I believe in the impossibility of reducing decisions or demands to facts, although they can, of course, be treated as facts.   More on this point will be said in chapters 5 (text to notes 4–5), 22, and 24.

[12] Evidence in support of this interpretation of Plato's theory of the best state will be supplied in the next three chapters ; I may refer, in the meanwhile, to *Statesman*, 293d/e ; 297c ; *Laws*, 713b/c ; 739d/e ; *Timaeus*, 22d ff., especially 25e and 26d.

[13] Cp. Aristotle's famous report, partly quoted later in this chapter (see especially note 25 to this chapter, and the text).

[14] This is shown in Grote's *Plato*, vol. III, note *u* on p. 267 f.

[15] The quotations are from the *Timaeus*, 50c/d and 51e–52b.   The simile which describes the Forms or Ideas as the fathers, and Space as the mother, of the sensible things, is important and has far-reaching connections.   Cp. also notes 17 and 19 to this chapter, and note 59 to chapter 10.

(1) It resembles Hesiod's *myth of chaos*, the yawning gap (space ; receptacle) which corresponds to the mother, and the God Eros, who corresponds to the father or to the Ideas.   Chaos is the origin, and the question of the causal explanation (chaos = cause) remains for a long time one of origin (archē) or birth or generation.

(2) The mother or space corresponds to the indefinite or boundless of Anaximander and of the Pythagoreans.   The Idea, which is male, must therefore correspond to the definite (or limited) of the Pythagoreans.   For the definite, as opposed to the boundless, the male, as opposed to the female, the light, as opposed to the dark, and the good, as opposed to the bad, all belong to the same side in the *Pythagorean table of opposites*.   (Cp. Aristotle's *Metaphysics*, 986a22 f.)   We also can therefore expect to see the Ideas associated with light and goodness.   (Cp. end of note 32 to chapter 8.)

(3) The Ideas are boundaries or limits, they are definite, as opposed to indefinite Space, and impress or imprint (cp. note 17 (2) to this chapter) themselves like rubber-stamps, or better, like moulds, upon Space (which is not only space but at the same time Anaximander's unformed matter— stuff without property), thus generating sensible things.   * J. D. Mabbott has kindly drawn my attention to the fact that the Forms or Ideas, according to Plato, do not impress themselves upon Space but are, rather, impressed or imprinted upon it by the Demiurge.   Traces of the theory that the Forms are 'causes both of being and of generation (or becoming)' can be found already in the *Phaedo* (100d), as Aristotle points out (in *Metaphysics* 1080a2).*

(4) In consequence of the act of generation, Space, i.e. the receptacle, begins to labour, so that all things are set in motion, in a Heraclitean or Empedoclean flux which is really universal in so far as the movement or flux extends even to the framework, i.e. (boundless) space itself.   (For the late Heraclitean idea of the receptacle, cp. the *Cratylus*, 412d.)

(5) This description is also reminiscent of Parmenides' ' Way of Delusive

Opinion', in which the world of experience and of flux is created by the mingling of two opposites, the light (or hot or fire) and the dark (or cold or earth). It is clear that Plato's Forms or Ideas would correspond to the former, and space or what is boundless to the latter ; especially if we consider that Plato's pure space is closely akin to indeterminate matter.

(6) The opposition between the determinate and indeterminate seems also to correspond, especially after the all-important discovery of the irrationality of the square root of two, to the opposition between the rational and the irrational. But since Parmenides identifies the rational with being, this would lead to an interpretation of space or the irrational as non-being. In other words, the Pythagorean table of opposites is to be extended to cover rationality, as opposed to irrationality, and being, as opposed to non-being. (This agrees with *Metaphysics*, 1004b27, where Aristotle says that ' all the contraries are reducible to being and non-being ' ; 1072a31, where one side of the table—that of being—is described as the object of (rational) thought ; and 1093b13, where the powers of certain numbers—presumably in opposition to their roots—are added to this side. This would further explain Aristotle's remark in *Metaphysics*, 986b27 ; and it would perhaps not be necessary to assume, as F. M. Cornford does in his excellent article ' Parmenides' Two Ways ', *Class. Quart.*, XVII, 1933, p. 108, that Parmenides, fr. 8, 53/54, ' has been misinterpreted by Aristotle and Theophrastus ' ; for if we expand the table of opposites in this way, Cornford's most convincing interpretation of the crucial passage of fr. 8 becomes compatible with Aristotle's remark.)

(7) Cornford has explained (*op. cit.*, 100) that there are three ' ways ' in Parmenides, the way of Truth, the way of Not-being, and the way of Seeming (or, if I may call it so, of delusive opinion). He shows (101) that they correspond to three regions discussed in the *Republic*, the perfectly real and rational world of the Ideas, the perfectly unreal, and the world of opinion (based on the perception of things in flux). He has also shown (102) that in the *Sophist*, Plato modifies his position. To this, some comments may be added from the point of view of the passages in the *Timaeus* to which this note is appended.

(8) The main difference between the Forms or Ideas of the *Republic* and those of the *Timaeus* is that in the former, the Forms (and also God ; cp. *Rep.*, 380d) are petrified, so to speak, while in the latter, they are deified. In the former, they bear a much closer resemblance to the Parmenidean One (cp. Adam's note to *Rep.*, 380d28, 31), than in the latter. This development leads to the *Laws*, where the Ideas are largely replaced by souls. The decisive difference is that the Ideas become more and more the starting points of motion and causes of generation, or as the *Timaeus* puts it, fathers of the moving things. The greatest contrast is perhaps between the *Phaedo*, 79e : ' The soul is infinitely more like the unchangeable ; even the most stupid person would not deny that ' (cp. also *Rep.*, 585c, 609b f.), and the *Laws*, 895e/896a (cp. *Phaedrus*, 245c ff.) : ' What is the definition of that which is named " soul " ? Can we imagine any other definition than . . " The motion that moves itself " ? ' The transition between these two positions is, perhaps, provided by the *Sophist* (which introduces the Form or Idea of motion itself) and by the *Timaeus*, 35a, which describes the ' divine and unchanging ' Forms and the changing and corruptible bodies. This seems to explain why, in the *Laws* (cp. 894d/e), the motion of the soul is said to be ' *first in origin and power* ' and why the soul is described (966e) as ' the most ancient and divine of all things whose motion is an ever-flowing source of real existence '. (Since, according to Plato, *all living things* have souls, it may be claimed that he admitted the presence of an at least partly formal principle in things ; a point of view which is very close to Aristotelianism, especially in the presence of the primitive and widespread belief that all things are alive.) (Cp. also note 7 to chapter 4.)

(9) In this development of Plato's thought, a development whose driving force is to explain the world of flux with the help of the Ideas, i.e. to make the break between the world of reason and the world of opinion at least understandable, even though it cannot be bridged, the *Sophist* seems to play a decisive rôle. Apart from making room, as Cornford mentions (*op. cit.*, 102), for the plurality of Ideas, it presents them, in an argument against Plato's own earlier position (248a ff.) : (*a*) as active causes, which may interact, for example, with mind ; (*b*) as unchanging in spite of that, although there is now an Idea of motion in which all moving things participate and which is not at rest ; (*c*) as capable of mingling with one another. It further introduces ' Not-being ', identified in the *Timaeus* with Space (cp. Cornford, *Plato's Theory of Knowledge*, 1935, note to 247), and thus makes it possible for the Ideas to mingle with it (cp. also *Philolaus*, fr. 2, 3, 5, Diels ⁵), and to produce the world of flux with its characteristic intermediate position between the being of Ideas and the not-being of Space or matter.

(10) Ultimately, I wish to defend my contention in the text that the Ideas are not only outside space, but also outside time, though they are in contact with the world at the beginning of time. This, I believe, makes it easier to understand how they act without being in motion ; for all motion or flux is in space and time. Plato, I believe, assumes that time has a beginning. I think that this is the most direct interpretation of *Laws*, 721c : ' the race of man is twin-born with all time ', considering the many indications that Plato believed man to be created as one of the first creatures. (In this point, I disagree slightly with Cornford, *Plato's Cosmology*, 1937, p. 145, and pp. 26 ff.)

(11) To sum up, the Ideas are earlier and better than their changing and decaying copies, and are themselves not in flux. (See also note 3 to chapter 4.)

¹⁶ Cp. note 4 to this chapter.

¹⁷ (1) The rôle of the gods in the *Timaeus* is similar to the one described in the text. Just as the Ideas stamp out things, so the gods form the *bodies* of men. Only the human *soul* is created by the Demiurge himself who also creates the world and the gods. (For another hint that the gods are patriarchs, see *Laws*, 713c/d.) Men, the weak, degenerate children of gods, are then liable to further degeneration ; cp. note 6 (7) to this chapter, and 37–41 to chapter 5.

(2) In an interesting passage of the *Laws* (681b ; cp. also note 32 (1, a) to chapter 4) we find another allusion to the parallelism between the relation *Idea—things* and the relation *parent—children*. In this passage, the origin of law is explained by the influence of tradition, and more especially, by the transmission of a rigid order from the parents to the children ; and the following remark is made : ' And they (the parents) would be sure to stamp upon their children, and upon their children's children, their own cast of mind.'

¹⁸ Cp. note 49, especially (3), to chapter 8.

¹⁹ Cp. *Timaeus*, 31a. The term which I have freely translated by ' superior thing which is their prototype ' is a term frequently used by Aristotle with the meaning ' universal ' or ' generic term '. It means a ' thing which is general ' or ' surpassing ' or ' embracing ' ; and I suspect that it originally means ' embracing ' or ' covering ' in the sense in which a mould embraces or covers what it moulds.

²⁰ Cp. *Republic*, 597c. See also 596a (and Adam's second note to 596a5) : ' For we are in the habit, you will remember, of postulating a Form or Idea— one for each group of many particular things to which we apply the same name.'

²¹ There are innumerable passages in Plato ; I mention only the *Phaedo*

(e.g. 79a), the *Republic*, 544a, the *Theaetetus* (152d/e, 179d/e), the *Timaeus* (28b/c, 29c/d, 51d f.). Aristotle mentions it in *Metaphysics*, 987a32 ; 999a25–999b10 ; 1010a6–15 ; 1078b15 ; see also notes 23 and 25 to this chapter.

²² Parmenides taught, as Burnet puts it (*Early Greek Philosophy* ², 208), that ' what is . . is finite, spherical, motionless, corporeal ', i.e. that the world is a full globe, a whole without any parts, and that ' there is nothing beyond it '. I am quoting Burnet because (*a*) his description is excellent and (*b*) it destroys his own interpretation (*E.G.P.*, 208–11) of what Parmenides calls the ' Opinion of the Mortals ' (or the Way of Delusive Opinion). For Burnet dismisses there all the interpretations of Aristotle, Theophrastus, Simplicius, Gomperz, and Meyer, as ' anachronisms ' or ' palpable anachronisms ', etc. Now the interpretation dismissed by Burnet is practically the same as the one here proposed in the text ; namely, that Parmenides believed in a world of reality behind this world of appearance. Such a dualism, which would allow Parmenides' description of the world of appearance to claim at least some kind of adequacy, is dismissed by Burnet as hopelessly anachronistic. I suggest, however, that if Parmenides had believed solely in his unmoving world, and not at all in the changing world, then he would have been really mad (as Empedocles hints). But in fact there is an indication of a similar dualism already in Xenophanes, fragm. 23–6, if confronted with fragm. 34 (esp. ' But all may have their fancy opinions '), so that we can hardly speak of an anachronism.—As indicated in note 15 (6–7), I follow Cornford's interpretation of Parmenides. (See also note 41 to chapter 10.)

²³ Cp. Aristotle's *Metaphysics*, 1078b23 ; the next quotation is : *op. cit.*, 1078b19.

²⁴ This valuable comparison is due to G. C. Field, *Plato and His Contemporaries*, 211.

²⁵ The preceding quotation is from Aristotle, *Metaphysics*, 1078b15 ; the next from *op. cit.*, 987b7.

²⁶ In Aristotle's analysis (in *Metaphysics*, 987a30–b18) of the arguments which led to the theory of Ideas (cp. also note 56 (6) to chapter 10), we can distinguish the following steps : (*a*) Heraclitus' flux, (*b*) the impossibility of true knowledge of things in flux, (*c*) the influence of Socrates' ethical essences, (*d*) the Ideas as objects of true knowledge, (*e*) the influence of the Pythagoreans, (*f*) the ' mathematicals ' as intermediate objects.—((*e*) and (*f*) I have not mentioned in the text, where I have mentioned instead (*g*) the Parmenidean influence.)

It may be worth while to show how these steps can be identified in Plato's own work, where he expounds his theory ; especially in the *Phaedo* and in the *Republic*, in the *Theaetetus* and in the *Sophist*, and in the *Timaeus*.

(1) In the *Phaedo*, we find indications of all the points up to and including (*e*). In 65a–66a, the steps (*d*) and (*c*) are prominent, with an allusion to (*b*). In 70e step (*a*), Heraclitus' theory appears, combined with an element of Pythagoreanism (*e*). This leads to 74a ff., and to a statement of step (*d*). 99–100 is an approach to (*d*) through (*c*), etc. For (*a*) to (*d*), cp. also the *Cratylus*, 439c ff.

In the *Republic*, it is of course especially Book VI that corresponds closely to Aristotle's report. (*a*) In the beginning of Book VI, 485a/b (cp. 527a/b), the Heraclitean flux is referred to (and contrasted with the unchanging world of Forms). Plato there speaks of ' a reality which exists for ever and *is exempt from generation and degeneration* '. (Cp. notes 2 (2) and 3 to chapter 4 and note 33 to chapter 8, and text.) The steps (*b*), (*d*) and especially (*f*) play a rather obvious rôle in the famous Simile of the Line (*Rep.*, 509c–511e ; cp. Adam's notes, and his appendix I to Book VII) ; Socrates' ethical influence, i.e. step (*c*), is of course alluded to throughout the *Republic*. It plays an important rôle within the Simile of the Line and especially immediately before, i.e. in 508b ff., where the rôle of the good is emphasized ; see in particular 508b/c : ' This is what I maintain regarding the offspring of the good. What the good has begotten in its own likeness is, in the intelligible world, related to reason (and its objects) in the same way as, in the visible world ', that which is the offspring of the sun, ' is related to sight (and its objects).' Step (e) is implied in (f), but more fully developed in Book VII, in the famous *Curriculum* (cp. especially 523a–527c), which is largely based on the Simile of the Line in Book VI.

(2) In the *Theaetetus*, (a) and (b) are treated extensively ; (c) is mentioned in 174b and 175c. In the *Sophist*, all the steps, including (g), are mentioned, only (e) and (f) being left out ; see especially 247a (step (c)) ; 249c (step (b)) ; 253d/e (step (d).) In the *Philebus*, we find indications of all steps except perhaps (f) ; steps (a) to (d) are especially emphasized in 59a–c.

(3) In the *Timaeus*, all the steps mentioned by Aristotle are indicated, with the possible exception of (c), which is alluded to only indirectly in the introductory recapitulation of the contents of the *Republic*, and in 29d. Step (e) is, as it were, alluded to throughout, since ' Timaeus ' is a ' western ' philosopher and strongly influenced by Pythagoreanism. The other steps occur twice in a form almost completely parallel to Aristotle's account ; first briefly in 28a–29d, and later, with more elaboration, in 48e–55c. Immediately after (a), i.e. a Heraclitean description (49a ff. ; cp. Cornford, *Plato's Cosmology*, 178) of the world in flux, the argument (b) is raised (51c–e) that if we are right in distinguishing between reason (or true knowledge) and mere opinion, we must admit the existence of the unchangeable Forms ; these are (51e f.) introduced next in accordance with step (d). The Heraclitean flux then comes again (as labouring space), but this time it is *explained*, as a consequence of the act of generation. And as a next step (f) appears, in 53c. (I suppose that the 'lines and planes and solids' mentioned by Aristotle in *Metaphysics*, 992b13, refer to 53c ff.)

(4) It seems that this parallelism between the *Timaeus* and Aristotle's report has not been sufficiently emphasized so far ; at least, it is not used by G. C. Field in his excellent and convincing analysis of Aristotle's report (*Plato and His Contemporaries*, 202 ff.). But it would have strengthened Field's arguments (arguments, however, which hardly need strengthening, since they are practically conclusive) against Burnet's and Taylor's views that the Theory of Ideas is Socratic (cp. note 56 to chapter 10). For in the *Timaeus*, Plato does not put this theory into the mouth of Socrates, a fact which according to Burnet's and Taylor's principles should prove that it was not Socrates' theory. (They avoid this inference by claiming that ' Timaeus ' is a Pythagorean, and that he develops not Plato's philosophy but his own. But Aristotle knew Plato personally for twenty years and should have been able to judge these matters ; and he wrote his *Metaphysics* at a time when members of the Academy could have contradicted his presentation of Platonism.)

(5) Burnet writes, in *Greek Philosophy*, I, 155 (cp. also p. xliv of his edition of the *Phaedo*, 1911) : ' the theory of forms in the sense in which it is maintained in the *Phaedo* and *Republic* is wholly absent from what we may fairly regard the most distinctively Platonic of the dialogues, those, namely, in which Socrates is no longer the chief speaker. In that sense it is never even mentioned in any dialogue later than the *Parmenides* . . with the single exception of the *Timaeus* (51c), where the speaker is a Pythagorean.' But if it is maintained in the *Timaeus* in the sense in which it is maintained in the *Republic*, then it is certainly so maintained in the *Sophist*, 257d/e ; and in the *Statesman*, 269c/d ; 286a ; 297b/c, and c/d ; 301a and e ; 302e ; and 303b ; and in the *Philebus*, 15a f., and 59a–d ; and in the *Laws*, 713b, 739d/e, 962c f., 963c ff., and, most important, 965c (cp. *Philebus*, 16d), 965d, and 966a ; see also the next note. (Burnet believes in the genuineness of the *Letters*, especially the *Seventh* ;

but the theory of Ideas is maintained there in 342a ff. ; see also note 56 (5, d) to chapter 10.)

²⁷ Cp. *Laws*, 895d–e. I do not agree with England's note (in his edition of the *Laws*, vol. II, 472) that ' the word " essence " will not help us '. True, if we meant by ' essence ' some important sensible part of the sensible thing (which might perhaps be purified and produced by some distillation), then ' essence ' would be misleading. But the word ' essential ' is widely used in a way which corresponds very well indeed with what we wish to express here ; something opposed to the accidental or unimportant or changing empirical aspect of the thing, whether it is conceived as dwelling in that thing, or in a metaphysical world of Ideas.

I am using the term ' *essentialism* ' in opposition to ' nominalism ', in order to avoid, and to replace, the misleading traditional term ' realism ', wherever it is opposed (not to ' idealism ' but) to ' nominalism '. (See also note 26 ff. to chapter 11, and text, and especially note 38.)

On Plato's application of his essentialist method, for instance, as mentioned in the text, to the theory of the soul, see *Laws*, 895e f., quoted in note 15 (8) to this chapter, and chapter 5, especially note 23. See also, for instance, *Meno*, 86d/e, and *Symposium*, 199c/d.

²⁸ On the theory of causal explanation, cp. my *The Logic of Scientific Discovery*, especially section 12, pp. 59 ff. See also note 6 to chapter 25, below.

²⁹ The theory of language here indicated is that of Semantics, as developed especially by A. Tarski and R. Carnap. Cp. Carnap, *Introduction to Semantics*, 1942, and note 23 to chapter 8.

³⁰ The theory that while the physical sciences are based on a methodological nominalism, the social sciences must adopt essentialist (' realistic ') methods, has been made clear to me by K. Polanyi (in 1925) ; he pointed out, at that time, that a reform of the methodology of the social sciences might conceivably be achieved by abandoning this theory.—The theory is held, to some extent, by most sociologists, especially by J. S. Mill (for instance, *Logic*, VI, ch. VI, 2 ; see also his historicist formulations, e.g. in VI, ch. X, 2, last paragraph : ' The fundamental problem . . of the social science is to find the laws according to which any state of society produces the state which succeeds it . .'), K. Marx (see below) ; M. Weber (cp., for example, his definitions in the beginning of *Methodische Grundlagen der Soziologie*, in *Wirtschaft und Gesellschaft*, I, and in *Ges. Aufsaetze zur Wissenschaftslehre*). G. Simmel, A. Vierkandt, R. M. MacIver, and many more.—The philosophical expression of all these tendencies is E. Husserl's ' Phaenomenology ', a systematic revival of the methodological essentialism of Plato and Aristotle. (See also chapter 11, especially note 44.)

The opposite, the *nominalist* attitude in sociology, can be developed, I think, only as a technological theory of social *institutions*.

In this context, I may mention how I came to trace historicism back to Plato and Heraclitus. In analysing historicism, I found that it needs what I call now methodological essentialism ; i.e. I saw that the typical arguments in favour of essentialism are bound up with historicism (cp. my *The Poverty of Historicism*). This led me to consider the history of essentialism. I was struck by the parallelism between Aristotle's report and the analysis which I had carried out originally without any reference to Platonism. In this way, I was reminded of the rôles of both Heraclitus and Plato in this development.

³¹ R. H. S. Crossman's *Plato To-day* (1937) was the first book (apart from G. Grote's *Plato*) I have found to contain a political interpretation of Plato which is partly similar to my own. See also notes 2–3 to chapter 6, and text. *Since then I have found that similar views of Plato have been expressed by various authors. C. M. Bowra (*Ancient Greek Literature*, 1933) is perhaps the first ; his brief but thorough criticism of Plato (pp. 186–90) is as fair as it is

penetrating.   The others are W. Fite (*The Platonic Legend*, 1934) ; B. Farrington (*Science and Politics in the Ancient World*, 1939) ; A. D. Winspear (*The
Genesis of Plato's Thought*, 1940) ; and H. Kelsen (*Platonic Justice*, 1933 ; now
in *What is Justice ?*, 1957, and *Platonic Love*, in *The American Imago*, vol. 3,
1942).*

NOTES TO CHAPTER 4

[1] Cp. *Republic*, 608e.   See also note 2 (2) to this chapter.

[2] In the *Laws*, the soul—' the most ancient and divine of all things in
motion' (966e)—is described as the 'starting point of all motion' (895b).
(1) With the Platonic theory, Aristotle contrasts his own, according to which
the ' good ' thing is not the starting point, but rather the end or aim of change,
since ' good ' *means* a thing aimed at—*the final cause of change*.   Thus he says of
the Platonists, i.e. of ' those who believe in Forms ', that they agree with
Empedocles (they speak ' in the same way ' as Empedocles) in so far as they
' do not speak as if anything came to pass *for the sake of these* ' (i.e. of things which
are ' good ') ' but as if all *movement started from them* '.   And he points out that
' good ' means therefore to the Platonists not ' a cause *qua* good ', i.e. an aim,
but that ' it is only incidentally a good '.   Cp. *Metaphysics*, 988a35 and b8 ff.
and 1075a, 34/35.   This criticism sounds as if Aristotle had sometimes held
views similar to those of Speusippus, which is indeed Zeller's opinion ; see
note 11 to chapter 11.

(2) Concerning the *movement towards corruption*, mentioned in the text in
this paragraph, and its general significance in the Platonic philosophy, we
must keep in mind the general opposition between the world of unchanging
things or Ideas, and the world of sensible things in flux.   Plato often expresses
this opposition as one between the world of unchanging things and the world
of *corruptible* things, or between *things that are ungenerated, and those that* are
generated and are doomed to *degenerate*, etc. ; see, for instance, *Republic*,
485a/b, quoted in note 26 (1) to chapter 3 and in text to note 33 to chapter 8 ;
Republic, 508d–e ; 527a/b ; and *Republic*, 546a, quoted in text to note 37 to
chapter 5 : ' All things that have been generated must degenerate ' (or
decay).   That this problem of the *generation and corruption* of the world of
things in flux was an important part of the Platonic School tradition is indicated
by the fact that Aristotle devoted a separate treatise to this problem.   Another
interesting indication is the way in which Aristotle talked about these matters
in the introduction to his *Politics*, contained in the concluding sentences of
the *Nicomachean Ethics* (1181b/15) : ' We shall try to . . find what it is that
preserves or corrupts the cities . .'   This passage is significant not only as a
general formulation of what Aristotle considered the main problem of his
Politics, but also because of its striking similarity to an important passage
in the *Laws*, viz. 676a, and 676b/c quoted below in text to notes 6 and 25 to
this chapter.   (See also notes 1, 3, and 24/25 to this chapter ; see note 32 to
chapter 8, and the passage from the *Laws* quoted in note 59 to chapter 8.)

[3] This quotation is from the *Statesman*, 269d.   (See also note 23 to this
chapter.)   For the hierarchy of motions, see *Laws*, 893c–895b.   For the theory
that perfect things (divine ' natures ' ; cp. the next chapter) can only become
less perfect when they change, see especially *Republic*, 380e–381c—in many
ways (note the examples in 380e) a parallel passage to *Laws*, 797d.   The
quotations from Aristotle are from the *Metaphysics*, 988b3, and from *De Gen. et
Corr.*, 335b14.   The last four quotations in this paragraph are from Plato's
Laws, 904c f., and 797d.   See also note 24 to this chapter, and text.   (It is
possible to interpret the remark about the evil objects as another allusion to a
cyclic development, as discussed in note 6 to chapter 2, i.e. as an allusion to

the belief that the trend of the development must reverse, and that things must begin to improve, once the world has reached the lowest depth of evilness.

* Since my interpretation of the Platonic theory of change and of the passages from the *Laws* has been challenged, I wish to add some further comments, especially on the two passages (1) *Laws*, 904c, f, and (2) 797d.

(1) The passage *Laws*, 904c, ' the less significant is the beginning decline in their level of rank ' may be translated more literally ' the less significant is the beginning movement *down* in the level of rank '. It seems to me certain, from the context, that ' *down* the level of rank ' is meant rather than ' *as to* level of rank ', which clearly is also a possible translation. (My reason is not only the whole dramatic context, down from 904a, but also more especially the series ' *kata* . . . *kata* . . . *katō* ' which, in a passage of gathering momentum, must colour the meaning of at least the second ' *kata* '.—Concerning the word I translate by ' level ', this *may*, admittedly, mean not only ' plane ' but also ' surface ' ; and the word I translate by ' rank ' *may* mean ' space ' ; yet Bury's translation : ' the smaller the change of character, the less is the movement over surface in space ' does not seem to me to yield much meaning in this context.)

(2) The continuation of this passage (*Laws*, 798) is most characteristic. It demands that ' the lawgiver must contrive, by whatever means at his disposal (' by hook or by crook ', as Bury well translates), a method which ensures for his state that the whole soul of every one of its citizens will, from reverence and fear, resist any change of any of the things that are established of old '. (Plato includes, explicitly, things which other lawgivers consider ' mere matters of play '—such, as, for example, changes in the games of children.)

(3) In general, the main evidence for my interpretation of Plato's theory of change—apart from a great number of minor passages referred to in the various notes in this chapter and the preceding one—is of course found in the historical or evolutionary passages of *all* the dialogues which contain such passages, especially the *Republic* (the decline and fall of the state from its near-perfect or Golden Age in Books VIII and IX), the *Statesman* (the theory of the Golden Age and its decline), the *Laws* (the story of the primitive patriarchy and of the Dorian conquest, and the story of the decline and fall of the Persian Empire), the *Timaeus* (the story of evolution by degeneration, which occurs twice, and the story of the Golden Age of Athens, which is continued in the *Critias*).

To this evidence Plato's frequent references to Hesiod must be added, and the undoubted fact that Plato's synthetic mind was not less keen than that of Empedocles (whose period of strife is the one ruling *now* ; cp. Aristotle, *De Gen. et Corr.*, 334a, b) in conceiving human affairs in a cosmic setting (*Statesman*, *Timaeus*).

(4) Ultimately, I may perhaps refer to general psychological considerations. On the one hand the fear of innovation (illustrated by many passages in the *Laws*, e.g. 758c/d) and, on the other hand, the idealization of the past (such as found in Hesiod or in the story of the lost paradise) are frequent and striking phenomena. It is perhaps not too far-fetched to connect the latter, or even both, with the idealization of one's childhood—one's home, one's parents, and with the nostalgic wish to return to these early stages of one's life, to one's origin. There are many passages in Plato in which he takes it for granted that the original state of affairs, or original nature, is a state of blessedness. I refer only to the speech of Aristophanes in the *Symposium* ; here it is taken for granted that the urge and the suffering of passionate love is sufficiently explained if it is shown that it derives from this nostalgia, and similarly, that the feelings of sexual gratification can be explained as those of a gratified nostalgia. Thus Plato says of Eros (*Symposium*, 193d) : ' He will

restore us *to our original nature* (see also 191d) and heal us and make us happy and blessed.' The same thought underlies many remarks such as the following from the *Philebus* (16c) : ' The men of old . . were better than we are now, and . . lived nearer to the gods . .' All this indicates the view that our unhappy and unblessed state is a consequence of the development which makes us different from our original nature—our Idea ; and it further indicates that the development is one from a state of goodness and blessedness to a state where goodness and blessedness are being lost ; but this means that the development is one of increasing corruption. Plato's theory of *anamnesis* —the theory that all knowledge is re-cognition or re-collection of the knowledge we had in our pre-natal past is part of the same view : in the past there resides not only the good, the noble, and the beautiful, but also all wisdom. Even the ancient change or motion is better than secondary motion ; for in the *Laws* the soul is said to be (895b) ' *the starting point* of all motion s the *first* to arise in things at rest . . the most ancient and potent motion ', and (966c) ' the most ancient and divine of all things '. (Cp. note 15 (8) to chapter 3.)

As pointed out before (cp. especially note 6 to chapter 3), the doctrine of an historical and cosmic tendency towards decay appears to be combined, in Plato, with a doctrine of an historical and cosmic cycle. (The period of decay, probably, is a part of this cycle.) *

⁴ Cp. *Timaeus*, 91d–92b/c. See also note 6 (7) to chapter 3 and note 11 to chapter 11.

⁵ See the beginning of chapter 2 above, and note 6 (1) to chapter 3. It is not a mere accident that Plato mentions Hesiod's story of ' metals ' when discussing his own theory of historical decay (*Rep.*, 546e/547a, esp. notes 39 and 40 to chapter 5) ; he clearly wishes to indicate how well his theory fits in with, and explains, that of Hesiod.

⁶ The historical part of the *Laws* is in Books Three and Four (see note 6 (5) and (8) to chapter 3). The two quotations in the text are from the beginning of this part, i.e. *Laws*, 676a. For the parallel passages mentioned, see *Republic*, 369b, f. (' The birth of a city . .') and 545d (' How will our city be changed . .').

It is often said that the *Laws* (and the *Statesman*) are less hostile towards democracy than the *Republic*, and it must be admitted that Plato's general tone is in fact less hostile (this is perhaps due to the increasing inner strength of democracy ; see chapter 10 and the beginning of chapter 11). But the only practical concession made to democracy in the *Laws* is that political officers are to be elected, by the members of the ruling (i.e. the military) class ; and since all important changes in the laws of the state are forbidden anyway (cp., for instance, the quotations in note 3 of this chapter), this does not mean very much. The fundamental tendency remains pro-Spartan, and this tendency was, as can be seen from Aristotle's *Politics*, 11, 6, 17 (1265b), compatible with a so-called ' mixed ' constitution. In fact, Plato in the *Laws* is, if anything, more hostile towards the spirit of democracy, i.e. towards the idea of the freedom of the individual, than he is in the *Republic* ; cp. especially the text to notes 32 and 33 to chapter 6 (i.e. *Laws*, 739c, ff., and 942a, f.) and to notes 19–22 to chapter 8 (i.e. *Laws*, 903c–909a).—See also next note.

⁷ It seems likely that it was largely this difficulty of explaining the first change (or the Fall of Man) that led Plato to transform his theory of Ideas, as mentioned in note 15 (8) to chapter 3 ; viz., to transform the Ideas into causes and active powers, capable of mingling with some of the other Ideas (cp. *Sophist*, 252e, ff.), and of rejecting the remaining ones (*Sophist*, 223c), and thus to transform them into something like gods, as opposed to the *Republic* which (cp. 380d) petrifies even the gods into unmoving and unmoved Parmenidean beings. An important turning point is, apparently, the *Sophist*,

248e–249c (note especially that here the Idea of motion is not at rest). The transformation seems to solve at the same time the difficulty of the so-called 'third man'; for if the Forms are, as in the *Timaeus*, fathers, then there is no 'third man' necessary to explain their similarity to their offspring.

Regarding the relation of the *Republic* to the *Statesman* and to the *Laws*, I think that Plato's attempt in the two latter dialogues to trace the origin of human society further and further back is likewise connected with the difficulties inherent in the problem of the first change. That it is difficult to conceive of a change overtaking a perfect city is clearly stated in *Republic*, 546a; Plato's attempt in the *Republic* to solve it will be discussed in the next chapter (cp. text to notes 37–40 to chapter 5). In the *Statesman*, Plato adopts the theory of a cosmic catastrophe which leads to the change from the (Empedoclean) half-circle of love to the present period, the half-circle of strife. This idea seems to have been dropped in the *Timaeus*, in order to be replaced by a theory (retained in the *Laws*) of more limited catastrophes, such as floods, which may destroy civilizations, but apparently do not affect the course of the universe. (It is possible that this solution of the problem was suggested to Plato by the fact that in 373–372 B.C., the ancient city of Helice was destroyed by earthquake and flood.) The earliest form of society, removed in the *Republic* only by one single step from the still existing Spartan state, is thrust back to a more and more distant past. Although Plato continues to believe that the first settlement must be the best city, he now discusses societies prior to the first settlement, i.e. nomad societies, 'hill shepherds'. (Cp. especially note 32 to this chapter.)

⁸ The quotation is from Marx-Engels, *The Communist Manifesto*; cp. *A Handbook of Marxism* (edited by E. Burns, 1935), 22.

⁹ The quotation is from Adam's comments on Book VIII of the *Republic*; see his edition, vol. II, 198, note to 544a3.

¹⁰ Cp. *Republic*, 544c.

¹¹ (1) As opposed to my contention that Plato, like many modern sociologists since Comte, tries to outline the typical stages of social development, most critics take Plato's story merely as a somewhat dramatic presentation of a purely logical classification of constitutions. But this not only contradicts what Plato says (cp. Adam's note to *Rep.*, 544c19, *op. cit.*, vol. II, 199), but it is also against the whole spirit of Plato's logic, according to which the essence of a thing is to be understood by its original nature, i.e. by its historical origin. And we must not forget that he uses the same word, 'genus', to mean a class in the logical sense and a race in the biological sense. The logical 'genus' is still identical with the 'race', in the sense of 'offspring of the same parent'. (With this, cp. notes 15–20 to chapter 3, and text, as well as notes 23–24 to chapter 5, and text, where the equation *nature = origin = race* is discussed.) Accordingly, there is every reason for taking what Plato says at its face value; for even if Adam were right when he says (*loc. cit.*) that Plato intends to give a 'logical order', this order would for him be at the same time that of a typical historical development. Adam's remark (*loc. cit.*) that the order 'is primarily determined by psychological and not by historical considerations' turns, I believe, against him. For he himself points out (for instance, *op. cit.*, vol. II, 195, note to 543a, ff.) that Plato 'retains throughout . . the analogy between the Soul and the City'. According to Plato's political theory of the soul (which will be discussed in the next chapter), the psychological history must run parallel to the social history, and the alleged opposition between psychological and historical considerations disappears, turning into another argument in favour of our interpretation.

(2) Exactly the same reply could be made if somebody should argue that Plato's order of the constitution is, fundamentally, not a logical but an ethical one; for the ethical order (and the aesthetic order as well) is, in Plato's

philosophy, indistinguishable from the historical order. In this connection, it may be remarked that this historicist view provides Plato with a theoretical background for Socrates' eudemonism, i.e. for the theory that goodness and happiness are identical. This theory is developed, in the *Republic* (cp. especially 580b), in the form of the doctrine that goodness and happiness, or badness and unhappiness, are proportional ; and so they must be, if the degree of the goodness as well as of the happiness of a man is to be measured by the degree in which he resembles our original blessed nature—the perfect Idea of man. (The fact that Plato's theory leads, in this point, to a theoretical justification of an apparently paradoxical Socratic doctrine may well have helped Plato to convince himself that he was only expounding the true Socratic creed ; see text to notes 56/57 to chapter 10.)

(3) Rousseau took over Plato's classification of institutions (*Social Contract*, Book II, ch. VII, Book III, ch. III ff., cp. also ch. X). It seems however that he was not directly influenced by Plato when he revived the Platonic Idea of a primitive society (cp., however, notes 1 to chapter 6 and 14 to chapter 9) ; but a direct product of the Platonic Renaissance in Italy was Sanazzaro's most influential *Arcadia*, with its revival of Plato's idea of a blessed primitive society of Greek (Dorian) hill shepherds. (For this idea of Plato's, cp. text to note 32 to this chapter.) Thus *Romanticism* (cp. also chapter 9) is historically indeed an offspring of Platonism.

(4) How far the modern historicism of Comte and Mill, and of Hegel and Marx, is influenced by the theistic historicism of Giambattista Vico's *New Science* (1725) is very hard to say : Vico himself was undoubtedly influenced by Plato, as well as by St. Augustine's *De Civitate Dei* and Machiavelli's *Discourses on Livy*. Like Plato (cp. ch. 5), Vico identified the 'nature' of a thing with its ' origin ' (cp. *Opere*, Ferrari's second ed., 1852-4, vol. V, p. 99) ; and he believed that all nations must pass through the same course of development, according to one universal law. His 'nations ' (like Hegel's) may thus be said to be one of the links between Plato's ' Cities ' and Toynbee's ' Civilizations '.

[12] Cp. *Republic*, 549c/d ; the next quotations are *op. cit.*, 550d-e, and later, *op. cit.*, 551a/b.

[13] Cp. *op. cit.*, 556e. (This passage should be compared with Thucydides, III, 82-4, quoted in chapter 10, text to note 12.) The next quotation is *op. cit.*, 557a.

[14] For Pericles' democratic programme, see text to note 31, chapter 10, note 17 to chapter 6, and note 34 to chapter 10.

[15] Adam, in his edition of *The Republic of Plato*, vol. II, 240, note to 559d22. (The italics in the second quotation are mine.) Adam admits that ' the picture is doubtless somewhat exaggerated ' ; but he leaves little doubt that he thinks it is, fundamentally, true ' for all time '.

[16] Adam, *loc. cit.*

[17] This quotation is from *Republic*, 560d (for this and the next quotation, cp. Lindsay's translation) ; the next two quotations are from the same work, 563 a-b, and d. (See also Adam's note to 563d25.) It is significant that Plato appeals here to the institution of private property, severely attacked in other parts of the *Republic*, as if it were an unchallenged principle of justice. It seems that when the property bought is a slave, an appeal to the lawful right of the buyer is adequate.

Another attack upon democracy is that ' it tramples under foot ' the educational principle that ' no one can grow up to be a good man unless his earliest years were given to noble games '. (*Rep.*, 558b ; see Lindsay's translation ; cp. note 68 to chapter 10.) See also the attacks upon equalitarianism quoted in note 14 to chapter 6.

* For Socrates' attitude towards his young companions see most of the earlier dialogues, but also the *Phaedo*, where Socrates' ' pleasant, kind, and respectful manner in which he listened to the young man's criticism ' is described. For Plato's contrasting attitude, see text to notes 19–21 to chapter 7 ; see also the excellent lectures by H. Cherniss, *The Riddle of the Early Academy* (1945), especially pp. 70 and 79 (on the *Parmenides* 135c–d), and cp. notes 18–21 to chapter 7, and text.

¹⁸ Slavery (see the preceding note) and the Athenian movement against it will be further discussed in chapters 5 (notes 13 and text), 10, and 11 ; see also note 29 to the present chapter. Like Plato, Aristotle (e.g. in *Pol.*, 1313b11, 1319b20 ; and in his *Constitution of Athens*, 59, 5) testifies to Athens' liberality towards slaves ; and so does the Pseudo-Xenophon (cp. his *Const. of Athens*, I, 10 f.)

¹⁹ Cp. *Republic*, 577a, f. ; see Adam's notes to 577a5 and b12 (*op. cit.*, vol. II, 332 f.). See now also the *Addendum III* (Reply to a Critic), below, especially pp. 330 f.

²⁰ *Republic*, 566e ; cp. note 63 to chapter 10.

²¹ Cp. *Statesman (Politicus)*, 301c/d. Although Plato distinguishes six types of debased states, he does not introduce any new terms ; the names ' monarchy ' (or ' kingship ') and ' aristocracy ' are used in the *Republic* (445d) of the best state itself, and not of the relatively best forms of debased states, as in the *Statesman*.

²² Cp. *Republic*, 544d.

²³ Cp. *Statesman*, 297c/d : ' If the government I have mentioned is the only true original, then the others ' (which are ' only copies of this ' ; cp. 297b/c) ' must use its laws, and write them down ; this is the only way in which they can be preserved '. (Cp. note 3 to this chapter, and note 18 to chapter 7.) ' And any violation of the laws should be punished with death, and the most severe punishments ; and this is very just and good, although, of course, only the second best thing.' (For the origin of the laws, cp. note 32 (1, a) to this chapter, and note 17 (2) to chapter 3.) And in 300e/301a, f., we read : ' The nearest approach of these lower forms of government to the true government . . is to follow these written laws and customs. . . When the rich rule and imitate the true Form, then the government is called aristocracy ; and when they do not heed the (ancient) laws oligarchy,' etc. It is important to note that not lawfulness or lawlessness in the abstract, but the preservation of the ancient institutions of the original or perfect state is the criterion of the classification. (This is in contrast to Aristotle's *Politics*, 1292a, where the main distinction is whether or not ' *the law* is supreme ', or, for instance, *the mob*.)

²⁴ The passage, *Laws*, 709e–714a, contains several allusions to the *Statesman* ; for instance, 710d–e, which introduces, following Herodotus III, 80–82, the *number of rulers* as the principle of classification ; the enumerations of the forms of government in 712c and d ; and 713b, ff., i.e. the myth of the perfect state in the day of Cronos, ' of which the best of our present states are imitations '. In view of these allusions, I little doubt that Plato intended his theory of the fitness of tyranny for Utopian experiments to be understood as a kind of continuation of the story of the *Statesman* (and thus also of the *Republic*).—The quotations in this paragraph are from the *Laws*, 709e, and 710c/d ; the ' remark from the *Laws* quoted above ' is 797d, quoted in the text to note 3, in this chapter. (I agree with E. B. England's note to this passage, in his edition of *The Laws of Plato*, 1921, vol. II, 258, that it is Plato's principle that ' *change is detrimental* to the power . . of anything ', and therefore also to the power of evil ; but I do not agree with him ' that change *from* bad ', viz., to good, is too self-evident to be mentioned as an exception ; it is *not* self-evident from the point of view of Plato's doctrine of the evil nature of change. See also next note.)

[25] Cp. *Laws*, 676b/c (cp. 676a quoted in the text to note 6). In spite of Plato's doctrine that ' change is detrimental ' (cp. the end of the last note), E. B. England interprets these passages on change and revolution by giving them an optimistic or progressive meaning. He suggests that the object of Plato's search is what ' we might call " the secret of political vitality " '. (Cp. *op. cit.*, vol. I, 344.) And he interprets this passage on the search for the true cause of (detrimental) change as dealing with a search for ' the cause and nature of the *true development* of a state, i.e. of its *progress towards perfection* '. (Italics his ; cp. vol. I, 345.) This interpretation cannot be correct, for the passage in question is an introduction to a story of political decline ; but it shows how much the tendency to idealize Plato and to represent him as a progressivist blinds even such an excellent critic to his own finding, namely, that Plato believed change to be detrimental.

[26] Cp. *Republic*, 545d (see also the parallel passage 465b). The next quotation is from the *Laws*, 683e. (Adam in his edition of the *Republic*, vol. II, 203, note to 545d21, refers to this passage in the *Laws*.) England, in his edition of the *Laws*, vol. I, 360 f., note to 683e5, mentions *Republic*, 609a, but neither 545d nor 465b, and supposes that the reference is ' to a *previous* discussion, or one recorded in a lost dialogue '. I do not see why Plato should not be alluding to the *Republic*, by using the fiction that some of its topics have been discussed by the present interlocutors. As Cornford says, in Plato's last group of dialogues there is ' no motive to keep up the illusion that the conversations had really taken place ' ; and he is also right when he says that Plato ' was not the slave of his own fictions '. (Cp. Cornford, *Plato's Cosmology*, pp. 5 and 4.) Plato's law of revolutions was rediscovered, without reference to Plato, by V. Pareto ; cp. his *Treatise on General Sociology*, §§ 2054, 2057, 2058. (At the end of § 2055, there is also a theory of arresting history.) Rousseau also rediscovered the law. (*Social Contract*, Book III, ch. X.)

[27] (1) It may be worth noting that the intentionally non-historical traits of the best state, especially the rule of the philosophers, are not mentioned by Plato in the summary at the beginning of the *Timaeus*, and that in Book VIII of the *Republic* he assumes that the rulers of the best state are not versed in Pythagorean number-mysticism ; cp. *Republic*, 546c/d, where the rulers are said to be ignorant of these matters. (Cp. also the remark, *Rep.*, 543d/544a, according to which the best state of Book VIII can still be surpassed, namely, as Adam says, by the city of Books V–VII—the ideal city in heaven.)

In his book, *Plato's Cosmology*, pp. 6 ff., Cornford reconstructs the outlines and contents of Plato's unfinished trilogy, *Timaeus—Critias—Hermocrates*, and shows how they are related to the historical parts of the *Laws* (Book III). This reconstruction is, I think, a valuable corroboration of my theory that Plato's view of the world was fundamentally historical, and that his interest in ' how it generated ' (and how it decays) is linked with his theory of Ideas, and indeed based on it. But if that is so, then there is no reason why we should assume that the later books of the *Republic* ' started from the question how it ' (i.e. the city) ' might be realized in the *future* and sketched its possible decline through lower forms of politics ' (Cornford, *op. cit.*, 6 ; italics mine) ; instead we should look upon the Books VIII and IX of the *Republic*, in view of their close parallelism with the Third Book of the *Laws*, as a simplified historical sketch of the actual decline of the ideal city of the *past*, and as an explanation of the origin of the existing states, analogous to the greater task set by Plato for himself in the *Timaeus*, in the unfinished trilogy, and in the *Laws*.

(2) In connection with my remark, later in the paragraph, that Plato ' certainly knew that he did not possess the necessary data ', see for instance *Laws*, 683d, and England's note to 683d2.

(3) To my remark, further down in the paragraph, that Plato recognized

the Cretan and Spartan societies as petrified or *arrested* forms (and to the remark in the next paragraph that Plato's best state is not only a class state but a *caste state*) the following may be added. (Cp. also note 20 to this chapter, and 24 to chapter 10.)

In *Laws*, 797d (in the introduction to the ' important pronouncement ', as England calls it, quoted in the text to note 3 to this chapter), Plato makes it perfectly clear that his Cretan and Spartan interlocutors are aware of the ' arrested ' character of their social institutions ; Clenias, the Cretan interlocutor, emphasizes that he is anxious to listen to any defence of the archaic character of a state. A little later (799a), and in the same context, a direct reference is made to the Egyptian method of arresting the development of institutions ; surely a clear indication that Plato recognized a tendency in Crete and Sparta parallel to that of Egypt, namely, to arrest all social change.

In this context, a passage in the *Timaeus* (see especially 24a–b) seems important. In this passage, Plato tries to show (*a*) that a class division very similar to that of the *Republic* was established in Athens at a very ancient period of its pre-historical development, and (*b*) that these institutions were closely akin to the caste system of Egypt (whose arrested caste institutions he assumes to have derived from his ancient Athenian state). Thus Plato himself acknowledges by implication that the ideal ancient and perfect state of the *Republic* is a caste state. It is interesting that Crantor, first commentator on the *Timaeus*, reports, only two generations after Plato, that Plato had been accused of deserting the Athenian tradition, and of becoming a disciple of the Egyptians. (Cp. Gomperz, *Greek Thinkers*, Germ. ed., II, 476.) Crantor alludes perhaps to Isocrates' *Busiris*, 8, quoted in note 3 to chapter 13.

For the problem of the castes in the *Republic*, see furthermore notes 31 and 32 (1, d) to this chapter, note 40 to chapter 6, and notes 11–14 to chapter 8. A. E. Taylor, *Plato : The Man and His Work*, p. 269 f., forcefully denounces the view that Plato favoured a caste state.

²⁸ Cp. *Republic*, 416a. The problem is considered more fully in this chapter, text to note 35. (For the problem of caste, mentioned in the next paragraph, see notes 27 (3) and 31 to this chapter.)

²⁹ For Plato's advice against legislating for the common people with their ' vulgar market quarrels ', etc., see *Republic*, 425b–427a/b ; especially 425d–e and 427a. These passages, of course, attack Athenian democracy, and all ' piecemeal ' legislation in the sense of chapter 9. * That this is so is also seen by Cornford, *The Republic of Plato* (1941) ; for he writes, in a note to a passage in which Plato recommends Utopian engineering (it is *Republic* 500d, f., the recommendation of ' canvas-cleaning ' and of a romantic radicalism ; cp. note 12 to chapter 9, and text) : ' Contrast the piecemeal tinkering at reform satirized at 425e . .'. Cornford does not seem to like piecemeal reforms, and he seems to prefer Plato's methods ; but his and my interpretation of Plato's intentions seem to coincide.*

The four quotations further down in this paragraph are from the *Republic*, 371d/e ; 463a–b (' supporters ' and ' employers ') ; 549a ; and 471b/c. Adam comments (*op. cit.*, vol. I, 97, note to 371e32): ' Plato does not admit slave labour in his city, unless perhaps in the persons of barbarians.' I agree that Plato opposes in the *Republic* (469b–470c) the enslavement of Greek prisoners of war ; but he goes on (in 471b–c) to encourage that of barbarians by Greeks, and especially by the citizens of his best city. (This appears to be also the opinion of Tarn ; cp. note 13 (2) to chapter 15.) And Plato violently attacked the Athenian movement against slavery, and insisted on the legal rights or property when the property was a slave (cp. text to notes 17 and 18 to this chapter). As is shown also by the third quotation (from *Rep.*, 548e/549a) in the paragraph to which this note is appended, he did *not* abolish slavery in his best city. (See also *Rep.*, 590c/d, where he defends the demand that the coarse and vulgar should be the slaves of the best man.)   A. E. Taylor is therefore wrong when he twice asserts (in his *Plato*, 1908 and 1914, pp. 197 and 118) that Plato implies ' that there is no class of slaves in the community '. For similar views in Taylor's *Plato : The Man and His Work* (1926), cp. end of note 27 to this chapter.

Plato's treatment of slavery in the *Statesman* throws, I think, much light on his attitude in the *Republic*.   For here, too, he does not speak much about slaves, although he clearly assumes that there are slaves in his state.   (See his characteristic remark, 289b/c, that ' all property in tame animals, except slaves ' has been already dealt with ; and a similarly characteristic remark, 309a, that true kingscraft ' makes slaves of those who wallow in ignorance and abject humility '.   The reason why Plato does not say very much about the slaves is quite clear from 289c, ff., especially 289d/e.   He does not see a major distinction between ' slaves and other servants ', such as labourers, tradesmen, merchants (i.e. all ' banausic ' persons who earn money ; cp. note 4 to chapter 11) ; slaves are distinguished from the others merely as ' servants acquired by purchase '.   In other words, he is so high above the baseborn that it is hardly worth his while to bother about subtle differences. All this is very similar to the *Republic*, only a little more explicit.   (See also note 57 (2) to chapter 8.)

For Plato's treatment of slavery in the *Laws*, see especially G. R. Morrow, ' Plato and Greek Slavery ' (*Mind*, N.S., vol. 48, 186–201 ; see also p. 402), an article which gives an excellent and critical survey of the subject, and reaches a very just conclusion, although the author is, in my opinion, still a little biased in favour of Plato.   (The article does not perhaps sufficiently stress the fact that in Plato's day an anti-slavery movement was well on the way ; cp. note 13 to chapter 5.)

[30] The quotation is from Plato's summary of the *Republic* in the *Timaeus* (18c/d).—With the remark concerning the lack of novelty of the suggested community of women and children, compare Adam's edition of *The Republic of Plato*, vol. I, p. 292 (note to 457b, ff.) and p. 308 (note to 463c17), as well as pp. 345–55, esp. 354 ; with the Pythagorean element in Plato's communism, cp. *op. cit.*, p. 199, note to 416d22.   (For the precious metals, see note 24 to chapter 10.   For the common meals, see note 34 to chapter 6 ; and for the communist principle in Plato and his successors, note 29 (2) to chapter 5, and the passages mentioned there.)

[31] The passage quoted is from *Republic*, 434b/c.   In demanding a caste state, Plato hesitates for a long time.   This is quite apart from the ' lengthy preface ' to the passage in question (which will be discussed in chapter 6 ; cp. notes 24 and 40 to that chapter) ; for when first speaking about these matters, in 415a, ff., he speaks as though a rise from the lower to the upper classes were permissible, provided that in the lower classes ' children were born with an admixture of gold and silver ' (415c), i.e. of upper class blood and virtue.   But in 434b–d, and, even more clearly, in 547a, this permission is, in effect, withdrawn ; and in 547a *any* admixture of the metals is declared an impurity which must be fatal to the state.   See also text to notes 11–14 to chapter 8 (and note 27 (3) to the present chapter).

[32] Cp. the *Statesman*, 271e.   The passages in the *Laws* about the primitive nomadic shepherds and their patriarchs are 677e–680e.   The passage quoted is *Laws*, 680e.   The passage quoted next is from the Myth of the Earthborn, *Republic*, 415d/e.   The concluding quotation of the paragraph is from *Republic*, 440d.—It may be necessary to add some comments on certain remarks in the paragraph to which this note is appended.

(1) It is stated in the text that it is not very clearly explained how the ' settlement ' came about.   Both in the *Laws* and in the *Republic* we first hear (see (*a*) and (*c*), below) of a kind of agreement or social contract (for the

social contract, cp. note 29 to chapter 5 and notes 43–54 to chapter 6, and text), and later (see (b) and (c), below) of a forceful subjugation.

(a) In the *Laws*, the various tribes of hill shepherds settle in the plains after having joined together to form larger war bands whose laws are arrived at by an agreement or contract, made by arbiters vested with royal powers (681b and c/d ; for the origin of the laws described in 681b, cp. note 17 (2) to chapter 3). But now Plato becomes evasive. Instead of describing how these bands settle in Greece, and how the Greek cities were founded, Plato switches over to Homer's story of the foundation of Troy, and to the Trojan war. From there, Plato says, the Achaeans returned under the name of Dorians, and ' the rest of the story . . is part of Lacedaemonian history ' (682e) ' for we have reached the settlement of Lacedaemon ' (682e/683a). So far we have heard nothing about the manner of this settlement, and there follows at once a further digression (Plato himself speaks about the ' roundabout track of the argument ') until we get ultimately (in 683c/d) the ' hint ' mentioned in the text ; see (b).

(b) The statement in the text that we get a hint that the Dorian ' settlement ' in the Peloponnese was in fact a violent subjugation, refers to the *Laws* (683c/d), where Plato introduces what are actually his first historical remarks on Sparta. He says that he begins at the time when the whole of the Peloponnese was ' practically subjugated ' by the Dorians. In the *Menexenus* (whose genuineness can hardly be doubted ; cp. note 35 to chapter 10) there is in 245c an allusion to the fact that the Peloponnesians were ' immigrants from abroad ' (as Grote puts it : cp. his *Plato*, III, p. 5).

(c) In the *Republic* (369b) the city is founded by workers with a view to the advantages of a division of labour and of co-operation, in accordance with the contract theory.

(d) But later (in *Rep.*, 415d/e ; see the quotation in the text, to this paragraph) we get a description of the triumphant invasion of a warrior class of somewhat mysterious origin—the ' earthborn '. The decisive passage of this description states that the earthborn must look round to find for their camp the most suitable spot (literally) ' for keeping down those within ', i.e. for keeping down those already living in the city, i.e. for *keeping down the inhabitants*.

(e) In the *Statesman* (271a, f.) these ' earthborn ' are identified with the very early nomad hill shepherds of the pre-settlement period. Cp. also the allusion to the autochthonous grasshoppers in the *Symposium*, 191b ; cp. note 6 (4) to chapter 3, and 11 (2) to chapter 8.

(f) To sum up, it seems that Plato had a fairly clear idea of the Dorian conquest, which he preferred, for obvious reasons, to veil in mystery. It also seems that there was a tradition that the conquering war hordes were of nomad descent.

(2) With the remark later in the text in this paragraph regarding Plato's ' continuous emphasis ' on the fact that *ruling is shepherding*, cp., for instance, the following passages : *Republic*, 343b, where the idea is introduced ; 345c, f., where, in the form of the simile of the good shepherd, it becomes one of the central topics of the investigation ; 375a–376b, 404a, 440d, 451b–e, 459a–460c, and 466c–d (quoted in note 30 to chapter 5), where the auxiliaries are likened to sheep-dogs and where their breeding and education are discussed accordingly ; 416a, ff., where the problem of the wolves without and within the state is introduced ; cp. furthermore the *Statesman*, where the idea is continued over many pages, especially 261d–276d. With regard to the *Laws*, I may refer to the passage (694e), where Plato says of Cyrus that he had acquired for his sons ' cattle and sheep and many herds of men and other animals '. (Cp. also *Laws*, 735, and *Theaet.*, 174d.)

(3) With all this, cp. also A. J. Toynbee, *A Study of History*, esp. vol. III,

pp. 32 (n. 1), where A. H. Lybyer, *The Government of the Ottoman Empire*, etc., is quoted, 33 (n. 2), 50–100 ; see more especially his remark on the conquering nomads (p. 22) who ' deal with . . men ', and on Plato's ' human watch-dogs' (p. 94, n. 2). I have been much stimulated by Toynbee's brilliant ideas and much encouraged by many of his remarks which I take as corroborating my interpretations, and which I can value the more highly the more Toynbee's and my fundamental assumptions seem to disagree. I also owe to Toynbee a number of terms used in my text, especially ' human cattle ', ' human herd ' and ' human watch-dog '.

Toynbee's *Study of History* is, from my point of view, a model of what I call historicism ; I need not say much more to express my fundamental disagreement with it ; and a number of special points of disagreement will be discussed at various places (cp. notes 43 and 45 (2) to this chapter, notes 7 and 8 to chapter 10, and chapter 24 ; also, my criticism of Toynbee in chapter 24, and in *The Poverty of Historicism*, p. 110 ff.). But it contains a wealth of interesting and stimulating ideas. Regarding Plato, Toynbee emphasizes a number of points in which I can follow him, especially that Plato's best state is inspired by his experience of social revolutions and by his wish to arrest all change, and that it is a kind of arrested Sparta (which itself was also arrested). In spite of these points of agreement, there is even in the inter-pretation of Plato a fundamental disagreement between Toynbee's views and my own. Toynbee regards Plato's best state as a typical (reactionary) Utopia, while I interpret its major part, in connection with what I consider as Plato's general theory of change, as an attempt to reconstruct a primi-tive form of society. Nor do I think that Toynbee would agree with my interpretation of Plato's story of the period prior to the settlement, and of the settlement itself, outlined in this note and the text ; for Toynbee says (*op. cit.*, vol. III, 80) that ' the Spartan society was not of nomadic origin '. Toynbee strongly emphasizes (*op. cit.*, III, 50 ff.) the peculiar character of the Spartan society, which, he says, was arrested in its development owing to a superhuman effort to keep down their ' human cattle '. But I think that this emphasis on the peculiar situation of Sparta makes it difficult to understand the similarities between the institutions of Sparta and Crete which Plato found so striking (*Rep.*, 544c ; *Laws*, 683a). These, I believe, can be explained only as arrested forms of very ancient tribal institutions, which must be considerably older than the effort of the Spartans in the second Messenian war (about 650–620 B.C. ; cp. Toynbee, *op. cit.*, III, 53). Since the conditions of the survival of these institutions were so very different in the two localities, their similarity is a strong argument in favour of their being primitive and against an explanation by a factor which affects only one of them.

* For problems of the Dorian Settlement, see also R. Eisler in *Caucasia*, vol. V, 1928, especially p. 113, note 84, where the term ' Hellenes ' is trans-lated as the 'settlers ', and ' Greeks ' as the ' graziers '—i.e. the cattle-breeders or nomads. The same author has shown (*Orphisch-Dionisische Mysterienge-danken*, 1925, p. 58, note 2) that the idea of the God-Shepherd is of Orphic origin. At the same place, the sheep-dogs of God (*Domini Canes*) are men-tioned.*

[33] The fact that education is in Plato's state a class prerogative has been overlooked by some enthusiastic educationists who credit Plato with the idea of making education independent of financial means ; they do not see that the evil is the class prerogative as such, and that it is comparatively unimportant whether this prerogative is based upon the possession of money or upon any other criterion by which membership of the ruling class is determined. Cp. notes 12 and 13 to chapter 7, and text. Concerning the carrying of arms, see also *Laws*, 753b.

[34] Cp. *Republic*, 460c. (See also note 31 to this chapter.) Regarding

Plato's recommendation of infanticide, see Adam, *op. cit.*, vol. I, p. 299, note to 460c18, and pp. 357 ff. Although Adam rightly insists that Plato was in favour of infanticide, and although he rejects as ' irrelevant ' all attempts ' to acquit Plato of sanctioning ' such a dreadful practice, he tries to excuse Plato by pointing out ' that the practice was widely prevalent in ancient Greece '. But it was not so in Athens. Plato chooses throughout to prefer the ancient Spartan barbarism and racialism to the enlightenment of Pericles' Athens ; and for this choice he must be held responsible. For a hypothesis explaining the Spartan practice, see note 7 to chapter 10 (and text) ; see also the cross references given there.

The later quotations in this paragraph which favour applying the principles of animal breeding to man are from *Republic*, 459b (cp. note 39 to chapter 8, and text) ; those on the analogy between dogs and warriors, etc., from the *Republic*, 404a ; 375a ; 376a/b ; and 376b. See also note 40 (2) to chapter 5, and the next note here.

³⁵ The two quotations before the note-number are both from *Republic*, 375b. The next following quotation is from 416a (cp. note 28 to this chapter) ; the remaining ones are from 375c–e. The problem of blending opposite ' natures ' (or even Forms ; cp. notes 18–20 and 40 (2) to chapter 5, and text and note 39 to chapter 8) is one of Plato's favourite topics. (In the *Statesman*, 283e, f., and later in Aristotle, it merges into the doctrine of the mean.)

³⁶ The quotations are from *Republic*, 410c ; 410d ; 410e ; 411e/412a and 412b.

³⁷ In the *Laws* (680b, ff.) Plato himself treats Crete with some irony because of its barbarous ignorance of literature. This ignorance extends even to Homer, whom the Cretan interlocutor does not know, and of whom he says : ' foreign poets are very little read by Cretans '. (' But they are read in Sparta ', rejoins the Spartan interlocutor.) For Plato's preference for Spartan customs, see also note 34 to chapter 6, and the text to note 30 to the present chapter.

³⁸ For Plato's view on Sparta's treatment of the human cattle, see note 29 to this chapter, *Republic*, 548e/549a, where the timocratic man is compared with Plato's brother Glaucon : ' He would be harder ' (than Glaucon) ' and less musical ' ; the continuation of this passage is quoted in the text to note 29. —Thucydides reports (IV, 80) the treacherous murder of the 2,000 helots ; the best of the helots were selected for death by a promise of freedom. It is almost certain that Plato knew Thucydides well, and we can be sure that he had in addition more direct sources of information.

For Plato's views on Athens' slack treatment of slaves, see note 18 to this chapter.

³⁹ Considering the decidedly anti-Athenian and therefore anti-literary tendency of the *Republic*, it is a little difficult to explain why so many educationists are so enthusiastic about Plato's educational theories. I can see only three likely explanations. Either they do not understand the *Republic*, in spite of its most outspoken hostility towards the then existing Athenian literary education ; or they are simply flattered by Plato's rhetorical emphasis upon the political power of education, just as so many philosophers are, and even some musicians (see text to note 41) ; or both.

It is also difficult to see how lovers of Greek art and literature can find encouragement in Plato, who, especially in the Tenth Book of the *Republic*, launched a most violent attack against all poets and tragedians, and especially against Homer (and even Hesiod). See *Republic*, 600a, where Homer is put below the level of a good technician or mechanic (who would be generally despised by Plato as banausic and depraved ; cp. *Rep.*, 495e and 590c, and note 4 to chapter 11) ; *Republic*, 600c, where Homer is put below the level of the Sophists Protagoras and Prodicus (see also Gomperz, *Greek Thinkers*,

German ed., II, 401) ; and *Republic*, 605a/b, where poets are bluntly forbidden to enter into any well-governed city.

These clear expressions of Plato's attitude, however, are usually passed over by the commentators, who dwell, on the other hand, on remarks like the one made by Plato in preparing his attack on Homer ('. . though love and admiration for Homer hardly allow me to say what I have to say ' ; *Rep.*, 595b). Adam comments on this (note to 595b11) by saying that ' Plato speaks with real feeling ' ; but I think that Plato's remark only illustrates a method fairly generally adopted in the *Republic*, namely, that of making some concession to the reader's sentiments (cp. chapter 10, especially text to note 65) before the main attack upon humanitarian ideas is launched.

[40] For the rigid censorship aimed at class discipline, see *Republic*, 377e, ff., and especially 378c : ' Those who are to be the guardians of our city ought to consider it the most pernicious crime to quarrel easily with one another.' It is interesting that Plato does not state this political principle at once, when introducing his theory of censorship in 376e, ff., but that he speaks first only of truth, beauty, etc. The censorship is further tightened up in 595a, ff., especially 605a/b (see the foregoing note, and notes 18–22 to chapter 7, and text). For the rôle of censorship in the *Laws*, see 801c/d.—See also the next note.

For Plato's forgetfulness of his principle (*Rep.*, 410c–412b, see note 36 to this chapter) that music has to strengthen the gentle element in man as opposed to the fierce, see especially 399a, f., where modes of music are demanded which do not make men soft, but are ' fit for men who are warriors '. Cp. also the next note, (2).—It must be made clear that Plato has not ' forgotten ' a *previously* announced principle, but only that principle to which his discussion is going to lead up.

[41] (1) For Plato's attitude towards music, especially music proper, see, for instance, *Republic*, 397b, ff. ; 398e, ff. ; 400a, ff. ; 410b, 424b, f., 546d. *Laws*, 657e, ff. ; 673a, 700b, ff., 798d, ff., 801d, ff., 802b, ff., 816c. His attitude is, fundamentally, that one must ' beware of changing to a new mode of music ; this endangers everything ' since ' any change in the style of music always leads to a change in the most important institutions of the whole state. So says Damon, and I believe him.' (*Rep.*, 424c.) Plato, as usual, follows the Spartan example. Adam (*op. cit.*, vol. I, p. 216, note to 424c20 ; italics mine ; cp. also his references) says that ' the connection between musical and political changes . . was recognized universally throughout Greece, and *particularly at Sparta*, where . . Timotheus had his lyre confiscated for adding to it four new strings '. That Sparta's procedure inspired Plato cannot be doubted ; its universal recognition throughout Greece, and especially in Periclean Athens, is most improbable. (Cp. (2) of this note.)

(2) In the text I have called Plato's attitude towards music (cp. especially *Rep.*, 398e, ff.) superstitious and backward if compared with ' a more enlightened contemporary criticism '. The criticism I have in mind is that of the anonymous writer, probably a musician of the fifth (or the early fourth) century, the author of an address (possibly an Olympian oration) which is now known as the thirteenth piece of Grenfell and Hunt, *The Hibeh Papyri*, 1906, pp. 45 ff. It seems possible that the writer is one of ' the various musicians who criticize Socrates ' (i.e. the ' Socrates ' of Plato's *Republic*), mentioned by Aristotle (in the equally superstitious passage of his *Politics*, 1342b, where he repeats most of Plato's arguments) ; but the criticism of the anonymous author goes much further than Aristotle indicates. Plato (and Aristotle) believed that certain musical modes, for instance, the ' slack ' Ionian and Lydian modes, made people soft and effeminate, while others, especially the Dorian mode, made them brave. This view is attacked by the anonymous author. ' They

say ', he writes, ' that some modes produce temperate and others just men ; others, again, heroes, and others cowards.' He brilliantly exposes the silliness of this view by pointing out that some of the most war-like of the Greek tribes use modes reputed to produce cowards, while certain professional (opera) singers habitually sing in the ' heroic ' mode without ever showing signs of becoming heroes. This criticism might have been directed against the Athenian musician Damon, often quoted by Plato as an authority, a friend of Pericles (who was liberal enough to tolerate a pro-Spartan attitude in the field of artistic criticism). But it might easily have been directed against Plato himself. For Damon, see Diels [5] ; for a hypothesis concerning the anonymous author, see *ibid.*, vol. II, p. 334, note.

(3) In view of the fact that I am attacking a ' reactionary ' attitude towards music, I may perhaps remark that my attack is in no way inspired by a personal sympathy for ' progress ' in music. In fact, I happen to like old music (the older the better) and to dislike modern music intensely (especially most works written since the day when Wagner began to write music). I am altogether against ' futurism ', whether in the field of art or of morals (cp. chapter 22, and note 19 to chapter 25.) But I am also against imposing one's likes and dislikes upon others, and against censorship in such matters. We can love and hate, especially in art, without favouring legal measures for suppressing what we hate, or for canonizing what we love.

[42] Cp. *Republic*, 537a ; and 466e–467e.

The characterization of modern totalitarian education is due to A. Kolnai, *The War against the West* (1938), p. 318.

[43] Plato's remarkable theory that the state, i.e. centralized and organized political power, originates through a conquest (the subjugation of a sedentary agricultural population by nomads or hunters) was, as far as I know, first re-discovered (if we discount some remarks by Machiavelli) by Hume in his criticism of the historical version of the contract theory (cp. his *Essays, Moral, Political, and Literary*, vol. II, 1752, Essay XII, *Of the Original Contract*) :—' Almost all the governments', Hume writes, ' which exist at present, or of which there remains any record in story, have been founded originally, either on usurpation or conquest, or both . .' And he points out that for ' an artful and bold man . . , it is often easy . . , by employing sometimes violence, sometimes false pretences, to establish his dominion over a people a hundred times more numerous than his partizans. . . By such arts as these, many governments have been established ; and this is all the *original contract*, which they have to boast of.' The theory was next revived by Renan, in *What is a Nation?* (1882), and by Nietzsche in his *Genealogy of Morals* (1887) ; see the third German edition of 1894, p. 98. The latter writes of the origin of the ' state ' (without reference to Hume) : ' Some horde of blonde beasts, a conquering master race with a war-like organization . . lay their terrifying paws heavily upon a population which is perhaps immensely superior in—numbers. . . This is the way in which the " state " originates upon earth ; I think that the sentimentality which lets it originate with a " contract ", is dead.' This theory appeals to Nietzsche because he likes these blonde beasts. But it has also been proffered more recently by F. Oppenheimer (*The State*, transl. Gitterman, 1914, p. 68) ; by a Marxist, K. Kautsky (in his book on *The Materialist Interpretation of History*) ; and by W. C. Macleod (*The Origin and History of Politics*, 1931). I think it very likely that something of the kind described by Plato, Hume, and Nietzsche has happened in many, if not in all, cases. I am speaking only about ' states ' in the sense of organized and even centralized political power.

I may mention that Toynbee has a very different theory. But before discussing it, I wish first to make it clear that from the anti-historicist point of view, the question is of no great importance. It is perhaps interesting in itself to consider how ' states ' originated, but it has no bearing whatever upon the sociology of states, as I understand it, i.e. upon political technology (see chapters 3, 9, and 25).

Toynbee's theory does not confine itself to ' states ' in the sense of organized and centralized political power. He discusses, rather, the ' origin of *civilizations* '. But here begins the difficulty ; for some of his ' civilizations ' are states (as here described), some are groups or sequences of states, and some are societies like that of the Eskimos, which are not states ; and if it is questionable whether ' states ' originate according to one single scheme, then it must be even more doubtful when we consider a class of such diverse social phenomena as the early Egyptian and Mesopotamian states and their institutions and technique on the one side, and the Eskimo way of living on the other.

But we may concentrate on Toynbee's description (*A Study of History*, vol. I, pp. 305 ff.) of the origin of the Egyptian and Mesopotamian ' civilizations '. His theory is that the challenge of a difficult jungle environment rouses a response from ingenious and enterprising leaders ; they lead their followers into the valleys which they begin to cultivate, and found states. This (Hegelian and Bergsonian) theory of the creative genius as a cultural and political leader appears to me most romantic. If we take Egypt, then we must look, first of all, for the origin of the caste system. This, I believe, is most likely the result of conquests, just as in India where every new wave of conquerors imposed a new caste upon the old ones. But there are other arguments. Toynbee himself favours a theory which is probably correct, namely, that animal breeding and especially animal training is a later, a more advanced and a more difficult stage of development than mere agriculture, and that this advanced step is taken by the nomads of the steppe. But in Egypt we find both agriculture and animal breeding, and the same holds for most of the early ' states ' (though not for all the American ones, I gather). This seems to be a sign that these states contain a nomadic element ; and it seems only natural to venture the hypothesis that this element is due to nomad invaders imposing their rule, a caste rule, upon the original agricultural population. This theory disagrees with Toynbee's contention (*op. cit.*, III, 23 f.) that nomad-built states usually wither away very quickly. But the fact that many of the early caste states go in for the breeding of animals has to be explained somehow.

The idea that nomads or even hunters constituted the original upper class is corroborated by the age-old and still surviving upper-class tradition according to which war, hunting, and horses are the symbols of the leisured classes ; a tradition which formed the basis of Aristotle's ethics and politics, and which is still alive, as Veblen (*The Theory of the Leisure Class*) and Toynbee have shown ; and to this evidence we can perhaps add the animal breeder's belief in racialism, and especially in the racial superiority of the upper class. The latter belief which is so pronounced in caste states and in Plato and in Aristotle is held by Toynbee to be ' one of the . . sins of our . . modern age ' and ' something alien from the Hellenic genius ' (*op. cit.*, III, 93). But although many Greeks may have developed beyond racialism, it seems likely that Plato's and Aristotle's theories are based on old traditions ; especially in view of the fact that racial ideas played such a rôle in Sparta.

⁴⁴ Cp. *Laws*, 694a–698a.

⁴⁵ (1) Spengler's *Decline of the West* is not in my opinion to be taken seriously. But it is a symptom ; it is the theory of one who believes in an upper class which is facing defeat. Like Plato, Spengler tries to show that ' the world ' is to be blamed, with its general law of decline and death. And like Plato, he demands (in his sequel, *Prussianism and Socialism*) a new order, a desperate experiment to stem the forces of history, a regeneration of the Prussian ruling class by the adoption of a ' socialism ' or communism, and of

economic abstinence.—Concerning Spengler, I largely agree with L. Nelson, who published his criticism under a long ironical title whose beginning may be translated : ' Witchcraft : Being an Initiation into the Secrets of Oswald Spengler's Art of Fortune Telling, and a Most Evident Proof of the Irrefutable Truth of His Soothsaying ', etc.   I think that this is a just characterization of Spengler.   Nelson, I may add, was one of the first to oppose what I call historicism (following here Kant in his criticism of Herder ; cp. chapter 12, note 56).

(2) My remark that Spengler's is not the last *Decline and Fall* is meant especially as an allusion to Toynbee.   Toynbee's work is so superior to Spengler's that I hesitate to mention it in the same context ; but the superiority is due mainly to Toynbee's wealth of ideas and to his superior knowledge (which manifests itself in the fact that he does not, as Spengler does, deal with everything under the sun at the same time).   But the aim and method of the investigation is similar.   It is most decidedly historicist.   (Cp. my criticism of Toynbee in *The Poverty of Historicism*, p. 110 ff.)   And it is, funda-mentally, Hegelian (although I do not see that Toynbee is aware of this fact).   His ' criterion of the growth of civilizations ' which is ' progress towards self-determination ' shows this clearly enough ; for Hegel's law of progress towards ' self-consciousness ' and ' freedom ' can be only too easily recognized.   (Toynbee's Hegelianism seems to come somehow through Bradley, as may be seen, for instance, by his remarks on relations, *op. cit.*, III, 223 : ' The very concept of " relations " between " things " or " beings " involves ' a ' logical contradiction. . . How is this contradiction to be transcended ? ' (I cannot enter here into a discussion of the problem of relations.   But I may state dogmatically that all problems concerning relations can be reduced, by certain simple methods of modern logic, to problems concerning properties, or classes ; in other words, *peculiar philosophical difficulties concerning relations do not exist*.   The method mentioned is due to N. Wiener and K. Kuratowski ; see Quine, *A System of Logistic*, 1934, pp. 16 ff.).   Now I do not believe that to classify a work as belonging to a certain school is to dismiss it ; but in the case of Hegelian historicism I think that it is so, for reasons to be discussed in the second volume of this book.

Concerning Toynbee's historicism, I wish to make it especially clear that I doubt very much indeed whether civilizations are born, grow, break down, and die.   I am obliged to stress this point because I myself use some of the terms used by Toynbee, in so far as I speak of the ' breakdown ' and of the ' arresting ' of societies.   But I wish to make it clear that my term ' break-down ' refers not to all kinds of civilizations but to one particular kind of phenomenon—to the *feeling* of bewilderment connected with the dissolution of the magical or tribal ' closed society '.   Accordingly, I do not believe, as Toynbee does, that Greek society suffered ' its breakdown ' in the period of the Peloponnesian war ; and I find the symptoms of the breakdown which Toynbee describes much earlier.   (Cp. with this notes 6 and 8 to chapter 10, and text.)   Regarding ' arrested ' societies, I apply this term exclusively, either to a society that clings to its magical forms through closing itself up, by force, against the influence of an open society, or to a society that attempts to *return to the tribal cage*.

Also I do not think that our Western civilization is just one member of a species.   I think that there are many closed societies who may suffer all kinds of fates ; but an ' open society ' can, I suppose, only go on, or be arrested and forced back into the cage, i.e. to the beasts.   (Cp. also chapter 10, especially the last note.)

(3) Regarding the Decline and Fall stories, I may mention that nearly all of them stand under the influence of Heraclitus' remark : ' They fill their bellies like the beasts ', and of Plato's theory of the low animal instincts.   I

mean to say that they all try to show that the decline is due to an adoption (by the ruling class) of these ' lower ' standards which are allegedly natural to the working classes.   In other words, and putting the matter crudely but bluntly, the theory is that civilizations, like the Persian and the Roman empires, decline owing to overfeeding.   (Cp. note 19 to chapter 10.)

NOTES TO CHAPTER 5

[1] The ' charmed circle ' is a quotation from Burnet, *Greek Philosophy*, I, 106, where similar problems are treated.   I do not, however, agree with Burnet that ' in early days the regularity of human life had been far more clearly apprehended than the even course of nature '.   This presupposes the establishment of a differentiation which, I believe, is characteristic of a later period, i.e. the period of the dissolution of the ' charmed circle of law and custom '.   Moreover, natural periods (the seasons, etc. ; cp. note 6 to chapter 2, and Plato (?), *Epinomis*, 978d, ff.) must have been apprehended in very early days.—For the distinction between natural and normative laws, see esp. note 18 (4) to this chapter.

[2] * Cp. R. Eisler, *The Royal Art of Astrology*.   Eisler says that the peculiarities of the movement of the planets were interpreted, by the Babylonian ' tablet writers who produced the Library of Assurbanipal' (*op. cit.*, 288), as 'dictated by the " laws " or " decisions " ruling " heaven and earth " (*pirishtē shamē u irsiti*), pronounced by the creator god at the beginning.' (*ibid.*, 232 f.).   And he points out (*ibid.*, 288) that the idea of ' universal laws ' (of nature) originates with this ' mythological . . concept of . . " decrees of heaven and earth ". . .'*

For the passage from Heraclitus, cp. D⁵, B 29, and note 7 (2) to chapter 2 ; also note 6 to that chapter, and text.   See also Burnet, *loc. cit.*, who gives a different interpretation ;   he thinks that ' when the regular course of nature began to be observed, no better name could be found for it than Right or Justice . . which properly meant the unchanging custom that guided human life.'   I do not believe that the term meant first something social and was then extended, but I think that both social and natural regularities (' order ') were originally undifferentiated, and interpreted as magical.

[3] The opposition is expressed sometimes as one between ' nature ' and ' law ' (or ' norm ' or ' convention '), sometimes as one between ' nature ' and the ' positing ' or ' laying down ' (viz., of normative laws), and sometimes as one between ' nature ' and ' art ', or ' natural ' and ' artificial '.

The antithesis between nature and convention is often said (on the authority of *Diogenes Laertius*, II, 16 and 4 ;   *Doxogr.*, 564b) to have been introduced by Archelaus, who is said to have been the teacher of Socrates.   But I think that, in the *Laws*, 690b, Plato makes it clear enough that he considers ' the Theban poet Pindar ' to be the originator of the antithesis (cp. notes 10 and 28 to this chapter).   Apart from Pindar's fragments (quoted by Plato ; see also Herodotus, III, 38), and some remarks by Herodotus (*loc. cit.*), one of the earliest original sources preserved is the Sophist Antiphon's fragments *On Truth* (see notes 11 and 12 to this chapter).   According to Plato's *Protagoras*, the Sophist Hippias seems to have been a pioneer of similar views (see note 13 to this chapter).   But the most influential early treatment of the problem seems to have been that of Protagoras himself, although he may possibly have used a different terminology.   (It may be mentioned that Democritus dealt with the antithesis which he applied also to such social ' institutions ' as language ;   and Plato did the same in the *Cratylus*, e.g. 384e.)

[4] A very similar point of view can be found in Russell's ' A Free Man's Worship ' (in *Mysticism and Logic*) ;   and in the last chapter of Sherrington's *Man on His Nature*.

⁵ (1) Positivists will reply, of course, that the reason why norms cannot be derived from factual propositions is that norms are meaningless ; but this shows only that (with Wittgenstein's *Tractatus*) they define ' meaning ' arbitrarily in such a way that only factual propositions are ' meaningful '. (See also my *The Logic of Scientific Discovery*, pp. 35 ff. and 51 f.)   The followers of ' psychologism ', on the other hand, will try to explain imperatives as expressions of emotions, norms as habits, and standards as points of view. But although the habit of not stealing certainly is a fact, it is necessary, as explained in the text, to distinguish this fact from the corresponding norm.— On the question of the logic of norms, I fully agree with most of the views expressed by K. Menger in his book, *Moral, Wille und Weltgestaltung*, 1935. He is one of the first, I believe, to develop the foundations of a *logic of norms*. I may perhaps express here my opinion that the reluctance to admit that norms are something important and irreducible is one of the main sources of the intellectual and other weaknesses of the more ' progressive ' circles in our present time.

(2) Concerning my contention that it is impossible to derive a sentence stating a norm or decision from a sentence stating a fact, the following may be added.   In analysing the relations between sentences and facts, we are moving in that field of logical inquiry which A. Tarski has called *Semantics* (cp. note 29 to chapter 3 and note 23 to chapter 8).   One of the fundamental concepts of semantics is the concept of *truth*.   As shown by Tarski, it is possible (within what Carnap calls a semantical system) to derive a descriptive state-ment like ' Napoleon died on St. Helena ' from the statement ' Mr. A said that Napoleon died on St. Helena ', in conjunction with the further statement that what Mr. A said was *true*.   (And if we use the term ' fact ' in such a wide sense that we not only speak about the fact described by a sentence but also about the *fact that this sentence is true*, then we could even say that it is possible to derive ' Napoleon died on St. Helena ' from the two ' facts ' that Mr. A said it, and that he spoke the truth.)   Now there is no reason why we should not proceed in an exactly analogous fashion in the realm of norms.   We might then introduce, in correspondence to the concept of truth, the concept of the *validity or rightness* of a norm.   This would mean that a certain norm N could be derived (in a kind of semantic of norms) from a sentence stating that N is valid or right ; or in other words, the norm or commandment ' Thou shalt not steal ' would be considered as equivalent to the assertion ' The norm " Thou shalt not steal " is valid or right '.   (And again, if we use the term ' fact ' in such a wide sense that we speak about the *fact that a norm is valid or right*, then we could even derive norms from facts.   This, however, does not impair the correctness of our considerations in the text which are con-cerned solely with the impossibility of deriving norms from psychological or sociological or similar, i.e. non-semantic, facts.)

* (3) In my first discussion of these problems, I spoke of norms or decisions but never of *proposals*.   The proposal to speak, instead, of ' proposals ' is due to L. J. Russell ; see his paper ' Propositions and Proposals ', in the *Library of the Tenth International Congress of Philosophy* (Amsterdam, August 11–18, 1948), vol. I, *Proceedings of the Congress*.   In this important paper, statements of fact or ' propositions ' are distinguished from suggestions for the adoption of a line of conduct (of a certain policy, or of certain norms, or of certain aims or ends), and the latter are called ' proposals '.   The great advantage of this termin-ology is that, as everybody knows, one can *discuss* a proposal, while it is not so clear whether, and in which sense, one can discuss a decision or a norm ; thus by talking of ' norms ' or ' decisions ', one is liable to support those who say that these things are beyond discussion (either above it, as some dogmatic theologians or metaphysicians may say, or—as nonsensical—below it, as some positivists may say).

Adopting Russell's terminology, we could say that a proposition may be *asserted* or *stated* (or a hypothesis *accepted*) while a proposal is *adopted* ; and we shall distinguish the *fact of its adoption* from the *proposal* which has been adopted.

Our dualistic thesis then becomes the thesis that *proposals are not reducible to facts* (or to statements of facts, or to propositions) *even though they pertain to facts.* *

⁶ Cp. also the last note (71) to chapter 10.

Although my own position is, I believe, clearly enough implied in the text, I may perhaps briefly formulate what seems to me the most important principles of humanitarian and equalitarian ethics.

(1) Tolerance towards all who are not intolerant and who do not propagate intolerance. (For this exception, cp. what is said in notes 4 and 6 to chapter 7.) This implies, especially, that the moral decisions of others should be treated with respect, as long as such decisions do not conflict with the principle of tolerance.

(2) The recognition that all moral urgency has its basis in the urgency of suffering or pain. I suggest, for this reason, to replace the utilitarian formula ' Aim at the greatest amount of happiness for the greatₑst number ', or briefly, ' Maximize happiness ', by the formula ' The least amount of avoidable suffering for all ', or briefly, ' Minimize suffering '. Such a simple formula can, I believe, be made one of the fundamental principles (admittedly not the only one) of public policy. (The principle ' Maximize happiness ', in contrast, seems to be apt to produce a benevolent dictatorship.) We should realize that from the moral point of view suffering and happiness must not be treated as symmetrical ; that is to say, the promotion of happiness is in any case much less urgent than the rendering of help to those who suffer, and the attempt to prevent suffering. (The latter task has little to do with ' matters of taste ', the former much.) Cp. also note 2 to chapter 9.

(3) The fight against tyranny ; or in other words, the attempt to safeguard the other principles by the institutional means of a legislation rather than by the benevolence of persons in power. (Cp. section 11 of chapter 7.)

⁷ Cp. Burnet, *Greek Philosophy*, I, 117.—Protagoras' doctrine referred to in this paragraph is to be found in Plato's dialogue *Protagoras*, 322a, ff. ; cp. also the *Theaetetus*, esp. 172b (see also note 27 to this chapter).

The difference between Platonism and Protagoreanism can perhaps be briefly expressed as follows :

(Platonism.) There is an inherent ' natural ' order of justice in the world, i.e. the original or first order in which nature was created. Thus the past is good, and any development leading to new norms is bad.

(Protagoreanism.) Man is the moral being in this world. Nature is neither moral nor immoral. Thus it is possible for man also to improve things.—It is not unlikely that Protagoras was influenced by Xenophanes, one of the first to express the attitude of the open society, and to criticize Hesiod's historical pessimism : ' In the beginning, the Gods did not show to man all he was wanting ; but in the course of time, he may search for the better, and find it.' (Cp. Diels ⁵, 18.) It seems that Plato's nephew and successor Speusippus returned to this progressive view (cp. Aristotle's *Metaphysics*, 1072b30 and note 11 to chapter 11) and that the Academy adopted with him a more liberal attitude in the field of politics also.

Concerning the relation of the doctrine of Protagoras to the tenets of religion, it may be remarked that he believed God to work through man. I do not see how this position can contradict that of Christianity. Compare with it for instance K. Barth's statement (*Credo*, 1936, p. 188) : ' The Bible is a *human* document' (i.e. man is God's instrument).

⁸ Socrates' advocacy of the autonomy of ethics (closely related to his insistence that problems of nature do not matter) is expressed especially in

his doctrine of the self-sufficiency or autarky of the 'virtuous' individual. That this theory contrasts strongly with Plato's views of the individual will be seen later ; cp. especially notes 25 to this chapter and 36 to the next, and text. (Cp. also note 56 to chapter 10.)

⁹ We cannot, for instance, construct institutions which work independently of how they are being 'manned'. With these problems, cp. chapter 7 (text to notes 7–8, 22–23), and especially chapter 9.

¹⁰ For Plato's discussion of Pindar's naturalism, see esp. *Gorgias*, 484b ; 488b ; *Laws*, 690b (quoted below in this chapter ; cp. note 28) ; 714e/715a ; cp. also 890a/b. (See also Adam's note to *Rep.*, 359c20.)

¹¹ Antiphon uses the term which, in connection with Parmenides and Plato, I have translated above by 'delusive opinion' (cp. note 15 to chapter 3); and he likewise opposes it to 'truth'. Cp. also Barker's translation in *Greek Political Theory*, I—*Plato and His Predecessors* (1918), 83.

¹² See Antiphon, *On Truth*; cp. Barker, *op. cit.*, 83–5. See also next note, (2).

¹³ Hippias is quoted in Plato's *Protagoras*, 337e. For the next four quotations, cp. (1) Euripides *Ion*, 854 ff. ; and (2) his *Phoenissae*, 538 ; cp. also Gomperz, *Greek Thinkers* (German ed., I, 325) ; and Barker, *op. cit.*, 75 ; cp. also Plato's violent attack upon Euripides in *Republic*, 568a–d. Furthermore (3) Alcidamas in *Schol. to Aristotle's Rhet.*, I, 13, 1373b18. (4) Lycophron in Aristotle's *Fragm.*, 91 (Rose) ; (cp. also the Pseudo-Plutarch, *De Nobil.*, 18.2). For the Athenian movement against slavery, cp. text to note 18 to chapter 4, and note 29 (with further references) to the same chapter ; also note 18 to chapter 10 and *Addendum III* (Reply to a Critic) below, especially pp. 330 f.

(1) is It worth noting that most Platonists show little sympathy with this equalitarian movement. Barker, for instance, discusses it under the heading 'General Iconoclasm' ; cp. *op. cit.*, 75. (See also the second quotation from Field's *Plato* quoted in text to note 3, chapter 6.) This lack of sympathy is due, undoubtedly, to Plato's influence.

(2) For Plato's and Aristotle's anti-equalitarianism mentioned in the text, next paragraph, cp. also especially note 49 (and text) to chapter 8, and notes 3–4 (and text) to chapter 11.

This anti-equalitarianism and its devastating effects has been clearly described by W. W. Tarn in his excellent paper 'Alexander the Great and the Unity of Mankind' (*Proc. of the British Acad.*, XIX, 1933, pp. 123 ff.). Tarn recognizes that in the fifth century, there may have been a movement towards 'something better than the hard-and-fast division of Greeks and barbarians ; but', he says, 'this had no importance for history, *because anything of the sort was strangled by the idealist philosophies*. Plato and Aristotle left no doubt about their views. Plato said that all barbarians were enemies by nature ; it was proper to wage war upon them, even to the point of enslaving . . them. Aristotle said that all barbarians were slaves by nature . .' (p. 124, italics mine). I fully agree with Tarn's appraisal of the pernicious anti-humanitarian influence of the idealist philosophers, i.e. of Plato and Aristotle. I also agree with Tarn's emphasis upon the immense significance of equalitarianism, of the idea of the unity of mankind (cp. *op. cit.*, p. 147). The main point in which I cannot fully agree is Tarn's estimate of the fifth-century equalitarian movement, and of the early cynics. He may or may not be right in holding that the historical influence of these movements was small in comparison with that of Alexander. But I believe that he would have rated these movements more highly if he had only followed up the parallelism between the cosmopolitan and the anti-slavery movement. The parallelism between the relations *Greeks : barbarians* and *free men : slaves* is clearly enough shown by Tarn in the passage here quoted ; and if we consider the unquestionable strength of the movement against slavery (see esp. note 18 to chapter 4) then the scattered remarks against the distinction between Greeks and barbarians gain much in significance. Cp. also Aristotle, *Politics*, III, 5, 7 (1278a) ; IV (VI), 4, 16 (1319b) ; and III, 2, 2 (1275b). See also note 48 to chapter 8, and the reference to E. Badian at the end of that note.

¹⁴ For the theme ' return to the beasts ', cp. chapter 10, note 71, and text.

¹⁵ For Socrates' doctrine of the soul, see text to note 44 to chapter 10.

¹⁶ The term ' natural right ' in an equalitarian sense came to Rome through the Stoics (there is the influence of Antisthenes to be considered ; cp. note 48 to chapter 8) and was popularized by Roman Law (cp. *Institutiones*, II, 1, 2 ; I, 2, 2). It is used by Thomas Aquinas also (*Summa*, II, 91, 2). The confusing use of the term ' natural law ' instead of ' natural right ' by modern Thomists is to be regretted, as well as the small emphasis they put upon equalitarianism.

¹⁷ The monistic tendency which first led to the attempt to interpret norms as natural has recently led to the opposite attempt, namely, to interpret natural laws as conventional. This (physical) type of *conventionalism* has been based, by Poincaré, on the recognition of the conventional or verbal character of definitions. Poincaré, and more recently Eddington, point out that we define natural entities by the laws they obey. From this the conclusion is drawn that these laws, i.e. the laws of nature, are definitions, i.e. verbal conventions. Cp. Eddington's letter in *Nature*, 148 (1941), 141 : ' The elements ' (of physical theory) ' . . can only be defined . . by the laws they obey ; so that we find ourselves chasing our own tails in a purely formal system.'—An analysis and a criticism of this form of conventionalism can be found in my *The Logic of Scientific Discovery*, especially pp. 78 ff.

¹⁸ (1) The hope of getting some argument or theory to share our responsibilities is, I believe, one of the basic motives of ' scientifio ' ethics. ' Scientific ' ethics is in its absolute barrenness one of the most amazing of social phenomena. What does it aim at ? At telling us what we ought to do, i.e. at constructing a code of norms upon a scientific basis, so that we need only look up the index of the code if we are faced with a difficult moral decision ? This clearly would be absurd ; quite apart from the fact that if it could be achieved, it would destroy all personal responsibility and therefore all ethics. Or would it give scientific criteria of the truth and falsity of moral judgements, i.e. of judgements involving such terms as ' good ' or ' bad ' ? But it is clear that moral *judgements* are absolutely irrelevant. Only a scandalmonger is interested in judging people or their actions ; ' judge not ' appears to some of us one of the fundamental and much too little appreciated laws of humanitarian ethics. (We may have to disarm and to imprison a criminal in order to prevent him from repeating his crimes, but too much of moral judgement and especially of moral indignation is always a sign of hypocrisy and pharisaism.) Thus an ethics of moral judgements would be not only irrelevant but indeed an immoral affair. The all-importance of moral problems rests, of course, on the fact that we can act with intelligent foresight, and that we can ask ourselves what our aims ought to be, i.e. how we ought to act.

Nearly all moral philosophers who have dealt with the problem of how we ought to act (with the possible exception of Kant) have tried to answer it either by reference to ' human nature ' (as did even Kant, when he referred to human reason) or to the nature of ' the good '. The first of these ways leads nowhere, since all actions possible to us are founded upon ' human nature ', so that the problem of ethics could also be put by asking which elements in human nature I ought to approve and to develop, and which sides I ought to suppress or to control. But the second of these ways also leads nowhere ; for given an analysis of ' the good ' in form of a sentence like : ' The good is such and such ' (or ' such and such is good '), we would always have

to ask : What about it ? Why should this concern me ? Only if the word
' good ' is used in an ethical sense, i.e. only if it is used to mean ' that which
I ought to do ', could I derive from the information ' x is good ' the conclusion
that I ought to do x. In other words, if the word ' good ' is to have any ethical
significance at all, it must be defined as ' that which I (or we) ought to do
(or to promote) '. But if it is so defined, then its whole meaning is exhausted
by the defining phrase, and it can in every context be replaced by this phrase,
i.e. the introduction of the term ' good ' cannot materially contribute to our
problem. (Cp. also note 49 (3) to chapter 11.)

All the discussions about the definition of the good, or about the possibility
of defining it, are therefore quite useless. They only show how far ' scientific '
ethics is removed from the urgent problems of moral life. And they thus
indicate that ' scientific ' ethics is a form of escape, and escape from the
realities of moral life, i.e. from our moral responsibilities. (In view of these
considerations it is not surprising to find that the beginning of ' scientific '
ethics, in the form of ethical naturalism, coincides in time with what may be
called the discovery of personal responsibility. Cp. what is said in chapter 10,
text to notes 27–38 and 55–7, on the open society and the Great Generation.)

(2) It may be fitting in this connection to refer to a particular form of
the escape from responsibility discussed here, as exhibited especially by the
juridical positivism of the Hegelian school, as well as by a closely allied
spiritual naturalism. That the problem is still significant may be seen from
the fact that an author of the excellence of Catlin remains on this important
point (as on a number of others) dependent upon Hegel ; and my analysis
will take the form of a criticism of Catlin's arguments in favour of spiritual
naturalism, and against the distinction between laws of nature and normative
laws (cp. G. E. G. Catlin, *A Study of the Principles of Politics*, 1930, pp. 96–99).

Catlin begins by making a clear distinction between the laws of nature
and ' laws . . which human legislators make ' ; and he admits that, at first
sight the phrase ' natural law ', if applied to norms, ' appears to be patently
unscientific, since it seems to fail to make a distinction between that human
law which requires enforcement and the physical laws which are incapable
of breach '. But he tries to show that it only *appears* to be so, and that ' our
criticism ' of this way of using the term ' natural law ' was ' too hasty '. And
he proceeds to a clear statement of spiritual naturalism, i.e. to a distinction
between ' sound law ' which is ' according to nature ', and other law : ' Sound
law, then, involves a formulation of human tendencies, or, in brief, is a copy
of the " natural " law to be " found " by political science. Sound law is
in this sense emphatically found and not made. It is a copy of natural social
law ' (i.e. of what I called ' sociological laws ' ; cp. text to note 8 to this
chapter). And he concludes by insisting that in so far as the legal system
becomes more rational, its rules ' cease to assume the character of arbitrary
commands and become mere deductions drawn from the primary social laws '
(i.e. from what I should call ' sociological laws ').

(3) This is a very strong statement of spiritual naturalism. Its criticism
is the more important as Catlin combines his doctrine with a theory of ' social
engineering ' which may perhaps at first sight appear similar to the one
advocated here (cp. text to note 9 to chapter 3 and text to notes 1–3 and 8–11
to chapter 9). Before discussing it, I wish to explain why I consider Catlin's
view to be dependent on Hegel's positivism. Such an explanation is necessary,
because Catlin uses his naturalism in order to distinguish between ' sound '
and other law ; in other words, he uses it in order to distinguish between
' just ' and ' unjust ' law ; and this distinction certainly does not look like
positivism, i.e. the recognition of the existing law as the sole standard of justice.
In spite of all that, I believe that Catlin's views are very close to positivism ;
my reason being that he believes that only ' sound ' law can be effective, and

in so far ' existent ' in precisely Hegel's sense. For Catlin says that when our legal code is not ' sound ', i.e. not in accordance with the laws of human nature, then ' our statute remains paper '. This statement is purest positivism ; for it allows us to deduce from the fact that a certain code is not only ' paper ' but successfully enforced, that it is ' sound ' ; or in other words, that all legislation which does not turn out to be merely paper is a copy of human nature and therefore just.

(4) I now proceed to a brief criticism of the argument proffered by Catlin against the distinction between (a) laws of nature which cannot be broken, and (b) normative laws, which are man-made, i.e. enforced by sanctions ; a distinction which he himself makes so very clearly at first. Catlin's argument is a twofold one. He shows (a^1) that laws of nature also are man-made, in a certain sense, and that they can, in a sense, be broken ; and (b^1) that in a certain sense normative laws cannot be broken. I begin with (a^1) ' The natural laws of the physicist ', writes Catlin, ' are not brute facts, they are rationalizations of the physical world, whether superimposed by man or justified because the world is inherently rational and orderly.' And he proceeds to show that natural laws ' can be nullified ' when ' fresh facts ' compel us to recast the law. My reply to this argument is this. A statement intended as a formulation of a law of nature is certainly man-made. We *make* the hypothesis that there is a certain invariable regularity, i.e. we describe the supposed regularity with the help of a statement, the natural law. But, as scientists, we are prepared to learn from nature that we have been wrong ; we are prepared to recast the law if fresh facts which contradict our hypothesis show that *our supposed law was no law, since it has been broken*. In other words, by accepting nature's nullification, the scientist shows that he accepts a hypothesis only as long as it has not been falsified ; which is the same as to say that he regards a law of nature as a rule which cannot be broken, since he accepts the breaking of his rule as proof that his rule did not formulate a law of nature. Furthermore : although the hypothesis is man-made, we may be unable to prevent its falsification. This shows that, by creating the hypothesis, we have not created the regularity which it is intended to describe (although we did create a new set of problems, and may have suggested new observations and interpretations). (b^1) ' It is not true ', says Catlin, ' that the criminal " breaks " the law when he does the forbidden act . . the statute does not say : " Thou canst not " ; it says, " Thou shalt not, or this punishment will be inflicted." As command ', Catlin continues, ' it may be broken, but as law, in a very real sense, it is only broken when the punishment is not inflicted. . . So far as the law is perfected and its sanctions executed, . . it approximates to physical law.' The reply to this is simple. In whichever sense we speak of ' breaking ' the law, the juridical law *can* be broken ; no verbal adjustment can alter that. Let us accept Catlin's view that a criminal cannot ' break ' the law, and that it is only ' broken ' if the criminal does not receive the punishment prescribed by the law. But even from this point of view, the law *can* be broken ; for instance, by officers of the state who refuse to punish the criminal. And even in a state where all sanctions are, *in fact*, executed, the officers *could*, if they chose, prevent such execution, and so ' break ' the law in Catlin's sense. (That they would thereby ' break ' the law in the ordinary sense, also, i.e. that they would become criminals, and that they might ultimately perhaps be punished is quite another question.) In other words : A normative law is always enforced *by men* and by their sanctions, and it is therefore fundamentally different from a hypothesis. Legally, we can enforce the suppression of murder, or of acts of kindness ; of falsity, or of truth ; of justice, or of injustice. But we cannot force the sun to alter its course. No amount of argument can bridge this gap.

¹⁹ The ' nature of happiness and misery ' is referred to in the *Theaetetus*, 175c. For the close relationship between ' nature ' and ' Form ' or ' Idea ', cp. especially *Republic*, 597a–d, where Plato first discusses the Form or Idea of a bed, and then refers to it as ' the bed which exists by nature, and which was made by God ' (597b). In the same place, he proffers the corresponding distinction between the ' artificial ' (or the ' fabricated ' thing, which is an ' imitation ') and ' truth '. Cp. also Adam's note to *Republic*, 597b10 (with the quotation from Burnet given there), and the notes to 476b13, 501b9, 525c15 ; furthermore *Theaetetus*, 174b (and Cornford's note 1 to p. 85 in his *Plato's Theory of Knowledge*). See also Aristotle's *Metaphysics*, 1015a14.

²⁰ For Plato's attack upon art, see the last book of the *Republic*, and especially the passages *Republic*, 600a–605b, mentioned in note 39 to chapter 4.

²¹ Cp. notes 11, 12 and 13 to this chapter, and text. My contention that Plato agrees at least partly with Antiphon's naturalist theories (although he does not, of course, agree with Antiphon's equalitarianism) will appear strange to many, especially to the readers of Barker, *op. cit*. And it may surprise them even more to hear the opinion that the main disagreement was not so much a theoretical one, but rather one of moral practice, and that Antiphon and not Plato was morally in the right, as far as the practical issue of equalitarianism is concerned. (For Plato's agreement with Antiphon's principle that nature is true and right, see also text to notes 23 and 28, and note 30 to this chapter.)

²² These quotations are from *Sophist*, 266b and 265e. But the passage also contains (265c) a criticism (similar to *Laws*, quoted in text to notes 23 and 30 in this chapter) of what may be described as a materialist interpretation of naturalism such as was held, perhaps, by Antiphon ; I mean ' the belief . . that nature . . generates without intelligence '.

²³ Cp. *Laws*, 892a and c. For the doctrine of the affinity of the soul to the Ideas, see also note 15 (8) to chapter 3. For the affinity of ' natures ' and ' souls ', see Aristotle's *Metaphysics*, 1015a14, with the passages of the *Laws* quoted, and with 896d/e : ' the soul dwells in all things that move . .'

Compare further especially the following passages in which ' natures ' and ' souls ' are used in a way that is obviously synonymous : *Republic*, 485a/b, 485e/486a and d, 486b (' nature ') ; 486b and d (' soul '), 490e/491a (both), 491b (both), and many other places (cp. also Adam's note to 370a7). The affinity is directly stated in 490b(10). For the affinity between ' nature ' and ' soul ' and ' race ', cp. 501e where the phrase ' philosophic natures ' or ' souls ' found in analogous passages is replaced by ' race of philosophers '.

There is also an affinity between ' soul ' or ' nature ' and the social class or caste ; see for instance *Republic*, 435b. The connection between caste and race is fundamental, for from the beginning (415a), caste is identified with race.

' Nature ' is used in the sense of ' talent ' or ' condition of the soul ' in *Laws*, 648d, 650b, 655e, 710b, 766a, 875c. The priority and superiority of nature over art is stated in *Laws*, 889a, ff. For ' natural ' in the sense of ' right ', or ' true ', see *Laws*, 686d and 818e, respectively.

²⁴ Cp. the passages quoted in note 32 (1), (*a*) and (*c*), to chapter 4.

²⁵ The Socratic doctrine of autarky is mentioned in *Republic*, 387d/e (cp. *Apology*, 41c, ff., and Adam's note to *Rep.*, 387d25). This is only one of the few scattered passages reminiscent of Socratic teaching ; but it is in direct contradiction to the main doctrine of the *Republic*, as it is expounded in the text (see also note 36 to chapter 6, and text) ; this may be seen by contrasting the quoted passage with 369c, ff., and very many similar passages.

²⁶ Cp. for instance the passage quoted in the text to note 29 to chapter 4. For the ' rare and uncommon natures ', cp. *Republic*, 491a/b, and many other

passages, for instance *Timaeus*, 51e : ' reason is shared by the gods with very few men '. For the ' social habitat ', see 491d (cp. also chapter 23).

While Plato (and Aristotle ; cp. especially note 4 to chapter 11, and text) insisted that manual work is degrading, Socrates seems to have adopted a very different attitude. (Cp. Xenophon, *Memorabilia*, II, 7 ; 7–10 ; Xenophon's story is, to some extent, corroborated by Antisthenes' and Diogenes' attitude towards manual work ; cp. also note 56 to chapter 10.)

²⁷ See especially *Theaetetus*, 172b (cp. also Cornford's comments on this passage in *Plato's Theory of Knowledge*). See also note 7 to this chapter. The elements of conventionalism in Plato's teaching may perhaps explain why the *Republic* was said, by some who still possessed Protagoras' writings, to resemble these. (Cp. *Diogenes Laertius*, III, 37.) For Lycophron's contract theory, see notes 43–54 to chapter 6 (especially note 46), and text.

²⁸ Cp. *Laws*, 690b/c ; see note 10 to this chapter. Plato mentions Pindar's naturalism also in *Gorgias*, 484b, 488b ; *Laws*, 714c, 890a. For the opposition between ' external compulsion ' on the one hand, and (*a*) ' free action ', (*b*) ' nature ', on the other, cp. also *Republic*, 603c, and *Timaeus*, 64d. (Cp. also *Rep.*, 466c–d, quoted in note 30 to this chapter.)

²⁹ Cp. *Republic*, 369b–c. This is part of the *contract theory*. The next quotation, which is the first statement of the *naturalist principle* in the perfect state, is 370a/b–c. (Naturalism is in the *Republic* first mentioned by Glaucon in 358e, ff. ; but this is, of course, not Plato's own doctrine of naturalism.)

(1) For the further development of the naturalistic principle of the division of labour and the part played by this principle in Plato's theory of justice, cp. especially text to notes 6, 23 and 40 to chapter 6.

(2) For a modern radical version of the naturalistic 'principle, see Marx's formula of the communist society (adopted from Louis Blanc) : ' From each according to his ability : to each according to his needs ! ' (Cp. for instance *A Handbook of Marxism*, E. Burns, 1935, p. 752 ; and note 8 to chapter 13 ; see also note 3 to chapter 13, and note 48 to chapter 24, and text.)

For the historical roots of this ' principle of communism ', see Plato's maxim ' Friends have in common all things they possess ' (see note 36 to chapter 6, and text ; for Plato's communism see also notes 34 to chapter 6 and 30 to chapter 4, and text), and compare these passages with the *Acts* : ' And all that believed were together, and had all things in common ; . . and parted them to all men, as every man had need.' (2, 44–45).—' Neither was there any among them that lacked : for . . distribution was made unto every man according as he had need '. (4, 34–35).

³⁰ See note 23, and text. The quotations in the present paragraph are all from the *Laws* : (1) 889, a–d (cp. the very similar passage in the *Theaetetus*, 172b) ; (2) 896c–e ; (3) 890e/891a.

For the next paragraph in the text (i.e. for my contention that Plato's naturalism is incapable of solving practical problems) the following may serve as an illustration. Many naturalists have contended that men and women are ' by nature ' different, both physically and spiritually, and that they should therefore fulfil different functions in social life. Plato, however, uses the same naturalistic argument to prove the opposite ; for, he argues, are not dogs of both sexes useful for watching as well as hunting ? ' Do you agree ', he writes (*Rep.*, 466c–d), ' that women . . must participate with men in guarding as well as in hunting, as it is with dogs ; . . and that in so doing, they will be acting in the most desirable manner, since this will be not contrary to nature, but in accordance with the natural relations of the sexes ? ' (See also text to note 28 to this chapter ; for the dog as ideal guardian, cp. chapter 4, especially note 32 (2), and text.)

³¹ For a brief criticism of the biological theory of the state, see note 7 to

chapter 10, and text.   * For the oriental origin of the theory, see R. Eisler, *Revue de Synthèse Historique*, vol. 41, p. 15.*

32 For some applications of Plato's political theory of the soul, and for the inferences drawn from it, see notes 58–9 to chapter 10, and text.   For the fundamental methodological analogy between city and individual, see especially *Republic*, 368e, 445c, 577c.   For Alcmaeon's political theory of the human individual, or of human physiology, cp. note 13 to chapter 6.

33 Cp. *Republic*, 423, b and d.

34 This quotation as well as the next is from G. Grote, *Plato and the Other Companions of Socrates* (1875), vol. III, 124.—The main passages of the *Republic* are 439c, f. (the story of Leontius) ; 571c, f. (the bestial part versus the reasoning part) ; 588c (the Apocalyptic Monster ; cp. the ' Beast ' which possesses a Platonic Number, in the *Revelation* 13, 17 and 18) ; 603d and 604b (man at war with himself).   See also *Laws*, 689a–b, and notes 58–9 to chapter 10.

35 Cp. *Republic*, 519e, f. (cp. also note 10 to chapter 8) ;   the next two quotations are both from the *Laws*, 903c.   (I have reversed their order.)   It may be mentioned that the ' whole ' referred to in these two passages ('*pan*' and ' *holon* ') is not the *state* but the *world* ;   yet there is no doubt that the underlying tendency of this cosmological holism is a political holism ;   cp. *Laws*, 903d–e (where the physician and craftsman is associated with the statesman), and the fact that Plato often uses ' *holon* ' (especially the plural of it) to mean ' state ' as well as ' world '.   Furthermore, the first of these two passages (in my order of quoting) is a shorter version of *Republic*, 420b–421c ; the second of *Republic*, 520b, ff.   (' We have created you for the sake of the state, as well as for your own sake.')   Further *passages on holism or collectivism* are :   *Republic*, 424a, 449e, 462a, f., *Laws*, 715b, 739c, 875a, f., 903b, 923b, 942a, f.   (See also notes 31/32 to chapter 6.)   For the remark in this paragraph that Plato spoke of the state as an organism, cp. *Republic*, 462c, and *Laws*, 964e, where the state is even compared with the human *body*.

36 Cp. Adam in his edition of the *Republic*, vol. II, 303 ; see also note 3 to chapter 4, and text.

37 This point is emphasized by Adam, *op. cit.*, note 546a, b7, and pp. 288 and 307.   The next quotation in this paragraph is *Republic*, 546a ; cp. *Republic*, 485a/b, quoted in note 26 (1) to chapter 3 and in text to note 33 to chapter 8.

38 This is the main point in which I must deviate from Adam's interpretation.   I believe Plato to indicate that the philosopher king of Books VI–VII, whose main interest is in the things that are not generated and do not decay (*Rep.*, 485b ; see the last note and the passages there referred to), obtains with his mathematical and dialectical training the knowledge of the Platonic Number and with it the means of arresting social degeneration and thereby the decay of the state.   See especially the text to note 39.

The quotations that follow in this paragraph are :   ' keeping pure the race of the guardians ' ; cp. *Republic*, 460c, and text to note 34 to chapter 4. ' A city thus constituted, etc.' :   546a.

The reference to Plato's distinction, in the field of mathematics, acoustics, and astronomy, between *rational knowledge* and delusive opinion based upon *experience or perception* is to *Republic*, 523a, ff., 525d, ff. (where ' *calculation* ' is discussed ;   see especially 526a) ; 527d, ff., 529b, f., 531a, ff. (down to 534a and 537d) ;   see also 509d–511e.

39 * I have been blamed for ' adding ' the words (which I never placed in quotation marks) ' lacking a purely rational method ' ;   but in view of *Rep.*, 523a to 537d, it seems to me clear that Plato's reference to ' *perception* ' implies just this contrast.*   The quotations in this paragraph are from *Rep.*, 546b, ff.   Note that, throughout this passage, it is ' *The Muses* ' who speak through the mouth of ' Socrates '.

In my interpretation of the Story of the Fall and the Number, I have carefully avoided the difficult, undecided, and perhaps undecidable problem of the computation of the Number itself. (It may be undecidable since Plato may not have revealed his secret in full.) I confine my interpretation entirely to the passages immediately before and after the one that describes the Number itself; these passages are, I believe, clear enough. In spite of that, my interpretation deviates, as far as I know, from previous attempts.

(1) The crucial statement on which I base my interpretation is (A) that the guardians work by ' *calculation aided by perception* '. Next to this, I am using the statements (B) that they will not ' *accidentally hit* upon (the correct way of) obtaining good offspring ' ; (C) that they will ' *blunder*, and beget children in the wrong way ' ; (D) that they are ' *ignorant* ' of such matters (that is, such matters as the Number).

Regarding (A), it should be clear to every careful reader of Plato that such a reference to perception is intended to express a criticism of the method in question. This view of the passage under consideration (546a, f.) is supported by the fact that it comes so soon after the passages 523a–537d (see the end of the last note), in which the opposition between pure rational knowledge and opinion based on perception is one of the main themes, and in which, more especially, the term ' calculation ' is used in a context emphasizing the opposition between rational knowledge and experience, while the term ' perception ' (see also 511c/d) is given a definite technical and deprecatory sense. (Cp. also, for instance, Plutarch's wording in his discussion of this opposition : in his *Life of Marcellus*, 306.) I am therefore of the opinion, and this opinion is enforced by the context, especially by (B), (C), (D), that Plato's remark (A) implies (a) that ' calculation based upon perception ' is a poor method, and (b) that there are better methods, namely the methods of mathematics and dialectics, which yield pure rational knowledge. The point I am trying to elaborate is, indeed, so plain, that I should not have troubled so much about it were it not for the fact that even Adam has missed it. In his note to 546a, b7, he interprets ' calculation ' as a reference to the rulers' task of determining the number of marriages they should permit, and ' perception ' as the means by which they ' decide what couples should be joined, what children be reared, etc.' That is to say, Adam takes Plato's remark to be a simple description and not as a polemic against the weakness of the empirical method. Accordingly, he relates neither the statement (C) that the rulers will ' blunder ' nor the remark (D) that they are ' ignorant ' nor to the fact that they use empirical methods. (The remark (B) that they will not ' hit ' upon the right method ' by accident ' would simply be left untranslated, if we follow Adam's suggestion.)

In interpreting our passage we must keep it in mind that in Book VIII, immediately before the passage in question, Plato returns to the question of the first city of Books II to IV. (See Adam's notes to 449a, ff., and 543a, ff.) But the guardians of this city are neither mathematicians nor dialecticians. Thus they have no idea of the purely rational methods emphasized so much in Book VII, 525–534. In this connection, the import of the remarks on perception, i.e. on the poverty of empirical methods, and on the resulting ignorance of the guardians, is unmistakable.

The statement (B) that the rulers will not ' hit accidentally upon ' (the correct way of) ' obtaining good offspring, or none at all ', is perfectly clear in my interpretation. Since the rulers have merely empirical methods at their disposal, it would be only a lucky accident if they did hit upon a method whose determination needs mathematical or other rational methods. Adam suggests (note to 546a, b7) the translation : ' none the more will they by calculation together with perception obtain good offspring ' ; and only in brackets, he adds : ' lit. hit the obtaining of '. I think that his failure to make any sense of the ' hit ' is a consequence of his failure to see the implications of (A).

The interpretation here suggested makes (C) and (D) perfectly understandable ; and Plato's remark that his Number is ' master over better or
worse birth ', fits in perfectly. It may be remarked that Adam does not
comment on (D), i.e. the ignorance, although such a comment would be
most necessary in view of his theory (note to 546d22) that ' the number is
not a nuptial . . number ', and that it has no technical eugenic meaning.

That the meaning of the Number is indeed technical and eugenic is, I
think, clear, if we consider that the passage containing the Number is enclosed
in passages containing references to eugenic knowledge, or rather, lack of
eugenic knowledge. Immediately before the Number, (A), (B), (C), occur,
and immediately afterwards, (D), as well as the story of the bride and bridegroom and their degenerate offspring. Besides, (C) before the Number and
(D) after the Number refer to each other ; for (C), the ' blunder ', is connected
with a reference to ' begetting in the wrong way ', and (D), the ' ignorance ',
is connected with an exactly analogous reference, viz., ' uniting bride and
bridegroom in the wrong manner '. (See also next note.)

The last point in which I must defend my interpretation is my contention
that those who *know* the Number thereby obtain the power to influence ' better
or worse births '. This does not of course follow from Plato's statement that
the Number itself has such power ; for if Adam's interpretation is right, then
the Number regulates the births because it determines an unalterable period
after which degeneration is bound to set in. But I assert that Plato's
references to ' perception ', to ' blunder ' and to ' ignorance ' as the immediate
cause of the eugenic mistakes would be pointless if he did not mean that,
had they possessed an adequate knowledge of the appropriate mathematical
and purely rational methods, the guardians would not have blundered. But
this makes the inference inevitable that the Number has a *technical* eugenic
meaning, and that its knowledge is the key to the power of arresting degeneration. (This inference also seems to me the only one compatible with all we
know about this type of superstition ; all astrology, for instance, involves the
apparently somewhat contradictory conception that the knowledge of our
fate may help us to influence this fate.)

I think that the rejection of the explanation of the Number as a secret
breeding taboo arises from a reluctance to credit Plato with such crude ideas,
however clearly he may express them. In other words, they arise from the
tendency to idealize Plato.

(2) In this connection, I must refer to an article by A. E. Taylor, ' The
Decline and Fall of The State in *Republic*, VIII ' (*Mind*, N.S. 48, 1939, pp.
23 ff.). In this article, Taylor attacks Adam (in my opinion not justly), and
argues against him : ' It is true, of course, that the decay of the ideal
State is expressly said in 546b to begin when the ruling class " beget children
out of due season " . . But this need not mean, and in my opinion does
not mean, that Plato is concerning himself here with problems of the hygiene
of reproduction. The main thought is the simple one that if, like everything
of man's making, the State carries the seeds of its own dissolution within it,
this must, of course, mean that sooner or later the persons wielding supreme
power will be inferior to those who preceded them ' (pp. 25 ff.). Now this
interpretation seems to me not only untenable, in view of Plato's fairly definite
statements, but also a typical example of the attempt to eliminate from Plato's
writing such embarrassing elements as racialism or superstition. Adam
began by denying that the Number has technical eugenic importance, and by
asserting that it is not a ' nuptial number ', but merely a cosmological
period. Taylor now continues by denying that Plato is here at all interested
in ' problems of the hygiene of the reproduction '. But Plato's passage is
thronged with allusions to these problems, and Taylor himself admits two
pages before (p. 23) that it is ' nowhere suggested ' that the Number ' is a

determinant of anything but the " better and worse births " '. Besides, not only the passage in question but the whole of the *Republic* (and similarly the *Statesman*, especially 310b, 310e) is simply full of emphasis upon the ' problems of the hygiene of reproduction '. Taylor's theory that Plato, when speaking of the ' human creature ' (or, as Taylor puts it, of a ' thing of human generation '), means *the state*, and that Plato wishes to allude to the fact that the state is the creation of a human lawgiver, is, I think, without support in Plato's text. The whole passage begins with a reference to the things of the sensible world in flux, to the things that are generated and that decay (see notes 37 and 38 to this chapter), and more especially, to living things, plants as well as animals, and to their racial problems. Besides, a thing ' of man's making ' would, if emphasized by Plato in such a context, mean an ' artificial ' thing which is inferior because it is ' twice removed ' from reality. (Cp. text to notes 20–23 to this chapter, and the whole Tenth Book of the *Republic* down to the end of 608b.) Plato would never expect anybody to interpret the phrase ' a thing of man's making ' as meaning the perfect, the ' natural ' state ; rather he would expect them to think of something very inferior (like poetry ; cp. note 39 to chapter 4). The phrase which Taylor translates ' thing of human generation ' is usually simply translated by ' human creature ', and this removes all difficulties.

(3) Assuming that my interpretation of the passage in question is correct, a suggestion may be made with the intention of connecting Plato's belief in the significance of racial degeneration with his repeated advice that the number of the members of the ruling class should be kept constant (advice that shows that the sociologist Plato understood the unsettling effect of population increase). Plato's way of thinking, described at the end of the present chapter (cp. text to note 45 ; and note 37 to chapter 8), especially the way he opposes The One monarch, The Few timocrats, to The Many who are nothing but a mob, may have suggested to him the belief that *an increase in numbers is equivalent to a decline in quality*. (Something on these lines is indeed suggested in the *Laws*, 710d.) If this hypothesis is correct, then he may easily have concluded *that population increase is interdependent with, or perhaps even caused by, racial degeneration*. Since population increase was in fact the main cause of the instability and dissolution of the early Greek tribal societies (cp. notes 6, 7, and 63 to chapter 10, and text), this hypothesis would explain why Plato believed that the ' real ' cause was racial degeneration (in keeping with his general theories of ' nature ', and of ' change ').

⁴⁰ (1) Or ' at the wrong time '. Adam insists (note to 546d22) that we must not translate ' at the wrong time ' but ' inopportunely '. I may remark that my interpretation is quite independent of this question ; it is fully compatible with ' inopportunely ' or ' wrongly ' or ' at the wrong time ' or ' out of due season '. (The phrase in question means, originally, something like ' contrary to the proper measure ' ; usually it means ' at the wrong time '.)

* (2) Concerning Plato's remarks about ' mingling ' and ' mixture ', it may be observed that Plato seems to have held a primitive but popular theory of heredity (apparently still held by race-horse breeders) according to which the offspring is an even mixture or blend of the characters or ' natures ' of his two parents, and that their characters, or natures, or ' virtues ' (stamina, speed, etc., or, according to the *Republic*, the *Statesman*, and the *Laws*, gentleness, fierceness, boldness, self-restraint, etc.) are mixed in him in proportion to the number of ancestors (grandparents, great-grandparents, etc.) who possessed these characters. Accordingly, the art of breeding is one of a judicious and scientific—mathematical or harmonious—blending or mixing of natures. See especially the *Statesman*, where the royal craft of statesmanship or herdsmanship is likened to that of weaving, and where the kingly weaver must blend boldness with self-restraint. (See also *Republic*, 375c–e, and 410c, ff. ; *Laws*, 731b ; and notes 34 f. to chapter 4 ; 13 and 39 f. to chapter 8 ; and text.) *

⁴¹ For Plato's law of social revolutions, see especially note 26 to chapter 4, and text.

⁴² The term 'meta-biology' is used by G. B. Shaw in this sense, i.e. as denoting a kind of religion. (Cp. the preface to *Back to Methuselah* ; see also note 66 to chapter 12.)

⁴³ Cp. Adam's note to *Republic*, 547a 3.

⁴⁴ For a criticism of what I call ' psychologism ' in the method of sociology, cp. text to note 19 to chapter 13 and chapter 14, where Mill's still popular methodological psychologism is discussed.

⁴⁵ It has often been said that Plato's thought must not be squeezed into a ' system ' ; accordingly, my attempts in this paragraph (and not only in this paragraph) to show the systematic unity of Plato's thought, which is obviously based on the Pythagorean table of opposites, will probably arouse criticism. But I believe that such a systematization is a necessary test of any interpretation. Those who believe that they do not need an interpretation, and that they can ' know ' a philosopher or his work, and take him just ' as he was ', or his work just ' as it was ', are mistaken. They cannot but interpret both the man and his work ; but since they are not aware of the fact that they interpret (that their view is coloured by tradition, temperament, etc.), their interpretation must necessarily be naïve and uncritical. (Cp. also chapter 10 (notes 1–5 and 56), and chapter 25.) A critical interpretation, however, must take the form of a rational reconstruction, and must be systematic ; it must try to reconstruct the philosopher's thought as a consistent edifice. Cp. also what A. C. Ewing says of Kant (*A Short Commentary on Kant's Critique of Pure Reason*, 1938, p. 4) : ' . . we ought to start with the assumption that a great philosopher is not likely to be always contradicting himself, and consequently, wherever there are two interpretations, one of which will make Kant consistent and the other inconsistent, prefer the former to the latter, if reasonably possible.' This surely applies also to Plato, and even to interpretation in general.

NOTES TO CHAPTER 6

¹ Cp. note 3 to chapter 4 and text, especially the end of that paragraph Furthermore, note 2 (2) to that chapter. Concerning the formula *Back to Nature*, I wish to draw attention to the fact that Rousseau was greatly influenced by Plato. Indeed, a glance at the *Social Contract* will reveal a wealth of analogies especially with those Platonic passages on naturalism which have been commented upon in the last chapter. Cp. especially note 14 to chapter 9. . There is also an interesting similarity between *Republic*, 591a, ff. (and *Gorgias*, 472e, ff., where a similar idea occurs in an individualist context), and Rousseau's (and Hegel's) famous theory of punishment. (Barker, *Greek Political Theory*, I, 388 ff., rightly emphasizes Plato's influence upon Rousseau. But he does not see the strong element of romanticism in Plato ; and it is not generally appreciated that the rural romanticism which influenced both France and Shakespeare's England through the medium of Sanazzaro's *Arcadia*, has its origin in Plato's Dorian shepherds ; cp. notes 11 (3), 26, and 32 to chapter 4, and note 14 to chapter 9.)

² Cp. R. H. S. Crossman, *Plato To-Day* (1937), 132 ; the next quotation is from p. 111. This interesting book (like the works of Grote and T. Gomperz) has greatly encouraged me to develop my rather unorthodox views on Plato, and to follow them up to their rather unpleasant conclusions. For the quotations from C. E. M. Joad, cp. his *Guide to the Philosophy of Morals and*

Politics (1938), 661, and 660. I may also refer here to the very interesting remarks on Plato's views on justice by C. L. Stevenson, in his article ' Persuasive Definitions ' (*Mind*, N.S., vol. 47, 1938, pp. 331 ff.).

³ Cp. Crossman, *op. cit.*, 132 f. The next two quotations are : Field, *Plato*, etc., 91 ; cp. similar remarks in Barker, *Greek Political Theory*, etc. (see note 13 to chapter 5).

The idealization of Plato has played a considerable part in the debates on the genuineness of the various works transmitted under his name. Many of them have been rejected by some of the critics simply because they contained passages which did not fit in with their idealized view of Plato. A rather naïve as well as typical expression of this attitude can be found in Davies' and Vaughan's ' Introductory Notice ' (cp. the Golden Treasury edition of the *Republic*, p. vi) : ' Mr. Grote, in his zeal to take Plato down from his super-human pedestal, may be somewhat too ready to attribute to him the compositions which have been judged unworthy of so divine a philosopher.' It does not seem to occur to the writers that their judgement of Plato should depend on what he wrote, and not vice versa ; and that, if these compositions are genuine *and* unworthy, Plato was not quite so divine a philosopher. (For Plato's divinity, see also Simplicius in *Arist. de coelo*, 32b44, 319a15, etc.)

⁴ The formulation of (*a*) emulates one of Kant's, who describes a *just constitution* as ' a constitution that achieves *the greatest possible freedom of human individuals* by framing the laws in such a way that *the freedom of each can co-exist with that of all others* '. (*Critique of Pure Reason* ², 373) ; see also his *Theory of Right*, where he says : ' Right (or justice) is the sum total of the conditions which are necessary for everybody's free choice to co-exist with that of everybody else, in accordance with a general law of liberty.' Kant believed that this was the aim pursued by Plato in the *Republic* ; from which we may see that Kant was one of the many philosophers who either were deceived by Plato or who idealized him by imputing to him their own humanitarian ideas. I may remark, in this connection, that Kant's ardent liberalism is very little appreciated in English and American writings on political philosophy (in spite of Hastie's *Kant's Principles of Politics*). He is only too often claimed to be a forerunner of Hegel ; but in view of the fact that he recognized in the romanticism of both Herder and Fichte a doctrine diametrically opposed to his own, this claim is grossly unjust to Kant, and there can be no doubt that he would have strongly resented it. It is the tremendous influence of Hegelianism that led to a wide acceptance of this, I believe, completely untenable claim.

⁵ Cp. text to notes 32/33 to chapter 5.

⁶ Cp. text to notes 25–29, chapter 5. The quotations in the present paragraph are : (1) *Republic*, 433a ; (2) *Republic*, 434a/b ; (3) *Republic*, 441d. With Plato's statement, in the first quotation, ' we have repeated over and again ', cp. also esp. *Republic*, 397e, where the theory of justice is carefully prepared, and, of course, *Republic*, 369b–c, quoted in text to note 29, chapter 5. See also notes 23 and 40 to the present chapter.

⁷ As pointed out in chapter 4 (note 18 and text, and note 29), Plato does not say much about slaves in the *Republic*, although what he says is significant enough ; but he dispels all doubts about his attitude in the *Laws* (cp. especially G. R. Morrow's article in *Mind*, referred to in note 29 to chapter 4).

⁸ The quotations are from Barker, *Greek Political Theory*, I, p. 180. Barker states (p. 176 f.) that ' Platonic Justice ' is ' social justice ', and correctly emphasizes its holistic nature. He mentions (178 f.) the possible criticism that this formula does ' not . . touch the essence of what men generally mean by justice ', i.e. ' a principle for dealing with the clash of wills ', i.e. justice as pertaining to individuals. But he thinks that ' such an objection is beside the point ', and that Plato's idea is ' not a matter of law ' but ' a conception

of social morality' (179) ; and he goes on to assert that this treatment of justice corresponded, in a way, to the current Greek ideas of justice : ' Nor was Plato, in conceiving justice in this sense, very far removed from the current ideas in Greece.' He does not even mention that there exists some evidence to the contrary, as here discussed in the next notes, and text.

⁹ Cp. *Gorgias*, 488e, ff. ; the passage is more fully quoted and discussed in section VIII below (see note 48 to this chapter, and text). For Aristotle's theory of slavery, see note 3 to chapter 11 and text. The quotations from Aristotle in this paragraph are : (1) and (2) *Nicom. Ethics*, V, 4, 7, and 8 ; (3) *Politics*, III, 12, 1 (1282b ; see also notes 20 and 30 to this chapter. The passage contains a reference to the *Nicom. Eth.*) ; (4) *Nicom. Ethics*, V, 4, 9 ; (5) *Politics*, IV (VI), 2, 1 (1317b).—In the *Nicom. Ethics*, V, 3, 7 (cp. also *Pol.*, III, 9, 1 ; 1280a), Aristotle also mentions that the meaning of ' justice ' varies in democratic, oligarchic, and aristocratic states, according to their different ideas of 'merit'. *(What follows here was first added in the American edition of 1950.)

For Plato's views, in the *Laws*, on *political justice and equality*, see especially the passage on the two kinds of equality (*Laws*, 757b–d) quoted below under (1). For the fact, mentioned here in the text, that not only virtue and breeding but also wealth should count in the distribution of honours and of spoils (and even size and good looks), see *Laws*, 744c, quoted in note 20 (1) to the present chapter, where other relevant passages are also discussed.

(1) In the *Laws*, 757b–d, Plato discusses ' *two kinds of equality* '. ' The one of these . . is equality of measure, weight, or number [i.e. numerical or arithmetical equality] ; but the truest and best equality . . distributes more to the greater and less to the smaller, giving each his due measure, in *accordance with nature.* . . By granting the greater honour to those who are superior in virtue, and the lesser honour to those who are inferior in virtue and breeding, *it distributes to each what is proper, according to this principle of* [*rational*] *proportions.* And this is precisely what we shall call " *political justice* ". And whoever may found a state must make this the sole aim of his legislation . . : this justice alone which, as stated, is *natural equality*, and which is distributed, as the situation requires, to unequals.' This second of the two equalities which constitutes what Plato here calls ' political justice ' (and what Aristotle calls ' distributive justice '), and which is described by Plato (and Aristotle) as ' *proportionate equality* '—the truest, best, and most natural equality—was later called ' geometrical ' (*Gorgias* 508a ; see also 465b/c, and Plutarch, *Moralia* 719b, f.), as opposed to the lower and democratic ' *arithmetical* ' equality. On this identification, the remarks under (2) may throw some light.

(2) According to tradition (see *Comm. in Arist. Graeca*, *pars* XV, Berlin, 1897, p. 117, 29, and *pars* XVIII, Berlin, 1900, p. 118, 18), an inscription over the door of Plato's academy said : ' Nobody untrained in geometry may enter my house ! ' I suspect that the meaning of this is not merely an emphasis upon the importance of mathematical studies, but that it means : ' Arithmetic (i.e. more precisely, Pythagorean number theory) is not enough ; you must know geometry ! ' And I shall attempt to sketch the reasons which make me believe that the latter phrase adequately sums up one of Plato's most important contributions to science. See also *Addendum*, p. 319.

As is now generally believed, the earlier Pythagorean treatment of geometry adopted a method somewhat similar to the one nowadays called ' arithmetization '. Geometry was treated as part of the theory of integers (or ' natural ' numbers, i.e. of numbers composed of monads or ' indivisible units ' ; cp. *Republic*, 525e) and of their ' *logoi* ', i.e. their ' rational ' proportions. For example, the Pythagorean rectangular triangles were those with sides in such rational proportions. (Examples are 3 : 4 : 5 ; or 5 : 12 : 13.) A general formula ascribed to Pythagoras is this : $2n + 1 : 2n(n + 1) :$

2n(n + 1) + 1. But this formula, derived from the ' *gnomōn* ', is not general enough, as the example 8 : 15 : 17 shows. A *general formula*, from which the Pythagorean can be obtained by putting m = n + 1, is this : $m^2 - n^2$: $2mn$: $m^2 + n^2$ (where m > n). Since this formula is a close consequence of the so-called ' Theorem of Pythagoras ' (if taken together with that kind of Algebra which seems to have been known to the early Pythagoreans), and since this formula was, apparently, not only unknown to Pythagoras but even to Plato (who proposed, according to Proclus, another non-general formula), it seems that the ' Theorem of Pythagoras ' was not known, in its general form, to either Pythagoras or even to Plato. (See for a less radical view on this matter T. Heath, *A History of Greek Mathematics*, 1921, vol. I, pp. 80–2. The formula described by me as ' general ' is essentially that of Euclid ; it can be obtained from Heath's unnecessarily complicated formula on p. 82 by first obtaining the three sides of the triangle and by multiplying them by $2/mn$, and then by substituting in the result *m* and *n* and *p* and *q*.)

The discovery of the irrationality of the square root of two (alluded to by Plato in the *Greater Hippias* and in the *Meno* ; cp. note 10 to chapter 8 ; see also Aristotle, *Anal. Priora*, 41a26 f.) destroyed the Pythagorean programme of ' arithmetizing ' geometry, and with it, it appears, the vitality of the Pythagorean Order itself. The tradition that this discovery was at first kept secret is, it seems, supported by the fact that Plato still calls the irrational at first ' *arrhētos* ', i.e. the secret, the unmentionable mystery ; cp. the *Greater Hippias*, 303b/c ; *Republic*, 546c. (A later term is ' the non-commensurable ' ; cp. *Theaetetus*, 147c, and *Laws*, 820c. The term ' *alogos* ' seems to occur first in Democritus, who wrote two books *On Illogical Lines and Atoms* (or *and Full Bodies*) which are lost ; Plato knew the term, as proved by his somewhat disrespectful allusion to Democritus' title in the *Republic*, 534d, but never used it himself as a synonym for ' *arrhētos* '. The first extant and indubitable use in this sense is in Aristotle's *Anal. Post.*, 76b9. See also T. Heath, *op. cit.*, vol. I, pp. 84 f., 156 f. and my first *Addendum* on p. 319, below.)

It appears that the breakdown of the Pythagorean programme, i.e. of the arithmetical method of geometry, led to the development of the axiomatic method of Euclid, that is to say, of a new method which was on the one side designed to rescue, from the breakdown, what could be rescued (including the method of rational proof), and on the other side to accept the irreducibility of geometry to arithmetic. Assuming all this, it would seem highly probable that Plato's role in the transition from the older Pythagorean method to that of Euclid was an exceedingly important one—in fact, that Plato was *one of the first to develop a specifically geometrical method* aiming at rescuing what could be rescued from, and at cutting the losses of, the breakdown of Pythagoreanism. Much of this must be considered as a highly uncertain historical hypothesis, but some confirmation may be found in Aristotle, *Anal. Post.*, 76b9 (mentioned above), especially if this passage is compared with the *Laws*, 818c, 895e (even and odd), and 819e/820a, 820c (incommensurable). The passage reads : ' Arithmetic assumes the meaning of " odd " and " even ", geometry that of " irrational " . .' (Or ' incommensurable ' ; cp. *Anal. Priora*, 41a26 f., 50a37. See also *Metaphysics*, 983a20, 1061b1–3, where the problem of irrationality is treated as if it were the *proprium* of geometry, and 1089a, where, as in *Anal. Post.*, 76b40, there is an allusion to the ' square foot ' method of the *Theaetetus*, 147d.) Plato's great interest in the problem of irrationality is shown especially in two of the passages mentioned above, the *Theaetetus*, 147c–148a, and *Laws*, 819d–822d, where Plato declares that he is ashamed of the Greeks for not being alive to the great problem of incommensurable magnitudes.

Now I suggest that the ' Theory of the Primary Bodies ' (in the *Timaeus*, 53c to 62c, and perhaps even down to 64a ; see also *Republic*, 528b–d) was part of Plato's answer to the challenge. It preserves, on the one hand, the atomistic character of Pythagoreanism—the indivisible units (' monads ') which also play a role in the school of the Atomists—and it introduces, on the other hand, the irrationalities (of the square roots of two and three) whose admission into the world had become unavoidable. It does so by taking two of the offending rectangular triangles—the one which is half of a square and incorporates the square root of two, and the one which is half of an equilateral triangle and incorporates the square root of three—as the units of which everything else is composed. Indeed, the doctrine that these two irrational triangles are the limits (*peras* ; cp. *Meno*, 75d–76a) or Forms of all elementary physical bodies may be said to be one of the central physical doctrines of the *Timaeus*.

All this would suggest that the warning against those untrained in geometry (an allusion to it may perhaps be found in the *Timaeus*, 54a) might have had the more pointed significance mentioned above, and that it may have been connected with the belief that geometry is something of higher importance than is arithmetic. (Cp. *Timaeus*, 31c.) And this, in turn, would explain why Plato's ' proportionate equality ', said by him to be something more aristocratic than the democratic arithmetical or numerical equality, was later identified with the ' geometrical equality ', mentioned by Plato in the *Gorgias*, 508a (cp. note 48 to this chapter), and why (for example by Plutarch, *loc. cit.*) arithmetic and geometry were associated with democracy and Spartan aristocracy respectively—in spite of the fact, then apparently forgotten, that the Pythagoreans had been as aristocratically minded as Plato himself; that their programme had stressed arithmetic ; and that ' geometrical ', in their language, is the name of a certain kind of numerical (i.e. arithmetical) proportion.

(3) In the *Timaeus*, Plato needs for the construction of the Primary Bodies an Elementary Square and an Elementary Equilateral Triangle. These two, in turn, are composed of two different kinds of *sub-elementary triangles*—the half-square which incorporates $\sqrt{2}$, and the half-equilateral which incorporates $\sqrt{3}$ respectively. The question why he chooses these two sub-elementary triangles, instead of the Square and the Equilateral itself, has been much discussed ; and similarly a second question—see below under (4)—why he constructs his Elementary Squares out of four sub-elementary half-squares instead of two, and the Elementary Equilateral out of six sub-elementary half-equilaterals instead of two. (See the first two of the three figures below.)

Concerning the first of these two questions, it seems to have been generally overlooked that Plato, with his burning interest in the problem of irrationality, would not have introduced the two irrationalities $\sqrt{2}$ and $\sqrt{3}$ (which he explicitly mentions in 54b) *had he not been anxious to introduce precisely these irrationalities as irreducible elements into his world.* (Cornford, *Plato's Cosmology*, pp. 214 and 231 ff., gives a long discussion of both questions, but the common solution which he offers for both—his ' hypothesis ' as he calls it on p. 234 —appears to me quite unacceptable ; had Plato wanted to achieve some ' grading ' like the one discussed by Cornford—note that there is no hint in Plato that anything smaller than what Cornford calls ' Grade B ' exists—it would have been sufficient to divide into two the *sides* of the *Elementary Squares* and Equilaterals of what Cornford calls ' Grade B ', building each of them up from four elementary figures *which do not contain any irrationalities.*) But if Plato was anxious to introduce these irrationalities into the world, as the sides of sub-elementary triangles of which everything else is composed, then he must have believed that he could, in this way, solve a problem ; and this problem, I suggest, was that of ' the nature of (the commensurable and) the uncommensurable ' (*Laws*, 820c). This problem, clearly, was particularly hard to solve on the basis of a cosmology which made use of anything like atomistic ideas, since irrationals are not multiples of any unit able to measure rationals ; but if the unit measures themselves contain sides in 'irrational ratios ', then the great paradox might be solved ; for then they can measure both, and the existence of irrationals was no longer incomprehensible or 'irrational '.

But Plato knew that there were more irrationalities than $\sqrt{2}$ and $\sqrt{3}$, for he mentions in the *Theaetetus* the discovery of an infinite sequence of irrational square roots (he also speaks, 148b, of 'similar considerations concerning solids ', but this need not refer to cubic roots but could refer to the cubic diagonal, i.e. to $\sqrt{3}$) ; and he also mentions in the *Greater Hippias* (303b–c ; cp. Heath, *op. cit.*, 304) the fact that by adding (or otherwise composing) irrationals, other irrational numbers may be obtained (but also rational numbers—probably an allusion to the fact that, for example, 2 minus $\sqrt{2}$ is irrational ; for this number, plus $\sqrt{2}$, gives of course a rational number). In view of these circumstances it appears that, if Plato wanted to solve the problem of irrationality by way of introducing his elementary triangles, he must have thought that all irrationals (or at least their multiples) can be composed by adding up (*a*) units ; (*b*) $\sqrt{2}$; (*c*) $\sqrt{3}$; and multiples of these. This, of course, would have been a mistake, but we have every reason to believe that no disproof existed at the time ; and the proposition that there are only two kinds of atomic irrationalities—the diagonals of the squares and of cubes—and that all other irrationalities are commensurable relative to (*a*) the unit; (*b*) $\sqrt{2}$; and (*c*) $\sqrt{3}$, has a certain amount of plausibility in it if we consider the relative character of irrationalities. (I mean the fact that we may say with equal justification that the diagonal of a square with unit side is irrational or that the side of a square with a unit diagonal is irrational. We should also remember that Euclid, in Book X, def. 2, still calls all incommensurable square roots 'commensurable by their squares '.) Thus Plato may well have believed in this proposition, even though he could not possibly have been in the possession of a valid proof of his conjecture. (A disproof was apparently first given by Euclid.) Now there is undoubtedly a reference to some unproved conjecture in the very passage in the *Timaeus* in which Plato refers to the reason for choosing his sub-elementary triangles, for he writes (*Timaeus*, 53c/d) : 'all triangles are derived from two, each having one right angle . . ; of these triangles, one [the half-square] has on either side half of a right angle, . . and equal sides ; the other [the scalene] . . has unequal sides. These two we assume as the first principles . . according to an account which combines likelihood [or likely conjecture] with necessity [proof]. Principles which are still further removed than these are known to heaven, and to such men as heaven favours.' And later, after explaining that there is an endless number of scalene triangles, of which ' the best ' must be selected, and after explaining that he takes the half-equilateral as the best, Plato says (*Timaeus*, 54a/b ; Cornford had to emend the passage in order to fit it into his interpretation ; cp. his note 3 to p. 214) : ' The reason is too long a story ; but if anybody puts this matter to the test, and proves that it has this property, then the prize is his, with all our good will.' Plato does not say clearly what ' this property ' means ; it must be a (provable or refutable) mathematical property which justifies that, having chosen the triangle incorporating $\sqrt{2}$, the choice of that incorporating $\sqrt{3}$ is ' the best ' ; and I think that, in view of the foregoing considerations, the property which he had in mind was the conjectured relative rationality of the other irrationals, i.e. relative to the unit, and the square roots of two and three.

(4) An additional reason for our interpretation, although one for which I do not find any further evidence in Plato's text, may perhaps emerge from

the following consideration. It is a curious fact that $\sqrt{2} + \sqrt{3}$ very nearly approximates π. (Cp. E. Borel, *Space and Time*, 1926, 1960, p. 216 ; my attention was drawn to this fact, in a different context, by W. Marinelli.) The excess is less than 0·0047, i.e. less than $1\frac{1}{2}$ pro mille of π, and a better approximation to π was hardly known at the time. A kind of explanation of this

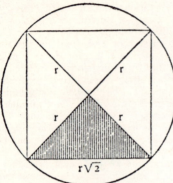

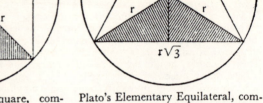

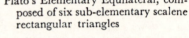

Plato's Elementary Square, composed of four sub-elementary isosceles rectangular triangles

Plato's Elementary Equilateral, composed of six sub-elementary scalene rectangular triangles

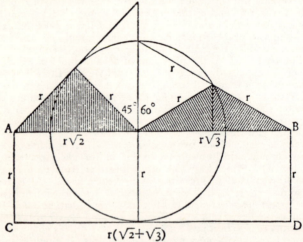

The rectangle ABCD has an area exceeding that of the circle by less than $1\frac{1}{2}$ pro mille

curious fact is that the arithmetical mean of the areas of the circumscribed hexagon and the inscribed octagon is a good approximation of the area of the circle. Now it appears, on the one hand, that Bryson operated with the means of circumscribed and inscribed polygons (cp. Heath, *op. cit.*, 224), and we know, on the other hand (from the *Greater Hippias*), that Plato was interested in the adding of irrationals, so that he must have added $\sqrt{2} + \sqrt{3}$. There are thus two ways by which Plato may have found out the approximate equation $\sqrt{2} + \sqrt{3} \approx \pi$, and the second of these ways seems almost in-escapable. It seems a plausible hypothesis that Plato knew of this equation, but was unable to prove whether or not it was a strict equality or only an approximation.

But if this is so, then we can perhaps answer the 'second question' mentioned above under (3), i.e. the question why Plato composed his elementary square of four sub-elementary triangles (half-squares) instead of two, and his elementary equilateral of six sub-elementary triangles (half-equilaterals) instead of two. If we look at the first two of the figures above, then we see that this construction emphasizes the centre of the circumscribed and inscribed circles, and, in both cases, the radii of the circumscribed circle. (In the case of the equilateral, the radius of the inscribed circle appears also ; but it seems that Plato had that of the circumscribed circle in mind, since he mentions it, in his description of the method of composing the equilateral, as the 'diagonal' ; cp. the *Timaeus*, 54d/e ; cp. also 54b.)

If we now draw these two circumscribed circles, or more precisely, if we inscribe the elementary square and equilateral into a circle with the radius r, then we find that the sum of the sides of these two figures approximates rπ ; in other words, Plato's construction suggests one of the simplest approximate solutions of the squaring of the circle, as our three figures show. In view of all this, it may easily be the case that Plato's conjecture and his offer of 'a prize with all our good will', quoted above under (3), involved not only the general problem of the commensurability of the irrationalities, but also the special problem whether $\sqrt{2} + \sqrt{3}$ squares the unit circle.

I must again emphasize that no direct evidence is known to me to show that this was in Plato's mind ; but if we consider the indirect evidence here marshalled, then the hypothesis does perhaps not seem too far-fetched. I do not think that it is more so than Cornford's hypothesis ; and if true, it would give a better explanation of the relevant passages.

(5) If there is anything in our contention, developed in section (2) of this note, that Plato's inscription meant 'Arithmetic is not enough ; you must know geometry !' and in our contention that this emphasis was connected with the discovery of the irrationality of the square roots of 2 and 3, then this might throw some light on the Theory of Ideas, and on Aristotle's much debated reports. It would explain why, in view of this discovery, the Pythagorean view that things (forms, shapes) are numbers, and moral ideas ratios of numbers, had to disappear—perhaps to be replaced, as in the *Timaeus*, by the doctrine that the elementary forms, or limits ('peras' ; cp. the passage from the *Meno*, 75d–76a, referred to above), or shapes, or ideas of things, are triangles. But it would also explain why, one generation later, the Academy could return to the Pythagorean doctrine. Once the shock caused by the discovery of irrationality had worn off, mathematicians began to get used to the idea that *the irrationals must be numbers*, in spite of everything, since they stand in the elementary relations of greater or less to other (rational) numbers. This stage reached, the reasons against Pythagoreanism disappeared, although the theory that shapes are numbers or ratios of numbers meant, after the admission of irrationals, something different from what it had meant before (a point which possibly was not fully appreciated by the adherents of the new theory). See also *Addendum I*, p. 319, below.*

[10] The well-known representation of Themis as blindfolded, i.e. disregarding the suppliant's station, and as carrying scales, i.e. as distributing equality or as balancing the claims and interests of the contesting individuals, is a symbolic representation of the equalitarian idea of justice. This representation cannot, however, be used here as an argument in favour of the contention that this idea was current in Plato's time ; for, as Prof. E. H. Gombrich kindly informs me, it dates from the Renaissance, and is inspired by a passage

in Plutarch's *De Iside et Osiride*, but not by classical Greece. ∗ On the other hand, the representation of Dikē with scales is classical (for such a representation, by Timochares, one generation after Plato, see R. Eisler, *The Royal Art of Astrology*, 1946, pp. 100, 266, and Plate 5), and goes back, probably, to Hesiod's identification of the constellation of Virgo with Dikē (in view of the neighbouring scales). And in view of the other evidence given here to show the association of Justice or Dikē with distributive equality, the scales are likely to mean the same as in the case of Themis.∗

[11] *Republic*, 440c–d. The passage concludes with a characteristic sheep-dog metaphor : ' Or else, until he has been called back, and calmed down, by the voice of his own reason, like a dog by his shepherd ? ' Cp. note 32 (2) to chapter 4.

[12] Plato, in fact, implies this when he twice presents Socrates as rather doubtful where he should now look out for justice. (Cp. 368b, ff., 432b, ff.)

[13] Adam obviously overlooks (under the influence of Plato) the equalitarian theory in his note to *Republic*, 331e, ff., where he, probably correctly, says that ' the view that Justice consists in doing good to friends and harm to enemies, is a faithful reflection of prevalent Greek morality '. But he is wrong when he adds that this was ' an all but universal view ' ; for he forgets his own evidence (note to 561e28), which shows that equality before the laws (' isonomy ') ' was the proud claim of democracy '. See also notes 14 and 17 to this chapter.

One of the oldest (if not the oldest) reference to ' isonomy ' is to be found in a fragment due to Alcmaeon the physician (early fifth century ; see Diels [5], chapter 24, fr. 4) ; he speaks of isonomy as a condition of health, and opposes it to ' monarchy '—the dominance of one over many. Here we have a political theory of the body, or more precisely, of human physiology. Cp. also notes 32 to chapter 5 and 59 to chapter 10.

[14] A passing reference to *equality* (similar to that in the *Gorgias*, 483c/d ; see also this note, below, and note 47 to this chapter) is made in Glaucon's speech in *Republic*, 359c ; but the issue is not taken up. (For this passage cp. note 50 to this chapter.)

In Plato's abusive attack upon democracy (see text to notes 14–18, chapter 4), three scornful jocular references to equalitarianism occur. The *first* is a remark to the effect that democracy ' distributes equality to equals and to unequals alike ' (558c ; cp. Adam's note to 558c16 ; see also note 21 to this chapter) ; this is intended as an ironical criticism. (Equality has been connected with democracy before, viz. in the description of the democratic revolution ; cp. *Rep.*, 557a, quoted in the text to note 13, chapter 4.) The *second* characterizes the ' democratic man ' as gratifying all his desires ' equally ', whether they may be good or bad ; he is therefore called an ' equalitarianist ' (' isonomist '), a punning allusion to the idea of ' equal laws for all ' or ' equality before the law ' (' isonomy ' ; cp. notes 13 and 17 to this chapter). This pun occurs in *Republic*, 561e. ' The way for it is well paved, since the word ' equal ' has already been used three times (*Rep.*, 561b and c) to characterize an attitude of the man to whom all desires and whims are ' equal '. The *third* of these cheap cracks is an appeal to the reader's imagination, typical even nowadays of this kind of propaganda : ' I nearly forgot to mention the great role played by these famous " equal laws ", and by this famous " liberty ", in the interrelations between men and women . . ' (*Rep.*, 563b).

Besides the evidence of the importance of equalitarianism mentioned here (and in the text to notes 9–10 to this chapter), we must consider especially Plato's own testimony in (1) the *Gorgias*, where he writes (488e/489a ; see also notes 47, 48, and 50 to the present chapter) : ' Does not the multitude (i.e. here : the majority of the people) believe . . that justice is equality ? '

(2) The *Menexenus* (238e–239a ; see note 19 to this chapter, and text). The passages in the *Laws* on equality are later than the *Republic*, and cannot be used as testimony for Plato's awareness of the issue when writing the *Republic* ; but see text to notes 9, 20 and 21 to this chapter.

¹⁵ Plato himself says, in connection with the *third* remark (563b ; cp. the last note) : ' Shall we utter whatever rises to our lips ? ' ; by which he apparently wishes to indicate that he does not see any reason to suppress the joke.

¹⁶ I believe that Thucydides' (II, 37 ff.) version of Pericles' oration can be taken as practically authentic. In all likelihood, he was present when Pericles spoke ; and in any case he would have reconstructed it as faithfully as possible. There is much reason to believe that in those times it was not extraordinary for a man to learn another's oration even by heart (cp. Plato's *Phaedrus*), and a faithful reconstruction of a speech of this kind is indeed not as difficult as one might think. Plato knew the oration, taking either Thucydides' version or another source, which must have been extremely similar to it, as authentic. Cp. also notes 31 and 34/35 to chapter 10. (It may be mentioned here that early in his career, Pericles had made rather dubious concessions to the popular tribal instincts and to the equally popular group egoism of the people ; I have in mind the legislation concerning citizenship in 451 B.C. But later he revised his attitude towards these matters, probably under the influence of such men as Protagoras.)

¹⁷ Cp. *Herodotus*, III, 80, and especially the eulogy on ' isonomy ', i.e. equality before the law (III, 80, 6) ; see also notes 13 and 14 to this chapter. The passage from Herodotus, which influenced Plato in other ways also (cp. note 24 to chapter 4), is one which Plato ridicules in the *Republic* just as he ridicules Pericles' oration ; cp. note 14 to chapter 4, and 34 to chapter 10.

¹⁸ Even the naturalist Aristotle does not always refer to this naturalistic version of equalitarianism ; for instance, his formulation of the principles of democracy in *Politics*, 1317b (cp. note 9 to this chapter, and text), is quite independent of it. But it is perhaps even more interesting that in the *Gorgias*, in which the opposition of nature and convention plays such an important rôle, Plato presents equalitarianism without burdening it with the dubious theory of the natural equality of all men (see 488e/489a, quoted in note 14 to this chapter, and 483d, 484a, and 508a).

¹⁹ Cp. *Menexenus*, 238e/239a. The passage immediately follows a clear allusion to Pericles' oration (viz., to the second sentence quoted in the text to note 17, in this chapter).—It seems not improbable that the reiteration of the term ' equal birth ' in that passage is meant as a scornful allusion to the ' low ' birth of Pericles' and Aspasia's sons, who were recognized as Athenian citizens only by special legislation in 429 B.C. (Cp. E. Meyer, *Gesch. d. Altertums*, vol. IV, p. 14, note to No. 392, and p. 323, No. 558.)

It has been held (even by Grote ; cp. his *Plato*, III, p. 11) that Plato in the *Menexenus*, ' in his own rhetorical discourse, . . drops the ironical vein ', i.e. that the middle part of the *Menexenus*, from which the quotation in the text is taken, is not meant ironically. But in view of the quoted passage on equality, and in view of Plato's open scorn in the *Republic* when he deals with this point (cp. note 14 to this chapter), this opinion seems to me untenable. And it appears to me equally impossible to doubt the ironical character of the passage immediately preceding the one quoted in the text where Plato says of Athens (cp. 238c/d) : ' In this time *as well as at present* . . our government was always an aristocracy . . ; though it is sometimes called a democracy, it is really an aristocracy, that is to say, a rule of the best, with the approval of the many . .' In view of Plato's hatred of democracy, this description needs no further comment. * Another undoubtedly ironical passage is 245c–d (cp. note 48 to chapter 8) where ' Socrates ' praises Athens for its consistent

hatred of foreigners and barbarians. Since elsewhere (in the *Republic*, 562e, f., quoted in note 48 to chapter 8) in an attack on democracy—and this means Athenian democracy—Plato scorns Athens because of its liberal treatment of foreigners, his praise in the *Menexenus* cannot be anything but irony ; again the liberality of Athens is ridiculed by a pro-Spartan partisan. (Strangers were forbidden to reside in Sparta, by a law of Lycurgus ; cp. Aristophanes' *Birds*, 1012.) It is interesting, in this connection, that in the *Menexenus* (236a ; cp. note 15 (1) to chapter 10) where ' Socrates ' is an orator who attacks Athens, Plato says of ' Socrates ' that he was a pupil of the oligarchic party leader Antiphon the Orator (of Rhamnus ; not to be confused with Antiphon the Sophist, who was an Athenian) ; especially in view of the fact that 'Socrates' produces a parody of a speech recorded by Thucydides, who in fact seems to have been a pupil of Antiphon whom he greatly admired.*
For the genuineness of the *Menexenus*, see also note 35 to chapter 10.

²⁰ *Laws*, 757a ; cp. the whole passage, 757a–e, of which the main parts are quoted above, in note 9 (1) to this chapter.

(1) For what I call the standard objection against equalitarianism, cp. also *Laws*, 744b, ff. ' It would be excellent if everybody could . . have all things equal ; but since this is impossible . .', etc. The passage is especially interesting in view of the fact that Plato is often described as an enemy of plutocracy by many writers who judge him only by the *Republic*. But in this important passage of the *Laws* (i.e. 744b, ff.) Plato demands that ' political offices, and contributions, as well as distributions, should be proportional to the value of a citizen's wealth. And they should depend not only on his virtue or that of his ancestors or on the size of his body and his good looks, but also upon his wealth or his poverty. In this way, a man will receive honours and offices as equitably as possible, i.e. in proportion to his wealth, although according to a principle of unequal distribution.' * The doctrine of the unequal distribution of honour and, we may assume, of spoils, in proportion to wealth and bodily size, is probably a residue from the heroic age of conquest. The wealthy who are heavily and expensively armed, and those who are strong, contribute more to the victory than the others. (The principle was accepted in Homeric times, and it can be found, as R. Eisler assures me, in practically all known cases of conquering war hordes.) * The basic idea of this attitude, viz., that it is unjust to treat unequals equally, can be found, in a passing remark, as early as the *Protagoras*, 337a (see also *Gorgias*, 508a, f., mentioned in notes 9 and 48 to this chapter) ; but Plato did not make much use of the idea before writing the *Laws*.

(2) For Aristotle's elaboration of these ideas, cp. esp. his *Politics*, III, 9, 1, 1280a (see also 1282b–1284b and 1301b29), where he writes : ' All men cling to justice of some kind, but their conceptions are imperfect, and do not embrace the whole Idea. For example, justice is thought (by democrats) to be equality ; and so it is, although it is not equality for all, but only for equals. And justice is thought (by oligarchs) to be inequality ; and so it is, although it is not inequality for all, but only for unequals.' Cp. also *Nichom. Eth.*, 1131b27, 1158b30 ff.

(3) Against all this anti-equalitarianism, I hold, with Kant, that it must be the principle of all morality that no man should consider himself more valuable than any other person. And I assert that this principle is the only one acceptable, considering the notorious impossibility of judging oneself impartially. I am therefore at a loss to understand the following remark of an excellent writer like Catlin (*Principles*, 314) : ' There is something profoundly immoral in the morality of Kant which endeavours to roll all personalities level . . and which ignores the Aristotelian precept to render equals to equals and unequals to unequals. One man has not socially the same rights as another . . The present writer would by no means be prepared

to deny that . . there is something in " blood ".' Now I ask : If there were
something in ' blood ', or in inequality of talents, etc. ; and even if it were
worth while to waste one's time in assessing these differences ; and even
if one could assess them ; why, then, should they be made the ground of
greater rights and not only of heavier duties ? (Cp. text to notes 31/32 to
chapter 4.) I fail to see the profound immorality of Kant's equalitarianism.
And I fail to see on what Catlin bases his moral judgement, since he considers
morals to be a matter of taste. Why should Kant's ' taste ' be profoundly
immoral ? (It is also the Christian ' taste '.) The only reply to this question
that I can think of is that Catlin judges from his positivistic point of view
(cp. note 18 (2) to chapter 5), and that he thinks the Christian and Kantian
demand immoral because it contradicts the positively enforced moral valuations
of our contemporary society.

(4) One of the best answers ever given to all these anti-equalitarianists is
due to Rousseau. I say this in spite of my opinion that his romanticism
(cp. note 1 to this chapter) was one of the most pernicious influences in the
history of social philosophy. But he was also one of the few really brilliant
writers in this field. I quote one of his excellent remarks from the *Origin of
Inequality* (see, for instance, the Everyman edition of the *Social Contract*, p. 174 ;
the italics are mine) ; and I wish to draw the reader's attention to the dignified
formulation of the last sentence of this passage. ' I conceive that there are
two kinds of inequality among the human species ; one, which I call natural
or physical because it is established by nature, and consists in a difference of
age, health, bodily strength, and the qualities of the mind or of the soul ;
and another, which may be called moral or political inequality, because it
depends on a kind of convention, and is established, or at least authorized,
by the consent of men. This latter consists of the different privileges, which
some men enjoy . . ; such as that of being more rich, more honoured, or
more powerful. . . It is useless to ask what is the source of natural inequality,
because that question is answered by the simple definition of the word. Again,
*it is still more useless to inquire whether there is any essential connection between the two
inequalities* ; for this would be only asking, in other words, whether those
who command are necessarily better than those who obey, and whether
strength of body or of mind, or wisdom, or virtue, are always found . . in
proportion to the power or wealth of a man ; *a question fit perhaps to be discussed
by slaves in the hearing of their masters, but highly unbecoming to reasonable and free
men in search of the truth.*'

[21] *Republic*, 558c ; cp. note 14 to this chapter (the first passage in the attack
on democracy).

[22] *Republic*, 433b. Adam, who also recognizes that the passage is intended
as an argument, tries to reconstruct the argument (note to 433b11) ; but he
confesses that ' Plato seldom leaves so much to be mentally supplied in his
reasoning '.

[23] *Republic*, 433e/434a.—For a continuation of the passage, cp. text to
note 40 to this chapter ; for the preparation for it in earlier parts of the
Republic, see note 6 to this chapter.—Adam comments on the passage which
I call the ' second argument ' as follows (note to 433e35) : ' Plato is looking
for a point of contact between his own view of Justice and the popular judicial
meaning of the word . .' (See the passage quoted in the next paragraph in
the text.) Adam tries to defend Plato's argument against a critic (Krohn)
who saw, though perhaps not very clearly, that there was something wrong
with it.

[24] The quotations in this paragraph are from *Republic*, 430d, ff.

[25] This device seems to have been successful even with a keen critic such as
Gomperz, who, in his brief criticism (*Greek Thinkers*, Book V, II, 10 ; Germ. ed.,
vol. II, pp. 378/379), fails to mention the weaknesses of the argument ; and

he even says, commenting upon the first two books (V, II, 5 ; p. 368) : 'An exposition follows which might be described as a miracle of clarity, precision, and genuine scientific character . .', adding that Plato's interlocutors Glaucon and Adeimantus, 'driven by their burning enthusiasm . . dismiss and forestall all superficial solutions '.

For my remarks on temperance, in the next paragraph of the text, see the following passage from Davies' and Vaughan's 'Analysis' (cp. the Golden Treasury edition of the *Republic*, p. xviii ; italics mine) : 'The essence of temperance is restraint. The essence of political temperance lies in recognizing *the right of the governing body to the allegiance and obedience of the governed.*' This may show that my interpretation of Plato's idea of temperance is shared (though expressed in a different terminology) by followers of Plato. I may add that ' temperance ', i.e. being satisfied with one's place, is a virtue in which all three classes share, although it is the only virtue in which the workers may participate. Thus the virtue attainable by the workers or money-earners is temperance ; the virtues attainable by the auxiliaries are temperance and courage ; by the guardians, temperance, courage, and wisdom.

The ' lengthy preface ', also quoted in the next paragraph, is from *Republic*, 432b, ff.

[26] On the term ' collectivism ', a terminological comment may be made here. What H. G. Wells calls ' collectivism ' has nothing to do with what I call by that name. Wells is an individualist (in my sense of the word), as is shown especially by his *Rights of Man* and his *Common Sense of War and Peace*, which contain very acceptable formulations of the demands of an equalitarian individualism. But he also believes, rightly, in the rational planning of political institutions, with the aim of furthering the freedom and the welfare of individual human beings. This he calls ' collectivism '; to describe what I believe to be the same thing as his ' collectivism ', I should use an expression like : ' rational institutional planning for freedom '. This expression may be long and clumsy, but it avoids the danger that ' collectivism ' may be interpreted in the anti-individualistic sense in which it is often used, not only in the present book.

[27] *Laws*, 903c ; cp. text to note 35, chapter 5. The ' preamble ' mentioned in the text (' But he needs . . some words of counsel to act as a charm upon him ', etc.) is *Laws*, 903b.

[28] There are innumerable places in the *Republic* and in the *Laws* where Plato gives a warning against unbridled group egoism ; cp., for instance, *Republic*, 519e, and the passages referred to in note 41 to this chapter. Regarding the identity often alleged to exist between collectivism and altruism, I may refer, in this connection, to the very pertinent question of Sherrington, who asks in *Man on His Nature* (p. 388) : ' Are the shoal and the herd altruism ? '

[29] For Dickens' mistaken contempt of Parliament, cp. also note 23 to chapter 7.

[30] Aristotle's *Politics*, III, 12, 1 (1282b) ; cp. text to notes 9 and 20, to this chapter. (Cp. also Aristotle's remark in *Pol.*, III, 9, 3, 1280a, to the effect that justice pertains to persons as well as to things.) With the quotation from Pericles later in this paragraph, cp. text to note 16 to this chapter, and to note 31 to chapter 10.

[31] This remark is from a passage (*Rep.*, 519e, f.) quoted in the text to note 35 to chapter 5.

[32] The important passages from the *Laws* quoted (1) in the present and (2) in the next paragraph are :

(1) *Laws*, 739c, ff. Plato refers here to the *Republic*, and apparently especially to *Republic*, 462a ff., 424a, and 449e. (A list of passages on collectivism and holism can be found in note 35 to chapter 5. On his com-

munism, see note 29 (2) to chapter 5 and other places there mentioned.) The passage here quoted begins, characteristically, with a quotation of the Pythagorean maxim ' Friends have in common all things they possess '. Cp. note 36 and text ; also the ' common meals ' mentioned in note 34.

(2) *Laws*, 942a, f. ; see next note. Both these passages are referred to as anti-individualistic by Gomperz (*op. cit.*, vol. II, 406). See also *Laws*, 807d/e.

³³ Cp. note 42, chapter 4, and text.—The quotation which follows in the present paragraph is *Laws*, 942a, f. (see the preceding note).

We must not forget that military education in the *Laws* (as in the *Republic*) is obligatory for all those allowed to carry arms, i.e. for all citizens—for all those who have anything like civil rights (cp. *Laws*, 753b). All others are ' banausic ', if not slaves (cp. *Laws*, 741e and 743d, and note 4 to chapter 11).

It is interesting that Barker, who hates militarism, believes that Plato held similar views (*Greek Political Theory*, 298–301). It is true that Plato did not eulogize war, and that he even spoke against war. But many militarists have talked peace and practised war ; and Plato's state is ruled by the military caste, i.e. by the wise ex-soldiers. This remark is as true for the *Laws* (cp. 753b) as it is for the *Republic*.

³⁴ Strictest legislation about meals—especially ' *common meals* '—and also about drinking habits plays a considerable part in Plato ; cp., for instance, *Republic*, 416e, 458c, 547d/e; *Laws*, 625e, 633a (where the obligatory common meals are said to be instituted with a view to war), 762b, 780–783, 806c, f, 839c, 842b. Plato always emphasizes the importance of common meals, in accordance with Cretan and Spartan customs. Interesting also is the preoccupation of Plato's uncle Critias with these matters. (Cp. Diels ², Critias, fr. 33.)

With the allusion to the anarchy of the ' wild beasts ', at the end of the present quotation, cp. also *Republic*, 563c.

³⁵ Cp. E. B. England's edition of the *Laws*, vol. I, p. 514, note to 739b8 ff. The quotations from Barker are from *op. cit.* ; pp. 149 and 148. Countless similar passages can be found in the writings of most Platonists. See however Sherrington's remark (cp. note 28 to this chapter) that it is hardly correct to say that a shoal or a herd is inspired by altruism. Herd instinct and tribal egoism, and the appeal to these instincts, should not be mixed up with unselfishness.

³⁶ Cp. *Republic*, 424a, 449c ; *Phaedrus*, 279c ; *Laws*, 739c ; see note 32 (1). (Cp. also *Lysis*, 207c, and Euripides, *Orest.*, 725.) For the possible connection of this principle with early Christian and Marxian communism, see note 29 (2) to chapter 5.

Regarding the individualistic theory of justice and injustice of the *Gorgias*, cp. for instance the examples given in the *Gorgias*, 468b, ff., 508d/e. These passages probably still show Socratic influence (cp. note 56 to chapter 10). Socrates' individualism is most clearly expressed in his famous doctrine of the self-sufficiency of the good man ; a doctrine which is mentioned by Plato in the *Republic* (387d/e) in spite of the fact that it flatly contradicts one of the main theses of the *Republic*, viz., that the state alone can be self-sufficient. (Cp. chapter 5, note 25, and the text to that and the following notes.)

³⁷ *Republic*, 368b/c.

³⁸ Cp. especially *Republic*, 344a, ff.

³⁹ Cp. *Laws*, 923b.

⁴⁰ *Republic*, 434a–c. (Cp. also text to note 6 and note 23 to this chapter, and notes 27 (3) and 31 to chapter 4.)

⁴¹ *Republic*, 466b/c. Cp. also the *Laws*, 715b/c, and many other passages against the anti-holistic misuse of class prerogatives. See also note 28 to this chapter, and note 25 (4) to chapter 7.

⁴² The problem here alluded to is that of the ' *paradox of freedom* ' ; cp. note 4 to chapter 7.—For the problem of state control in education, see note 13 to chapter 7.

⁴³ Cp. Aristotle, *Politics*, III, 9, 6 ff. (1280a). Cp. Burke, *French Revolution* (ed. 1815 ; vol. V, 184 ; the passage is aptly quoted by Jowett in his notes to the passage of Aristotle's ; see his edition of Aristotle's *Politics*, vol. II, 126).

The quotation from Aristotle later in the paragraph is *op. cit.*, III, 9, 8, (1280b).

Field, for instance, proffers a similar criticism (in his *Plato and His Contemporaries*, 117) : ' There is no question of the city and its laws exercising any educative effect on the moral character of its citizens.' However, Green has clearly shown (in his *Lectures on Political Obligation*) that it is impossible for the state to enforce morality by law. He would certainly have agreed with the formula : ' We want to moralize politics, and not to politicize morals.' (See end of this paragraph in the text.) Green's view is foreshadowed by Spinoza (*Tract. Theol. Pol.*, chapter 20) : ' He who seeks to regulate everything by law is more likely to encourage vice than to smother it.'

⁴⁴ I consider the analogy between civil peace and international peace, and between ordinary crime and international crime, as fundamental for any attempt to get international crime under control. For this analogy and its limitations as well as for the poverty of the historicist method in such problems, cp. not. 7 to chapter 9.

* Among those who consider rational methods for the establishment of international peace as a Utopian dream, H. J. Morgenthau may be mentioned (cp. his book, *Scientific Man versus Power Politics*, English edition, 1947). Morgenthau's position can be summed up as that of a disappointed historicist. He realizes that historical predictions are impossible ; but since he assumes (with, for example, the Marxists) that the field of applicability of *reason* (or of the scientific method) is limited to the field of *predictability*, he concludes from the impredictability of historical events that reason is inapplicable to the field of international affairs.

The conclusion does not follow, because scientific prediction and prediction in the sense of historical prophecy are not the same. (None of the natural sciences, with practically the sole exception of the theory of the solar system, attempts anything resembling historical prophecy.) The task of the social sciences is not to predict ' trends ' or ' tendencies ' of development, nor is this the task of the natural sciences. ' The best the so-called " social laws " can do is exactly the best the so-called " natural laws " can do, namely, to indicate certain *trends* . . Which conditions will actually occur and help one particular *trend* to materialize, neither the natural nor the social sciences are able to foretell. Nor are they able to forecast with more than a high degree of probability that in the presence of certain conditions a certain trend will materialize ', writes Morgenthau (pp. 120 ff. ; italics mine). But the natural sciences do not attempt the prediction of trends, and only historicists believe that they, and the social sciences, have such aims. Accordingly, the realization that these aims are not realizable will disappoint only the historicist. ' Many . . political scientists, however, claim that they can . . actually . . predict social events with a high degree of certainty. In fact, they . . are the victims of . . delusions ', writes Morgenthau. I certainly agree ; but this merely shows that historicism is to be repudiated. To assume, however, that the repudiation of historicism means the repudiation of rationalism in politics reveals a fundamentally historicist prejudice—the prejudice, namely, that historical prophecy is the basis of any rational politics. (I have mentioned this view as characteristic of historicism in the beginning of chapter 1.)

Morgenthau ridicules all attempts to bring power under the control of reason, and to suppress war, as springing from a rationalism and scientism which is inapplicable to society by its very essence. But clearly, he proves too much. Civil peace has been established in many societies, in spite of that essential lust for power which, according to Morgenthau's theory, should prevent it. He admits the fact, of course, but does not see that it destroys the theoretical basis of his romantic contentions.*

⁴⁵ The quotation is from Aristotle's *Politics*, III, 9, 8, (1280).

(1) I say in the text 'furthermore' because I believe that the passages alluded to in the text, i.e. *Politics*, III, 9, 6, and III, 9, 12, are likely to represent Lycophron's views also. My reasons for believing this are the following. From III, 9, 6, to III, 9, 12, Aristotle is engaged in a criticism of the doctrine I have called protectionism. In III, 9, 8, quoted in the text, he directly attributes to Lycophron a concise and perfectly clear formulation of this doctrine. From Aristotle's other references to Lycophron (see (2) in this note), it is probable that Lycophron's age was such that he must have been, if not the first, at least one of the first to formulate protectionism. Thus it seems reasonable to assume (although it is anything but certain) that the whole attack upon protectionism, i.e. III, 9, 6, to III, 9, 12, is directed against Lycophron, and that the various but equivalent formulations of protectionism are all his. (It may also be mentioned that Plato describes protectionism as a 'common view' in *Rep.*, 358c.)

Aristotle's objections are all intended to show that the protectionist theory is unable to account for the local as well as the internal unity of the state. It overlooks, he holds (III, 9, 6), the fact that the state exists for the sake of the good life in which neither slaves nor beasts can have a share (i.e. for the good life of the virtuous landed proprietor, for everybody who earns money is by his 'banausic' occupation prevented from citizenship). It also overlooks the *tribal unity* of the 'true' state which is (III, 9, 12) 'a community of well-being in families, and an *aggregation of families*, for the sake of a complete and self-sufficient life . . established among men who live in the same place, and *who intermarry*'.

(2) For Lycophron's equalitarianism, see note 13 to chapter 5.—Jowett (in *Aristotle's Politics*, II, 126) describes Lycophron as ' an obscure rhetorician ' ; but Aristotle must have thought otherwise, since in his extant writings he mentions Lycophron at least six times. (In *Pol.*, *Rhet.*, *Fragm.*, *Metaph.*, *Phys.*, *Soph. El.*)

It is unlikely that Lycophron was much younger than Alcidamas, his colleague in Gorgias' school, since his equalitarianism would hardly have attracted so much attention if it had become known after Alcidamas had succeeded Gorgias as the head of the school. Lycophron's epistemological interests (mentioned by Aristotle in *Metaphysics*, 1045b9, and *Physics*, 185b27) are also a case in point, since they make it probable that he was a pupil of Gorgias' earlier period, i.e. before Gorgias confined himself practically exclusively to rhetoric. Of course, any opinion on Lycophron must be highly speculative, owing to the scanty information we have.

⁴⁶ Barker, *Greek Political Theory*, I, p. 160. For Hume's criticism of the historical version of the contract theory, see note 43 to chapter 4. Concerning Barker's further contention (p. 161) that Plato's justice, as opposed to that of the contract theory, is not 'something external ', but rather, internal to the soul, I may remind the reader of Plato's frequent recommendations of most severe sanctions by which justice may be achieved ; he always recommends the use of ' persuasion *and force* ' (cp. notes 5, 10 and 18 to chapter 8). On the other hand, some modern democratic states have shown that it is possible to be liberal and lenient without increasing criminality.

With my remark that Barker sees in Lycophron (as I do) the originator of the contract theory, cp. Barker, *op cit.*, p. 63 : ' Protagoras did not anticipate the Sophist Lycophron in founding the doctrine of Contract.' (Cp. with this the text to note 27 to chapter 5.)

[47] Cp. *Gorgias*, 483b, f.

[48] Cp. *Gorgias*, 488e–489b ; see also 527b.
From the way in which Socrates replies here to Callicles, it seems possible that the historical Socrates (cp. note 56 to chapter 10) may have countered the arguments in support of a biological naturalism of Pindar's type by arguing like this : If it is natural that the stronger should rule, then it is also natural that equality should rule, since the multitude which shows its strength by the fact that it rules demands equality.   In other words, he may have shown the empty, ambiguous character of the naturalistic demand.   And his success might have inspired Plato to proffer his own version of naturalism.

I do not wish to assert that Socrates' later remark (508a) on ' geometrical equality ' must necessarily be interpreted as anti-equalitarian, i.e. why it must mean the same as the ' proportionate equity ' of the *Laws*, 744b, ff., and 757a–e (cp. notes 9 and 20 (1) to this chapter).   This is what Adam suggests in his second note to *Republic*, 558c15.   But perhaps there is something in his suggestion ; for the ' geometrical ' equality of the *Gorgias*, 508a, seems to allude to Pythagorean problems (cp. note 56 (6) to chapter 10 ; see also the remarks in that note on the *Cratylus*) and may well be an allusion to ' geometrical proportions '.

[49] *Republic*, 358e.   Glaucon disclaims the authorship in 358c.   In reading this passage, the reader's attention is easily distracted by the issue ' nature versus convention ', which plays a major rôle in this passage as well as in Callicles' speech in the *Gorgias*.   However, Plato's major concern in the *Republic* is not to defeat conventionalism, but to denounce the rational protectionist approach as selfish.   (That the conventionalist contract theory was not Plato's main enemy emerges from notes 27–28 to chapter 5, and text.)

[50] If we compare Plato's presentation of protectionism in the *Republic* with that in the *Gorgias*, then we find that it is indeed the same theory, although in the *Republic* much less emphasis is laid on *equality*.   But even equality is mentioned, although only in passing, viz., in *Republic*, 359c : ' Nature . . , by conventional law, is twisted round and compelled by force to honour equality.'   This remark increases the similarity with Callicles' speech.   (See *Gorgias*, esp. 483c/d.)   But as opposed to the *Gorgias*, Plato drops equality at once (or rather, he does not even take the issue up) and never returns to it ; which makes it only the more obvious that he was at pains to avoid the problem.   Instead, Plato revels in the description of the cynical egoism which he presents as the only source from which protectionism springs.   (For Plato's silence on equalitarianism, cp. especially note 14 to this chapter, and text.)   A. E. Taylor, *Plato : The Man and His Work* (1926), p. 268, contends that while Callicles starts from ' nature ', Glaucon starts from ' convention '.

[51] Cp. *Republic*, 359a ; my further allusions in the text are to 359b, 360d, ff. ; see also 358c.   For the ' rubbing in ', cp. 359a–362c, and the elaboration down to 367e.   Plato's description of the nihilistic tendencies of protectionism fills altogether nine pages in the Everyman edition of the *Republic* ; an indication of the significance Plato attached to it.   (There is a parallel passage in the *Laws*, 890a, f.)

[52] When Glaucon has finished his presentation, Adeimantus takes his place (with a very interesting and indeed most pertinent challenge to Socrates to criticize utilitarianism), yet not until Socrates has stated that he thinks Glaucon's presentation an excellent one (362d).   Adeimantus' speech is an amendment of Glaucon's, and it reiterates the claim that what I call protectionism derives from Thrasymachus' nihilism (see especially 367a, ff.)   After

Adeimantus, Socrates himself speaks, full of admiration for Glaucon as well as Adeimantus, because their belief in justice is unshaken in spite of the fact that *they presented the case for injustice so excellently*, i.e. the theory that it is good to inflict injustice as long as one can ' get away with it '. By emphasizing the excellence of the arguments proffered by Glaucon and Adeimantus, ' Socrates ' (i.e. Plato) implies that these arguments are a fair presentation of the views discussed ; and he ultimately states his own theory, not in order to show that Glaucon's representation needs emendation, but, as he emphasizes, in order to show that, contrary to the opinions of the protectionists, justice is good, and injustice evil. (It should not be forgotten—cp. note 49 to this chapter—that Plato's attack is not directed against the contract theory as such but solely against protectionism ; for the contract theory is soon (*Rep.*, 369b–c ; cp. text to note 29 to chapter 5) adopted by Plato himself, at least partially ; including the theory that people ' gather into settlements ' because ' every one expects in this way to further his own interests '.)

It must also be mentioned that the passage culminates with the impressive remark of ' Socrates ' quoted in the text to note 37 to this chapter. This shows that Plato combats protectionism only by presenting it as an immoral and indeed unholy form of egoism.

Finally, in forming our judgement on Plato's procedure, we must not forget that Plato likes to argue against rhetoric and sophistry ; and indeed, that he is the man who by his attacks on the ' Sophists ' created the bad associations connected with that word. I believe that we therefore have every reason to censor him when he himself makes use of rhetoric and sophistry in place of argument. (Cp. also note 10 to chapter 8.)

[53] We may take Adam and Barker as representative of the Platonists mentioned here. Adam says (note to 358e, ff.) of Glaucon that he resuscitates Thrasymachus' theory, and he says (note to 373a, ff.) of Thrasymachus that his is ' the same theory which is afterwards (in 358e, ff.) represented by Glaucon '. Barker says (*op. cit.*, 159) of the theory which I call protectionism and which he calls ' pragmatism ', that it is ' in the same spirit as Thrasymachus '.

[54] That the great sceptic Carneades believed in Plato's presentation can be seen from Cicero (*De Republica*, III, 8 ; 13 ; 23), where Glaucon's version is presented, practically without alteration, as the theory adopted by Carneades. (See also text to notes 65 and 66 and note 56 to chapter 10.)

In this connection I may express my opinion, that one can find a great deal of comfort in the fact that anti-humanitarians have always found it necessary to appeal to our humanitarian sentiments ; and also in the fact that they have frequently succeeded in persuading us of their sincerity. It shows that they are well aware that these sentiments are deeply rooted in most of us, and that the despised ' many ' are too good, too candid, and too guileless, rather than too bad ; while they are even ready to be told by their often unscrupulous ' betters ' that they are unworthy and materialistically minded egoists who only want to ' fill their bellies like the beasts '.

NOTES TO CHAPTER 7

The motto to this chapter is from the *Laws*, 690b. (Cp. note 28 to chapter 5.)

[1] Cp. text to notes 2/3 to chapter 6.

[2] Similar ideas have been expressed by J. S. Mill ; thus he writes in his *Logic* (1st ed., p. 557 f.) : ' Although the actions of rulers are by no means wholly determined by their selfish interests, it is as security against those selfish interests that constitutional checks are required.' Similarly he writes

in *The Subjection of Women* (p. 251 of the Everyman edition ; italics mine) :
' Who doubts that there may be great goodness, and great happiness and
great affection, under the absolute government of a good man ?   Meanwhile *laws and institutions require to be adapted, not to good men, but to bad.*'   Much
as I agree with the sentence in italics, I feel that the admission contained in
the first part of the sentence is not really called for.   (Cp. especially note 25 (3)
to this chapter.)   A similar admission may be found in an excellent passage
of his *Representative Government* (1861 ; see especially p. 49) where Mill combats
the Platonic ideal of the philosopher king because, *especially if his rule should
be a benevolent one*, it will involve the ' abdication ' of the ordinary citizen's will,
and ability, to judge a policy.

It may be remarked that this admission of J. S. Mill's was part of
an attempt to resolve the conflict between James Mill's *Essay on Government*
and ' Macaulay's famous attack ' on it (as J. S. Mill calls it ; cp. his *Autobiography*, chapter V, One Stage Onward ; 1st edition, 1873, pp. 157–61 ;
Macaulay's criticisms were first published in the *Edinburgh Review*, March
1829, June 1829, and October 1829).   This conflict played a great rôle in
J. S. Mill's development ; his attempt to resolve it determined, indeed, the
ultimate aim and character of his *Logic* (' the principle chapters of what I
afterwards published on the Logic of the Moral Sciences ') as we hear from
his *Autobiography*.

The resolution of the conflict between his father and Macaulay which
J. S. Mill proposes is this.   He says that his father was right in believing that
politics was a deductive science, but wrong in believing that ' the type of
deduction (was) that of . . pure geometry ', while Macaulay was right in
believing that it was more experimental than this, but wrong in believing that
it was like ' the purely experimental method of chemistry '.   The true solution
according to J. S. Mill (*Autobiography*, pp. 159 ff.) is this : the appropriate
method of politics is the deductive one of dynamics—a method which, he
believes, is characterized by the summation of effects as exemplified in the
' principle of the Composition of Forces '.   (That this idea of J. S. Mill survived at any rate down to 1937 is shown in my *The Poverty of Historicism*, p. 63.)

I do not think that there is very much in this analysis (which is based,
apart from other things, upon a misinterpretation of dynamics and chemistry).
Yet so much would seem to be defensible.

James Mill, like many before and after him, tried to ' deduce the science
of government from the principles of human nature ' as Macaulay said
(towards the end of his first paper), and Macaulay was right, I think, to describe this attempt as ' utterly impossible '.   Also, Macaulay's method could
perhaps be described as more empirical, in so far as he made full use of historical facts for the purpose of refuting J. Mill's dogmatic theories.   But the
method which he practised has nothing to do with that of chemistry, or with
that which J. S. Mill believed to be the method of chemistry (or with the
Baconian inductive method which, irritated by J. Mill's syllogisms, Macaulay
praised).   It was simply the method of rejecting invalid logical demonstra-
tions in a field in which nothing of interest can be logically demonstrated,
and of discussing theories and possible situations, in the light of alternative
theories and of alternative possibilities, and of factual historical evidence.
One of the main points at issue was that J. Mill believed that he had demonstrated the necessity for monarchy and aristocracy to produce a rule of terror
—a point which was easily refuted by examples.   J. S. Mill's two passages
quoted at the beginning of this note show the influence of this refutation.

Macaulay always emphasized that he only wanted to reject Mill's proofs,
and not to pronounce on the truth or falsity of his alleged conclusions.   This
alone should have made it clear that he did not attempt to practise the inductive method which he praised.

³ Cp. for instance E. Meyer's remark (*Gesch. d. Altertums*, V, p. 4) that 'power is, in its very essence, indivisible'.

⁴ Cp. *Republic*, 562b-565e. In the text, I am alluding especially to 562c : 'Does not the excess' (of liberty) ' bring men to such a state that they badly want a tyranny ? ' Cp. furthermore 563d/e : ' And in the end, as you know well enough, they just do not take any notice of the laws, whether written or unwritten, since they want to have no despot of any kind over them. This then is the origin out of which tyranny springs.' (For the beginning of this passage, see note 19 to chapter 4.)

Other remarks of Plato's on the *paradoxes of freedom and of democracy* are : *Republic*, 564a : ' Then too much freedom is liable to change into nothing else but too much slavery, in the individual as well as in the state . . Hence it is reasonable to assume that tyranny is enthroned by no other form of government than by democracy. Out of what I believe is the greatest possible excess of freedom springs what is the hardest and most savage form of slavery.' See also *Republic*, 565c/d : ' And are not the common people in the habit of making one man their champion or party leader, and of exalting his position and making him great ? '—' This is their habit.'—' Then it seems clear that whenever a tyranny grows up, this democratic party-leadership is the origin from which it springs.'

The so-called *paradox of freedom* is the argument that freedom in the sense of absence of any restraining control must lead to very great restraint, since it makes the bully free to enslave the meek. This idea is, in a slightly different form, and with a very different tendency, clearly expressed by Plato.

Less well known is the *paradox of tolerance* : Unlimited tolerance must lead to the disappearance of tolerance. If we extend unlimited tolerance even to those who are intolerant, if we are not prepared to defend a tolerant society against the onslaught of the intolerant, then the tolerant will be destroyed, and tolerance with them.—In this formulation, I do not imply, for instance, that we should always suppress the utterance of intolerant philosophies ; as long as we can counter them by rational argument and keep them in check by public opinion, suppression would certainly be most unwise. But we should claim the *right* to suppress them if necessary even by force ; for it may easily turn out that they are not prepared to meet us on the level of rational argument, but begin by denouncing all argument ; they may forbid their followers to listen to rational argument, because it is deceptive, and teach them to answer arguments by the use of their fists or pistols. We should therefore claim, in the name of tolerance, the right not to tolerate the intolerant. We should claim that any movement preaching intolerance places itself outside the law, and we should consider incitement to intolerance and persecution as criminal, in the same way as we should consider incitement to murder, or to kidnapping, or to the revival of the slave trade, as criminal.

Another of the less well-known paradoxes is the *paradox of democracy*, or more precisely, of majority-rule ; i.e. the possibility that the majority may decide that a tyrant should rule. That Plato's criticism of democracy can be interpreted in the way sketched here, and that the principle of majority-rule may lead to self-contradictions, was first suggested, as far as I know, by Leonard Nelson (cp. note 25 (2) to this chapter). I do not think, however, that Nelson, who, in spite of his passionate humanitarianism and his ardent fight for freedom, adopted much of Plato's political theory, and especially Plato's principle of leadership, was aware of the fact that analogous arguments can be raised against all the different particular forms of the *theory of sovereignty*.

All these paradoxes can easily be avoided if we frame our political demands in the way suggested in section II of this chapter, or perhaps in some such manner as this. We demand a government that rules according to the principles of equalitarianism and protectionism ; that tolerates all who are prepared to reciprocate, i.e. who are tolerant ; that is controlled by, and accountable to, the public.   And we may add that some form of majority vote, together with institutions for keeping the public well informed, is the best, though not infallible, means of controlling such a government.   (No infallible means exist.)   Cp. also chapter 6, the last four paragraphs in the text prior to note 42 ; text to note 20 to chapter 17 ; note 7 (4) to chapter 24 ; and note 6 to the present chapter.

⁵ Further remarks on this point will be found in chapter 19, below.

⁶ Cp. passage (7) in note 4 to chapter 2.

The following remarks on the *paradoxes of freedom and of sovereignty* may possibly appear to carry the argument too far ; since, however, the arguments discussed in this place are of a somewhat formal character, it may be just as well to make them more watertight, even if it involves something approaching hair-splitting.   Moreover, my experience in debates of this kind leads me to expect that the defenders of the leader-principle, i.e. of the sovereignty of the best or the wisest, may actually offer the following counter-argument : (*a*) if ' the wisest ' should decide that the majority should rule, then he was not really wise.   As a further consideration they may support this by the assertion (*b*) that a wise man would never establish a principle which might lead to contradictions, like that of majority-rule.   My reply to (*b*) would be that we need only to alter this decision of the ' wise ' man in such a way that it becomes free from contradictions.   (For instance, he could decide in favour of a government bound to rule according to the principle of equalitarianism and protectionism, and controlled by majority vote.   This decision of the wise man would give up the sovereignty-principle ; and since it would thereby become free from contradictions, it may be made by a ' wise ' man.   But of course, this would not free the principle that the wisest should rule from *its* contradictions. The other argument, namely (*a*), is a different matter.   It comes dangerously close to defining the ' wisdom ' or ' goodness ' of a politician in such a way that he is called ' wise ' or ' good ' only if he is determined not to give up his power.   And indeed, the only sovereignty-theory which is free from contradictions would be the theory which demands that only a man who is absolutely determined to cling to his power should rule.   Those who believe in the leader-principle should frankly face this logical consequence of their creed.   If freed from contradictions it implies, not the rule of the best or wisest, but the rule of the strong man, of the man of power.   (Cp. also note 7 to chapter 24.)

⁷ * Cp. my lecture *Towards a Rational Theory of Tradition* (first published in *The Rationalist Yearbook*, 1949 ; now in my *Conjectures and Refutations*), where I try to show that traditions play a kind of intermediate and intermediary rôle between *persons* (and personal decisions) and *institutions*.*

⁸ For Socrates' behaviour under the Thirty, see *Apology*, 32c.   The Thirty tried to implicate Socrates in their crimes, but he resisted.   This would have meant death to him if the rule of the Thirty had continued a little longer. Cp. also notes 53 and 56 to chapter 10.

For the contention, later in the paragraph, that wisdom means knowing the limitations of one's knowledge, see the *Charmides*, 167a, 170a, where the meaning of ' know thyself ' is explained in this way ; the *Apology* (cp. especially 23a–b) exhibits a similar tendency (of which there is still an echo in the *Timaeus*, 72a).   For the important modification in the interpretation of ' know thyself ' which takes place in the *Philebus*, see note 26 to the present chapter.   (Cp. also note 15 to chapter 8.)

⁹ Cp. Plato's *Phaedo*, 96–99.   The *Phaedo* is, I believe, still partly Socratic, but very largely Platonic.   The story of his philosophical development told by the Socrates of the *Phaedo* has given rise to much discussion.   It is,

I believe, an authentic autobiography neither of Socrates nor of Plato. I suggest that it is simply *Plato's interpretation* of Socrates' development. Socrates' attitude towards science (an attitude which combined the keenest interest in rational argument with a kind of modest agnosticism) was incomprehensible to Plato. He tried to explain it by referring to the backwardness of Athenian science in Socrates' day, as opposed to Pythagoreanism. Plato thus presents this agnostic attitude in such a way that it is no longer justified in the light of his newly acquired Pythagoreanism. (And he tries to show how much the new metaphysical theories of the soul would have appealed to Socrates' burning interest in the individual ; cp. notes 44 and 56 to chapter 10, and note 58 to chapter 8.)

[10] It is the version that involves the square root of two, and the problem of irrationality ; i.e. it is the very problem that precipitated the dissolution of Pythagoreanism. By refuting the Pythagorean arithmetization of geometry, it gave rise to the specific deductive-geometrical methods which we know from Euclid. (Cp. note 9 (2) to chapter 6.) The use of this problem in the *Meno* might be connected with the fact that there is a tendency in some parts of this dialogue to ' show off ' the author's (hardly Socrates') acquaintance with the 'latest' philosophical developments and methods.

[11] *Gorgias*, 521d, f.

[12] Cp. Crossman, *Plato To-Day*, 118. ' Faced by these three cardinal errors of Athenian Democracy . .'—How truly Crossman understands Socrates may be seen from *op. cit.*, 93 : ' All that is good in our Western culture has sprung from this spirit, whether it is found in scientists, or priests, or politicians, or quite ordinary men and women who have refused to prefer political falsehoods to simple truth . . in the end, their example is the only force which can break the dictatorship of force and greed . . . Socrates showed that philosophy is nothing else than conscientious objection to prejudice and unreason.'

[13] Cp. Crossman, *op. cit.*, 117 f. (first group of italics mine). It seems that Crossman has for the moment forgotten that, in Plato's state, education is a class monopoly. It is true that in the *Republic* the possession of money is not a key to higher education. But this is quite unimportant. The important point is that only the members of the ruling class are educated. (Cp. note 33 to chapter 4.) Besides, Plato was, at least in his later life, anything but an opponent of plutocracy, which he much preferred to a classless or equalitarian society : cp. the passage from the *Laws*, 744b, ff., quoted in note 20 (1) to chapter 6. For the problem of state control in education, cp. also note 42 to that chapter, and notes 39–41, chapter 4.

[14] Burnet takes (*Greek Philosophy*, I, 178) the *Republic* to be purely Socratic (or even pre-Socratic—a view which may be nearer to the truth ; cp. especially A. D. Winspear, *The Genesis of Plato's Thought*, 1940). But he does not even seriously attempt to reconcile this opinion with an important statement which he quotes from Plato's *Seventh Letter* (326a, cp. *Greek Philosophy*, I, 218) which he believes to be authentic. Cp. note 56 (5, d) to chapter 10.

[15] *Laws*, 942c, quoted more fully in text to note 33, chapter 6.

[16] *Republic*, 540c.

[17] Cp. the quotations from the *Republic*, 473c–e, quoted in text to note 44, chapter 8.

[18] *Republic*, 498b/c. Cp. the *Laws*, 634d/e, in which Plato praises the Dorian law that ' forbids any young man to question which of the laws are right and which are wrong, and makes them all unanimous in proclaiming that the laws are all good '. Only an old man may criticize a law, adds the old writer ; and even he may do so only when no young man can hear him. See also text to note 21 to this chapter, and notes 17, 23 and 40 to chapter 4.

[19] *Republic*, 497d.

[20] *Op. cit.*, 537c. The next quotations are from 537d–e, and 539d. The

'continuation of this passage' is 540b–c. Another most interesting remark is 536c–d, where Plato says that the persons selected (in the previous passage) for dialectical studies are decidedly too old for learning new subjects.

²¹ * Cp. H. Cherniss, *The Riddle of the Early Academy*, p. 79 ; and the *Parmenides*, 135c–d.*

Grote, the great democrat, strongly comments on this point (i.e. on the 'brighter' passages of the *Republic*, 537c–540) : 'The dictum forbidding dialectic debate with youth . . is decidedly anti-Socratic. . . It belongs indeed to the case of Meletus and Anytus, in their indictment against Socrates. . . It is identical with their charge against him, of corrupting the youth. . . And when we find him (= Plato) forbidding all such discourse at an earlier age than thirty years—we remark as a singular coincidence that this is the exact prohibition which Critias and Charicles actually imposed upon Socrates himself, during the short-lived dominion of the Thirty Oligarchs at Athens.' (Grote, *Plato, and the Other Companions of Socrates*, ed. 1875, vol. III, 239.)

²² The idea, contested in the text, that those who are good in obeying will also be good in commanding is Platonic. Cp. *Laws*, 762e.

Toynbee has admirably shown how successfully a Platonic system of educating rulers may work—in an arrested society ; cp. *A Study of History*, III, especially 33 ff. ; cp. notes 32 (3) and 45 (2) to chapter 4.

²³ Some may perhaps ask how an individualist can demand devotion to any cause, and especially to such an abstract cause as scientific inquiry. But such a question would only reveal the old mistake (discussed in the foregoing chapter), the identification of individualism and egoism. An individualist can be unselfish, and he can devote himself not only to the help of individuals, but also to the development of the institutional means for helping other people. (Apart from that, I do not think that devotion should be *demanded*, but only that it should be *encouraged*.) I believe that devotion to certain institutions, for instance, to those of a democratic state, and even to certain traditions, may fall well within the realm of individualism, provided that the humanitarian aims of these institutions are not lost sight of. Individualism must not be identified with an anti-institutional personalism. This is a mistake frequently made by individualists. They are right in their hostility to collectivism, but they mistake institutions for collectives (which claim to be aims in themselves), and therefore become anti-institutional personalists ; which leads them dangerously close to the leader-principle. (I believe that this partly explains Dickens' hostile attitude towards Parliament.) For my terminology (' individualism ' and ' collectivism ') see text to notes 26–29 to chapter 6.

²⁴ Cp. Samuel Butler, *Erewhon* (1872), p. 135 of the Everyman's edition.

²⁵ Cp. for these events : Meyer, *Gesch. d. Altertums*, V, pp. 522–525, and 488 f. ; see also note 69 to chapter 10. The Academy was notorious for breeding tyrants. Among Plato's pupils were Chairon, later the tyrant of Pellene ; Eurastus and Coriscus, the tyrants of Skepsis (near Atarneus) ; and Hermias, later tyrant of Atarneus and Assos. (Cp. *Athen.*, XI, 508, and Strabo, XIII, 610.) Hermias was, according to some sources, a direct pupil of Plato's ; according to the so-called ' Sixth Platonic Letter ', whose authenticity is questionable, he was perhaps only an admirer of Plato's, ready to accept his advice. Hermias became a patron of Aristotle, and of the third head of the Academy, Plato's pupil Xenocrates.

For Perdiccas III, and his relations to Plato's pupil Euphacus, see *Athen.*, XI, 508 ff., where Callippus is also referred to as Plato's pupil.

(1) Plato's lack of success as an educator is not very surprising if we look at the principles of education and selection developed in the First Book of the *Laws* (from 637d and especially 643a : ' Let me define the nature and meaning of education ' to the end of 650b). For in this long passage he shows that

there is one great instrument of educating, or rather, of selecting the man one can trust. It is wine, drunkenness, which will loose his tongue, and give you an idea of what he is really like. ' What is more fitting than to make use of wine, first of all to test the character of a man, and secondly, to train him? What is cheaper, and less objectionable? ' (649d/e). So far, I have not seen the method of drinking discussed by any of the educationists who glorify Plato. This is strange, for the method is still widely in use, even though it is perhaps no longer so cheap, especially in the universities.

(2) In fairness to the leader-principle, it must be admitted, however, that others have been more fortunate than Plato in their selection. Leonard Nelson (cp. note 4 to this chapter), for instance, who believed in this principle, seems to have had a unique power both of attracting and of selecting a number of men and women who have remained true to their cause, in the most trying and tempting circumstances. But theirs was a better cause than Plato's ; it was the humanitarian idea of freedom and equalitarian justice. * (Some of Nelson's essays have just been published in an English translation, by Yale University Press, under the title *Socratic Method and Critical Philosophy*, 1949. The very interesting introductory essay is by Julius Kraft.) *

(3) There remains this fundamental weakness in the theory of the benevolent dictator, a theory still flourishing even among some democrats. I have in mind the theory of the leading personality whose intentions are for the best of his people and who can be trusted. Even if that theory were in order ; even if we believe that a man can continue, without being controlled or checked, in such an attitude : how can we assume that he will detect a successor of the same rare excellence ? (Cp. also notes 3 and 4 to chapter 9, and note 69 to chapter 10.)

(4) Concerning the problem of power, mentioned in the text, it is interesting to compare the *Gorgias* (525e, f.) with the *Republic* (615d, f.). The two passages are closely parallel. But the *Gorgias* insists that the greatest criminals are *always* ' men who come from the class which possesses power ' ; private persons may be bad, it is said, but not incurable. In the *Republic*, this clear warning against the corrupting influence of power is omitted. Most of the greatest sinners are still tyrants ; but, it is said, ' there are also some private people among them '. (In the *Republic*, Plato relies on self-interest which, he trusts, will prevent the guardians from misusing their power ; cp. *Rep.*, 466b/c, quoted in text to note 41, chapter 6. It is not quite clear why self-interest should have such a beneficial effect on guardians, but not on tyrants.)

²⁶ * In the early (Socratic) dialogues (e.g. in the *Apology* and the *Charmides* ; cp. note 8 to the present chapter, note 15 to chapter 8 and note 56 (5) to chapter 10), the saying ' know thyself ' is interpreted as ' know how little you know '. The late (Platonic) dialogue *Philebus*, however, introduces a subtle but very important change. At first (48c/d, f.), the saying is here interpreted, by implication, in the same way ; for the many who do not know themselves are said to be ' claiming, . . and lying, that they are wise '. But this interpretation is now developed as follows. Plato divides men into two classes, the weak and the powerful. The ignorance and folly of the weak man is described as laughable, while ' *the ignorance of the strong* ' is ' appropriately called " evil " and " hateful " . .'. But this implies the Platonic doctrine that *he who wields power ought to be wise rather than ignorant* (or that only he who is wise ought to wield power) ; in opposition to the original Socratic doctrine that (everybody, and especially) *he who wields power ought to be aware of his ignorance*. (There is, of course, no suggestion in the *Philebus* that ' wisdom ' in its turn ought to be interpreted as ' awareness of one's limitations ' ; on the contrary, wisdom involves here an expert knowledge of Pythagorean teaching, and of the Platonic Theory of Forms, as developed in the *Sophist*.)*

NOTES TO CHAPTER 8

With the motto for this chapter, taken from *Republic* 540c–d, cp. note 37 to this chapter, and note 12 to chapter 9, where the passage is quoted more fully.

[1] *Republic*, 475e ; cp. for instance also 485c, f., 501c.

[2] *Op. cit.*, 389b, f.

[3] *Op. cit.*, 389c/d ; cp. also *Laws*, 730b, ff.

[4] With this and the three following quotations, cp. *Republic*, 407e and 406c. See also *Statesman*, 293a, f., 295b–296e, etc.

[5] Cp. *Laws*, 720c. It is interesting to note that the passage (718c–722b) serves to introduce the idea that the statesman should use *persuasion*, together with force (722b) ; and since by ' persuasion ' of the masses, Plato means largely lying propaganda—cp. notes 9 and 10 to this chapter and the quotation from *Republic*, 414b/c, quoted there in the text—it turns out that Plato's thought in our passage from the *Laws*, in spite of this novel gentleness, is still pervaded by the old associations—the doctor-politician administering lies. Later on (*Laws*, 857c/d), Plato complains about an opposite type of doctor : one who talks too much philosophy to his patient, instead of concentrating on the cure. It seems likely enough that Plato reports here some of his experiences when he fell ill while writing the *Laws*.

[6] *Republic*, 389b.—With the following short quotations cp. *Republic*, 459c.

[7] Cp. Kant, *On Eternal Peace*, Appendix. (*Werke*, ed. Cassirer, 1914, vol. VI, 457.) Cp. M. Campbell Smith's translation (1903), pp. 162 ff.

[8] Cp. Crossman, *Plato To-Day* (1937), 130 ; cp. also the immediately preceding pages. It seems that Crossman still believes that lying propaganda was intended only for the consumption of the ruled, and that Plato intended to educate the rulers to a full use of their critical faculties ; for I find now (in *The Listener*, vol. 27, p. 750) that he writes : ' Plato believed in free speech, free discussion only for the select few.' But the fact is that he did not believe in it at all. Both in the *Republic* and in the *Laws* (cp. the passages quoted in notes 18–21 to chapter 7, and text), he expresses his fear lest anybody who is not yet on the verge of old age should think or speak freely, and thus endanger the rigidity of the arrested doctrine, and therefore the petrifaction of the arrested society. See also the next two notes.

[9] *Republic*, 414b/c. In 414d, Plato reaffirms his hope of persuading ' the rulers themselves and the military class, and then the rest of the city ', of the truth of his lie. Later he seems to have regretted his frankness ; for in the *Statesman*, 269b, ff. (see especially 271b ; cp. also note 6 (4) to chapter 3), he speaks as if he believed in the truth of the same Myth of the Earthborn which, in the *Republic*, he had been reluctant (see note 11 to this chapter) to introduce even as a lordly ' lie '.

* What I translate as a ' lordly lie ' is usually translated ' noble lie ' or ' noble falsehood ' or even ' spirited fiction '.

The literal translation of the word ' *gennaios* ' which I now translate by ' lordly ' is ' high born ' or ' of noble descent '. Thus ' lordly lie ' is at least as literal as ' noble lie ', but it avoids the associations which the term ' noble lie ' might suggest, and which are in no way warranted by the situation, viz. a lie by which a man nobly takes something upon himself which endangers him—such as Tom Sawyer's lie by which he takes Becky's guilt upon himself and which Judge Thatcher (in chapter XXXV) describes as ' a noble, a generous, a magnanimous lie '. There is no reason whatever why the ' lordly lie ' should be considered in this light ; thus the translation ' noble lie ' is just one of the typical attempts at idealizing Plato.—Cornford translates ' a . . bold flight of invention ', and argues in a footnote against the translation ' noble lie ' ; he gives passages where ' *gennaios* ' means ' on a generous scale ' ; and indeed, ' big lie ' or ' grand lie ' would be a perfectly appropriate translation. But Cornford at the same time argues against the use of the term ' lie ' ; he describes the myth as ' Plato's harmless allegory ' and argues against the idea that Plato ' would countenance lies, for the most part ignoble, now called propaganda ' ; and in the next footnote he says : ' Note that the Guardians themselves are to accept this allegory, if possible. It is not " propaganda " foisted on the masses by the Rulers.' But all these attempts at idealization fail. Plato himself makes it quite clear that the lie is one for which one ought to feel ashamed ; see the last quotation in note 11, below. (In the first edition of this book, I translated ' inspired lie ', alluding to its ' high birth ', and suggested ' ingenious lie ' as an alternative ; this was criticized both as too free and as tendentious by some of my Platonic friends. But Cornford's ' bold flight of invention ' takes ' *gennaios* ' in precisely the same sense.)

See also notes 10 and 18 to this chapter.*

¹⁰ Cp. *Republic*, 519e, f., quoted in the text to note 35 to chapter 5 ; on *persuasion and force*, see also *Republic*, 366d, discussed in the present note, below, and the passages referred to in notes 5 and 18 to this chapter.

The Greek word (' peithō '; its personification is an alluring goddess, an attendant of Aphroditē) usually translated by *persuasion* can mean (*a*) ' persuasion by fair means ' and (*b*) ' talking over by foul means ', i.e. ' make-believe ' (see below, sub. (D), i.e. *Rep.*, 414c), and sometimes it means even ' persuasion by gifts ', i.e. bribery (see below, sub. (D), i.e. *Rep.*, 390e). Especially in the phrase ' persuasion and force ', the term ' persuasion ' is often (*Rep.* 548b) interpreted in sense (*a*), and the phrase is often (and often appropriately) translated ' by fair means or foul ' (cp. Davies' and Vaughan's translation ' by fair means or foul ', of the passage (C), *Rep.*, 365d, quoted below). I believe, however, that Plato, when recommending ' persuasion and force ' as instruments of political technique, uses the words in a more literal sense, and that he recommends the use of rhetorical propaganda together with violence. (Cp. *Laws*, 661c, 711c, 722b, 753a.)

The following passages are significant for Plato's use of the term ' persuasion ' in sense (*b*), and especially in connection with political propaganda. (*A*) *Gorgias*, 453a to 466a, especially 454b–455a ; *Phaedrus*, 260b, ff., *Theaetetus*, 201a ; *Sophist*, 222c ; *Statesman*, 296b, ff., 304c/d ; *Philebus*, 58a. In all these passages, persuasion (the ' art of persuasion ' as opposed to the ' art of imparting true knowledge ') is associated with rhetoric, make-believe, and propaganda. In the *Republic*, 364b, f., especially 364e–365d (cp. *Laws*, 909b), deserves attention. (*B*) In 364e (' they persuade ', i.e. mislead into believing, ' not only individuals, but whole cities '), the term is used much in the same sense as in 414b/c (quoted in the text to note 9, this chapter), the passage of the ' lordly lie '. (*C*) 365d is interesting because it uses a term which Lindsay translates very aptly by ' cheating ' as a kind of paraphrase for ' persuading '. (' In order not to be caught .. we have the masters of persuasion at our disposal ; .. thus by *persuasion and force*, we shall escape punishment. But, it may be objected, one cannot *cheat, or force*, the gods .. .') Furthermore (*D*) in *Republic*, 390e, f., the term ' persuasion ' is used in the sense of bribery. (This must be an old use ; the passage is supposed to be a quotation from Hesiod. It is interesting that Plato, who so often argues against the idea that men can ' persuade ' or bribe the gods, makes some concession to it in the next passage, 399a/b.) Next we come to 414b/c, the passage of the ' lordly lie ' ; immediately after this passage, in 414c (cp. also the next note in this chapter), ' Socrates ' makes the cynical remark (*E*) : ' It would need much persuading to make anybody believe in this story.' Lastly, I may mention (*F*) *Republic*, 511d and 533e, where Plato speaks of

persuasion or belief or faith (the root of the Greek word for ' persuasion ' is
the same as that of our ' faith ') as a lower cognitive faculty of the soul,
corresponding to the formation of (delusive) opinion about things in flux
(cp. note 21 to chapter 3, and especially the use of ' persuasion ' in *Tim.*, 51e),
as opposed to rational knowledge of the unchanging Forms. For the problem
of ' moral ' persuasion, see also chapter 6, especially notes 52/54 and text,
and chapter 10, especially text to notes 56 and 65, and note 69.

¹¹ *Republic*, 415a. The next quotation is from 415c. (See also the
Cratylus, 398a.) Cp. notes 12–14 to the present chapter and text, and notes
27 (3), 29, and 31 to chapter 4.

(1) For my remark in the text, earlier in this paragraph, concerning Plato's
uneasiness, see *Republic*, 414c–d, and last note, (*E*) : ' It would need much
persuading to make anybody believe in this story,' says Socrates.—' You seem
to be rather reluctant to tell it,' replies Glaucon.—' You will understand my
reluctance ', says Socrates, ' when I have told it.'—' Speak and don't be
frightened ', says Glaucon. This dialogue introduces what I call the *first idea
of the Myth* (proffered by Plato in the *Statesman* as a true story ; cp. note 9 to
this chapter ; see also *Laws*, 740a). As mentioned in the text, Plato suggests
that it is this ' first idea ' which is the reason for his hesitation, for Glaucon
replies to this idea : ' Not without reason were you so long ashamed to tell
your lie.' No similar rhetorical remark is made after Socrates has told ' the
rest of the story ', i.e., the Myth of Racialism.

* (2) Concerning the autochthonous warriors, we must remember that
the Athenian nobility claimed (as opposed to the Dorians) to be the aborigines
of their country, born of the earth ' like grasshoppers ' (as Plato says in the
Symposium, 191b ; see also end of note 52 to the present chapter). It has
been suggested to me by a friendly critic that Socrates' uneasiness, and
Glaucon's comment that Socrates had reason to be ashamed, mentioned here-
under (1), is to be interpreted as an ironical allusion of Plato's to the Athenians
who, in spite of their claim to be autochthonous, did not defend their country
as they would defend a mother. But this ingenious suggestion does not appear
to me a tenable one. Plato, with his openly admitted preference of Sparta,
would be the last to charge the Athenians with lack of patriotism ; and there
would be no justice in such a charge, for in the Peloponnesian war, the
Athenian democrats never gave in to Sparta (as will be shown in chapter 10),
while Plato's own beloved uncle Critias did give in, and became the leader
of a puppet government under the protection of the Spartans. If Plato
intended to allude ironically to an inadequate defence of Athens, then it could
be only an allusion to the Peloponnesian war, and thus a criticism of Critias—
the last person whom Plato would criticize in this way.

(3) Plato calls his Myth a ' Phoenician lie '. A suggestion which may
explain this is due to R. Eisler. He points out that the Ethiopians, Greeks
(the silver mines), Sudanese, and Syrians (Damascus) were in the Orient
described, respectively, as golden, silver, bronze, and iron races, and that this
description was utilized in Egypt for purposes of political propaganda (cp.
also Daniel, ii. 31–45) ; and he suggests that the story of these four races was
brought to Greece in Hesiod's time by the Phoenicians (as might be expected),
and that Plato alludes to this fact.*

¹² The passage is from the *Republic*, 546a, ff. ; cp. text to notes 36–40 to
chapter 5. The intermixture of classes is clearly forbidden in 434c also ;
cp. notes 27 (3), 31 and 34 to chapter 4, and note 40 to chapter 6.

The passage from the *Laws* (930d–e) contains the principle that the child
of a mixed marriage inherits the caste of his lesser parent.

¹³ *Republic*, 547a. (For the mixture theory of heredity, see also text to
note 39/40 to chapter 5, especially 40 (2), and to notes 39–43, and 52, to
the present chapter.)

¹⁴ *Op. cit.*, 415c.

¹⁵ Cp. Adam's note to *Republic*, 414b, ff., italics mine.   The great exception is Grote (*Plato, and the Other Companions of Socrates*, London, 1875, III, 240), who sums up the spirit of the *Republic*, and its opposition to that of the *Apology* : 'In the . . Apology, we find Socrates confessing his own ignorance. . . But the Republic presents him in a new character. . . He is himself on the throne of King Nomos : the infallible authority, temporal as well as spiritual, from which all public sentiment emanates, and by whom orthodoxy is determined. . . He now expects every individual to fall into the place, and contract the opinions, prescribed by authority ; *including among these opinions deliberate ethical and political fictions*, such as about the . . earthborn men. . . Neither the Socrates of the Apology, nor his negative Dialectic, could be allowed to exist in the Platonic Republic.' (Italics mine ; see also Grote, *op. cit.*, p. 188.)

The doctrine that *religion is opium for the people*, although not in this particular formulation, turns out to be one of the tenets of Plato and the Platonists. (Cp. also note 17 and text, and especially note 18 to this chapter.)   It is, apparently, one of the more esoteric doctrines of the school, i.e. it may be discussed only by sufficiently elderly members (cp. note 18 to chapter 7) of the upper class.   But those who let the cat out of the bag are prosecuted for atheism by the idealists.

¹⁶ For instance Adam, Barker, Field.

¹⁷ Cp. Diels, *Vorsokratiker* ⁵, Critias fragm. 25.   (I have picked about eleven characteristic lines out of more than forty.)—It may be remarked that the passage commences with a sketch of the social contract (which even somewhat resembles Lycophron's equalitarianism ; cp. note 45 to chapter 6). On Critias, cp. especially note 48 to chapter 10.   Since Burnet has suggested that the poetic and dramatic fragments known under the name of Critias should be attributed to the grandfather of the leader of the Thirty, it should be noted that Plato attributes to the latter poetic gifts in the *Charmides*, 157e ; and in 162d, he alludes even to the fact that Critias was a dramatist.   (Cp. also Xenophon's *Memorabilia*, I, iv, 18.)

¹⁸ Cp. the *Laws*, 909e.   It seems that Critias' view later even became part of the Platonic school tradition, as indicated by the following passage from Aristotle's *Metaphysics* (1074b3) which at the same time provides another example of the use of the term ' persuasion ' for ' propaganda ' (cp. notes 5 and 10 to this chapter).   ' The rest . . has been added in the form of a myth, with a view to the persuasion of the mob, and to legal and general (political) expediency . .'   Cp. also Plato's attempt in the *Statesman*, 271a, f., to argue in favour of the truth of a myth in which he certainly did not believe.   (See notes 9 and 15 to this chapter.)

¹⁹ *Laws*, 908b.

²⁰ *Op. cit.*, 909a.

²¹ For the conflict between good and evil, see *op. cit.*, 904–906.   See especially 906a/b (justice versus injustice ; ' justice ' means here, still, the collectivist justice of the *Republic*).   Immediately preceding is 903c, a passage quoted above in the text to note 35 to chapter 5 and to note 27 to chapter 6. See also note 32 to the present chapter.

²² *Op. cit.*, 905d–907b.

²³ The paragraph to which this note is appended indicates my adherence to an ' absolutist ' theory of truth which is in accordance with the common idea that *a statement is true if* (and only if) *it agrees with the facts* it describes. This ' absolute ' or ' correspondence theory of truth ' (which goes back to Aristotle) was first clearly developed by A. Tarski (*Der Wahrheitsbegriff in den formalisierten Sprachen*, Polish ed. 1933, German translation 1936), and is the basis of a theory of logic called by him Semantics (cp. note 29 to chapter 3

and note 5 (2) to chapter 5) ; see also R. Carnap's *Introduction to Semantics*, 1942, which develops the theory of truth in detail.	I am quoting from p. 28 : ' It is especially to be noticed that the concept of truth in the sense just explained —we may call it the semantical concept of truth—is fundamentally different from concepts like " believed ", " verified ", " highly confirmed ", etc.'— A similar, though undeveloped view can be found in my *Logik der Forschung*, (translated, 1959, as *The Logic of Scientific Discovery*), section 84 ; this was written before I became acquainted with Tarski's Semantics, which is the reason why my theory is only rudimentary.	The pragmatist theory of truth (which derives from Hegelianism) was criticized by Bertrand Russell from the point of view of an absolutist theory of truth as early as 1907 ; and recently he has shown the connection between a relativist theory of truth and the creed of fascism. See Russell, *Let the People Think*, pp. 77, 79.

²⁴ Especially *Rep.*, 474c–502d.	The following quotation is *Rep.*, 475e.

²⁵ For the seven quotations which follow, in this paragraph, see : (1) and (2), *Republic*, 476b ; (3), (4), (5), *op. cit.*, 500d–e ; (6) and (7) : *op. cit.*, 501a/b ; with (7), cp. also the parallel passage, *op. cit.*, 484c. See, furthermore, *Sophist*, 253d/e ; *Laws*, 964a–966a (esp. 965b/c).

²⁶ Cp. *op. cit.*, 501c.

²⁷ Cp. especially *Republic*, 509a, f.—See 509b : ' The sun induces the sensible things to generate ' (although he is not himself involved in the process of generation) ; similarly, ' you may say of the objects of rational knowledge that not only do they owe it to the Good that they can be known, but their reality and even their essence flows from it ; although the Good is not itself an essence but transcends even essences in dignity and power.' (With 509b, cp. Aristotle, *De Gen. et Corr.*, 336a 15, 31, and *Phys.*, 194b 13.)—In 510b, the Good is described as the absolute origin (not merely postulated or assumed), and in 511b, it is described as ' the first origin of everything '.

²⁸ Cp. especially *Republic*, 508b, ff.—See 508b/c : ' What the Good has begotten in its own likeness ' (viz. *truth*) ' is the link, in the intelligible world between reason and its objects ' (i.e. the Ideas) ' in the same way as, in the visible world, that thing ' (viz. *light* which is the offspring of the sun) ' which is the link between sight and its objects ' (i.e. sensible things).

²⁹ Cp. *op. cit.*, 505a ; 534b, ff.

³⁰ Cp. *op. cit.*, 505d.

³¹ *Philebus*, 66a.

³² *Republic*, 506d, ff., and 509–511.

The definition of the Good, here quoted, as ' the class of the determinate (or finite, or limited) conceived as a unity ' is, I believe, not so hard to understand, and is in full agreement with others of Plato's remarks.	The ' class of the determinate ' is the class of the Forms or Ideas, conceived as male principles, or progenitors, as opposed to the female, unlimited or indeterminate space (cp. note 15 (2) to chapter 3). These Forms or primogenitors are, of course, good, in so far as they are ancient and unchanging originals, and in so far as each of them is one as opposed to the many sensible things which it generates.	If we conceive the class or race of the progenitors as many, then they are not absolutely good ; thus the absolute Good can be visualized if we conceive them as a unity, as One—as the One primogenitor. (Cp. also Arist., *Met.*, 988a 10.)

Plato's Idea of the Good is practically empty.	It gives us no indication of what is good, in a moral sense, i.e. what we ought to do.	As can be seen especially from notes 27 and 28 to this chapter, all we hear is that the Good is highest in the realm of Form or Ideas, a kind of super-Idea, from which the Ideas originate, and receive their existence.	All we could possibly derive from this is that the Good is unchangeable and prior or primary and therefore ancient (cp. note 3 to chapter 4), and One Whole ; and, therefore, that those things participate in it which do not change, i.e., the good is what preserves (cp. notes 2 and 3 to chapter 4), and what is ancient, especially the ancient laws (cp. note 23 to chapter 4, note 7, paragraph on Platonism, to chapter 5, and note 18 to chapter 7), and that holism is good (cp. note 21 to the present chapter) ; i.e., we are again thrown back, in practice, to totalitarian morality (cp. text to notes 40/41 to chapter 6).

If the *Seventh Letter* is genuine, then we have there (314b/c) another statement by Plato that his doctrine of the Good cannot be formulated ; for he says of this doctrine : ' It is not capable of expression like other branches of study.' (Cp. also note 57 to chapter 10.)

It is again Grote who clearly saw and criticized the emptiness of the Platonic Idea or Form of Good. After asking what this Good is, he says (*Plato*, III, 241 f.) : 'This question is put . . But unfortunately it remains unanswered. . . In describing the condition of other men's minds—that they divine a Real Good . . do everything in order to obtain it, but puzzle themselves in vain to grasp and determine what it is—he' (Plato) 'has unconsciously described the condition of his own.' It is surprising to see how few modern writers have taken any notice of Grote's excellent criticism of Plato.

For the quotations in the next pa ragraph of the text, see (1) : *Republic*, 500b–c ; (2) : *op. cit.*, 485a/b. This second passage is very interesting. It is, as Adam reaffirms (note to 485b9), the first passage in which ' generation ' and ' degeneration ' are employed in this half-technical sense. It refers to the flux, and to Parmenides' changeless entities. And it introduces the main argument in favour of the rule of the philosophers. See also note 26 (1) to chapter 3 and note 2 (2) to chapter 4. In the *Laws*, 689c–d, when discussing the ' degeneration ' (688c) of the Dorian kingdom brought about by the ' worst ignorance ' (the ignorance, namely, of not knowing how to obey those who are rulers by nature ; see 689b), Plato explains what he means by wisdom : only such wisdom as aims at the greatest unity or ' unisonity ' entitles a man to authority. And the term ' unisonity ' is explained in the *Republic*, 591b and d, as the harmony of the ideas of justice (i.e. of keeping one's place) and of temperance (of being satisfied with it). Thus we are again thrown back to our starting point.

[33] * A critic of this passage asserted that he could find no trace, in Plato, of any fear of independent thought. But we should remember Plato's insistence on censorship (see notes 40 and 41 to chapter 4) and his prohibition of higher dialectical studies for anybody under 50 years of age in the *Republic* (see notes 19 to 21 to chapter 7), to say nothing of the *Laws* (see note 18 to chapter 7, and many other passages).*

[34] For the problem of the priest caste, see the *Timaeus*, 24a. In a passage which clearly alludes to the best or ' ancient ' state of the *Republic*, the priest caste takes the place of the ' philosophic race ' of the *Republic*. Cp. also the attacks on priests (and even on Egyptian priests), diviners, and shamans, in the *Statesman*, 290c, f. ; see also note 57 (2) to chapter 8, and note 29 to chapter 4.

The remark of Adam's, quoted in the text in the paragraph after the next, is from his note to *Republic*, 547a3 (quoted above in text to note 43 to chapter 5).

[35] Cp. for instance *Republic*, 484c, 500e, ff.

[36] *Republic*, 535a/b. All that Adam says (cp. his note to 535b8) about the term which I have translated by ' awe-inspiring ' supports the usual view that the term means ' stern ' or ' awful ', especially in the sense of ' inspiring terror '. Adam's suggestion that we translate ' masculine ' or ' virile ' follows the general tendency to tone down what Plato says, and it clashes strangely with *Theaetetus* 149a. Lindsay translates : ' of . . sturdy morals '.

[37] *Op. cit.*, 540c ; see also 500c–d : ' the philosopher himself . . becomes

godlike ', and note 12 to chapter 9, where 540c, f., is quoted more fully.—
It is most interesting to note how Plato transforms the Parmenidian One
when arguing in favour of an aristocratic hierarchy. The opposition *one*
—*many* is not preserved, but gives rise to a system of grades : the one
Idea—the few who come close to it—the more who are their helpers—
the many, i.e. the mob (this division is fundamental in the *Statesman*). As
opposed to this, Antisthenes' monotheism preserves the original Eleatic
opposition between the One (God) and the Many (whom he probable
considered as brothers because of their equal distance from God).—Antisthenes
was influenced by Parmenides through Zeno's influence upon Gorgias. Probably
there was also the influence of Democritus, who had taught : ' The wise may
belongs to all countries alike, for the home of a great soul is the whole world.'

[38] *Republic*, 500d.

[39] The quotations are from *Republic*, 459b, and ff. ; cp. also notes 34 f. to
chapter 4, and especially 40 (2) to chapter 5. Cp. also the three similes of
the *Statesman*, where the ruler is compared with (1) the shepherd, (2) the
doctor, (3) the weaver whose functions are explained as those of a man who
blends characters by skilful breeding (310b, f.).

[40] *Op. cit.*, 460a. My statement that Plato considers this law very important
is based on the fact that Plato mentions it in the outline of the *Republic* in the
Timaeus, 18d/e.

[41] *Op. cit.*, 460b. The ' suggestion is taken up ' in 468c ; see the next note.

[42] *Op. cit.*, 468c. Though it has been denied by my critics, my translation
is correct, and so is my remark about ' the latter benefit '. Shorey calls the
passage ' deplorable '.

[43] For the Story of the Number and the Fall, cp. notes 13 and 52 to this
chapter, notes 39/40 to chapter 5, and text.

[44] *Republic*, 473c–e. Note the opposition between (divine) *rest*, and the
evil, i.e. change in the form of corruption, or degeneration. Concerning the
term translated here by ' oligarchs ' cp. the end of note 57, below. It is
equivalent to ' hereditary aristocrats '.

The phrase which, for stylistic reasons, I have put in brackets, is important,
for in it *Plato demands the suppression of all ' pure ' philosophers* (and unphilosophical
politicians). A more literal translation of the phrase would be this : ' while
the many ' (who have) ' natures ' (disposed or gifted) ' for drifting along,
nowadays, in one alone of these two, *are eliminated by force* '. Adam admits
that the meaning of Plato's phrase is ' that Plato refuses to sanction the exclusive
pursuit of knowledge ' ; but his suggestion that we soften the meaning of
the last words of the phrase by translating : ' are forcibly debarred from
exclusively pursuing either ' (italics his ; cp. note to 473d24, vol. I, 330, of his
ed. of the *Republic*) has no foundation in the original,—only in his tendency
to idealize Plato. The same holds for Lindsay's translation (' are forcibly
debarred from this behaviour ').—Whom does Plato wish to suppress ? I
believe that ' the many ' whose limited or incomplete talents or ' natures '
Plato condemns here are identical (as far as philosophers are concerned)
with the ' many whose natures are incomplete ', mentioned in *Republic*, 495d ;
and also with the ' many ' (professed philosophers) ' whose wickedness is
inevitable ', mentioned in 489e (cp. also 490e/491a) ; cp. notes 47, 56, and 59
to this chapter (and note 23 to chapter 5). The attack is, therefore, directed
on the one hand against the ' uneducated ' democratic politicians, on the
other hand most probably mainly against the half-Thracian Antisthenes, the
' uneducated bastard ', the equalitarian philosopher ; cp. note 47, below.

[45] Kant, *On Eternal Peace*, Second Supplement (*Werke*, ed. Cassirer, 1914,
vol. VI, 456). Italics mine ; I have also abbreviated the passage. (The
' possession of power ' may well allude to Frederick the Great.)

[46] Cp. for instance Gomperz, *Greek Thinkers*, V, 12, 2 (German ed.,

vol. II ², 382) ; or Lindsay's translation of the *Republic*. (For a criticism of this interpretation, cp. note 50, below.)

⁴⁷ It must be admitted that Plato's attitude towards Antisthenes raises a highly speculative problem ; this is of course connected with the fact that very little is known about Antisthenes from first-rate sources. Even the old Stoic tradition that the Cynic school or movement can be traced back to Antisthenes is at present often questioned (cp., for instance, G. C. Field's *Plato*, 1930, or D. R. Dudley, *A History of Cynicism*, 1937) although perhaps not on quite sufficient grounds (cp. Fritz's review of the last-mentioned book in *Mind*, vol. 47, p. 390). In view of what we know, especially from Aristotle, about Antisthenes, it appears to me highly probable that there are many allusions to him in Plato's writings ; and even the one fact that Antisthenes was, apart from Plato, the only member of Socrates' inner circle who taught philosophy at Athens, would be a sufficient justification for searching Plato's work for such allusions. Now it seems to me rather probable that a series of attacks in Plato's work first pointed out by Duemmler (especially *Rep.*, 495d/e, mentioned below in note 56 to this chapter ; *Rep.*, 535e, f., *Soph.*, 251b–e) represents these allusions. There is a definite resemblance (or so at least it appears to me) between these passages and Aristotle's scornful attacks on Antisthenes. Aristotle, who mentions Antisthenes' name, speaks of him as of a simpleton, and he speaks of ' uneducated people such as the Antistheneans ' (cp. note 54 to chapter 11). Plato, in the passages mentioned, speaks in a similar way, but more sharply. The first passage I have in mind is from the *Sophist*, 251b, f., which corresponds very closely indeed to Aristotle's first passage. Regarding the two passages from the *Republic*, we must remember that, according to the tradition, Antisthenes was a ' bastard ' (his mother came from barbarian Thrace), and that he taught in the Athenian gymnasium reserved for ' bastards '. Now we find, in *Republic*, 535e, f. (cp. end of note 52 to this chapter), an attack which is so specific that an individual person must be intended. Plato speaks of ' people who dabble in philosophy without being restrained by a feeling of their own unworthiness', and he contends that ' the baseborn should be debarred ' from doing so. He speaks of the people as ' unbalanced ' (or ' skew ' or ' limping ') in their love of work and of relaxation ; and becoming more personal, he alludes to somebody with a ' crippled soul ' who, though he loves truth (as a Socratic would), does not attain it, since he ' wallows in ignorance ' (probably because he does not accept the theory of Forms) ; and he warns the city not to trust such limping ' bastards '. I think it likely that Antisthenes is the object of this undoubtedly personal attack ; the admission that the enemy loves truth seems to me an especially strong argument, occurring as it does in an attack of extreme violence. But if this passage refers to Antisthenes, then it is very likely that a very similar passage refers to him also, viz. *Republic*, 495d/e, where Plato again describes his victim as possessing a disfigured or crippled soul as well as body. He insists in this passage that the object of his contempt, in spite of aspiring to be a philosopher, is so depraved that he is not even ashamed of doing degrading (' banausic ' ; cp. note 4 to chapter 11) manual labour. Now we know of Antisthenes that he recommended manual labour, which he held in high esteem (for Socrates' attitude, cp. Xenophon, *Mem.*, II, 7, 10), and that he practised what he taught ; a further strong argument that the man with the crippled soul is Antisthenes.

Now in the same passage, *Republic*, 495d, there is also a remark about ' the many whose natures are incomplete', and who nevertheless aspire to philosophy. This seems to refer to the same group (the ' Antistheneans ' of Aristotle) of ' many natures ' whose suppression is demanded in *Republic*, 473c–e, discussed in note 44 to this chapter.—Cp. also *Republic*, 489e, mentioned in notes 59 and 56 to this chapter.

⁴⁸ We know (from Cicero, *De Natura Deorum*, and Philodemus, *De Pietate*) that Antisthenes was a monotheist ; and the form in which he expressed his monotheism (there is only One God ' according to nature ', i.e., to truth, although there are many ' according to convention ') shows that he had in mind the opposition *nature—convention* which, in the mind of a former member of the school of Gorgias and contemporary of Alcidamas and Lycophron (cp. note 13 to chapter 5), must have been connected with *equalitarianism*.

This in itself does not of course establish the conclusion that the half-barbarian Antisthenes believed in the brotherhood of Greeks and barbarians. Yet it seems to me extremely likely that he did.

W. W. Tarn (*Alexander the Great and the Unity of Mankind* ; cp. note 13 (2) to chapter 5) has tried to show—I once thought successfully—that the idea of the unity of mankind can be traced back at least to Alexander the Great.   I think that by a very similar line of reasoning, we can trace it back farther ; to Diogenes, Antisthenes, and even to Socrates and the ' Great Generation ' of the Periclean age (cp. note 27 to chapter 10, and text).   This seems, even without considering the more detailed evidence, likely enough ; for a cosmopolitan idea can be expected to occur as a corollary of such imperialist tendencies as those of the Periclean age (cp. *Rep.*, 494c/d, mentioned in note 50 (5) to this chapter, and the *First Alcibiades*, 105b, ff. ; see also text to notes 9–22, 36 and 47 to chapter 10).   This is especially likely if other equalitarian tendencies exist. I do not intend to belittle the significance of Alexander's deeds, but the ideas ascribed to him by Tarn seem to me, in a way, a renaissance of some of the best ideas of fifth-century Athenian imperialism. See also *Addendum III*, below, pp. 329 f.

Proceeding to details, I may first say that there is strong evidence that at least in Plato's (and Aristotle's) time, the problem of equalitarianism was clearly seen to be concerned with two fully analogous distinctions, that between *Greeks and barbarians* on the one side and that between *masters (or free men) and slaves* on the other ; cp. with this note 13 to chapter 5.   Now we have very strong evidence that the fifth-century Athenian movement against slavery was not confined to a few intellectualists like Euripides, Alcidamas, Lycophron, Antiphon, Hippias, etc., but that it had considerable practical success.   This evidence is contained in the unanimous reports of the enemies of Athenian democracy (especially the ' Old Oligarch ', Plato, Aristotle ; cp. notes 17, 18 and 29 to chapter 4, and 36 to chapter 10).

If we now consider in this light the admittedly scanty available evidence for the existence of *cosmopolitism*, it appears, I believe, reasonably strong—*provided that we include the attacks of the enemies of this movement among the evidence*.   In other words, we must make full use of the attacks of the Old Oligarch, of Plato, and of Aristotle against the humanitarian movement, if we wish to assess its real significance.   Thus the Old Oligarch (2, 7) attacks Athens for an eclectic cosmopolitan way of life.   Plato's attacks on cosmopolitan and similar tendencies, although not frequent, are especially valuable.   (I have in mind passages like *Rep.*, 562e/563a—' citizens, resident aliens, and strangers from abroad, are all on a footing of equality '—a passage which should be compared with the ironical description in *Menexenus*, 245c–d, in which Plato sarcastically eulogizes Athens for its consistent hatred of barbarians ; *Rep.*, 494c/d ; of course, the passage *Rep.*, 469b–471c, must be considered in this context too.   See also end of note 19 to chapter 6.) Whether or not Tarn is right on Alexander, he hardly does full justice to the various extant statements of this fifth-century movement, for instance to Antiphon (cp. p. 149, note 6 of his paper) or Euripides or Hippias, or Democritus (cp. note 29 to chapter 10), or to Diogenes (p. 150, note 12) and Antisthenes.   I do not think that Antiphon wanted only to stress the biological kinship between men, for he was undoubtedly a social reformer ; and ' by nature ' meant to him ' in truth '.   It therefore seems to me practically certain that he attacked the distinction between Greeks and barbarians as being fictitious. Tarn comments on Euripides' fragment which states that a noble man can range the world like an eagle the air by remarking that ' he knew that an eagle has a permanent home-rock ' ; but this remark does not do full justice to the fragment ; for in order to be a cosmopolitan, one need not give up one's permanent home. In the light of all this, I do not see why Diogenes' meaning was purely ' negative' when he replied to the question ' where are you from ? ' by saying that he was a cosmopolite, a citizen of the whole world ; especially if we consider that a similar answer (' I am a man of the world ') is reported of Socrates, and another (' The wise man belongs to all countries, for the home of a great soul is the whole world ' ; cp. Diels [5], fr. 247 ; genuineness questioned by Tarn and Diels) of Democritus.

Antisthenes' monotheism also must be considered in the light of this evidence. There is no doubt that this monotheism was not of the Jewish, i.e. tribal and exclusive, type. (Should the story of *Diog. Laert.*, VI, 13, that Antisthenes taught in the Cynosarges, the gymnasium for ' bastards ', be true, then he must have deliberately emphasized his own mixed and barbarian descent.) Tarn is certainly right when he points out (p. 145) that Alexander's monotheism was connected with his idea of the unity of mankind. But the same should be said of the Cynic ideas, which were influenced, as I believe (see the last note), by Antisthenes, and in this way by Socrates. (Cp. especially the evidence of Cicero, *Tuscul.*, V., 37, and of Epictetus, I, 9, 1, with *D.L.*, VI, 2, 63–71 ; also *Gorgias*, 492e, with *D.L.*, VI, 105. See also Epictetus, III, 22 and 24.)

All this made it once appear to me not too unlikely that Alexander may have been genuinely inspired, as the tradition reports, by Diogenes' ideas ; and thus by the equalitarian tradition. But in view of E. Badian's criticism of Tarn (*Historia*, 7, 1958, pp. 425 ff.) I feel now inclined to reject Tarn's claim ; but not, of course, my views on the fifth-century movement.

[49] Cp. *Republic*, 469b–471c, especially 470b–d, and 469b/c. Here indeed we have (cp. the next note) a trace of something like the introduction of a new ethical whole, more embracing than the city ; namely the unity of Hellenic superiority. As was to be expected (see the next note (1) (b)), Plato elaborates the point in some detail. * (Cornford justly summarizes this passage when he says that Plato ' expresses no humanitarian sympathies extending beyond the borders of Hellas ' ; cp. *The Republic of Plato*, 1941, p. 165.)*

[50] In this note, further arguments are collected bearing on the interpretation of *Republic*, 473e, and the *problem of Plato's humanitarianism*. I wish to express my thanks to my colleague, Prof. H. D. Broadhead, whose criticism has greatly helped me to complete and clarify my argument.

(1) One of Plato's standard topics (cp. the methodological remarks, *Rep.*, 368e, 445c, 577c, and note 32 to chapter 5) is the opposition and comparison between the individual and the whole, i.e. the city. The introduction of a new whole, even more comprehensive than the city, viz. mankind, would be a most important step for a holist to take ; it would need (a) preparation and (b) elaboration. (a) Instead of such a preparation we get the above mentioned passage on the opposition between Greeks and barbarians (*Rep.*, 469b–471c). (b) Instead of an elaboration, we find, if anything, a withdrawal of the ambiguous expression ' race of men '. First, in the immediate continuation of the key-passage under consideration, i.e. of the passage of the philosopher king (*Republic*, 473d/e), there occurs a paraphrase of the questionable expression, in form of a summary or winding up of the whole speech ; and this paraphrase, Plato's standard opposition, *city—individual*, replaces that of *city—human race*. The paraphrase reads : ' No other constitution can establish a state of happiness, neither in *private* affairs nor in those of the city.' Secondly, a similar result is found if we analyse the six repetitions or variations (viz.

487e, 499b, 500e, 501e, 536a–b, discussed in note 52 below, and the summary 540d/e with the afterthought 541b) of the key-passage under consideration (i.e. of *Rep.*, 473d/e). In two of them (487e, 500e) the city alone is mentioned ; in all the others, Plato's standard opposition *city—individual* again replaces that of *city—human race*. Nowhere is there a further allusion to the allegedly Platonic idea that sophocracy alone can save, not only the suffering *cities*, but all suffering *mankind*.—In view of all this it seems clear that in *all* these places only his standard opposition lingered in Plato's mind (without, however, the wish to give it any prominence in this connection), probably in the sense that sophocracy alone can attain the stability and the happiness—the divine rest—of any *state*, as well as that of all its *individual citizens and their progeny* (in which otherwise evil must grow—the evil of degeneration).

(2) The term ' human ' (' anthrōpinos ') is used by Plato, as a rule, either in opposition to ' divine ' (and, accordingly, sometimes in a slightly disparaging sense, especially if the limitations of human knowledge or human art are to be stressed, cp. *Timaeus*, 29c/d ; 77a, or *Sophist*, 266c, 268d, or *Laws*, 691e, f., 854a), or in a *zoological* sense, in opposition, or with reference to, animals, for example, eagles. Nowhere except in the early Socratic dialogues (for one further exception, see this note under (6), below) do I find this term (or the term ' man ') used in a humanitarian sense, i.e. indicating something that transcends the distinction of nation, race, or class. Even a ' mental ' use of the term ' human ' is rare. (I have in mind a use such as in *Laws*, 737b : ' a humanly impossible piece of folly '.) In fact, the extreme nationalist views of Fichte and Spengler, quoted in chapter 12, text to note 79, are a pointed expression of the Platonic usage of the term ' human ', as signifying a zoological rather than a moral category. A number of Platonic passages indicating this and similar usages may be given : *Republic*, 365d ; 486a ; 459b/c ; 514b ; 522c ; 606e, f. (where Homer as a guide to human affairs is opposed to the composer of hymns to the gods) ; 620b.—*Phaedo*, 82b.—*Cratylus*, 392b.—*Parmenides*, 134e.—*Theaetetus*, 107b.—*Crito*, 46e.—*Protagoras*, 344c.—*Statesman*, 274d (the shepherd of the human flock who is a god, not a man).—*Laws* 673d ; 688d ; 737b (890b is perhaps another example of a disparaging use—' the men ' seems here nearly equivalent with ' the many ').

(3) It is of course true that Plato assumes a *Form or Idea of Man* ; but it is a mistake to think that it represents what all men have in common ; rather, it is an aristocratic ideal of a proud super-Greek ; and on this is based a belief, not in the brotherhood of men, but in a hierarchy of ' natures ', aristocratic or slavish, in accordance with their greater or lesser likeness to the original, the ancient primogenitor of the human race. (The Greeks are more like him than any other race.) Thus ' intelligence is shared by the gods with only a very few men ' (*Tim.*, 51e ; cp. Aristotle, in the text to note 3, chapter 11).

(4) The ' City in Heaven ' (*Rep.*, 592b) and its citizens are, as Adam rightly points out, not Greek ; but this does not imply that they belong to ' humanity ' as he thinks (note to 470e30, and others) ; they are rather super-exclusive, super-Greek (they are ' above ' the Greek city of 470e, ff.)—more remote from the barbarians than ever. (This remark does not imply that the idea of the City in Heaven—as those of the Lion in Heaven, for example, and of other constellations—may not have been of oriental origin.)

(5) Finally, it may be mentioned that the passage 499c/d rescinds the distinction between Greeks and barbarians no more than that between the past, the present, and the future : Plato tries here to give drastic expression to a sweeping generalization in regard to time and space ; he wishes to say no more than : ' If at any time whatever, or if at any place whatever ' (we may add : even in such an extremely unlikely place as a barbarian

country) 'such a thing did happen, then. . .' The remark, *Republic*, 494c/d, expresses a similar, though stronger, feeling of being faced with something approaching impious absurdity, a feeling here aroused by Alcibiades' hopes for a universal empire of Greeks and foreigners. (I agree with the views expressed by Field, *Plato and His Contemporaries*, 130, note 1, and by Tarn; cp. note 13 (2) to chapter 5.)

To sum up, I am unable to find anything but hostility towards the humanitarian idea of a unity of mankind which transcends race and class, and I believe that those who find the opposite idealize Plato (cp. note 3 to chapter 6, and text) and fail to see the link between his aristocratic and anti-humanitarian exclusiveness and his theory of Ideas. See also this chapter, notes 51, 52, and 57, below.

* (6) There is, to my knowledge, only one real exception, one passage which stands in flagrant contrast to all this. In a passage (*Theaetetus*, 174e, f.), designed to illustrate the broad-mindedness and the universalistic outlook of the philosopher, we read : ' Every man has had countless ancestors, and among them are in any case rich and poor, kings and slaves, barbarians and Greeks.' I do not know how to reconcile this interesting and definitely humanitarian passage—its emphasis on the parallelism master *v.* slave and Greek *v.* barbarian is reminiscent of all those theories which Plato opposes—with Plato's other views. Perhaps it is, like so much in the *Gorgias*, Socratic ; and the *Theaetetus* is perhaps (as against the usual assumption) earlier than the *Republic*. See also my *Addendum II* p. 320 below.*

⁵¹ The allusion is, I believe, to two places in the Story of the Number where Plato (by speaking of ' your race ') refers to the race of men : ' concerning your own race ' (546a/b ; cp. note 39 to chapter 5, and text) and ' testing the metals within your races ' (546d/e, f. ; cp. notes 39 and 40 to chapter 5, and the next passage). Cp. also the arguments in note 52 to this chapter, concerning a ' bridge ' between the two passages, i.e. the key passage of the philosopher king, and the Story of the Number.

⁵² *Republic*, 546d/e, f. The passage quoted here is part of the Story of the Number and the Fall of Man, 546a–547a, quoted in text to notes 39/40 to chapter 5 ; see also notes 13 and 43 to the present chapter.—My contention (cp. text to the last note) that the remark in the key-passage of the philosopher king, *Republic*, 473e (cp. notes 44 and 50 to this chapter), foreshadows the Story of the Number, is strengthened by the observation that there exists a bridge, as it were, between the two passages. The Story of the Number is undoubtedly foreshadowed by *Republic*, 536a/b, a passage which, on the other hand, may be described as the converse (and so as a variation) of the philosopher king passage ; for it says in effect that the worst must happen if the wrong men are selected as rulers, and it even finishes up with a direct reminiscence of the great wave : ' if we take men of another kind . . then we shall bring down upon philosophy another deluge of laughter '. This clear reminiscence is, I believe, an indication that Plato was conscious of the character of the passage (which proceeds, as it were, from the end of 473c–e back to its beginning), which shows what must happen if the advice given in the passage of the philosopher king is neglected. Now this ' converse ' passage (536a/b) may be described as a bridge between the ' key passage ' (473e) and the ' Number-passage ' (546a, ff.) ; for it contains unambiguous references to racialism, foreshadowing the passage (546d, f.) on the same subject to which the present note is appended. (This may be interpreted as additional evidence that racialism was in Plato's mind, and alluded to, when he wrote the passage of the philosopher king.) I now quote the beginning of the ' converse' passage (536a/b) : ' We must distinguish carefully between the true-born and the bastard. For if an individual or a city does not know how to look upon matters such as these, they will quite innocently accept the services

of the unbalanced (or limping) bastards in any capacity ; perhaps as friends, or even as rulers.' (Cp. also note 47 to this chapter.)

For something like an explanation of Plato's preoccupation with matters of racial degeneration and racial breeding, see text to notes 6, 7, and 63 to chapter 10, in connection with note 39 (3) and 40 (2) to chapter 5.

* For the passage about Codrus the martyr, quoted in the next paragraph of the text, see the *Symposium*, 208d, quoted more fully in note 4 to chapter 3.— R. Eisler (*Caucasica*, 5, 1928, p. 129, note 237) asserts that ' Codrus ' is a pre-Hellenic word for ' king '. This would give some further colour to the tradition that Athens' nobility was autochthonous. (See note 11 (2) to this chapter ; 52 to chapter 8 ; and *Republic* 368a and 580b/c.) *

⁵³ A. E. Taylor, *Plato* (1908, 1914), p. 122 f. I agree with this interesting passage as far as it is quoted in the text. I have, however, omitted the word ' patriot ' after ' Athenian ' since I do not fully agree with this characterization of Plato in the sense in which it is used by Taylor. For Plato's ' patriotism ' cp. text to notes 14–18 to chapter 4. For the term ' patriotism ', and the ' paternal state ', cp. notes 23–26 and 45 to chapter 10.

⁵⁴ *Republic*, 494b : ' But will not one who is of this type be first in everything, from childhood on ? '

⁵⁵ *Op. cit.*, 496c : ' Of my own spiritual sign, I need not speak.'

⁵⁶ Cp. what Adam says in his ed. of the *Republic*, notes to 495d23 and 495e31, and my note 47 to the present chapter. (See also note 59 to this chapter.)

⁵⁷ *Republic*, 496c–d ; cp. the *Seventh Letter*, 325d. (I do not think that Barker, *Greek Political Theory*, I, 107, n. 2, makes a good guess when he says of the passage quoted that ' it is possible . . that Plato is thinking of the Cynics '. The passage certainly does not refer to Antisthenes ; and Diogenes, whom Barker must have in mind, was hardly famous when it was written, quite apart from the fact that Plato would not have referred to him in this way.)

(1) Earlier in the same passage of the *Republic*, there is another remark which may be a reference to Plato himself. Speaking of the small band of the worthy and those who belong to it, he mentions ' a nobly-born and well-bred character who was saved by flight ' (or ' by exile ' ; saved, that is, from the fate of Alcibiades, who became a victim of flattery and deserted Socratic philosophy). Adam thinks (note to 496b9) that ' Plato was hardly exiled '; but the flight to Megara of Socrates' disciples after the death of their master may well stand out in Plato's memory as one of the turning-points of his life. That the passage refers to Dio is hardly possible since Dio was about 40 when he went into exile, and therefore well beyond the critical youthful age ; and there was not (as in Plato's case) a parallelism with the Socratic companion Alcibiades (quite apart from the fact that Plato had resisted Dio's banishment, and had tried to get it rescinded). If we assume that the passage refers to Plato, then we shall have to assume the same of 502a : ' Who will doubt the possibility that kings or aristocrats may have a descendant who is a born philosopher ? ' ; for the continuation of that passage is so similar to the previous one that they seem to refer to the same ' nobly-born character '. This interpretation of 502a is probable in itself, for we must remember that Plato always showed his family pride, for instance, in the eulogy on his father and on his brothers, whom he calls ' divine '. (*Rep.*, 368a ; I cannot agree with Adam, who takes the remark as ironical ; cp. also the remark on Plato's alleged ancestor Codrus in *Symp.*, 208d, together with his alleged descent from Attica's tribal kings.) If this interpretation is adopted, the reference in 499b–c to ' rulers, kings, or their sons ', which fits Plato perfectly (he was not only a Codride, but also a descendant of the ruler Dropides), would have to be considered in the same light, i.e. as a

preparation for 502a. But this would solve another puzzle. I have in mind 499b and 502a. It is difficult, if not impossible, to interpret these passages as attempts to flatter the younger Dionysius, since such an interpretation could hardly be reconciled with the unmitigated violence and the admittedly (576a) personal background of Plato's attacks (572–580) upon the older Dionysius. It is important to note that Plato speaks in all three passages (473d, 499b, 502a) about hereditary kingdoms (which he opposes so strongly to tyrannies) and about ' dynasties ' ; but we know from Aristotle's *Politics*, 1292b2 (cp. Meyer, *Gesch. d. Altertums*, V, p. 56) and 1293a11, that ' dynasties ' are hereditary oligarchic families, and therefore not so much the families of a tyrant like Dionysius, but rather what we call now *aristocratic* families, like that of Plato himself. Aristotle's statement is supported by Thucydides, IV, 78, and Xenophon, *Hellenica*, V, 4, 46. (These arguments are directed against Adam's second note to 499b13.) See also note 4 to chapter 3.

＊ (2) Another important passage which contains a revealing self-reference is to be found in the *Statesman*. Here the essential characteristic of the royal statesman is assumed (258b, 292c) to be his *knowledge or science* ; and the result is another plea for sophocracy : ' The only right government is that in which the rulers are true Masters of Science ' (293c). And Plato proves that ' the man who possesses the Royal Science, *whether he rules or does not rule*, must, as our argument shows, be proclaimed royal ' (292e/293a). Plato certainly claimed to possess the Royal Science ; accordingly, this passage implies unequivocally that he considered himself a ' man who must be proclaimed royal '. This illuminating passage must not be neglected in any attempt to interpret the *Republic*. (The Royal Science, of course, is again that of the romantic pedagogue and breeder of a master class which must provide the fabric for covering and holding together the other classes—the slaves, labourers, clerks, etc., discussed in 289c, ff. The task of the Royal Science is thus described as that of ' interweaving ' (blending, mixing) ' of the characters of temperate and courageous men, when they have been drawn together, by kingscraft, into a community life of unanimity and friendship '. See also notes 40 (2) to chapter 5 ; 29 to chapter 4 ; and note 34 to the present chapter.) ＊

[58] In a famous passage in the *Phaedo* (89d) Socrates warns against misanthropy or hatred of men (with which he compares misology or distrust in rational argument). See also note 28 and 56 to chapter 10, and note 9 to chapter 7.

The next quotation in this paragraph is from *Republic*, 489b/c.—The connection with the previous passages is more obvious if the whole of 488 and 489 is considered, and especially the attack in 489e upon the ' many ' philosophers whose wickedness is inevitable, i.e. the same ' many ' and ' incomplete natures ' whose suppression is discussed in notes 44 and 47 to this chapter.

An indication that Plato had once dreamt of becoming the philosopher king and saviour of Athens can be found, I believe, in the *Laws*, 704a–707c, where Plato tries to point out the moral dangers of the sea, of seafaring, trade, and imperialism. (Cp. Aristotle, *Pol.*, 1326b–1327a, and my notes 9–22 and 36 to chapter 10, and text.)

See especially *Laws*, 704d : ' If the city were to be built on the coast, and well supplied with natural harbours . . then it would need a mighty saviour, and indeed, a super-human legislator, to make her escape variability and degeneration.' Does this not read as if Plato wanted to show that his failure in Athens was due to the super-human difficulties created by the geography of the place ? (But in spite of all disappointments—cp. note 25 to chapter 7— Plato still believes in the method of winning over a tyrant ; cp. *Laws*, 710c/d, quoted in text to note 24 to chapter 4.)

[59] There is a passage (beginning in *Republic*, 498d/e ; cp. note 12 to

chapter 9) in which Plato even expresses his hope that 'the many' may change their minds and accept philosophers as rulers, once they have learned (perhaps from the *Republic*?) to distinguish between the genuine philosopher and the pseudo-philosopher.

With the last two lines of the paragraph in the text, cp. *Republic*, 473e–474a, and 517a/b.

[60] Sometimes such dreams have even been openly confessed. F. Nietzsche, *The Will to Power* (ed. 1911, Book IV, Aphor. 958 ; the reference is to *Theages*, 125e/126a), writes : ' In Plato's Theages it is written : " Every one of us wants to be the lord of all men, if it were only possible—and most of all he would like to be the Lord God Himself." This is the spirit which must come again.' I need not comment upon Nietzsche's political views ; but there are other philosophers, Platonists, who have naïvely hinted that if a Platonist were, by some lucky accident, to gain power in a modern state, he would move towards the Platonic Ideal, and leave things at least nearer perfection than he found them. ' . . men born into an " oligarchy " or " democracy " ', we read (in the context this may well be an allusion to England in 1939), ' with the ideals of Platonic philosophers and finding themselves, by some fortunate turn of circumstance, possessed of supreme political power, would certainly try to actualise the Platonic State, and even if they were not completely successful, as they might be, would at least leave the commonwealth nearer to that model than they found it.' (Quoted from A. E. Taylor, ' The Decline and Fall of the State in *Republic*, VIII ', *Mind*, N.S. 48, 1939, p. 31.) The argument in the next chapter is directed against such romantic dreams.

* A searching analysis of the Platonic lust for power can be found in H. Kelsen's brilliant article *Platonic Love* (*The American Imago*, vol. III, 1942, pp. 1 ff.).*

[61] *Op. cit.*, 520a–521c, the quotation is from 520d.

[62] Cp. G. B. Stern, *The Ugly Dachshund*, 1938.

NOTES TO CHAPTER 9

The motto, from *Les Thibaults*, by Roger Martin du Gard, is quoted from p. 575 of the English edition (*Summer 1914*, London, 1940).

[1] My description of Utopian social engineering seems to coincide with that kind of social engineering advocated by M. Eastman in *Marxism: is it Science?* ; see especially pp. 22 ff. I have the impression that Eastman's views represent the swing of the pendulum from historicism to Utopian engineering. But I may possibly be mistaken, and what Eastman really has in mind may be more in the direction of what I call piecemeal engineering. Roscoe Pound's conception of ' social engineering ' is clearly ' piecemeal ' ; cp. note 9 to chapter 3. See also note 18 (3) to chapter 5.

[2] I believe that there is, from the ethical point of view, no symmetry between suffering and happiness, or between pain and pleasure. Both the greatest happiness principle of the Utilitarians and Kant's principle ' Promote other people's happiness . .' seem to me (at least in their formulations) wrong on this point which, however, is not completely decidable by rational argument. (For the irrational aspect of ethical beliefs, see note 11 to the present chapter, and for the rational aspect, sections ii and especially iii of chapter 24). In my opinion (cp. note 6 (2) to chapter 5) human suffering makes a direct moral appeal, namely, the appeal for help, while there is no similar call to increase the happiness of a man who is doing well anyway. (A further criticism of the Utilitarian formula ' Maximize pleasure ' is that it assumes, in principle, a continuous pleasure-pain scale which allows us to treat degrees of pain as negative degrees of pleasure. But, from the moral

point of view, pain cannot be outweighed by pleasure, and especially not one man's pain by another man's pleasure. Instead of the greatest happiness for the greatest number, one should demand, more modestly, the least amount of avoidable suffering for all ; and further, that unavoidable suffering—such as hunger in times of an unavoidable shortage of food—should be distributed as equally as possible.) There is some kind of analogy between this view of ethics and the view of scientific methodology which I have advocated in my *The Logic of Scientific Discovery*. It adds to clarity in the field of ethics if we formulate our demands negatively, i.e. if we demand the elimination of suffering rather than the promotion of happiness. Similarly, it is helpful to formulate the task of scientific method as the elimination of false theories (from the various theories tentatively proffered) rather than the attainment of established truths.

³ A very good example of this kind of piecemeal engineering, or perhaps of the corresponding piecemeal technology, are C. G. F. Simkin's two articles on 'Budgetary Reform' in the Australian *Economic Record* (1941, pp. 192 ff., and 1942, pp. 16 ff.) I am glad to be able to refer to these two articles since they make conscious use of the methodological principles which I advocate ; they thus show that these principles are useful in the practice of technological research.

I do not suggest that piecemeal engineering cannot be bold, or that it must be confined to 'smallish' problems. But I think that the degree of complication which we can tackle is governed by the degree of our experience gained in conscious and systematic piecemeal engineering.

⁴ This view has recently been emphasized by F. A. von Hayek in various interesting papers (cp. for instance his *Freedom and the Economic System*, Public Policy Pamphlets, Chicago, 1939). What I call 'Utopian engineering' corresponds largely, I believe, to what Hayek would call 'centralized' or 'collectivist' planning. Hayek himself recommends what he calls 'planning for freedom'. I suppose he would agree that this would take the character of 'piecemeal engineering'. One could, I believe, formulate Hayek's objections to collectivist planning somewhat like this. If we try to construct society according to a blueprint, then we may find that we cannot incorporate individual freedom in our blueprint ; or if we do, that we cannot realize it. The reason is that centralized economic planning eliminates from economic life one of the most important functions of the individual, namely his function as a chooser of the product, as a free consumer. In other words, Hayek's criticism belongs to the realm of social technology. He points out a certain technological impossibility, namely that of drafting a plan for a society which is at once economically centralized *and* individualistic.

* Readers of Hayek's *The Road to Serfdom* (1944) may feel puzzled by this note ; for Hayek's attitude in this book is so explicit that no room is left for the somewhat vague comments of my note. But my note was printed before Hayek's book was published ; and although many of his leading ideas were foreshadowed in his earlier writings, they were not yet quite as explicit as in *The Road to Serfdom*. And many ideas which, as a matter of course, we now associate with Hayek's name were unknown to me when I wrote my note.

In the light of what I know now about Hayek's position, my summary of it does not appear to me to be mistaken, although it is, no doubt, an under-statement of his position. The following modifications may perhaps put the matter right.

(a) Hayek would not himself use the word 'social engineering' for any political activity which he would be prepared to advocate. He objects to this term because it is associated with a general tendency which he has called 'scientism'—the naïve belief that the methods of the natural sciences (or, rather, what many people believe to be the methods of the natural sciences) must produce similarly impressive results in the social field. (Cp. Hayek's two series of articles, *Scientism and the Study of Society, Economica*, IX–XI 1942–44, and *The Counter-revolution of Science, ibid.*, VIII, 1941.)

If by 'scientism' we mean a tendency to ape, in the field of social science, what are supposed to be the methods of the natural sciences, then *historicism can be described as a form of scientism.* A typical and influential scientistic argument in favour of historicism is, in brief, this : ' We can predict eclipses ; why should we not be able to predict revolutions? ' ; or, in a more elaborate form : ' The task of science is to predict ; thus the task of the social sciences must be to make social, i.e. historical, predictions.' I have tried to refute this kind of argument (cp. my *The Poverty of Historicism*, and *Prediction and Prophecy, and their Significance for Social Theory, Proceedings of the Xth International Congress of Philosophy, Amsterdam*, 1948 ; now in my *Conjectures and Refutations*) ; and in this sense, I am opposed to scientism.

But if by 'scientism' we should mean the view that the methods of the social sciences are, to a very considerable extent, the same as those of the natural sciences, then I should be obliged to plead 'guilty' to being an adherent of 'scientism' ; indeed, I believe that the similarity between the social and the natural sciences can even be used for correcting wrong ideas about the natural sciences by showing that these are much more similar to the social sciences than is generally supposed.

It is for this reason that I have continued to use Roscoe Pound's term ' social engineering ' in Roscoe Pound's sense, which as far as I can see, is free of that ' scientism ' which, I think, must be rejected.

Terminology apart, I still think that Hayek's views can be interpreted as favourable to what I call 'piecemeal engineering'. On the other hand, Hayek has given a much clearer formulation of his views than my old outline indicates. The part of his views which corresponds to what I should call ' social engineering ' (in Pound's sense) is his suggestion that there is an urgent need, in a free society, to reconstruct what he describes as its ' *legal framework* '.*

⁵ Bryan Magee has drawn my attention to what he rightly calls ' de Tocqueville's superbly put argument ' in *L'ancien régime.*

⁶ The problem whether or not a good end justifies bad means seems to arise out of such cases as whether one should lie to a sick man in order to set his mind at rest ; or whether one should keep a people in ignorance in order to make them happy ; or whether one should begin a long and bloody civil war in order to establish a world of peace and beauty.

In all these cases the action contemplated is to bring about first a more immediate result (called ' the means ') which is considered an evil, in order that a secondary result (called ' the end ') may be brought about which is considered a good.

I think that in all such cases three different kinds of questions arise.

(*a*) How far are we entitled to assume that the means will in fact lead to the expected end ? Since the means are the more immediate result, they will in most cases be the more certain result of the contemplated action, and the end, which is more remote, will be less certain.

The question here raised is a factual question rather than one of moral valuations. It is the question whether, as a matter of fact, the assumed causal connection between the means and the end can be relied upon ; and one might therefore reply that, if the assumed causal connection does not hold, the case was simply not one of means and ends.

This may be true. But in practice, the point here considered contains what is perhaps the most important moral issue. For although the question (whether the contemplated means will bring about the contemplated end) is a factual one, *our attitude towards this question raises some of the most fundamental moral problems*—the problem whether we ought to rely, in such cases, on our conviction that such a causal connection holds ; or in other words, whether we ought to rely, dogmatically, on causal theories, or whether we should adopt a sceptical attitude towards them, especially where the immediate result of our action is, in itself, considered evil.

This question is perhaps not so important in the first of our three examples, but it is so in the two others. Some people may feel very certain that the causal connections assumed in these two cases hold ; but the connection may be a very remote one ; and even the emotional certainty of their belief may itself be the result of an attempt to suppress their doubts. (The issue, in other words, is that between the fanatic and the rationalist in the Socratic sense— the man who tries to know his intellectual limitations.) The issue will be the more important the greater the evil of ' the means '. However that may be, to educate oneself so as to adopt an attitude of scepticism towards one's causal theories, and one of intellectual modesty, is, without doubt, one of the most important moral duties.

But let us assume that the assumed causal connection holds, or in other words, that there is a situation in which one can properly speak of means and ends. Then we have to distinguish between two further questions, (b) and (c).

(b) Assuming that the causal relation holds, and that we can be reasonably certain of it, the problem becomes, in the main, one of choosing the lesser of two evils—that of the contemplated means and that which must arise if these means are not adopted. In other words, the best of ends do not as such justify bad means, but the attempt to avoid results may justify actions which are in themselves producing bad results. (Most of us do not doubt that it is right to cut off a man's limb in order to save his life.)

In this connection it may become very important that we are not really able to assess the evils in question. Some Marxists, for example (cp. note 9 to chapter 19), believe that there would be far less suffering involved in a violent social revolution than in the chronic evils inherent in what they call ' Capitalism '. But even assuming that this revolution leads to a better state of affairs—how can they evaluate the suffering in the one state and in the other ? Here, again, a factual question arises, and it is again our duty not to over-estimate our factual knowledge. Besides, granted that the contemplated means will on balance improve the situation—have we ascertained whether other means would not achieve better results, at a lesser price ?

But the same example raises another very important question. Assuming, again, that the sum total of suffering under ' Capitalism ' would, if it continues for several generations, outweigh the suffering of civil war—can we condemn one generation to suffer for the sake of later generations ? (There is a great difference between sacrificing oneself for the sake of others, and between sacrificing others—or oneself *and* others—for some such end.)

(c) The third point of importance is that we must not think that the so-called ' end ', as a final result, is more important than the intermediate result, the ' means '. This idea, which is suggested by such sayings as ' All is well that ends well', is most misleading. First, the so-called ' end' is hardly ever the end of the matter. Secondly, the means are not, as it were, superseded once the end is achieved. For example, ' bad ' means, such as a new powerful weapon used in war for the sake of victory, may, after this ' end ' is achieved, create new trouble. In other words, even if something can be correctly described as a means to an end, it is, very often, much more than this. It produces other results apart from the end in question ; and what we have to balance is not the (past or present) means against (future) ends, but the total results, as far as they can be foreseen, of one course of action against those of another. These results spread over a period of time which includes intermediate results ; and the contemplated ' end ' will not be the last to be considered.

⁷ (1) I believe that the parallelism between the institutional problems of civil and of international peace is most important.   Any international organization which has legislative, administrative and judicial institutions *as well as an armed executive which is prepared to act* should be as successful in upholding international peace as are the analogous institutions within the state.   But it seems to me important not to expect more.   We have been able to reduce crime within the states to something comparatively unimportant, but we have not been able to stamp it out entirely.   Therefore we shall, for a long time to come, need a police force which is ready to strike, and which sometimes does strike.   Similarly, I believe that we must be prepared for the probability that we may not be able to stamp out international crime.   If we declare that our aim is to make war impossible once and for all, then we may undertake too much, with the fatal result that we may not have a force which is ready to strike when these hopes are disappointed.   (The failure of the League of Nations to take action against aggressors was, at least in the case of the attack on Manchukuo, due largely to the general feeling that the League had been established in order to end *all* wars and not to wage them.   This shows that propaganda for ending *all* wars is self-defeating.   We must end international anarchy, and be ready to go to war against any international crime. (Cp. especially H. Mannheim, *War and Crime*, 1941 ; and A. D. Lindsay, ' War to End War ', in *Background and Issues*, 1940.)

But it is also important to search for the weak spot in the analogy between civil and international peace, that is to say, for the point where the analogy breaks down.   In the case of civil peace, upheld by the state, there is the individual citizen to be protected by the state.   The citizen is, as it were, a ' natural ' unit or atom (although there is a certain ' conventional ' element even in the conditions of citizenship).   On the other hand, the members or units or atoms of our international order will be states.   But a state can never be a ' natural ' unit like the citizen ; *there are no natural boundaries to a state.*   The boundaries of a state change, and can be defined only by applying the principle of a *status quo* ; and since every *status quo* must refer to an arbitrarily chosen date, the determination of the boundaries of a state is purely conventional.

The attempt to find some ' natural ' boundaries for states, and accordingly, to look upon the state as a ' natural ' unit, leads to the *principle of the national state* and to the romantic fictions of nationalism, racialism, and tribalism. But this principle is not ' natural ', and the idea that there exist natural units like nations, or linguistic or racial groups, is entirely fictitious.   Here, if anywhere, we should learn from history ; for since the dawn of history, men have been continually mixed, unified, broken up, and mixed again ; and this cannot be undone, even if it were desirable.

There is a second point in which the analogy between civil and international peace breaks down.   The state must protect the individual citizen, its units or atoms ; but the international organization also must ultimately protect human individuals, and not its units or atoms, i.e. states or nations.

The complete renunciation of the principle of the national state (a principle which owes its popularity solely to the fact that it appeals to tribal instincts and that it is the cheapest and surest method by which a politician who has nothing better to offer can make his way), and the recognition of the necessarily conventional demarcation of *all* states, together with the further insight that *human individuals and not states or nations must be the ultimate concern even of international organizations*, will help us to realize clearly, and to get over, the difficulties arising from the breakdown of our fundamental analogy.   (Cp. also chapter 12, notes 51–64 and text, and note 2 to chapter 13.)

(2) It seems to me that the remark that human individuals must be recognized to be the ultimate concern not only of international organizations,

but of all politics, international as well as ' national ' or parochial, has important applications. We must realize that *we can treat individuals fairly, even if we decide to break up the power-organization of an aggressive state* or ' nation ' to which these individuals belong. It is a widely held prejudice that the destruction and control of the military, political and even of the economic power of a state or ' nation ' implies misery or subjugation for its individual citizens. But this prejudice is as unwarranted as it is dangerous.

It is unwarranted provided that an international organization protects the citizens of the thus weakened state against exploitation of their political and military weakness. The only damage to the individual citizen that cannot be avoided is one to his national pride ; and if we assume that he was a citizen of an aggressor country, then this is a damage which will be unavodable in any case, provided the aggression has been warded off.

The prejudice that we cannot distinguish between the treatment of a state and of its individual citizens is also very dangerous, for when it comes to the problem of dealing with an aggressor country, it necessarily creates two factions in the victorious countries, viz., the faction of those who demand harsh treatment and those who demand leniency. As a rule, both overlook the possibility of treating a state harshly, and, at the same time, its citizens leniently.

But if this possibility is overlooked, then the following is likely to happen. Immediately after the victory the aggressor state *and* its citizens will be treated comparatively harshly. But the state, the power-organization, will probably not be treated as harshly as might be reasonable because of a reluctance to treat innocent individuals harshly, that is to say, because the influence of the faction for leniency will make itself felt somehow. In spite of this reluctance, it is likely that individuals will suffer beyond what they deserve. After a short time, therefore, a reaction is likely to occur in the victorious countries. Equalitarian and humanitarian tendencies are likely to strengthen the faction for leniency until the harsh policy is reversed. But this development is not only likely to give the aggressor state a chance for a new aggression ; it will also provide it with the weapon of the moral indignation of one who has been wronged, while the victorious countries are likely to become afflicted with the diffidence of those who feel that they may have done wrong.

This very undesirable development must in the end lead to a new aggression. It can be avoided if, and only if, from the start, a clear distinction is made between the aggressor state (and those responsible for its acts) on the one hand, and its citizens on the other hand. Harshness towards the aggressor state, and even the radical destruction of its power apparatus, will not produce this moral reaction of humanitarian feelings in the victorious countries if it is combined with a policy of fairness towards the individual citizens.

But is it possible to break the political power of a state without injuring its citizens indiscriminately ? In order to prove that this is possible I shall construct an example of a policy which breaks the political and military power of an aggressor state without violating the interests of its individual citizens.

The fringe of the aggressor country, including its sea-coast and its main (not all) sources of water power, coal, and steel, could be severed from the state, and administered as an international territory, never to be returned. Harbours as well as the raw materials could be made accessible to the citizens of the state for their legitimate economic activities, without imposing any economic disadvantages on them, on the condition that they *invite* international commissions to control the proper use of these facilities. Any use which may help to build up a new war potential is forbidden, and if there is reason for suspicion that the internationalized facilities and raw materials may be so used, their use has at once to be stopped. It then rests with the suspect party to *invite* and to facilitate a thorough investigation, and to offer satisfactory guarantees for a proper use of its resources.

Such a procedure would not eliminate the possibility of a new attack but it would force the aggressor state to make its attack on the internationalized territories previous to building up a new war potential. Thus such an attack would be hopeless provided the other countries have retained and developed their war potential. Faced with this situation the former aggressor state would be forced to change its attitude radically, and adopt one of co-operation. It would be forced to *invite* the international control of its industry and to facilitate the investigation of the international controlling authority (instead of obstructing them) because only such an attitude would guarantee its use of the facilities needed by its industries ; and such a development would be likely to take place without any further interference with the internal politics of the state.

The danger that the internationalization of these facilities might be mis-used for the purpose of exploiting or of humiliating the population of the defeated country can be counter-acted by international legal measures that provide for courts of appeal, etc.

This example shows that it is not impossible to treat a state harshly and its citizens leniently.

* (I have left parts (1) and (2) of this note exactly as they were written in 1942. Only in part (3), which is non-topical, have I made an addition, after the first two paragraphs.) *

(3) But is such an engineering approach towards the problem of peace scientific ? Many will contend, I am sure, that a truly scientific attitude towards the problems of war and peace must be different. They will say that *we must first study the causes of war*. We must study the forces that lead to war, and also those that may lead to peace. It has been recently claimed, for instance, that ' lasting peace ' can come only if we consider fully the ' under-lying dynamic forces ' in society that may produce war or peace. In order to find out these forces, we must, of course, study history. In other words, we must approach the problem of peace by a historicist method, and not by a technological method. This, it is claimed, is the only scientific approach.

The historicist may, with the help of history, show that the causes of war can be found in the clash of economic interests ; or in the clash of classes ; or of ideologies, for instance, freedom versus tyranny ; or 'n the clash of races, or of nations, or of imperialisms, or of militarist systems ; or in hate ; or in fear ; or in envy ; or in the wish to take revenge ; or in all these things together, and in countless others. And he will thereby show that the task of removing these causes is extremely difficult. And he will show that there is no point in constructing an international organization, as long as we have not removed the causes of war, for instance the economic causes, etc.

Similarly, psychologism may argue that the causes of war are to be found in ' human nature ', or, more specifically, in its aggressiveness, and that the way to peace is that of preparing for other outlets for aggression. (The reading of thrillers has been suggested in all seriousness—in spite of the fact that some of our late dictators were addicted to them.)

I do not think that these methods of dealing with this important problem are very promising. And I do not believe, more especially, in the plausible argument that in order to establish peace we must ascertain the cause or the causes of war.

Admittedly, there are cases where the method of searching for the causes of some evil, and of removing them, may be successful. If I feel a pain in my foot I may find that it is caused by a pebble and remove it. But we must not generalize from this. The method of removing pebbles does not even cover all cases of pains in my foot.   In some such cases I may not find 'the cause'; and in others I may be unable to remove it.

In general, the method of removing causes of some undesirable event is applicable only if we know a short list of necessary conditions (i.e. a list of conditions such that the event in question never happens except if one at least of the conditions on the list is present) and if all of these conditions can be controlled, or, more precisely, prevented.   (It may be remarked that necessary conditions are hardly what one describes by the vague term 'causes'; they are, rather, what are usually called 'contributing causes'; as a rule, where we speak of 'causes' we mean a set of sufficient conditions.) But I do not think that we can hope to construct such a list of the necessary conditions of war.   Wars have broken out under the most varying circumstances.   Wars are not simple phenomena, such as, perhaps, thunderstorms. There is no reason to believe that by calling a vast variety of phenomena 'wars', we ensure that they are all 'caused' in the same way.

All this shows that the apparently unprejudiced and convincingly scientific approach, the study of the 'causes of war', is, in fact, not only prejudiced, but also liable to bar the way to a reasonable solution ; it is, in fact, pseudo-scientific.

How far should we get if, instead of introducing laws and a police force, we approached the problem of criminality 'scientifically', i.e. by trying to find out what precisely are the causes of crime?   I do not imply that we cannot here or there discover important factors contributing to crime or to war, and that we cannot avert much harm in this way ; but this can well be done after we have got crime under control, i.e. after we have introduced our police force.   On the other hand, the study of economic, psychological, hereditary, moral, etc., 'causes' of crime, and the attempt to remove these causes, would hardly have led us to find out that a police force (which does not remove the cause) can bring crime under control.   Quite apart from the vagueness of such phrases as 'the cause of war', the whole approach is anything but scientific.   It is as if one insisted that it is unscientific to wear an overcoat when it is cold ; and that we should rather study the causes of cold weather, and remove them.   Or, perhaps, that lubricating is unscientific, since we should rather find out the causes of friction and remove them.   This latter example shows, I believe, the absurdity of the apparently scientific criticism ; for just as lubrication certainly reduces the 'causes' of friction, so an international police force (or another armed body of this kind) may reduce an important 'cause' of war, namely the hope of 'getting away with it '.

[8] I have tried to show this in my *The Logic of Scientific Discovery*.   I believe, in accordance with the methodology outlined, that systematic piecemeal engineering will help us to build an empirical social technology, reached by the method of trial and error.   Only in this way, I believe, can we begin to build an empirical social science.   The fact that such a social science hardly exists so far, and that the historical method is incapable of furthering it much, is one of the strongest arguments against the possibility of large-scale or Utopian social engineering.   See also my *The Poverty of Historicism*.

[9] For a very similar formulation, see John Carruthers' lecture *Socialism & Radicalism* (published as a pamphlet by the Hammersmith Socialist Society, London, 1894).   He argues in a typical manner against piecemeal reform : 'Every palliative measure brings its own evil with it, and the evil is generally greater than that it was intended to cure.   Unless we make up our minds to have a new garment altogether, we must be prepared to go in rags, for patching will not improve the old one.'   (It should be noted that by 'radicalism ', used by Carruthers in the title of his lecture, he means about the opposite of what is meant here.   Carruthers advocates an uncompromising programme

of canvas-cleaning and attacks 'radicalism', i.e. the programme of 'progressive' reforms advocated by the 'radical liberals'. This use of the term 'radical' is, of course, more customary than mine ; nevertheless, the term means originally ' going to the root '—of the evil, for instance—or ' eradicating the evil ' ; and there is no proper substitute for it.)

For the quotations in the next paragraph of the text (the ' divine original ' which the artist-politician must ' copy '), see *Republic*, 500e/501a. See also notes 25 and 26 to chapter 8.

In Plato's Theory of Forms are, I believe, elements which are of great importance for the understanding, and for the theory, of art. This aspect of Platonism is treated by J. A. Stewart, in his book *Plato's Doctrine of Ideas* (1909), 128 ff. I believe, however, that he stresses too much the object of pure contemplation (as opposed to that ' pattern ' which the artist not only visualizes, but which he labours to reproduce, on his canvas).

[10] *Republic*, 520c. For the ' Royal Art ', see especially the *Statesman* ; cp. note 57 (2) to chapter 8.

[11] It has often been said that ethics is only a part of aesthetics, since ethical questions are ultimately a matter of taste. (Cp. for instance G. E. G. Catlin, *The Science and Methods of Politics*, 315 ff.) If by saying this, no more is meant than that ethical problems cannot be solved by the rational methods of science, I agree. But we must not overlook the vast difference between moral ' problems of taste ' and problems of taste in aesthetics. If I dislike a novel, a piece of music, or perhaps a picture, I need not read it, or listen to it, or look at it. Aesthetic problems (with the possible exception of architecture) are largely of a private character, but ethical problems concern men, and their lives. To this extent, there is a fundamental difference between them.

[12] For this and the preceding quotations, cp. *Republic*, 500d–501a (italics mine) : cp. also notes 29 (end) to chapter 4, and 25, 26, 37, 38 (especially 25 and 38) to chapter 8.

The two quotations in the next paragraph are from the *Republic*, 541a, and from the *Statesman*, 293c–e.

It is interesting (because it is, I believe, characteristic of the hysteria of romantic radicalism with its *hubris*—its ambitious arrogance of godlikeness) to see that both passages of the *Republic*—the canvas-cleaning of 500d, ff., and the purge of 541a—are preceded by reference to the godlikeness of the philosophers ; cp. 500c–d, ' the philosopher becomes . . godlike himself ', and 540c–d (cp. note 37 to chapter 8 and text), ' And the state will erect monuments, at the expense of the public, to commemorate them ; and sacrifices will be offered to them, as demigods, . . or at least as men who are blessed by grace, and godlike.'

It is also interesting (for the same reasons) that the first of these passages is preceded by the passage (498d/e, f. ; see note 59 to chapter 8) in which Plato expresses his hope that philosophers may become, as rulers, acceptable even to ' the many '.

* Concerning the term ' liquidate ' the following modern outburst of radicalism may be quoted : ' Is it not obvious that if we are to have socialism —real and permanent socialism—all the fundamental opposition must be " liquidated " (i.e. rendered politically inactive by disfranchisement, and if necessary by imprisonment) ? ' This remarkable rhetorical question is printed on p. 18 of the still more remarkable pamphlet *Christians in the Class Struggle*, by Gilbert Cope, with a Foreword by the Bishop of Bradford. (1942 ; for the historicism of this pamphlet, see note 3 to chapter 1.) The Bishop, in his Foreword, denounces ' our present economic system ' as ' immoral and un-Christian ', and he says that ' when something is so plainly the work of the devil. . . nothing can excuse a minister of the Church from working for its destruction '. Accordingly, he recommends the pamphlet ' as a lucid and penetrating analysis '.

A few more sentences may be quoted from the pamphlet. ' Two parties may ensure partial democracy, but a full democracy can be established only by a single party. . .' (p. 17).—' In the period of transition . . the workers . . must be led and organized by a single party which tolerates the existence of no other party fundamentally opposed to it. . .' (p. 19).—' Freedom in the socialist state means that no one is allowed to attack the principle of common ownership, but everyone is encouraged to work for its more effective realization and operation. . . The important matter of how the opposition is to be nullified depends upon the methods used by the opposition itself ' (p. 18).

Most interesting of all is perhaps the following argument (also to be found on p. 18) which deserves to be read carefully : ' Why is it possible to have a socialist party in a capitalist country if it is not possible to have a capitalist party in a socialist state ? The answer is simply that the one is a movement involving all the productive forces of a great majority against a small minority, while the other is an attempt of a minority to restore their position of power and privilege by renewed exploitation of the majority.' In other words, a ruling ' small minority ' can afford to be tolerant, while a ' great majority ' cannot afford to tolerate a ' small minority '. This simple answer is indeed a model of ' a lucid and penetrating analysis ', as the Bishop puts it.*

[13] Cp. for this development also chapter 13, especially note 7, and text.

[14] It seems that romanticism, in literature as well as in philosophy, may be traced back to Plato. It is well known that Rousseau was directly influenced by him (cp. note 1 to chapter 6). Rousseau also knew Plato's *Statesman* (cp. the *Social Contract*, Book II, ch. VII, and Book III, ch. VI) with its eulogy of the early hill-shepherds. But apart from this direct influence, it is probable that Rousseau derived his pastoral romanticism and love for primitivity indirectly from Plato ; for he was certainly influenced by the Italian Renaissance, which had rediscovered Plato, and especially his naturalism and his dreams of a perfect society of primitive shepherds (cp. notes 11 (3) and 32 to chapter 4 and note 1 to chapter 6).—It is interesting that Voltaire recognized at once the dangers of Rousseau's romantic obscurantism ; just as Kant was not prevented by his admiration for Rousseau from recognizing this danger when he was faced with it in Herder's ' Ideas ' (cp. also note 56 to chapter 12, and text).

NOTES TO CHAPTER 10

This chapter's motto is taken from the *Symposium*, 193d.

[1] Cp. *Republic*, 419a, ff., 421b, 465c, ff., and 519e ; see also chapter 6, especially sections II and IV.

[2] I am thinking not only of the medieval attempts to arrest society, attempts that were based on the Platonic theory that the rulers are responsible for the souls, the spiritual welfare of the ruled (and on many practical devices developed by Plato in the *Republic* and in the *Laws*), but I am thinking also of many later developments.

[3] I have tried, in other words, to apply as far as possible the method which I have described in my *The Logic of Scientific Discovery*.

[4] Cp. especially *Republic*, 566e ; see also below, note 63 to this chapter.

[5] In my story there should be ' no villains . . Crime is not interesting . . It is what men do at their best, with good intentions . . that really concerns us '. I have tried as far as possible to apply this methodological principle to my interpretation of Plato. (The formulation of the principle quoted in this

note I have taken from G. B. Shaw's Preface to *Saint Joan*; see the first sentences in the section 'Tragedy, not Melodrama'.)

⁶ For Heraclitus, see chapter 2. For Alcmaeon's and Herodotus' theories of isonomy, see notes 13, 14, and 17, to chapter 6. For Phaleas of Chalcedon's economic equalitarianism, see Aristotle's *Politics*, 1266a, and Diels ⁵, chapter 39 (also on Hippodamus). For Hippodamus of Miletus, see Aristotle's *Politics*, 1267b22, and note 9 to chapter 3. Among the first political theorists, we must, of course, also count the Sophists, Protagoras, Antiphon, Hippias, Alcidamas, Lycophron ; Critias (cp. Diels ⁵, fr. 6, 30–38, and note 17 to chapter 8), and the Old Oligarch (if these were two persons) ; and Democritus.

For the terms 'closed society' and 'open society', and their use in a somewhat similar sense by Bergson, see the Note to the Introduction. My characterization of the closed society as magical and of the open society as rational and critical of course makes it impossible to apply these terms without idealizing the society in question. The magical attitude has by no means disappeared from our life, not even in the most ' open ' societies so far realized, and I think it unlikely that it can ever completely disappear. In spite of this, it seems to be possible to give some useful criterion of the transition from the closed society to the open. The transition takes place when social institutions are first consciously recognized as man-made, and when their conscious alteration is discussed in terms of their suitability for the achievement of human aims or purposes. Or, putting the matter in a less abstract way, the closed society breaks down when the supernatural awe with which the social order is considered gives way to active interference, and to the conscious pursuit of personal or group interests. It is clear that cultural contact through civilization may engender such a breakdown, and, even more, the development of an impoverished, i.e. landless, section of the ruling class.

I may mention here that I do not like to speak of 'social breakdown' in a general way. I think that the breakdown of a closed society, as described here, is a fairly clear affair, but in general the term 'social breakdown' seems to me to convey very little more than that the observer does not like the course of the development he describes. I think that the term is much misused. But I admit that, with or without reason, the member of a certain society might have the feeling that 'everything is breaking down'. There is little doubt that to the members of the *ancien régime* or of the Russian nobility, the French or the Russian revolution must have appeared as a complete social breakdown ; but to the new rulers it appeared very differently.

Toynbee (cp. *A Study of History*, V, 23–35 ; 338) describes ' the appearance of schism in the body social ' as a criterion of a society which has broken down. Since schism, in the form of class disunion, undoubtedly occurred in Greek society long before the Peloponnesian war, it is not quite clear why he holds that this war (and not the breakdown of tribalism) marks what he describes as the breakdown of Hellenic civilization. (Cp. also note 45 (2) to chapter 4, and note 8 to the present chapter.)

Concerning the similarity between the Greeks and the Maoris, some remarks can be found in Burnet's *Early Greek Philosophy* ²,·especially pp. 2 and 9.

⁷ I owe this criticism of the organic theory of the state, together with many other suggestions, to J. Popper-Lynkeus ; he writes (*Die allgemeine Nährpflicht*, 2nd ed., 1923, pp. 71 f.) : ' The excellent Menenius Agrippa . . persuaded the insurgent plebs to return ' (to Rome) ' by telling them his simile of the body's members who rebelled against the belly. . . Why did not one of them say : " Right, Agrippa ! If there must be a belly, then we, the plebs, want to be the belly from now on ; and you . . may play the rôle of the members ! " ' (For the simile, see Livy II, 32, and Shakespeare's *Coriolanus*, Act 1, Scene 1.) It is perhaps interesting to note that even a

modern and apparently progressive movement like ' Mass-Observation ' makes propaganda for the organic theory of society (on the cover of its pamphlet, *First Year's Work*, 1937–38). See also note 31 to chapter 5.

On the other hand, it must be admitted that the tribal ' closed society ' has something like an ' organic ' character, just because of the absence of social tension. The fact that such a society may be based on slavery (as it was the case with the Greeks) does not create in itself a social tension, because slaves sometimes form no more part of society than its cattle ; their aspirations and problems do not necessarily create anything that is felt by the rulers as a problem within society. *Population growth*, however, does create such a problem. In Sparta, which did not send out colonies, it led first to the subjugation of neighbouring tribes for the sake of winning their territory, and then to a conscious effort to arrest all change by measures that included the control of population increase through the institution of infanticide, birth control, and homosexuality. All this was seen quite clearly by Plato, who always insisted (perhaps under the influence of Hippodamus) on the need for a fixed number of citizens, and who recommended in the *Laws* colonization and birth control, as he had earlier recommended homosexuality (explained in the same way in Aristotle's *Politics*, 1272a23) as means for keeping the population constant ; see *Laws*, 740d–741a, and 838e. (For Plato's recommendation of infanticide in the *Republic*, and for similar problems, see especially note 34 to chapter 4 ; furthermore, notes 22 and 63 to chapter 10, and 39 (3) to chapter 5.)

Of course, all these practices are far from being completely explicable in rational terms ; and the Dorian homosexuality, more especially, is closely connected with the practice of war, and with the attempts to recapture, in the life of the war horde, an emotional satisfaction which had been largely destroyed by the breakdown of tribalism ; see especially the ' war horde composed of lovers ', glorified by Plato in the *Symposium*, 178e. In the *Laws*, 636b, f., 836b/c, Plato deprecates homosexuality (cp., however, 838e).

[8] I suppose that what I call the ' strain of civilization ' is similar to the phenomenon which Freud had in mind when writing *Civilization and its Discontents*. Toynbee speaks of a Sense of Drift (*A Study of History*, V, 412 ff.), but he confines it to ' ages of disintegration ', while I find my strain very clearly expressed in Heraclitus (in fact, traces can be found in Hesiod)—long before the time when, according to Toynbee, his ' Hellenic society ' begins to ' disintegrate '. Meyer speaks of the disappearance of ' The status of birth, which had determined every man's place in life, his civil and social rights and duties, together with the security of earning his living ' (*Geschichte des Altertums*, III, 542). This gives an apt description of the strain in Greek society of the fifth century B.C.

[9] Another profession of this kind which led to comparative intellectual independence, was that of a wandering bard. I am thinking here mainly of Xenophanes, the progressivist ; cp. the paragraph on ' Protagoreanism ' in note 7 to chapter 5. (Homer also may be a case in point.) It is clear that this profession was accessible to very few men.

I happen to have no personal interest in matters of commerce, or in commercially minded people. But the influence of commercial initiative seems to me rather important. It is hardly an accident that the oldest known civilization, that of Sumer, was, as far as we know, a commercial civilization with strong democratic features ; and that the arts of writing and arithmetic, and the beginnings of science, were closely connected with its commercial life. (Cp. also text to note 24 to this chapter.)

[10] *Thucydides*, I, 93 (I mostly follow Jowett's translation). For the problem of Thucydides' bias, cp. note 15 (1) to this chapter.

[11] This and the next quotation : *op. cit.*, I, 107. Thucydides' story of the

treacherous oligarchs can hardly be recognized in Meyer's apologetic version (*Gesch. d. Altertums*, III, 594), in spite of the fact that he has no better sources ; it is simply distorted beyond recognition. (For Meyer's partiality, see note 15 (2) to the present chapter.)—For a similar treachery (in 479 B.C., on the eve of Plataea) cp. Plutarch's *Aristides*, 13.

¹² *Thucydides*, III, 82–84. The following conclusion of the passage is characteristic of the element of individualism and humanitarianism present in Thucydides, a member of the Great Generation (see below, and note 27 to this chapter) and, as mentioned above, a moderate : ' When men take revenge, they are reckless ; they do not consider the future, and do not hesitate to annul those common laws of humanity on which every individual must rely for his own deliverance should he ever be overtaken by calamity ; they forget that in their own hour of need they will look for them in vain.' For a further discussion of Thucydides' bias see note 15 (1) to this chapter.

¹³ Aristotle, *Politics*, VIII, (V), 9, 10/11 ; 1310a. Aristotle does not agree with such open hostility ; he thinks it wiser that ' true Oligarchs should *affect* to be advocates of the people's cause ' ; and he is anxious to give them good advice : ' They should take, or they should at least *pretend* to take, the opposite line, by including in their oath the pledge : I shall do no harm to the people.'

¹⁴ *Thucydides*, II, 9.

¹⁵ Cp. E. Meyer, *Geschichte des Altertums*, IV (1915), 368.

(1) In order to judge Thucydides' alleged impartiality, or rather, his involuntary bias, one must compare his treatment of the most important affair of Plataea which marked the outbreak of the first part of the Peloponnesian war (Meyer, following Lysias, calls this part the Archidamian war ; cp. Meyer, *Gesch. d. Altertums*, IV, 307, and V, p. VII) with his treatment of the Melian affair, Athens' first aggressive move in the second part (the war of Alcibiades). The Archidamian war broke out with an attack on democratic Plataea—a lightning attack made without declaration of war by Thebes, a partner of totalitarian Sparta, whose friends inside Plataea, the oligarchic fifth column, had by night opened the doors of Plataea to the enemy. Though most important as the immediate cause of the war, the incident is comparatively briefly related by Thucydides (II, 1–7) ; he does not comment upon the moral aspect, apart from calling ' the affair of Plataea a glaring violation of the thirty years truce ' ; but he censures (II, 5) the democrats of Plataea for their harsh treatment of the invaders, and even expresses doubts whether they did not break an oath. This method of presentation contrasts strongly with the famous and most elaborate, though of course fictitious, Melian Dialogue (*Thuc.*, V, 85–113) in which Thucydides tries to brand Athenian imperialism. Shocking as the Melian affair seems to have been (Alcibiades may have been responsible ; cp. Plutarch, *Alc.*, 16), the Athenians did *not* attack without warning, and tried to negotiate before using force.

Another case in point, bearing on Thucydides' attitude, is his eulogy (in VIII, 68) of the oligarchic party leader, the orator Antiphon (who is mentioned in Plato's *Menexenus*, 236a, as a teacher of Socrates ; cp. end of note 19 to chapter 6).

(2) E. Meyer is one of the greatest modern authorities on this period. But to appreciate his point of view one must read the following scornful remarks on democratic governments (there are a great many passages of this kind) : ' Much more important ' (viz., than to arm) ' was it to continue the entertaining game of party-quarrels, and to secure unlimited freedom, as interpreted by everybody according to his particular interests.' (V, 61.) But is it more, I ask, than an ' interpretation according to his particular interests ' when Meyer writes : ' The wonderful freedom of democracy, and of her leaders, have manifestly proved their inefficiency.' (V, 69.) About

the Athenian democratic leaders who in 403 B.C. refused to surrender to Sparta (and whose refusal was later even justified by success—although no such justification is necessary), Meyer says : ' Some of these leaders might have been honest fanatics ; . . they might have been so utterly incapable of any sound judgement that they really believed ' (what they said, namely :) ' that Athens must never capitulate.' (IV, 659.) Meyer censures other historians in the strongest terms for being biased. (Cp. e.g. the notes in V, 89 and 102, where he defends the older tyrant Dionysius against allegedly biased attacks, and 113 bottom to 114 top, where he is also exasperated by some anti-Dionysian ' parroting historians '.) Thus he calls Grote ' an English radical leader ', and his work ' not a history, but an apology for Athens ', and he proudly contrasts himself with such men : ' It will hardly be possible to deny that we have become more impartial in questions of politics, and that we have arrived thereby at a more correct and more comprehensive historical judgement.' (All this in III, 239.)

Behind Meyer's point of view stands—Hegel. This explains everything (as will be clear, I hope, to readers of chapter 12). Meyer's Hegelianism becomes obvious in the following remark, which is an unconscious but nearly literal quotation from Hegel ; it is in III, 256, when Meyer speaks of a ' flat and moralizing evaluation, which judges great political undertakings with the yardstick of civil morality ' (Hegel speaks of ' the litany of private virtues '), ' ignoring the deeper, the truly moral factors of the state, and of historical responsibilities '. (This corresponds exactly to the passages from Hegel quoted in chapter 12, below ; cp. note 75 to chapter 12.) I wish to use this opportunity once more to make it clear that I do not pretend to be impartial in my historical judgement. Of course I do what I can to ascertain the relevant facts. But I am aware that my evaluations (like anybody else's) must depend entirely on my point of view. This I admit, although I fully believe in my point of view, i.e. that my evaluations are right.

[16] Cp. Meyer, *op. cit.*, IV, 367.

[17] Cp. Meyer, *op. cit.*, IV, 464.

[18] It must however be kept in mind that, as the reactionaries complained, slavery was in Athens on the verge of dissolution. Cp. the evidence mentioned in notes 17, 18 and 29 to chapter 4 ; furthermore, notes 13 to chapter 5, 48 to chapter 8, and 27–37 to the present chapter.

[19] Cp. Meyer, *op. cit.*, IV, 659.

Meyer comments upon this move of the Athenian democrats : ' Now when it was too late they made a move towards a political constitution which later helped Rome . . to lay the foundations of its greatness.' In other words, instead of crediting the Athenians with a constitutional invention of the first order, he reproaches them ; and the credit goes to Rome, whose conservatism is more to Meyer's taste.

The incident in Roman history to which Meyer alludes is Rome's alliance, or federation, with Gabii. But immediately before, and on the very page on which Meyer describes this federation (in V, 135) we can read also : ' All these towns, when incorporated with Rome, lost their existence . . without even receiving a political organization of the type of Attica's " demes ".' A little later, in V, 147, Gabii is again referred to, and Rome in her generous ' liberality ' again contrasted with Athens ; but at the turn of the same page Meyer reports without criticism Rome's looting and total destruction of Veii, which meant the end of Etruscan civilization.

The worst perhaps of all these Roman destructions is that of Carthage. It took place at a moment when Carthage was no longer a danger to Rome, and it robbed Rome, and us, of most valuable contributions which Carthage could have made to civilization. I only mention the great treasures of geographical information which were destroyed there. (The story of the decline of Carthage is not unlike that of the fall of Athens in 404 B.C., discussed in this chapter below ; see note 48.   The oligarchs of Carthage preferred the fall of their city to the victory of democracy.)

Later, under the influence of Stoicism, derived indirectly from Antisthenes, Rome began to develop a very liberal and humanitarian outlook.   It reached the height of this development in those centuries of peace after Augustus (cp. for instance Toynbee, *A Study of History*, V, pp. 343–346), but it is here that some romantic historians see the beginning of her decline.

Regarding this decline itself, it is, of course, naïve and romantic to believe, as many still do, that it was due to the degeneration caused by long-continued peace, or to demoralization, or to the superiority of the younger barbarian peoples, etc. ; in brief, to over-feeding. (Cp. note 45 (3) to chapter 4.) The devastating result of violent epidemics (cp. H. Zinsser, *Rats, Lice, and History*, 1937, pp. 131 ff.) and the unchecked and progressive exhaustion of the soil, and with it a breakdown of the agricultural basis of the Roman economic system (cp. V. G. Simkhovitch, ' Hay and History ', and ' Rome's Fall Reconsidered ', in *Towards the Understanding of Jesus*, 1927), seem to have been some of the main causes. Cp. also W. Hegemann, *Entlarvte Geschichte* (1934).

[20] *Thucydides*, VII, 28 ; cp. Meyer, *op. cit.*, IV, 535. The important remark that ' this would yield more ' enables us, of course, to fix an approximate upper limit for the ratio between the taxes previously imposed and the volume of trade.

[21] This is an allusion to a grim little pun which I owe to P. Milford : ' A Plutocracy is preferable to a Lootocracy.'

[22] Plato, *Republic*, 423b. For the problem of keeping the size of the population constant, cp. note 7, above.

[23] Cp. Meyer, *Geschichte des Altertums*, IV, 577.

[24] *Op. cit.*, V, 27. Cp. also note 9 to this chapter, and text to note 30 to chapter 4. * For the passage from the *Laws*, see 742a–c. Plato elaborates here the Spartan attitude. He lays down ' a law that forbids private citizens to possess any gold or silver. . . Our citizens should be allowed only such coins as are legal tender among ourselves, but valueless elsewhere. . . For the sake of an expeditionary force, or official visit abroad, such as embassies or other necessary missions . . it is necessary that the state should always possess Hellenic (gold) coinage. And if a private citizen should ever be obliged to go abroad, he may do so, provided he has duly obtained permission from the magistrates. And should he have, upon his return, any foreign money left, then he must surrender it to the state, and accept its equivalent in home currency. And should anybody be found to keep it, then it must be confiscated, and he who imported it, and anybody who failed to inform against him, should be liable to curses and condemnations, and, in addition, to a fine of not less than the amount of the money involved.' Reading this passage, one wonders whether one does not wrong Plato in describing him as a reactionary who copied the laws of the totalitarian township of Sparta ; for here he anticipates by more than 2000 years the principles and practices which nowadays are nearly universally accepted as sound policy by the most progressive Western European democratic governments (who, like Plato, hope that some other government will look after the ' Universal Hellenic gold currency ').

A later passage (*Laws*, 950d) has, however, less of a liberal Western ring. ' First, no man under forty years shall obtain permission for going abroad to whatever place it may be. Secondly, nobody shall obtain such permission in a private capacity : in a public capacity, permission may be granted only to heralds, ambassadors, and to certain missions of inspection. . . And *these men, after their return, will teach the young that the political institutions of other countries are inferior to their own.*'

Similar laws are laid down for the reception of strangers. For 'inter-communication between states necessarily results in a mixing of characters . . and in importing novel customs ; and this must cause the greatest harm to people who enjoy . . the right laws ' (949e/950a).*

²⁵ This is admitted by Meyer (*op. cit.*, IV, 433 f.), who in a very interesting passage says of the two parties : ' each of them claims that it defends " the paternal state " . . , and that the opponent is infected with the modern spirit of selfishness and revolutionary violence. In reality, both are infected. . . The traditional customs and religion are more deeply rooted in the democratic party ; its aristocratic enemies who fight under the flag of the restoration of the ancient times are . . entirely modernized.' Cp. also *op. cit.*, V, 4 f., 14, and the next note.

²⁶ From Aristotle's *Athenian Constitution*, ch. 34, §3, we learn that the Thirty Tyrants professed at first what appeared to Aristotle a ' moderate ' programme, viz., that of the ' paternal state '.—For the nihilism and the modernity of Critias, cp. his theory of religion discussed in chapter 8 (see especially note 17 to that chapter) and note 48 to the present chapter.

²⁷ It is most interesting to contrast Sophocles' attitude towards the new faith with that of Euripides. Sophocles complains (cp. Meyer, *op. cit.*, IV, III) : ' It is wrong that . . the lowly born should flourish, while the brave and nobly born are unfortunate.' Euripides replies (with Antiphon ; cp. note 13 to chapter 5) that the distinction between the nobly and the low born (especially slaves) is merely verbal : ' The name alone brings shame upon the slave.'—For the humanitarian element in Thucydides, cp. the quotation in note 12 to this chapter. For the question how far the Great Generation was connected with cosmopolitan tendencies, see the evidence marshalled in note 48 to chapter 8—especially the hostile witnesses, i.e. the Old Oligarch, Plato, and Aristotle.

²⁸ ' Misologists ', or haters of rational argument, are compared by Socrates to ' misanthropists ', or haters of men ; cp. the *Phaedo*, 89c. In contrast, cp. Plato's misanthropic remark in the *Republic*, 496c–d (cp. notes 57 and 58 to chapter 8).

²⁹ The quotations in this paragraph are from Democritus' fragments, Diels, *Vorsokratiker* ⁵, fragments number 41 ; 179 ; 34 ; 261 ; 62 ; 55 ; 251 ; 247 (genuineness questioned by Diels and by Tarn, cp. note 48 to chapter 8) ; 118.

³⁰ Cp. text to note 16, chapter 6.

³¹ Cp. *Thucydides*, II, 37–41. Cp. also the remarks in note 16 to chapter 6.

³² Cp. T. Gomperz, *Greek Thinkers*, Book V, ch. 13, 3 (Germ. ed., II, 407).

³³ Herodotus' work with its pro-democratic tendency (cp., for example, III, 80) appeared about a year or two after Pericles' oration (cp. Meyer, *Gesch. d. Altertums*, IV, 369).

³⁴ This has been pointed out for instance by T. Gomperz, *Greek Thinkers*, V, 13, 2 (Germ. ed., II, 406 f.) ; the passages in the *Republic* to which he draws attention are : 557d and 561c, ff. The similarity is undoubtedly intentional. Cp. also Adam's edition of the *Republic*, vol. II, 235, note to 557d26. See also the *Laws*, 699d/e, ff., and 704d–707d. For a similar observation regarding Herodotus III, 80, see note 17 to chapter 6.

³⁵ Some hold the *Menexenus* to be spurious, but I believe that this shows only their tendency to idealize Plato. The *Menexenus* is vouched for by Aristotle, who quotes a remark from it as due to the ' Socrates of the Funeral Dialogue ' (*Rhetoric*, I, 9, 30 = 1367b8 ; and III, 14, 11 = 1415b30). See especially also end of note 19 to chapter 6 ; also note 48 to chapter 8 and notes 15 (1) and 61 to the present chapter.

³⁶ The Old Oligarch's (or the Pseudo-Xenophon's) *Constitution of Athens* was published in 424 B.C. (according to Kirchhoff, quoted by Gomperz,

Greek Thinkers, Germ. ed., I, 477). For its attribution to Critias, cp. J. E. Sandys, *Aristotle's Constitution of Athens*, Introduction IX, especially note 3. See also notes 18 and 48 to this chapter. Its influence upon Thucydides is, I think, noticeable in the passages quoted in notes 10 and 11 to this chapter. For its influence upon Plato, see especially note 59 to chapter 8, and *Laws*, 704a–707d. (Cp. Aristotle, *Politics*, 1326b–1327a ; Cicero, *De Republica*, II, 3 and 4.)

³⁷ I am alluding to M. M. Rader's book, *No Compromise—The Conflict between Two Worlds* (1939), an excellent criticism of the ideology of fascism.

With the allusion, later in this paragraph, to Socrates' warning against misanthropy and misology, cp. note 28, above.

³⁸ *(1) For the theory that what may be called ' the invention of critical thought' consists in the foundation of a new tradition—the tradition of critically discussing the traditional myths and theories—see my *Towards a Rational Theory of Tradition*, *The Rationalist Annual*, 1949 ; now in *Conjectures and Refutations*. (Only such a new tradition can explain the fact that, in the Ionian School, the three first generations produced three different philosophies.) *

(2) Schools (especially Universities) have retained certain aspects of tribalism ever since. But we must think not only of their emblems, or of the Old School Tie with all its social implications of caste, etc., but also of the patriarchal and authoritarian character of so many schools. It was not just an accident that Plato, when he had failed to re-establish tribalism, founded a school instead ; nor is it an accident that schools are so often bastions of reaction, and school teachers dictators in pocket edition.

As an illustration of the tribalistic character of these early schools, I give here a list of some of the taboos of the early Pythagoreans. (The list is from Burnet's *Early Greek Philosophy* ², 106, who takes it from Diels ; cp. *Vorsokratiker* ⁵, vol. I, pp. 97 ff. ; but see also Aristoxenus' evidence in *op. cit.*, p. 101.) Burnet speaks of ' genuine taboos of a thoroughly primitive type '. —To abstain from beans.—Not to pick up what has fallen.—Not to touch a white cock.—Not to break bread.—Not to step over a crossbar.—Not to stir the fire with iron.—Not to eat from a whole loaf.—Not to pluck a garland. —Not to sit on a quart measure.—Not to eat the heart.—Not to walk on highways.—Not to let the swallows share one's roof.—When the pot is taken off the fire, not to leave the mark of it in the ashes, but to stir them together.— Not to look in a mirror beside a light.—After rising from the bedclothes, to roll them together and to smooth out the impress of the body.

³⁹ An interesting parallelism to this development is the destruction of tribalism through the Persian conquests. This social revolution led, as Meyer points out (*op. cit.*, vol. III, 167 ff.), to the emergence of a number of prophetic, i.e. in our terminology, of historicist, religions of destiny, degeneration, and salvation, among them that of the ' chosen people ', the Jews (cp. chapter 1).

Some of these religions were also characterized by the doctrine that the creation of the world is not yet concluded, but still going on. This must be compared with the early Greek conception of the world as an edifice and with the Heraclitean destruction of this conception, described in chapter 2 (see note 1 to that chapter). It may be mentioned here that even Anaximander felt uneasy about the edifice. His stress upon the boundless or indeterminate or indefinite character of the building-material may have been the expression of a feeling that the building may possess no definite framework, that it may be in flux (cp. next note).

The development of the Dionysian and the Orphic mysteries in Greece is probably dependent upon the religious development of the east (cp. *Herodotus*, II, 81). Pythagoreanism, as is well known, had much in common with Orphic teaching, especially regarding the theory of the soul (see also note 44 below). But Pythagoreanism had a definitely ' aristocratic ' flavour, as opposed to the Orphic teaching which represented a kind of ' proletarian ' version of this movement. Meyer (*op. cit.*, III, p. 428, § 246) is probably right when he describes the beginnings of philosophy as a rational counter-current against the movement of the mysteries ; cp. Heraclitus' attitude in these matters (fragm. 5, 14, 15 ; and 40, 129, Diels⁵ ; 124-129 ; and 16-17, Bywater). He hated the mysteries *and* Pythagoras ; the Pythagorean Plato despised the mysteries. (*Rep.*, 364e, f. ; cp. however Adam's Appendix IV to Book IX of the *Republic*, vol. II, 378 ff., of his edition.)

[40] For Anaximander (cp. the preceding note), see Diels⁵, fragm. 9 : ' The origin of things . . . is some indeterminate (or boundless) nature ; . . out of those things from which existing things are generated, into these they dissolve again, by necessity. For they do penance to one another for their offence (or injustice), according to the order of time.' That individual existence appeared to Anaximander as *injustice* was the interpretation of Gomperz (*Greek Thinkers*, Germ. ed., vol. I, p. 46 ; note the similarity to Plato's theory of justice) ; but this interpretation has been severely criticized.

[41] Parmenides was the first to seek his salvation from this strain by interpreting his dream of the arrested world as a revelation of true reality, and the world of flux in which he lived as a dream. ' The real being is indivisible. It is always an integrated whole, which never breaks away from its order ; it never disperses, and thus need not re-unite.' (D⁵, fragm. 4.) For Parmenides, cp. also note 22 to chapter 3, and text.

[42] Cp. note 9 to the present chapter (and note 7 to chapter 5).

[43] Cp. Meyer, *Geschichte des Altertums*, III, 443, and IV, 120 f.

[44] J. Burnet, ' The Socratic Doctrine of the Soul ', *Proceedings of the British Academy*, VIII (1915/16), 235 ff. I am the more anxious to stress this partial agreement since I cannot agree with Burnet in most of his other theories, especially those that concern Socrates' relations to Plato ; his opinion in particular that Socrates is politically the more reactionary of the two (*Greek Philosophy*, I, 210) appears to me untenable. Cp. note 56 to this chapter.

Regarding the Socratic doctrine of the soul, I believe that Burnet is right in insisting that the saying ' care for your souls ' is Socratic ; for this saying expresses Socrates' moral interests. But I think it highly improbable that Socrates held any metaphysical theory of the soul. The theories of the *Phaedo*, the *Republic*, etc., seem to me undoubtedly Pythagorean. (For the Orphic-Pythagorean theory that the body is the tomb of the soul, cp. Adam, Appendix IV to Book IX of the *Republic* ; see also note 39 to this chapter.) And in view of Socrates' clear statement in the *Apology*, 19c, that he had ' nothing whatever to do with such things ' (i.e. with speculations on nature ; see note 56 (5) to this chapter), I strongly disagree with Burnet's opinion that Socrates was a Pythagorean ; and also with the opinion that he held any definite metaphysical doctrine of the ' nature ' of the soul.

I believe that Socrates' saying ' care for your souls ' is an expression of his moral (and intellectual) individualism. Few of his doctrines seem to be so well attested as his individualistic theory of the moral self-sufficiency of the virtuous man. (See the evidence mentioned in notes 25 to chapter 5 and 36 to chapter 6.) But this is most closely connected with the idea expressed in the sentence ' care for your souls '. In his emphasis on self-sufficiency, Socrates wished to say : They can destroy your body, but they cannot destroy your moral integrity. If the latter is your main concern, they cannot do any really serious harm to you.

It appears that Plato, when becoming acquainted with the Pythagorean metaphysical theory of the soul, felt that Socrates' moral attitude needed a metaphysical foundation, especially a theory of survival. He therefore substituted for 'they cannot destroy your moral integrity' the idea of the indestructibility of the soul. (Cp. also notes 9 f. to chapter 7.)

Against my interpretation, it may be contended by both metaphysicians and positivists that there can be no such moral and non-metaphysical idea of the soul as I ascribe to Socrates, since any way of speaking of the soul must be metaphysical. I do not think that I have much hope of convincing Platonic metaphysicians ; but I shall attempt to show positivists (or materialists, etc.) that they too believe in a 'soul', in a sense very similar to that which I attribute to Socrates, and that most of them value that 'soul' more highly than the body.

First of all, even positivists may admit that we can make a perfectly empirical and 'meaningful', although somewhat unprecise, distinction between 'physical' and 'psychical' maladies. In fact, this distinction is of considerable practical importance for the organization of hospitals, etc. (It is quite probable that one day it may be superseded by something more precise, but that is a different question.) Now most of us, even positivists, would, if we had to choose, prefer a mild physical malady to a mild form of insanity. Even positivists would moreover probably prefer a lengthy and in the end incurable physical illness (provided it was not too painful, etc.) to an equally lengthy period of incurable insanity, and perhaps even to a period of curable insanity. In this way, I believe, we can say without using metaphysical terms that they care for their 'souls' more than for their 'bodies'. (Cp. *Phaedo*, 82d : they 'care for their souls and are not servants of their bodies' ; see also *Apology*, 29d–30b.) And this way of speaking would be quite independent of any theory they might have concerning the 'soul' ; even if they should maintain that, in the last analysis, it is only part of the body, and all insanity only a physical malady, our conclusion would still hold. (It would come to something like this : that they value their brains more highly than other parts of their bodies.)

We can now proceed to a similar consideration of an idea of the 'soul' which is closer still to the Socratic idea. Many of us are prepared to undergo considerable physical hardship for the sake of purely intellectual ends. We are, for example, ready to suffer in order to advance scientific knowledge ; and also for the sake of furthering our own intellectual development, i.e. for the sake of attaining 'wisdom'. (For Socrates' intellectualism, cp. for insta ce the *Crito*, 44d/e, and 47b.) Similar things could be said of the furthering of moral ends, for instance, equalitarian justice, peace, etc. (Cp. *Crito*, 47e/48a, where Socrates explains that he means by 'soul' that part of us which is 'improved by justice and depraved by injustice'.) And many of us would say, with Socrates, that these things are more important to us than things like health, even though we like to be in good health. And many may even agree with Socrates that the possibility of adopting such an attitude is what makes us proud to be men, and not animals.

All this, I believe, can be said without any reference to a metaphysical theory of the 'nature of the soul'. And I see no reason why we should attribute such a theory to Socrates in the face of his clear statement that he had nothing to do with speculations of that sort.

[45] In the *Gorgias*, which is, I believe, Socratic in parts (although the Pythagorean elements which Gomperz has noted show, I think, that it is largely Platonic ; cp. note 56 to this chapter), Plato puts into the mouth of Socrates an attack on 'the ports and ship-yards and walls' of Athens, and on the tributes or taxes imposed upon her Allies. These attacks, as they stand, are certainly Plato's, which may explain why they sound very much like those of the oligarchs. But I think it quite possible that Socrates may have made similar remarks, in his anxiety to stress the things which, in his opinion, mattered most. But he would, I believe, have loathed the idea that his

moral criticism could be turned into treacherous oligarchic propaganda against the open society, and especially, against its representative, Athens. (For the question of Socrates' loyalty, cp. esp. note 53 to this chapter, and text.)

⁴⁶ The typical figures, in Plato's works, are Callicles and Thrasymachus. Historically, the nearest realizations are perhaps Theramenes and Critias ; Alcibiades also, whose character and deeds, however, are very hard to judge.

⁴⁷ The following remarks are highly speculative and do not bear upon my arguments.

I consider it possible that the basis of the *First Alcibiades* is Plato's own conversion by Socrates, i.e. that Plato may in this dialogue have chosen the figure of Alcibiades to hide himself. There might have been a strong inducement for him to tell the story of his conversion ; for Socrates, when accused of being responsible for the misdeeds of Alcibiades, Critias, and Charmides (see below), had referred, in his defence before the court, to Plato as a living example, and as a witness, of his true educational influence. It seems not unlikely that Plato with his urge to literary testimony felt that he had to tell the tale of Socrates' relations with himself, a tale which he could not tell in court (cp. Taylor, *Socrates*, note 1 to p. 105). By using Alcibiades' name and the special circumstances surrounding him (e.g. his ambitious political dreams which might well have been similar to those of Plato before his conversion) he would attain his apologetic purpose (cp. text to notes 49–50), showing that Socrates' moral influence in general, and in particular on Alcibiades, was very different from what his prosecutors maintained it to be. I think it not unlikely that the *Charmides* is also, largely, a self-portrait. (It is not without interest to note that Plato himself undertook similar conversions, but as far as we can judge, in a different way ; not so much by direct personal moral appeal, but rather by an institutional teaching of Pythagorean mathematics, as a pre-requisite for the dialectical intuition of the Idea of the Good. Cp. the stories of his attempted conversion of the younger Dionysius.) For the *First Alcibiades* and related problems, see also Grote's *Plato*, I, especially pp. 351–355.

⁴⁸ Cp. Meyer, *Geschichte des Altertums*, V, 38 (and Xenophon's *Hellenica*, II, 4, 22). In the same volume, on pp. 19–23 and 36–44 (see especially p. 36) can be found all the evidence needed for justifying the interpretation given in the text. The *Cambridge Ancient History* (1927, vol. V ; cp. especially pp. 369 ff.) gives a very similar interpretation of the events.

It may be added that the number of full citizens killed by the Thirty during the eight months of terror approached probably 1,500, which is, as far as we know, not much less than one-tenth (probably about 8 per cent.) of the total number of full citizens left after the war, or 1 per cent. per month—an achievement hardly surpassed even in our own day.

Taylor writes of the Thirty (*Socrates*, Short Biographies, 1937, p. 100, note 1) : ' It is only fair to remember that these men probably " lost their heads " under the temptation presented by their situation. Critias had previously been known as a man of wide culture whose political leanings were decidedly democratic.' I believe that this attempt to minimize the responsibility of the puppet government, and especially of Plato's beloved uncle, must fail. We know well enough what to think of the shortlived democratic sentiments professed in those days at suitable occasions by the young aristocrats. Besides, Critias' father (cp. Meyer, vol. IV, p. 579, and *Lys.*, 12, 43, and 12, 66), and probably Critias himself, had belonged to the oligarchy of he Four Hundred ; and Critias' extant writings show his treacherous pro-Spartan leanings as well as his oligarchic outlook (cp., for instance, Diels ⁵, 45) and his blunt nihilism (cp. note 17 to chapter 8) and his ambition (cp. Diels ⁵, 15 ; cp. also Xenophon's *Memorabilia*, I, 2, 24 ;

and his *Hellenica*, II, 3, 36 and 47). But the decisive point is that he simply tried to give consistent effect to the programme of the ' Old Oligarch ', the author of the Pseudo-Xenophontic *Constitution of Athens* (cp. note 36 to the present chapter) : to eradicate democracy ; and to make a determined attempt to do so with Spartan help, should Athens be defeated. The degree of violence used is the logical result of the situation. It does not indicate that Critias lost his head ; rather, that he was very well aware of the difficulties, i.e. of the democrats' still formidable power of resistance.

Meyer, whose great sympathy for Dionysius I proves that he is at least not prejudiced *against* tyrants, says about Critias (*op. cit.*, V, p. 17), after a sketch of his amazingly opportunistic political career, that ' he was just as unscrupulous as Lysander ', the Spartan conqueror, and therefore the appropriate head of Lysander's puppet government.

It seems to me that there is a striking similarity between the characters of Critias, the soldier, æsthete, poet, and sceptical companion of Socrates, and of Frederick II of Prussia, called ' the Great ', who also was a soldier, an æsthete, a poet, and a sceptical disciple of Voltaire, as well as one of the worst tyrants and most ruthless oppressors in modern history. (On Frederick, cp. W. Hegemann, *Entlarvte Geschichte*, 1934 ; see especially p. 90 on his attitude towards religion, reminiscent of that of Critias.)

[49] This point is very well explained by Taylor, *Socrates*, Short Biographies, 1937, p. 103, who follows here Burnet's note to Plato's *Euthyphro*, 4c, 4.—The only point in which I feel inclined to deviate, but only very slightly, from Taylor's excellent treatment (*op. cit.*, 103, 120) of Socrates' trial is in the interpretation of the tendencies of the charge, especially of the charge concerning the introduction of ' novel religious practices ' (*op. cit.*, 109 and 111 f.).

[50] Evidence to show this can be found in Taylor's *Socrates*, 113–115 ; cp. especially 115, note 1, where *Aeschines*, I, 173, is quoted : ' You put Socrates the Sophist to death because he was shown to have educated Critias.'

[51] It was the policy of the Thirty to implicate as many people in their acts of terrorism as they could ; cp. the excellent remarks by Taylor in *Socrates*, 101 f. (especially note 3 to p. 101). For Chaerephon, see note 56, (5) e_6, to the present chapter.

[52] As Crossman and others do ; cp. Crossman, *Plato To-Day*, 91/92. I agree in this point with Taylor, *Socrates*, 116 ; see also his notes 1 and 2 to that page.

That the plan of the prosecution was not to make a martyr of Socrates ; that the trial could have been avoided, or managed differently, had Socrates been prepared to compromise, i.e. to leave Athens, or even to promise to keep quiet, all this seems fairly clear in view of Plato's (or Socrates') allusions in the *Apology* as well as in the *Crito*. (Cp. *Crito*, 45e and especially 52b/c, where Socrates says that he would have been permitted to emigrate had he offered to do so at the trial.)

[53] Cp. especially *Crito*, 53b/c, where Socrates explains that, if he were to accept the opportunity for escape, he would confirm his judges in their belief ; for he who corrupts the laws is likely to corrupt the young also.

The *Apology* and *Crito* were probably written not long after Socrates' death. The *Crito* (possibly the earlier of the two) was perhaps written upon Socrates' request that his motives in declining to escape should be made known. Indeed, such a wish may have been the first inspiration of the Socratic dialogues. T. Gomperz (*Greek Thinkers*, V, 11, 1, Germ. ed., II, 358) believes the *Crito* to be of later date and explains its tendency by assuming that it was Plato who was anxious to stress his loyalty. ' We do not know ' writes Gomperz, ' the immediate situation to which this small dialogue owes its existence ; but it is hard to resist the impression that Plato is here most interested in defending himself and his group against the suspicion of harbouring revolutionary views.' Although Gomperz's suggestion would easily fit into my general interpretation of Plato's views, I feel that the *Crito* is much more likely to be Socrates' defence than Plato's. But I agree with Gomperz's interpretation of its tendency. Socrates had certainly the greatest interest in defending himself against a suspicion which endangered his life's work.— Regarding this interpretation of the contents of the *Crito*, I again agree fully with Taylor (*Socrates*, 124 f.). But the loyalty of the *Crito* and its contrast to the obvious disloyalty of the *Republic* which quite openly takes sides with Sparta against Athens seems to refute Burnet's and Taylor's view that the *Republic* is Socratic, and that Socrates was more strongly opposed to democracy than Plato. (Cp. note 56 to this chapter.)

Concerning Socrates' affirmation of his loyalty to democracy, cp. especially the following passages of the *Crito* : 51d/e, where the democratic character of the laws is stressed, i.e. the possibility that the citizen might change the laws without violence, by rational argument (as Socrates puts it, he may try to convince the laws) ;—52b, f., where Socrates insists that he has no quarrel with the Athenian constitution ;—53c/d, where he describes not only virtue and justice but especially institutions and laws (those of Athens) as the best things among men ;—54c, where he says that he may be a victim of men, but insists that he is not a victim of the laws.

In view of all these passages (and especially of *Apology*, 32c ; cp. note 8 to chapter 7), we must, I believe, discount the one passage which looks very different, viz. 52e, where Socrates by implication praises the constitutions of Sparta and Crete. Considering especially 52b/c, where Socrates said that he was not curious to know other states *or their laws*, one may be tempted to suggest that the remark on Sparta and Crete in 52e is an interpolation, made by somebody who attempted to reconcile the *Crito* with later writings, especially with the *Republic*. Whether that is so or whether the passage is a Platonic addition, it seems extremely unlikely that it is Socratic. One need only remember Socrates' anxiety not to do anything which might be interpreted as pro-Spartan, an anxiety of which we know from Xenophon's *Anabasis*, III, 1, 5. There we read that ' Socrates feared that he ' (i.e. his friend, the young Xenophon—another of the young black sheep) ' might be blamed for being disloyal ; for Cyrus was known to have assisted the Spartans in the war against Athens.' (This passage is certainly much less suspect than the *Memorabilia* ; there is no influence of Plato here, and Xenophon actually accuses himself, by implication, of having taken his obligations to his country too lightly, and of having deserved his banishment, mentioned in *op. cit.*, V, 3, 7, and VII, 7. 57.)

⁵⁴ *Apology*, 30e/31a.

⁵⁵ Platonists, of course, would all agree with Taylor who says in the last sentence of his *Socrates* : ' Socrates had just one " successor "—Plato.' Only Grote seems sometimes to have held views similar to those stated in the text ; what he says, for instance, in the passage quoted here in note 21 to chapter 7 (see also note 15 to chapter 8) can be interpreted as at least an expression of doubt whether Plato did not betray Socrates. Grote makes it perfectly clear that the *Republic* (not only the *Laws*) would have furnished the theoretical basis for condemning the Socrates of the *Apology*, and that this Socrates would never have been tolerated in Plato's best state. And he even points out that Plato's theory agrees with the practical treatment meted out to Socrates by the Thirty. (An example showing that the perversion of his master's teaching by a pupil is a thing that can succeed, even if the master is still alive, famous, and protests in public, can be found in note 58 to chapter 12.)

For the remarks on the *Laws*, made later in this paragraph, see especially the passages of the *Laws* referred to in notes 19–23 to chapter 8. Even Taylor, whose opinions on these questions are diametrically opposed to those presented here (see also the next note), admits : ' The person who first proposed to make false opinions in theology an offence against the state, was Plato himself, in the tenth Book of the *Laws*.' (Taylor, *op. cit.*, 108, note 1.)

In the text, I contrast especially Plato's *Apology* and *Crito* with his *Laws*. The reason for this choice is that nearly everybody, even Burnet and Taylor (see the next note), would agree that the *Apology* and the *Crito* represent the *Socratic* doctrine, and that the *Laws* may be described as *Platonic*. It seems to me therefore very difficult to understand how Burnet and Taylor could possibly defend their opinion that Socrates' attitude towards democracy was more hostile than Plato's. (This opinion is expressed in Burnet's *Greek Philosophy*, I, 209 f., and in Taylor's *Socrates*, 150 f., and 170 f.). I have seen no attempt to defend this view of Socrates, who fought for freedom (cp. especially note 53 to this chapter) and died for it, and of Plato, who wrote the *Laws*.

Burnet and Taylor hold this strange view because they are committed to the opinion that the *Republic* is Socratic and not Platonic ; and because it may be said that the *Republic* is slightly less anti-democratic than the Platonic *Statesman* and the *Laws*. But the differences between the *Republic* and the *Statesman* as well as the *Laws* are very slight indeed, especially if not only the first books of the *Laws* are considered but also the last ; in fact, the agreement of doctrine is rather closer than one would expect in two books separated by at least one decade, and probably by three or more, and most dissimilar in temperament and style (see note 6 to chapter 4, and many other places in this book where the similarity, if not identity, between the doctrines of the *Laws* and the *Republic* is shown). There is not the slightest internal difficulty in assuming that the *Republic* and the *Laws* are both *Platonic* ; but Burnet's and Taylor's own admission that their theory leads to the conclusion that Socrates was not only an enemy of democracy but even a greater enemy than Plato shows the difficulty if not absurdity of their view that not only the *Apology* and the *Crito* are Socratic but the *Republic* as well. For all these questions, see also the next note, and the *Addenda*, III, B(2), below.

[56] I need hardly say that this sentence is an attempt to sum up my interpretation of the historical rôle of Plato's theory of justice (for the moral failure of the Thirty, cp. Xenophon's *Hellenica*, II, 4, 40–42) ; and particularly of the main political doctrines of the *Republic* ; an interpretation which tries to explain the contradictions among the early dialogues, especially the *Gorgias*, and the *Republic*, as arising from the fundamental difference between the views of Socrates and those of the later Plato. The cardinal importance of the question which is usually called the *Socratic Problem* may justify my entering here into a lengthy and partly methodological debate.

(1) The older solution of the Socratic Problem assumed that a group of the Platonic dialogues, especially the *Apology* and the *Crito*, is Socratic (i.e., in the main historically correct, and intended as such) while the majority of the dialogues are Platonic, including many of those in which Socrates is the main speaker, as for instance the *Phaedo* and the *Republic*. The older authorities justified this opinion often by referring to an ' independent witness ', Xenophon, and by pointing out the similarity between the Xenophontic Socrates and the Socrates of the ' Socratic ' group of dialogues, and the dissimilarities between the Xenophontic ' Socrates ' and the ' Socrates ' of the Platonic group of dialogues. The metaphysical theory of Forms or Ideas, more especially, was usually considered Platonic.

(2) Against this view, an attack was launched by J. Burnet, who was supported by A. E. Taylor. Burnet denounced the argument on which the ' older solution ' (as I call it) is based as circular and unconvincing. It is not sound, he held, to select a group of dialogues solely because the theory of Forms is less prominent in them, to call them Socratic, and then to say that the theory of Forms was not Socrates' but Plato's invention. And it is not

sound to claim Xenophon as an independent witness since we have no reason whatever to believe in his independence, and good reason to believe that he must have known a number of Plato's dialogues when he commenced writing the *Memorabilia*.   Burnet demanded that we should proceed from the assumption that *Plato really meant what he said*, and that, when he made Socrates pronounce a certain doctrine, he believed, and wished his readers to believe, that this doctrine was characteristic of Socrates' teaching.

(3) Although Burnet's views on the Socratic Problem appear to me untenable, they have been most valuable and stimulating.   A bold theory of this kind, even if it is false, always means progress ; and Burnet's books are full of bold and most unconventional views on his subject.   This is the more to be appreciated as a historical subject always shows a tendency to become stale.   But much as I admire Burnet for his brilliant and bold theories, and much as I appreciate their salutary effect, I am, considering the evidence available to me, unable to convince myself that these theories are tenable. In his invaluable enthusiasm, Burnet was, I believe, not always critical enough towards his own ideas.   This is why others have found it necessary to criticize these ideas instead.

Regarding the Socratic Problem, I believe with many others that the view which I have described as the ' older solution ' is fundamentally correct. This view has lately been well defended, against Burnet and Taylor, especially by G. C. Field (*Plato and His Contemporaries*, 1930) and A. K. Rogers (*The Socratic Problem*, 1933) ; and many other scholars seem to adhere to it.   In spite of the fact that the arguments so far offered appear to me convincing, I may be permitted to add to them, using some results of the present book. But before proceeding to criticize Burnet, I may state that it is to Burnet that we owe our insight into the following principle of method.   *Plato's evidence is the only first-rate evidence available to us* ; all other evidence is secondary.   (Burnet has applied this principle to Xenophon ; but we must apply it also to Aristophanes, whose evidence was rejected by Socrates himself, in the *Apology* ; see under (5), below.)

(4) Burnet explains that it is his method to assume ' that Plato really meant what he said '.   According to this methodological principle, Plato's ' Socrates ' must be intended as a *portrait of the historical Socrates*.   (Cp. *Greek Philosophy*, I, 128, 212 f., and note on p. 349/50 ; cp. Taylor's *Socrates*, 14 f., 32 f., 153.)   I admit that Burnet's methodological principle is a sound starting point.   But I shall try to show, under (5), that the facts are such that they soon force *everybody* to give it up, including Burnet and Taylor.   They are forced, like all others, to *interpret* what Plato says.   But while others become conscious of this fact, and therefore careful and critical in their interpretations, it is inevitable that those who cling to the belief that they do not interpret Plato but simply accept what he said make it impossible for themselves to examine their interpretations critically.

(5) The facts that make Burnet's methodology inapplicable and force him and all others to interpret what Plato said, are, of course, the contradictions in Plato's alleged portrait of Socrates.   Even if we accept the principle that we have no better evidence than Plato's, we are forced by the internal contradictions in his writing not to take him at his word, and to give up the assumption that he ' really meant what he said '.   If a witness involves himself in contradictions, then we cannot accept his testimony without interpreting it, even if he is the best witness available.   I give first only three examples of such internal contradictions.

(a) The Socrates of the *Apology* very impressively repeats three times (18b–c ; 19c–d ; 23d) that he is not interested in natural philosophy (and therefore not a Pythagorean) : ' I know nothing, neither much nor little, about such things ', he said (19c) ; ' I, men of Athens, have nothing whatever to

do with such things ' (i.e. with speculations about nature).   Socrates asserts
that many who are present at the trial could testify to the truth of this statement ; they have heard him speak, but neither in few nor in many words
has anybody ever heard him speak about matters of natural philosophy.
(*Ap.*, 19, c–d.)   On the other hand, we have (*a'*) the *Phaedo* (cp. especially
108d, f., with the passages of the *Apology* referred to) and the *Republic*.   In
these dialogues, Socrates appears as a Pythagorean philosopher of ' nature ' ;
so much so that both Burnet and Taylor could say that he was in fact a leading
member of the Pythagorean school of thought.   (Cp. Aristotle, who says of
the Pythagoreans ' their discussions . . are all about nature ' ; see *Metaphysics*, end of 989b.)

Now I hold that (*a*) and (*a'*) flatly contradict each other ; and this
situation is made worse by the fact that the dramatic date of the *Republic* is
earlier and that of the *Phaedo* later than that of the *Apology*.   This makes it
impossible to reconcile (*a*) with (*a'*) by assuming that Socrates either gave up
Pythagoreanism in the last years of his life, between the *Republic* and the
Apology, or that he was converted to Pythagoreanism in the last month of his
life.

I do not pretend that there is no way of removing this contradiction by
some assumption or *interpretation*.   Burnet and Taylor may have reasons,
perhaps even good reasons, for trusting the *Phaedo* and the *Republic* rather
than the *Apology*.   (But they ought to realize that, assuming the correctness
of Plato's portrait, any doubt of Socrates' veracity in the *Apology* makes of
him one who lies for the sake of saving his skin.)   Such questions, however,
do not concern me at the moment.   My point is rather that in accepting
evidence (*a'*) as against (*a*), Burnet and Taylor are forced to abandon their
fundamental methodological assumption ' that Plato really meant what he
said ' ; they must interpret.

But interpretations made unawares must be uncritical ; this can be
illustrated by the use made by Burnet and Taylor of Aristophanes' evidence.
They hold that Aristophanes' jests would be pointless if Socrates had not been
a natural philosopher.   But it so happens that Socrates (I always assume,
with Burnet and Taylor, that the *Apology* is historical) foresaw this very
argument.   In his apology, he warned his judges against precisely this very
interpretation of Aristophanes, insisting most earnestly (*Ap.*, 19c, ff. ; see also
20c–e) that he had neither little nor much to do with natural philosophy, but
simply nothing at all.   Socrates felt as if he were fighting against shadows
in this matter, against the shadows of the past (*Ap.*, 18d–e) ; but we can now
say that he was also fighting the shadows of the future.   For when he challenged his fellow-citizens to come forward—those who believed Aristophanes
and dared to call Socrates a liar—*not one came*.   It was 2,300 years before some
Platonists made up their minds to answer his challenge.

It may be mentioned, in this connection, that Aristophanes, a moderate
anti-democrat, attacked Socrates as a ' sophist ', and that most of the sophists
were democrats.

(*b*) In the *Apology* (40c, ff.) Socrates takes up an agnostic attitude towards
the problem of survival ; (*b'*) the *Phaedo* consists mainly of elaborate proofs
of the immortality of the soul.   This difficulty is discussed by Burnet (in his
edition of the *Phaedo*, 1911, pp. xlviii ff.), in a way which does not convince
me at all.   (Cp. notes 9 to chapter 7, and 44 to the present chapter.)   But
whether he is right or not, his own discussion proves that he is forced to give
up his methodological principle and to *interpret* what Plato says.

(*c*) The Socrates of the *Apology* holds that the wisdom even of the wisest
consists in the realization of how little he knows, and that, accordingly, the
Delphian saying ' know thyself ' must be interpreted as ' know thy limitations ; ' and he implies that the rulers, more than anybody else, ought to

know their limitations. Similar views can be found in other early dialogues. But the main speakers of the *Statesman* and the *Laws* propound the doctrine that the powerful ought to be wise ; and by wisdom they no longer mean a knowledge of one's limitations, but rather the initiation into the deeper mysteries of dialectic philosophy—the intuition of the world of Forms or Ideas, or the training in the Royal Science of politics. The same doctrine is expounded, in the *Philebus*, even as part of a discussion of the Delphian saying. (Cp. note 26 to chapter 7.)

(*d*) Apart from these three flagrant contradictions, I may mention two further contradictions which could easily be neglected by those who do not believe that the *Seventh Letter* is genuine, but which seem to me fatal to Burnet who maintains that the *Seventh Letter* is authentic. Burnet's view (untenable even if we neglect this letter ; cp. for the whole question note 26 (5) to chapter 3) that Socrates *but not Plato* held the theory of Forms, is contradicted in 342a, ff., of this letter ; and his view that the *Republic*, more especially, is Socratic, in 326a (cp. note 14 to chapter 7). Of course, all these difficulties could be removed, but only by interpretation.

(*e*) There are a number of similar although at the same time more subtle and more important contradictions which have been discussed at some length in previous chapters, especially in chapters 6, 7 and 8. I may sum up the most important of these.

(e_1) The attitude towards men, especially towards the young, changes in Plato's portrait in a way which cannot be Socrates' development. Socrates died for the right to talk freely to the young, whom he loved. But in the *Republic*, we find him taking up an attitude of condescension and distrust which resembles the disgruntled attitude of the Athenian Stranger (admittedly Plato himself) in the *Laws* and the general distrust of mankind expressed so often in this work. (Cp. text to notes 17–18 to chapter 4 ; 18–21 to chapter 7 ; and 57–58 to chapter 8.)

(e_2) The same sort of thing can be said about Socrates' attitude towards truth and free speech. He died for it. But in the *Republic*, ' Socrates ' advocates lying ; in the admittedly Platonic *Statesman*, a lie is offered as truth, and in the *Laws*, free thought is suppressed by the establishment of an Inquisition. (Cp. the same places as before, and furthermore notes 1–23 and 40–41 to chapter 8 ; and note 55 to the present chapter.)

(e_3) The Socrates of the *Apology* and some other dialogues is intellectually modest ; in the *Phaedo*, he changes into a man who is assured of the truth of his metaphysical speculations. In the *Republic*, he is a dogmatist, adopting an attitude not far removed from the petrified authoritarianism of the *Statesman* and of the *Laws*. (Cp. text to notes 8–14 and 26 to chapter 7 ; 15 and 33 to chapter 8 ; and (*c*) in the present note.)

(e_4) The Socrates of the *Apology* is an individualist ; he believes in the self-sufficiency of the human individual. In the *Gorgias*, he is still an individualist. In the *Republic*, he is a radical collectivist, very similar to Plato's position in the *Laws*. (Cp. notes 25 and 35 to chapter 5 ; text to notes 26, 32, 36 and 48–54 to chapter 6 and note 45 to the present chapter.)

(e_5) Again we can say similar things about Socrates' equalitarianism. In the *Meno*, he recognizes that a slave participates in the general intelligence of all human beings, and that he can be taught even pure mathematics ; in the *Gorgias*, he defends the equalitarian theory of justice. But in the *Republic*, he despises workers and slaves and is as much opposed to equalitarianism as is Plato in the *Timaeus* and in the *Laws*. (Cp. the passages mentioned under (e_4) ; furthermore, notes 18 and 29 to chapter 4 ; note 10 to chapter 7, and note 50 (3) to chapter 8, where *Timaeus*, 51e, is quoted.)

(e_6) The Socrates of the *Apology* and *Crito* is loyal to Athenian democracy. In the *Meno* and in the *Gorgias* (cp. note 45 to this chapter) there are suggestions

of a *hostile* criticism ; in the *Republic* (and, I believe, in the *Menexenus*), he is
an open enemy of democracy ; and although Plato expresses himself more
cautiously in the *Statesman* and in the beginning of the *Laws*, his political
tendencies in the later part of the *Laws* are admittedly (cp. text to note 32 to
chapter 6) identical with those of the ' Socrates ' of the *Republic*. (Cp. notes
53 and 55 to the present chapter and notes 7 and 14–18 to chapter 4.)

The last point may be further supported by the following. It seems that
Socrates, in the *Apology*, is not merely loyal to Athenian democracy, but that
he appeals directly to the democratic party by pointing out that Chaerephon,
one of the most ardent of his disciples, belonged to their ranks. Chaerephon
plays a decisive part in the *Apology*, since by approaching the Oracle, he is
instrumental in Socrates' recognition of his mission in life, and thereby ultimately in Socrates' refusal to compromise with the Demos. Socrates introduces this important person by emphasizing the fact (*Apol.*, 20e/21a) that
Chaerephon was not only his friend, but also a friend of the people, whose
exile he shared, and with whom he returned (presumably, he participated
in the fight against the Thirty) ; that is to say, Socrates chooses as the main
witness for his defence an ardent democrat. (There is some independent
evidence for Chaerephon's sympathies, such as in Aristophanes' *Clouds*, 104,
501 ff. Chaerephon's appearance in the *Charmides* may be intended to create
a kind of balance ; the prominence of Critias and Charmides would otherwise
create the impression of a pro-Thirty manifesto.) Why does Socrates emphasize
his intimacy with a militant member of the democratic party ? We cannot
assume that this was merely special pleading, intended to move his judges
to be more merciful : the whole spirit of his apology is against this assumption.
The most likely hypothesis is that Socrates, by pointing out that he had
disciples in the democratic camp, intended to deny, by implication, the
charge (which also was only implied) that he was a follower of the aristocratic
party and a teacher of tyrants. The spirit of the *Apology* excludes the
assumption that Socrates was pleading friendship with a democratic leader
without being truly sympathetic with the democratic cause. And the same
conclusion must be drawn from the passage (*Apol.*, 32b–d) in which he
emphasizes his faith in democratic legality, and denounces the Thirty in no
uncertain terms.

(6) It is simply the internal evidence of the Platonic dialogues which
forces us to assume that they are not entirely historical. We must therefore
attempt to interpret this evidence, by proffering theories which can be critically
compared with the evidence, using the method of trial and error. Now we
have very strong reason to believe that the *Apology* is in the main historical,
for it is the only dialogue which describes a public occurrence of considerable
importance and well known to a great number of people. On the other hand,
we know that the *Laws* are Plato's latest work (apart from the doubtful
Epinomis), and that they are frankly ' Platonic '. It is, therefore, the simplest
assumption that the dialogues will be historical or Socratic so far as they
agree with the tendencies of the *Apology*, and Platonic where they contradict
these tendencies. (This assumption brings us practically back to the position
which I have described above as the ' older solution ' of the Socratic Problem.)

If we consider the tendencies mentioned above under (e_1) to (e_6), we
find that we can easily order the most important of the dialogues in such a
way that for any single one of these tendencies the similarity with the Socratic
Apology decreases and that with the Platonic *Laws* increases. This is the series.

Apology and *Crito—Meno—Gorgias—Phaedo—Republic—Statesman—Timaeus
—Laws*.

Now the fact that this series orders the dialogues according to *all* the
tendencies (e_1) to (e_6) is in itself a corroboration of the theory that we are
here faced with a development in Plato's thought. But we can get quite

independent evidence. 'Stylometric' investigations show that our series agrees with the chronological order in which Plato wrote the dialogues. Lastly, the series, at least up to the *Timaeus*, exhibits also a continually increasing interest in Pythagoreanism (and Eleaticism). This must therefore be another tendency in the development of Plato's thought.

A very different argument is this. We know, from Plato's own testimony in the *Phaedo*, that Antisthenes was one of Socrates' most intimate friends ; and we also know that Antisthenes claimed to preserve the true Socratic creed. It is hard to believe that Antisthenes would have been a friend of the Socrates of the *Republic*. Thus we must find a common point of departure for the teaching of Antisthenes and Plato ; and this common point we find in the Socrates of the *Apology* and *Crito*, and in *some* of the doctrines put into the mouth of the 'Socrates' of the *Meno*, *Gorgias*, and *Phaedo*.

These arguments are entirely independent of any work of Plato's which has ever been seriously doubted (as the *Alcibiades I* or the *Theages* or the *Letters*). They are also independent of the testimony of Xenophon. They are based solely upon the internal evidence of some of the most famous Platonic dialogues. But they agree with this secondary evidence, especially with the *Seventh Letter*, where in a sketch of his own mental development (325 f.), Plato even refers, unmistakably, to the key-passage of the *Republic* as *his own central discovery* : 'I had to state . . that . . never will the race of men be saved from its plight before either the race of the genuine and true philosophers gains political power, or the ruling men in the cities become genuine philosophers, by the grace of God.' (326a ; cp. note 14 to chapter 7, and (*d*) in this note, above.) I cannot see how it is possible to accept, with Burnet, this letter as genuine without admitting that the central doctrine of the *Republic* is Plato's, not Socrates' ; that is to say, without giving up the fiction that Plato's portrait of Socrates in the *Republic* is historical. (For further evidence, cp. for instance Aristotle, *Sophist. El.*, 183b7 : 'Socrates raised questions, but gave no answers ; for he confessed that he did not know.' This agrees with the *Apology*, but hardly with the *Gorgias*, and certainly not with the *Phaedo* or the *Republic*. See furthermore Aristotle's famous report on the history of the theory of Ideas, admirably discussed by Field, *op. cit.* ; cp. also note 26 to chapter 3.)

(7) Against evidence of this character, the type of evidence used by Burnet and Taylor can have little weight. The following is an example. As evidence for his opinion that Plato was politically more moderate than Socrates, and that Plato's family was rather 'Whiggish', Burnet uses the argument that a member of Plato's family was named 'Demos'. (Cp. *Gorg.*, 481d, 513b.—It is not, however, certain, although probable, that Demos' father Pyrilampes here mentioned is really identical with Plato's uncle and stepfather mentioned in *Charm.*, 158a, and *Parm.*, 126b, i.e. that Demos was a relation of Plato's.) What weight can this have, I ask, compared with the historical record of Plato's two tyrant uncles ; with the extant political fragments of Critias (which remain in the family even if Burnet is right, which he hardly is, in attributing them to his grandfather ; cp. *Greek Phil.*, I, 338, note 1, with *Charmides*, 157e and 162d, where the poetical gifts of Critias the tyrant are alluded to) ; with the fact that Critias' father had belonged to the Oligarchy of the Four Hundred (*Lys.*, 12, 66) ; and with Plato's own writings which combine family pride with not only anti-democratic but even anti-Athenian tendencies? (Cp. the eulogy, in *Timaeus*, 20a, of an enemy of Athens like Hermocrates of Sicily, father-in-law of the older Dionysius.) The purpose behind Burnet's argument is, of course, to strengthen the theory that the *Republic* is Socratic. Another example of bad method may be taken from Taylor, who argues (*Socrates*, note 2 on p. 148 f. ; cp. also p. 162) in favour of the view that the *Phaedo* is Socratic (cp. my note 9 to chapter 7) :

' In the *Phaedo* [72e] . . the doctrine that " learning is just recognition " is expressly said by Simmias ' (this is a slip of Taylor's pen ; the speaker is Cebes) ' speaking to Socrates, to be " the doctrine *you* are so constantly repeating ". Unless we are willing to regard the *Phaedo* as a gigantic and unpardonable mystification, this seems to me proof that the theory really belongs to Socrates.' (For a similar argument, see Burnet's edition of the *Phaedo*, p. xii, end of chapter ii.) On this I wish to make the following comments : (*a*) It is here *assumed* that Plato considered himself a *historian* when writing this passage, for otherwise his statement would not be ' a gigantic and unpardonable mystification ' ; in other words, the most questionable and the most central point of the theory is assumed. (*b*) But even if Plato had considered himself a historian (I do not think that he did), the expression ' a gigantic . . etc.' seems to be too strong. Taylor, not Plato, puts ' you ' in italics. Plato might only have wished to indicate that he is going to assume that the readers of the dialogue are acquainted with this theory. Or he might have intended to refer to the *Meno*, and thus to himself. (This last explanation is I think almost certainly true, in view of *Phaedo*, 73a, f., with the allusion to diagrams.) Or his pen might have slipped, for some reason or other. Such things are bound to occur, even to historians. Burnet, for example, has to explain Socrates' Pythagoreanism ; to do this he makes Parmenides a Pythogorean rather than a pupil of Xenophanes, of whom he writes (*Greek Philosophy*, I, 64) : ' the story that he founded the Eleatic school seems to be derived from a playful remark of Plato's which would also prove Homer to have been a Heraclitean.' To this, Burnet adds the footnote : ' Plato, *Soph.*, 242d. See *E. Gr. Ph.*², p. 140'. Now I believe that this statement of a historian clearly implies four things, (1) that the passage of Plato which refers to Xenophanes is playful, i.e. not meant seriously, (2) that this playfulness manifests itself in the reference to Homer, that is, (3) by remarking that he was a Heraclitean, which would, of course, be a very playful remark since Homer lived long before Heraclitus, and (4) that there is no other serious evidence connecting Xenophanes with the Eleatic School. But none of these four implications can be upheld. For we find, (1) that the passage in the *Sophist* (242d) which refers to Xenophanes is not playful, but that it is recommended by Burnet himself, in the methodological appendix to his *Early Greek Philosophy*, as important and as full of valuable historical information ; (2) that it contains no reference at all to Homer ; and (3) that another passage which contains this reference (*Theaet.*, 179d/e ; cp. 152d/e, 160d) with which Burnet mistakenly identified *Sophist*, 242d, in *Greek Philosophy*, I (the mistake is not made in his *Early Greek Philosophy* ²), does not refer to Xenophanes ; nor does it call Homer a Heraclitean, but it says the opposite, namely, that some of Heraclitus' ideas are as old as Homer (which is, of course, much less playful) ; and (4), there is a clear and important passage in Theophrastus (*Phys. op.*, fragm. 8 = Simplicius, *Phys.*, 28, 4) ascribing to Xenophanes a number of opinions which we know Parmenides shared with him and linking him with Parmenides—to say nothing of D.L. ix, 21–3, or of Timaeus ap. Clement *Strom* 1, 64, 2. This heap of misunderstandings, misinterpretations, misquotations, and misleading omissions (for the created myth, see Kirk and Raven, p. 265) can be found in one single historical remark of a truly great historian such as Burnet. From this we must learn that such things do happen, even to the best of historians : all men are fallible. (A more serious example of this kind of fallibility is the one discussed in note 26 (5) to chapter 3.)

(8) The chronological order of those Platonic dialogues which play a rôle in these arguments is here assumed to be nearly the same as that of the stylometric list of Lutoslawski (*The Origin and Growth of Plato's Logic*, 1897). A list of those dialogues which play a rôle in the text of this book will be found in note 5 to chapter 3. It is drawn up in such a way that there is more uncertainty of date within each group than between the groups. A minor

deviation from the stylométric list is the position of the *Euthyphro* which for reasons of its content (discussed in text to note 60 to this chapter) appears to me to be probably later than the *Crito* ; but this point is of little importance. (Cp. also note 47 to this chapter.)

[57] There is a famous and rather puzzling passage in the *Second Letter* (314c) : ' There is no writing of Plato nor will there ever be. What goes by his name really belongs to Socrates turned young and handsome.' The most likely solution of this puzzle is that the passage, if not the whole letter, is spurious. (Cp. Field, *Plato and His Contemporaries*, 200 f., where he gives an admirable summary of the reasons for suspecting the letter, and especially the passages ' 312d–313c and possibly down to 314c ' ; concerning 314c, an additional reason is, perhaps, that the forger might have intended to allude to, or to give his interpretation of, a somewhat similar remark in the *Seventh Letter*, 341b/c, quoted in note 32 to chapter 8.)   But if for a moment we assume with Burnet (*Greek Philosophy*, I, 212) that the passage is genuine, then the remark ' turned young and handsome ' certainly raises a problem, especially as it cannot be taken literally since Socrates is presented in all the Platonic dialogues as old and ugly (the only exception is the *Parmenides*, where he is hardly handsome, although still young).   If genuine, the puzzling remark would mean that Plato quite intentionally gave an idealized and not an historical account of Socrates ; and it would fit our interpretation quite well to see that Plato was indeed conscious of re-interpreting Socrates as a young and handsome aristocrat who is, of course, Plato himself.   (Cp. also note 11 (2) to chapter 4, note 20 (1) to chapter 6, and note 50 (3) to chapter 8.)

[58] I am quoting from the first paragraph of Davies' and Vaughan's introduction to their translation of the *Republic*. Cp. Crossman, *Plato To-Day*, 96.

[59] (1) The ' division ' or ' split ' in Plato's soul is one of the most outstanding impressions of his work, and especially of the *Republic*. Only a man who had to struggle hard to uphold his self-control or the rule of his reason over his animal instincts could emphasize this point as much as Plato did ; cp. the passages referred to in note 34 to chapter 5, especially the story of the beast in man (*Rep.*, 588c), which is probably of Orphic origin, and in notes 15 (1)–(4), 17, and 19 to chapter 3, which not only show an astonishing similarity with psycho-analytical doctrines, but might also be claimed to exhibit strong symptoms of repression.   (See also the beginning of Book IX, 571d and 575a, which sound like an exposition of the doctrine of the Oedipus Complex. On Plato's attitude to his mother, some light is perhaps thrown by *Republic*, 548e–549d, especially in view of the fact that in 548e his brother Glaucon is identified with the son in question.) * An excellent statement of the conflicts in Plato, and an attempt at a psychological analysis of his will to power, are made by H. Kelsen in *The American Imago*, vol. 3, 1942, pp. 1–110, and Werner Fite, *The Platonic Legend*, 1939.*

Those Platonists who are not prepared to admit that from Plato's longing and clamouring for unity and harmony and unisonity, we may conclude that he was himself disunited and disharmonious, may be reminded that this way of arguing was invented by Plato. (Cp. *Symposium*, 200a, f., where Socrates argues that it is a necessary and not a probable inference that he who loves or desires does not possess what he loves and desires.)

What I have called Plato's *political theory of the soul* (see also text to note 32 to chapter 5), i.e. the division of the soul according to the class-divided society, has long remained the basis of most psychologies. It is the basis of psychoanalysis too.   According to Freud's theory, what Plato had called the ruling part of the soul tries to uphold its tyranny by a ' censorship ', while the rebellious proletarian animal-instincts, which correspond to the social underworld, really exercise a hidden dictatorship ; for they determine the policy of the apparent ruler.—Since Heraclitus' ' flux ' and ' war ', the realm of social experience has strongly influenced the theories, metaphors, and symbols by which we interpret the physical world around us (and ourselves) to ourselves. I mention only Darwin's adoption, under the influence of Malthus, of the theory of social competition.

(2) A remark may be added here on *mysticism*, in its relation to the closed and open society, and to the strain of civilization.

As McTaggart has shown, in his excellent study *Mysticism* (see his *Philosophical Studies*, edited by S. V. Keeling, 1934, esp. pp. 47 ff.), the fundamental ideas of mysticism are two : (a) the doctrine of the *mystic union*, i.e. the assertion that there is a greater unity in the world of realities than that which we recognize in the world of ordinary experience, and (b) the doctrine of the *mystic intuition*, i.e. the assertion that there is a way of knowing which ' brings the known into closer and more direct relation with what is known ' than is the relation between the knowing subject and the known object in ordinary experience. McTaggart rightly asserts (p. 48) that ' of these two characteristics the mystic unity is the more fundamental ', since the mystic intuition is ' an example of the mystic unity '. We may add that a third characteristic, less fundamental still, is (c) the *mystic love*, which is an example of mystic unity *and* mystic intuition.

Now it is interesting (and this has not been seen by McTaggart) that in the history of Greek Philosophy, the doctrine of the mystic unity was first clearly asserted by Parmenides in his holistic doctrine of the one (cp. note 41 to the present chapter) ; next by Plato, who added an elaborate doctrine of mystic intuition and communion with the divine (cp. chapter 8), of which doctrine there are just the very first beginnings in Parmenides ; next by Aristotle, e.g. in *De Anima*, 425b30 f. : ' The actual hearing and the actual sound are merged into one ' ; cp. *Rep.* 507c, ff., 430a20, and 431a1 : ' Actual knowledge is identical with its object ' (see also *De Anima*, 404b16, and *Metaphysics*, 1072b20 and 1075a2, and cp. Plato's *Timaeus*, 45b–c, 47a–d ; *Meno*, 81a, ff. ; *Phaedo*, 79d) ; and next by the Neo-Platonists, who elaborated the doctrine of the mystic love, of which only the beginning can be found in Plato (for example, in his doctrine, *Rep.*, 475 ff., that the philosophere *loves* truth, which is closely connected with the doctrines of holism and the philosopher's communion with the divine truth).

In view of these facts and of our historical analysis, we are led to interpret mysticism as one of the typical reactions to the breakdown of the closed society ; a reaction which, *in its origin*, was directed against the open society, and which may be described as an escape into the dream of a paradise in which the tribal unity reveals itself as the unchanging reality.

This interpretation is in direct conflict with that of Bergson in his *Two Sources of Morality and Religion* ; for Bergson asserts that it is mysticism which makes the leap from the closed to the open society.

* But it must of course be admitted (as Jacob Viner very kindly pointed out to me in a letter) that mysticism is versatile enough to work in any political direction ; and even among the apostles of the open society, mystics and mysticism have their representatives. It is the mystic inspiration of a better, a less divided, world which undoubtedly inspired not only Plato, but also Socrates.*

It may be remarked that in the nineteenth century, especially in Hegel and Bergson, we find an *evolutionary mysticism*, which, by extolling change, seems to stand in direct opposition to Parmenides' and Plato's hatred of change. And yet, the underlying experience of these two forms of mysticism seems to be the same, as shown by the fact, that an over-emphasis on change is common to both. Both are reactions to the frightening experience of social change : the one combined with the hope that change may be arrested; the other with a somewhat hysterical (and undoubtedly ambivalent) acceptance of change as real, essential and welcome.—Cp. also notes 32–33 to chapter 11, 36 to chapter 12, and 4, 6, 29, 32 and 58 to chapter 24.

[60] The *Euthyphro*, an early dialogue, is usually interpreted as an unsuccessful attempt of Socrates to define piety. Euthyphro himself is the caricature of a popular 'pietist' who knows exactly what the gods wish. To Socrates' question ' What is piety and what is impiety ? ' he is made to answer : ' Piety is acting as I do ! That is to say, prosecuting any one guilty of murder, sacrilege, or of any similar crime, whether he be your father or your mother . . ; while not to prosecute them is impiety' (5, d/e). Euthyphro is presented as prosecuting his father for having murdered a serf. (According to the evidence quoted by Grote, *Plato*, I, note to p. 312, every citizen was bound by Attic law to prosecute in such cases.)

[61] *Menexenus*, 235b. Cp. note 35 to this chapter, and the end of note 19 to chapter 6.

[62] The claim that if you want security you must give up liberty has become a mainstay of the revolt against freedom. But nothing is less true. There is, of course, no absolute security in life. But what security can be attained depends on our own watchfulness, enforced by institutions to help us watch— i.e. by *democratic institutions* which are devised (using Platonic language) to enable the herd to watch, and to judge, their watch-dogs.

[63] With the 'variations' and 'irregularities', cp. *Republic*, 547a, quoted in the text to notes 39 and 40 to chapter 5. Plato's obsession with the problems of propagation and birth control may perhaps be explained in part by the fact that he understood the implications of population growth. Indeed (cp. text to note 7 to this chapter) the ' Fall ', the loss of the tribal paradise, is caused by a ' natural ' or ' original ' fault of man, as it were : by a maladjustment in his natural rate of breeding. Cp. also notes 39 (3) to ch. 5, and 34 to ch. 4. With the next quotation further below in this paragraph, cp. *Republic*, 566e, and text to note 20 to chapter 4.—Crossman, whose treatment of the period of tyranny in Greek history is excellent (cp. *Plato To-Day*, 27–30), writes : ' Thus it was the tyrants' who really created the Greek *State*. They broke down the old tribal organization of primitive aristocracy . .' (*op. cit.*, 29). This explains why Plato hated tyranny, perhaps even more than freedom : cp. *Republic*, 577c.—(See, however, note 69 to this chapter.) His passages on tyranny, especially 565–568, are a brilliant sociological analysis of a consistent power-politics. I should like to call it the first attempt towards a *logic of power*. (I chose this term in analogy to F. A. von Hayek's use of the term *logic of choice* for the pure economic theory.)—The logic of power is fairly simple, and has often been applied in a masterly way. The opposite kind of politics is much more difficult ; partly because the logic of anti-power politics, i.e. the *logic of freedom*, is hardly understood yet.

[64] It is well known that most of Plato's political proposals, including the proposed communism of women and children, were ' in the air ' in the Periclean period. Cp. the excellent summary in Adam's edition of the *Republic*, vol. I, p. 354 f., * and A. D. Winspear, *The Genesis of Plato's Thought*, 1940.*

[65] Cp. V. Pareto, *Treatise on General Sociology*, §1843 (English translation : *The Mind and Society*, 1935, vol. III, pp. 1281) ; cp. note 1 to chapter 13, where the passage is quoted more fully.

[66] Cp. the effect which Glaucon's presentation of Lycophron's theory had on Carneades (cp. note 54 to chapter 6), and later, on Hobbes. The professed ' a-morality ' of so many Marxists is also a case in point. Leftists frequently believe in their own immorality. (This, although not much to the point, is sometimes more modest and more pleasant than the dogmatic self-righteousness of many reactionary moralists.)

[67] *Money* is one of the symbols as well as one of the difficulties of the open

society.   There is no doubt that we have not yet mastered the rational control of its use ; its greatest misuse is that it can buy political power.   (The most direct form of this misuse is the institution of the slave-market ; but just this institution is defended in *Republic*, 563b ; cp. note 17 to chapter 4 ; and in the *Laws*, Plato is not opposed to the political influence of wealth ; cp. note 20 (1) to chapter 6.)   From the point of view of an individualistic society, money is fairly important.   It is part of the institution of the (partially) *free market*, which gives the consumer some measure of control over production. Without some such institution, the producer may control the market to such a degree that he ceases to produce for the sake of consumption, while the consumer consumes largely for the sake of production.—The sometimes glaring misuse of money has made us rather sensitive, and Plato's opposition between money and friendship is only the first of many conscious or unconscious attempts to utilize these sentiments for the purpose of political propaganda.

⁶⁸ The group-spirit of tribalism is, of course, not entirely lost.   It manifests itself, for instance, in the most valuable experiences of *friendship and comradeship* ; also, in youthful tribalistic movements like the boy-scouts (or the German Youth Movement), and in certain clubs and adult societies, as described, for instance, by Sinclair Lewis in *Babbitt*.   The importance of this perhaps most universal of all emotional and æsthetic experiences must not be underrated. Nearly all social movements, totalitarian as well as humanitarian, are influenced by it.   It plays an important rôle in war, and is one of the most powerful weapons of the revolt against freedom ; admittedly also in peace, and in revolts against tyranny, but in these cases its humanitarianism is often endangered by its romantic tendencies.—A conscious and not unsuccessful attempt to revive it for the purpose of arresting society and of perpetuating a class rule seems to have been the English Public School System.   (' No one can grow up to be a good man unless his earliest years were given to noble games ' is its motto, taken from *Republic*, 558b.)

Another product and symptom of the loss of the tribalistic group-spirit is, of course, Plato's emphasis upon the analogy between politics and medicine (cp. chapter 8, especially note 4), an emphasis which expresses the feeling that the body of society is sick, i.e. the feeling of strain, of drift.   ' From the time of Plato on, the minds of political philosophers seem to have recurred to this comparison between medicine and politics,' says G. E. G. Catlin (*A Study of the Principles of Politics*, 1930, note to 458, where Thomas Aquinas, G. Santayana, and Dean Inge are quoted to support his statement ; cp. also the quotations in *op. cit.*, note to 37, from Mill's *Logic*).   Catlin also speaks most characteristically (*op. cit.*, 459) of ' harmony ' and of the ' desire for protection, whether assured by the mother or by society '.   (Cp. also note 18 to chapter 5.)

⁶⁹ Cp. chapter 7 (note 24 and text ; see *Athen.*, XI, 508) for the names of nine such disciples of Plato (including the younger Dionysius and Dio).   I suppose that Plato's repeated insistence upon the use, not only of force, but of ' *persuasion* and force ' (cp. *Laws*, 722b, and notes 5, 10, and 18 to chapter 8), was meant as a criticism of the tactics of the Thirty, whose propaganda was indeed primitive.   But this would imply that Plato was well aware of Pareto's recipe for utilizing sentiments instead of fighting them.   That Plato's friend Dio (cp. note 25 to chapter 7) ruled Syracuse as a tyrant is admitted even by Meyer in his defence of Dio whose fate he explains, in spite of his admiration for Plato as a politician, by pointing out the ' gulf between ' (the Platonic) ' theory and practice ' (*op. cit.*, V, 999).   Meyer says of Dio (*loc. cit.*), ' The ideal king had become, externally, indistinguishable from the contemptible tyrant.'   But he believes that, internally as it were, Dio remained an idealist, and that he suffered deeply when political necessity forced murder (especially that of his ally Heraclides) and similar measures upon him.   I think, however,

that Dio acted according to Plato's theory ; a theory which, by the logic of power, drove Plato in the *Laws* to admit even the goodness of tyranny (709e, ff. ; at the same place, there may also be a suggestion that the débâcle of the Thirty was due to their great number : Critias alone would have been all right).

⁷⁰ The tribal paradise is, of course, a myth (although some primitive people, most of all the Eskimos, seem to be happy enough). There may have been no sense of drift in the closed society, but there is ample evidence of other forms of fear—fear of demoniac powers behind nature. The attempt to revive this fear, and to use it against the intellectuals, the scientists, etc., characterizes many late manifestations of the revolt against freedom. It is to the credit of Plato, the disciple of Socrates, that it never occurred to him to present his enemies as the offspring of the sinister demons of darkness. In this point, he remained enlightened. He had little inclination to idealize the evil which was to him simply debased, or degenerate, or impoverished goodness. (Only in one passage in the *Laws*, 896e and 898c, there is what may be a suggestion of an abstract idealization of the evil.)

⁷¹ A final note may be added here in connection with my remark on *the return to the beasts*. Since the intrusion of Darwinism into the field of human problems (an intrusion for which Darwin should not be blamed) there have been many ' social zoologists ' who have proved that the human race is bound to degenerate physically, because insufficient physical competition, and the possibility of protecting the body by the efforts of the mind, prevent natural selection from acting upon our bodies. The first to formulate this idea (not that he believed in it) was Samuel Butler, who wrote : ' The one serious danger which this writer ' (an Erewhonian writer) ' apprehended was that the machines ' (and, we may add, civilization in general) ' would so . . lessen the severity of competition, that many persons of inferior physique would escape detection and transmit their inferiority to their descendants.' (*Erewhon*, 1872 ; cp. Everyman's edition, p. 161.) The first as far as I know to write a bulky volume on this theme was W. Schallmayer (cp. note 65 to chapter 12), one of the founders of modern racialism. In fact, Butler's theory has been continually rediscovered (especially by ' biological naturalists ' in the sense of chapter 5, above). According to some modern writers (see, for example, G. H. Estabrooks, *Man : The Mechanical Misfit*, 1941), man made the decisive mistake when he became civilized, and especially when he began to help the weak ; before this, he was an almost perfect man-beast ; but civilization, with its artificial methods of protecting the weak, lead to degeneration, and therefore must ultimately destroy itself. In reply to such arguments, we should, I think, first admit that man is likely to disappear one day from this world ; but we should add that this is also true of even the most perfect beasts, to say nothing of those which are only ' almost perfect '. The theory that the human race might live a little longer if it had not made the fatal mistake of helping the weak is most questionable ; but even if it were true —is mere length of survival of the race really all we want ? Or is the almost perfect man-beast so eminently valuable that we should prefer a prolongation of his existence (he did exist for quite a long time, anyway) to our experiment of helping the weak ?

Mankind, I believe, has not done so badly. In spite of the treason oɪ some of its intellectual leaders, in spite of the stupefying effects of Platonic methods in education and the devastating results of propaganda, there have been some surprising successes. Many weak men have been helped, and for nearly a hundred years slavery has been practically abolished. Some say it will soon be re-introduced. I feel more optimistic ; and, after all, it will depend on ourselves. But even if all this should be lost again, and even if we had to return to the almost perfect man-beast, this would not alter the fact that once upon a time (even if the time was short), slavery did disappear from the face of the earth.   This achievement and its memory may, I believe, compensate some of us for all our misfits, mechanical or otherwise ; and it may even compensate some of us for the fatal mistake made by our forefathers when they missed the golden opportunity of arresting all change—of returning to the cage of the closed society and establishing, for ever and ever, a perfect zoo of almost perfect monkeys.

ADDENDA

I

PLATO AND GEOMETRY (1957)

In the second edition of this book, I made a lengthy addition to note 9 to chapter 6 (pp. 248 to 253). The historical hypothesis propounded in this note was later amplified in my paper ' The Nature of Philosophical Problems and Their Roots in Science ' (*British Journal for the Philosophy of Science*, **3**, 1952, pp. 124 ff. ; now also in my *Conjectures and Refutations*). It may be restated as follows : (1) the discovery of the irrationality of the square root of two which led to the breakdown of the Pythagorean programme of reducing geometry and cosmology (and presumably all knowledge) to arithmetic, produced a crisis in Greek mathematics ; (2) Euclid's *Elements* are not a textbook of geometry, but rather the final attempt of the Platonic School to resolve this crisis by reconstructing the whole of mathematics and cosmology *on a geometrical basis*, in order to deal with the problem of irrationality systematically rather than *ad hoc*, thus inverting the Pythagorean programme of arithmetization ; (3) it was Plato who first conceived the programme later carried out by Euclid : it was Plato who first recognized the need for a reconstruction ; who chose geometry as the new basis, and the geometrical method of proportion as the new method ; who drew up the programme for a *geometrization of mathematics*, including arithmetic, astronomy, and cosmology ; and who became the founder of the geometrical picture of the world, and thereby also the founder of modern science—of the science of Copernicus, Galileo, Kepler, and Newton.

I suggested that the famous inscription over the door of Plato's Academy (p. 248, (2), above) alluded to this programme of geometrization. (That it was intended to announce an *inversion of the Pythagorean programme* seems likely in view of Archytas, fragment A, Diels-Kranz.)

In the middle of the last paragraph on p. 249 I suggested ' that Plato was *one of the first to develop a specifically geometrical method* aiming at rescuing what could be rescued . . . from the breakdown of Pythagoreanism ' ; and I described this suggestion as ' a highly uncertain historical hypothesis '. I no longer think that the hypothesis is so very uncertain. On the contrary, I now feel that a re-reading of Plato, Aristotle, Euclid, and Proclus, in the light of this hypothesis, would produce as much corroborating evidence as one could expect. In addition to the confirming evidence referred to in the paragraph quoted, I now wish to add that already the *Gorgias* (451a/b ; c ; 453e) takes the discussion of ' odd ' and ' even ' as characteristic of arithmetic, thereby clearly identifying arithmetic with Pythagorean number theory, while characterizing the geometer as the man who adopts the method of proportions (465b/c). Moreover, in the passage from the *Gorgias* (508a) Plato speaks not only of geometrical equality (cp. note 48 to chapter 8) but he also states implicitly the principle which he was later to develop fully in the *Timaeus* : that the cosmic order is a *geometrical order*. Incidentally, the *Gorgias* also proves that the word ' *alogos* ' was not associated in Plato's mind with irrational numbers, since 465a says that even a technique, or art, must not be *alogos* ; which would hold *a fortiori* for a science such as geometry. I think we may simply translate ' *alogos* ' as ' alogical '. (Cp. also *Gorgias* 496a/b ; and 522e.) The point is important for the interpretation of the title of Democritus's lost book, mentioned earlier on p. 249.

My paper on ' The Nature of Philosophical Problems ' (see above) contains some further suggestions concerning Plato's *geometrization of arithmetic* and of cosmology in general (his inversion of the Pythagorean programme), and his theory of forms.

Added in 1961

Since this *addendum* was first published in 1957, in the third edition of this book, I have found, almost by accident, some interesting corroboration of the historical hypothesis formulated above, in the first paragraph under (2). It is a passage in Proclus' commentaries to the First Book of Euclid's Elements (ed. Friedlein, 1873, Prologus ii, p. 71, 2-5) from which it becomes clear that there existed a tradition according to which Euclid's elements were a Platonic cosmology, a treatment of the problems of the *Timaeus*.

THE DATING OF THE THEAETETUS (1961)

There is a hint in note 50, (6), to chapter 8, p. 281, that ' the *Theaetetus* is perhaps (as against the usual assumption) earlier than the *Republic* '. This suggestion was made to me by the late Dr. Robert Eisler in a conversation not long before his death in 1949. But since he did not tell me any more about his conjecture than that it was partly based on *Theaetetus* 174e, f.—the crucial passage whose post-*Republican* dating did not seem to me to fit into my theory—I felt that there was not sufficient evidence for it, and that it was too *ad hoc* to justify me in publicly saddling Eisler with the responsibility for it.

However, I have since found quite a number of independent arguments in favour of an earlier dating of the *Theaetetus*, and I therefore wish now to acknowledge Eisler's original suggestion.

Since Eva Sachs (cp. *Socrates*, **5**, 1917, 531 f.) established that the proem of the *Theaetetus*, as we know it, was written after 369, the conjecture of a Socratic core and an early dating involves another—that of an earlier lost edition, revised by Plato after Theaetetus' death. The latter conjecture was proposed independently by various scholars, even before the discovery of a papyrus (ed. by Diels, *Berlin*, *Klassikerhefte*, **2**, 1905) that contains part of a *Commentary to the Theaetetus* and refers to two distinct editions. The following arguments seem to support both conjectures.

(1) Certain passages in Aristotle seem to allude to the *Theaetetus* : they fit the text of the *Theaetetus* perfectly, and they claim, at the same time, that the ideas there expressed belong to Socrates rather than to Plato. The passages I have in mind are the ascription to Socrates of the invention of *induction* (*Metaphysics* 1078b17–33 ; cp. 987b1 and 1086b3) which, I think, is an allusion to Socrates' *maieutic* (developed at length in the *Theaetetus*), his method of helping the pupil to perceive the true essence of a thing through purging his mind of his false prejudices ; and the further ascription to Socrates of the attitude so strongly expressed again and again in the *Theaetetus* : ' Socrates used to ask questions and not to answer them ; for he used to confess that he did not know ' (*Soph. El.* 183b7). (These passages are discussed, in a different context, in my lecture *On the Sources of Knowledge and of Ignorance, Proceedings of the British Academy*, **46**, 1960

(see especially p. 50) which is also separately published by Oxford University Press and is now included in my *Conjectures and Refutations*.)

(2) The *Theaetetus* has a surprisingly inconclusive ending, even though it turns out that it was so planned and prepared almost from the beginning. (In fact, as an attempt to solve the problem of knowledge which it ostensibly tries to do, this beautiful dialogue is a complete failure.) But endings of a similarly inconclusive nature are known to be characteristic of a number of early dialogues.

(3) ' Know thyself ' is interpreted, as in the *Apology*, as ' Know how little you know '. In his final speech Socrates says ' After this, *Theaetetus* . . . you will be less harsh and gentler to your associates, for you will have the wisdom not to think that you know what you do not know. So much my art [of *maieutic*] can accomplish ; nor do I know any of the things that are known by others . . .'

(4) That ours is a second edition, revised by Plato, seems likely, especially in view of the fact that the Introduction to the dialogue (142a to the end of 143c) which might well have been added as a memorial to a great man, actually contradicts a passage which may have survived the revision of the earlier edition of this dialogue ; I mean its very end which, like a number of other early dialogues, alludes to Socrates' trial as imminent. The contradiction consists in the fact that Euclid, who appears as a character in the Introduction and who narrates how the dialogue came to be written down, tells us (142c/d, 143a) that he went repeatedly to Athens (from Megara, presumably), using every time the opportunity of checking his notes with Socrates, and making ' *corrections* ' here and there. This is told in a way which makes it quite clear that the dialogue itself must have taken place *at least* several months before Socrates' trial and death ; but this is inconsistent with the ending of the dialogue. (I have not seen any reference to this point, but I cannot imagine that it has not been discussed by some Platonist.) It may even be that the reference to ' corrections ', in 143a, and also the much discussed description of the ' new style ' in 143b–c (see for example C. Ritter's *Plato*, vol. I, 1910, pp. 220 f.) were introduced in order to explain some deviations of the revised edition from the original edition. (This would make it possible to place the *revised* edition even after the *Sophist*.)

REPLY TO A CRITIC (1961)

I have been asked to say something in reply to the critics of this volume. But before doing so, I should like to thank again those whose criticism has helped me to improve the book in various ways.

Of the others—those I have come across—I feel reluctant to say much. In attacking Plato I have, as I now realize, offended and hurt many Platonists, and I am sorry for this. Still, I have been surprised by the violence of some of the reactions.

I think most of the defenders of Plato have denied facts which, it seems to me, cannot be seriously denied. This is true even of the best of them : Professor Ronald B. Levinson in his monumental book (645 closely printed pages) *In Defense of Plato*.

In trying to answer Professor Levinson I have before me two tasks of very unequal importance. The less important task—defending myself against a number of accusations—will be tackled first (in section A), so that the more important task—replying to Professor Levinson's defence of Plato (in section B)—will not be too much obscured by my personal defence.

A

The portrait of myself painted by Professor Levinson has caused me to doubt the truth of my own portrait of Plato ; for if it is possible to derive from a living author's book so distorted an image of his doctrines and intentions, what hope can there be of producing anything like a true portrait of an author born almost twenty-four centuries ago ?

Yet how can I defend myself against being identified with the supposed original of the portrait painted by Professor Levinson ? All I can do is to show that some at least of the mistranslations, misrepresentations, and distortions of Plato with which Professor Levinson charges me are really non-existent. And even this I can only do by analysing two or three representative samples, taken at random from hundreds : there seem to be more such charges in the book than there are pages. Thus all I can do is to prove that some at least of the most violent accusations levelled against me are baseless.

I should have liked to do this without raising any counter-accusation of misquotation, etc. ; but as this has turned out to be impossible, I wish to make it quite clear that I now see that Professor Levinson, like other Platonists, must have found my book not only exasperating, but almost sacrilegious. And since I am that man by whom the offence cometh, I must not complain if I am bitterly denounced.

So let us examine a few of the relevant passages.

Professor Levinson writes (p. 273, note 72) of me : ' As with others of whom he disapproves, so here with Critias, Popper has further blackened his character by exaggeration. For the verses cited represent religion, though a fabrication, as being aimed at the general good of society, not at the selfish benefit of the cunning fabricator himself.'

Now if this means anything, it must mean that I have asserted, or at least hinted, in the passages quoted by Professor Levinson (that is, pp. 179 and 140 of A, which corresponds to pp. 183–184, and pp. 142–143 of E [1]) that Critias' verses which I have quoted represent religion not only as a fabrication, but as a fabrication ' aimed . . . at the selfish benefit of the cunning fabricator himself '.

I deny that I either asserted, or even hinted at, anything of the kind. On the contrary, my concern has been to point out that the ' general good of society ' is one of the dominant preoccupations of Plato, and that his attitude in this respect ' is practically identical with that of Critias '. The basis of my criticism is clearly announced at the beginning of chapter 8 (second paragraph) where I write : ' " For the benefit of the city ", says Plato. Again we find that the appeal to the principle of collective utility is the ultimate ethical consideration.'

What I assert is that this moral principle which posits ' the general good of society ' as a moral aim, is not good enough as a basis of ethics ; for example, that it leads to lying—' for the general good of society ' or ' for the benefit of the city '. In other words, I try to show that ethical collectivism is mischievous, and that it corrupts. But I nowhere interpret Critias' quoted verses in the sense alleged by Professor Levinson. I should be inclined to ask ' Who blackens whose character by exaggeration ? ', were it not for the fact that I recognize that the severity of my attack was a provocation which excuses Professor Levinson's charges. But it does not make them true.

---

[1] ' A ' stands in this *Addendum* for the American editions of 1950 and 1956 ; ' E ' for the present edition and for the English editions from 1952 on.

A second example is this. Professor Levinson writes (pp. 354 f.) : 'One of Popper's most extravagant assertions is that Plato had viewed as a " favourable circumstance " the presence in Athens of Spartan troops, summoned to assist the Thirty in maintaining themselves and their iniquitous regime and had felt no other emotion than approval at the thought of Athens beneath the Spartan yoke ; he would have been prepared, we are led to suppose, to summon them again, if their presence could aid him in achieving his neo-oligarchical revolution. There is no text which Popper can cite in support of such a charge ; it arises solely from his picture of Plato as a third head upon the double-headed monster he has created, called " the Old Oligarch and Critias " ; it is guilt by association, the very ultimate example of the witch-hunt technique.'

To this my reply is : if this is one of my ' most extravagant assertions ', then I cannot have made any extravagant assertions. For this assertion was never made by me ; nor does it fit into the picture which I have of Plato, and which I have tried—not wholly successfully, it seems—to convey.

I do believe that Plato was led, by his distrust of the common man, and by his ethical collectivism, to approve of violence ; but I simply never have made any assertion about Plato even faintly similar to the one which Professor Levinson here asserts, somewhat extravagantly, that I have made. There is therefore no text which Professor Levinson can cite in support of his charge that I have made this assertion : it arises solely from his picture of Popper as a third head upon the double-headed monster of Otto Neurath and J. A. Lauwerys which Professor Levinson has created ; and as to ' guilt by association ', I can only refer to Professor Levinson's p. 441. There he is ' helped towards answering this question '—the question of ' the predisposing cause that leads Popper chronically to indulge these sinister imaginings ' —by associating me with ' an older compatriot of Popper's, the late versatile Austrian philosopher and sociologist, Otto Neurath '. (In fact neither Neurath nor I had any sympathy for the other's philosophy, as emerges only too clearly from Neurath's and my own writings ; Neurath, for example, defended Hegel, and attacked both Kantianism and my own praise of Kant. Of Neurath's attack on Plato I heard for the first time when I read about it in Professor Levinson's book ; and I have not yet seen Neurath's relevant papers.)

But to return to my alleged ' extravagant assertion ' : what I actually said (p. 195E = 190A) about Plato's feelings is almost the opposite of what Professor Levinson (p. 354) reports. I did not at all suggest that Plato viewed as a ' favourable circumstance ' the presence in Athens of Spartan troops, or that he ' felt no other emotion than approval at the thought of Athens beneath the Spartan yoke '. What I tried to convey, and what I said, was that the Thirty Tyrants had failed ' in spite of favourable circumstances in the shape of powerful support from victorious Sparta ' ; and I suggested that Plato saw the cause of their failure —just as I do—in the moral failure of the Thirty. I wrote : ' Plato felt that a complete reconstruction of the programme was needed. The Thirty had been beaten in the realm of power politics largely because they had offended the citizens' sense of justice. The defeat had been largely a moral defeat.'

This is all I say here of Plato's feelings. (I say twice ' Plato felt '.) I suggest that the failure of the Thirty induced a partial moral conversion in Plato—though not a sufficiently far-reaching one. There is no suggestion here of those feelings which Professor Levinson makes me attribute to Plato ; and I would never have dreamt that anybody could read this into my text.

I certainly do attribute to Plato a measure of sympathy with the Thirty Tyrants and especially with their pro-Spartan aims. But this is of course something completely different from the ' extravagant assertions ' which Professor Levinson attributes to me. I can only say that I did suggest that he admired his uncle Critias, the leader of the Thirty. I did suggest that he was in sympathy with some of Critias' aims and views. But I also said that he considered the oligarchy of the Thirty as a moral failure, and that this led him to reconstruct his collectivist morality.

It will be seen that my answer to two of Professor Levinson's charges has taken up almost as much space as the charges themselves. This is unavoidable ; and I must therefore confine myself to only two further examples (out of hundreds), both connected with my alleged mistranslations of Plato's text.

The first is Professor Levinson's allegation that I worsen, or exaggerate, Plato's text. ' Popper, however, as before, employs the unfavourable word " deport " in his translation, in place of " send out ",' writes Professor Levinson on p. 349, note 244. But this is simply a mistake—Professor Levinson's mistake. If he looks at the passage again, he will find that I employ the word ' deport ' where his translation—or rather Fowler's—uses ' banish '. (The part of the passage in which Fowler's translation uses ' send out ' simply does not occur in my quotation but is replaced by dots.)

As a consequence of this mistake, it turns out that, in this context, Professor Levinson's remark ' as before ' is highly appropriate. For before the passage just discussed he writes of me (p. 348, note 243) : ' Popper reënforces his interpretation [p. 166E = p. 162A] of the Platonic passage [*Rep.* 540e/541a] by slight inaccuracies in the translation, tending to give the impression of greater scorn or violence in Plato's attitude. Thus he translates " send away " (*apopempō*) as " expel and deport " . . .' Now first of all, there is another of Professor Levinson's slips here (which makes two in two consecutive footnotes) ; for Plato does *not* use here the word ' *apopempō* ', but the word ' *ekpempō* '. This certainly does not make much difference ; yet ' *ekpempō* ' has, at any rate, the ' *ex* ' of ' *expel* ' ; and one of its dictionary meanings is ' to drive away ' and another ' to send away in disgrace ' (or ' to send away with the collateral notion of disgrace ' as my edition of Liddell and Scott has it). The word is a somewhat stronger form of ' *pempō* '—' to send off ', ' to dispatch '—which, if used in connection with Hades (' to send to Hades ') ' commonly means to send a living man to Hades, i.e. to kill him '. (I am quoting Liddell and Scott. Nowadays some people might even ' commonly ' say ' to dispatch him '. Closely related is the meaning intended when Phaedrus tells us in Plato's *Symposium* 179e—a passage referred to by Professor Levinson on p. 348—that the gods, redeeming and honouring Achilles for his valour and his love of Patroclus, ' sent him to the Islands of the Blessed '—while Homer sent him to Hades.) It seems obvious that neither of the translations ' expel ' or ' deport ' is open to criticism here on scholarly grounds. Yet Professor Levinson is open to criticism when he quotes me as writing ' expel and deport ' for I do not use the words in this way. (He would have been at least technically correct had he quoted me ' must be expelled . . . and deported ' : the three dots make some difference here, for to write ' expel and deport ' *could* be an attempt to exaggerate, by way of ' re-enforcing ' the one expression with the other. Thus this slight inaccuracy tends to re-enforce my alleged misdeed— my alleged re-enforcing of my interpretation of this Platonic passage by slight inaccuracies in my translation.)

But anyhow, this case amounts to nothing. For take the passage in Shorey's translation. (Shorey is, rightly, accepted as an authority by Professor Levinson.) ' All inhabitants above the

age of ten ', Shorey translates, ' they [the ' philosophers ' who
have become ' masters of the state '] will send out into the fields,
and they will take over the children, remove them from the
manners and habits of their parents, and bring them up in their
own customs and laws which will be such as we have described.'
Now does this not say exactly what I said (though perhaps not
quite as clearly as I did on my p. 166E = 162A) ? For who can
believe that the ' sending out ' of ' all the inhabitants above the
age of ten ' can be anything but a violent expulsion and deporta-
tion ? Would they just meekly go, leaving their children behind,
when ' sent out ', if they were not threatened, and compelled, by
the ' philosophers' who have become ' masters of the state ' ?
(Professor Levinson's suggestion, p. 349, that they are sent to
' their . . . country estates, outside the city proper ' is supported
by him, ironically enough, with a reference to the *Symposium* 179e
and the ' Islands of the Blessed ', the place to which Achilles was
sent by the gods—or more precisely by Apollo's or Paris's arrow.
Gorgias, 526c, would have been a more appropriate reference.)

In all this, there is an important principle involved. I mean
the principle that *there is no such thing as a literal translation* ; that all
translations are interpretations ; and that we always have to take
the context into account, and even parallel passages.

That the passages with which (on p. 166E = p. 162A) I have
associated the one just quoted may indeed be so associated is
confirmed by Shorey's own footnotes : he refers, especially, to the
passage which I have called the ' canvas-cleaning ' passage, and
to the ' kill-and-banish ' passage from the *Statesman*, 293c–e.
' Whether they happen to rule by law or without law, over willing
or unwilling subjects ; . . . and whether they purge the state for
its good, by killing or by deporting [or, as Professor Levinson
translates with Fowler, ' by killing or banishing ' ; see above]
some of its citizens . . . this form of government must be declared to be the only one that is right.' (See my text, p. 166E
= p. 162A.)

Professor Levinson quotes (p. 349) part of this passage more
fully than I do. *Yet he omits to quote that part which I quoted as its
commencement*, ' Whether they happen to rule by law or without
law, over willing or unwilling subjects '. The point is interesting,
because it fits Professor Levinson's attempt to make the kill-and-
banish passage appear in an almost innocent light. Immediately
after quoting the passage, Professor Levinson writes : ' Fair interpretation of this stated principle [I do not see any ' principle '

here stated, unless it is that all is permitted if it is done *for the benefit of the state*] requires at least a brief indication of the general pattern of the dialogue.' In the course of this ' brief indication ' of Plato's aims and tendencies, we hear—without a direct quotation from Plato—that ' Other traditional and currently accepted criteria, such as whether rule be exercised . . . *over willing or unwilling subjects, or in accord or not in accord with law*, are rejected as irrelevant or non-essential '. The words from Professor Levinson's passage which I have here italicized will be seen to be a near-quotation of the commencement (not quoted by Professor Levinson) of my own quotation from Plato's kill-and-banish passage. Yet this commencement appears now in a very harmless light : no longer are the rulers told to kill and banish ' *with or without law* ', as I indicated ; and Professor Levinson's readers get the impression that this question is here merely dismissed as a side issue —as ' *irrelevant* ' to the problem in hand

But Plato's readers, and even the parti.cipants in his dialogue, get a different impression. Even the ' Younger Socrates ', who intervened just before (after the commencement of the passage as quoted by me) with the one exclamation ' Excellent ! ' is shocked by the lawlessness of the proposed killing ; for immediately after the enunciation of the kill-and-banish principle (perhaps it really is a ' principle ', after all) he says, in Fowler's translation (the italics are of course mine) : ' Everything else that you have said seems reasonable ; but that government [and such hard measures, too, it is implied] *should be carried out without laws* is a hard saying.'

I think that this remark proves that the commencement of my quotation—' by law or *without law* '—is really meant by Plato to be part of his kill-and-banish principle ; that I was right in commencing the quotation where I did ; and that Professor Levinson is simply mistaken when he suggests that ' with or without law ' is here merely intended to mean that this is a question which is here ' rejected as irrelevant ' to the essence of the problem in hand.

In interpreting the kill-and-banish passage, Professor Levinson is clearly deeply disturbed ; yet at the end of his elaborate attempt to defend Plato by comparing his practices with our own he arrives at the following view of the passage : ' Looked at in this context, Plato's statesman, with his apparent readiness to kill, banish, and enslave, where we should prescribe either the penitentiary, at one end, or psychiatric social service, at the other, loses much of his sanguinary coloration.'

Now I do not doubt that Professor Levinson is a genuine humanitarian—a democrat and a liberal. But is it not perturbing to see that a genuine humanitarian, in his eagerness to defend Plato, can be led to compare in this fashion our admittedly very faulty penal practices and our no less faulty social services with the avowedly *lawless* killing and banishing (and enslaving) of citizens by the ' true statesman '—a good and wise man—' for the benefit of the city ' ? Is this not a frightening example of the spell which Plato casts over many of his readers, and of the danger of Platonism ?

There is too much of this—all mixed with accusations against a largely imaginary Popper—for me to deal with. But I wish to say that I regard Professor Levinson's book not only as a very sincere attempt to defend Plato, but also as an attempt to see Plato in a new light. And though I have found only one passage —and quite an unimportant one—which has led me to think that, *in this place*, I interpreted Plato's text (though not his meaning) somewhat too freely, I do not wish to create the impression that Professor Levinson's is not a very good and interesting book— especially if we forget all about the scores of places where ' Popper ' is quoted, or (as I have shown) slightly misquoted, and very often radically misunderstood.

But more important than these personal questions is the question : how far does Professor Levinson's defence of Plato succeed ?

B

I have learnt that when faced with a new attack on my book by a defender of Plato it is best to disregard the smaller points and to look for answers to the following five cardinal points.

(1) How is my assertion met that the *Republic* and the *Laws* condemn the Socrates of the *Apology* (as pointed out in chapter 10, second paragraph of section vi) ? As explained in a note (note 55 to chapter 10) the assertion was in effect made by Grote, and supported by Taylor. If it is fair—and I think it is—then it supports also my assertion mentioned in my next point, (2).

(2) How is my assertion met that Plato's anti-liberal and anti-humanitarian attitude cannot possibly be explained by the alleged fact that better ideas were not known to him, or that he was, for those days, *comparatively* liberal and humanitarian ?

(3) How is my assertion met that Plato (for example in the

canvas-cleaning passage of the *Republic* and in the kill-and-banish passage of the *Statesman*) encouraged his rulers to use ruthless violence ' for the benefit of the state ' ?

(4) How is my assertion met that Plato established for his philosopher kings the duty and privilege of using lies and deceit for the benefit of the city, especially in connection with racial breeding, and that he was one of the founding fathers of racialism ?

(5) What is said in answer to my quotation of the passage from the *Laws* used as a motto for *The Spell of Plato* on p. 7 (and, as announced at the beginning of the Notes on p. 203, ' discussed in some detail in notes 33 and 34 to chapter 6 ') ?

I often tell my students that what I say about Plato is—necessarily—merely an interpretation, and that I should not be surprised if Plato (should I ever meet his shade) were to tell me, and to establish to my satisfaction, that it is a misrepresentation ; but I usually add that he would have quite a task to explain away a number of the things he had said.

Has Professor Levinson succeeded on Plato's behalf in this task, regarding any of the five points mentioned above ?

I really do not think he has.

(1') As to the first point, I ask anybody in doubt to read carefully the text of the last speech made by the Athenian Stranger in book X of the *Laws* (907d down to, say, 909d). The legislation there discussed is concerned with the type of crime of which Socrates was accused. My contention is that, while Socrates had a way out (most critics think, in view of the evidence of the *Apology*, that he would probably have escaped death had he been willing to accept banishment), Plato's *Laws* do not make any such provision. I shall quote from a passage in Bury's translation (which seems to be acceptable to Levinson) of this very long speech. After classifying his ' criminals ' (that is, those guilty of ' impiety ' or ' the disease of atheism ' : the translation is Bury's ; *cp.* 908c), the Athenian Stranger discusses first ' those who, though they utterly disbelieve the existence of gods, possess by nature a just character . . and . . . are incapable of being induced to commit unjust actions '. (908b-c ; this is almost a portrait—of course an unconscious one—of Socrates, apart from the important fact that he does not seem to have been an atheist, though accused of impiety and unorthodoxy.) About these Plato says :

' . . . those criminals . . . being devoid of evil disposition and character, shall be placed by the judge according to law in the reformatory for a period of not less than five years, during which time no other of the citizens shall hold intercourse with them save only those who take part in the nocturnal assembly, and they shall company with them [I should translate ' they shall attend to them '] to minister to their soul's salvation by admonition . . .' Thus the ' good ' among the impious men get a minimum of five years of solitary confinement, only relieved by ' attention ' to their sick souls from the members of the Nocturnal Council. ' . . . and when the period of their incarceration has expired, if any of them seems to be reformed, he shall dwell with those who are reformed, but if not, and if he be convicted again on a like charge, he shall be punished by death.'

I have nothing to add to this.

(2′) The second point is perhaps the most important from Professor Levinson's point of view : it is one of his main claims that I am mistaken in my assertion that there were humanitarians— better ones than Plato—among those whom I have called the ' Great Generation '.

He asserts, in particular, that my picture of Socrates as a man very different from Plato in this respect is quite fictitious.

Now I have devoted a very long footnote (note 56 to chapter 10), in fact quite an essay, to this problem—the *Socratic Problem* ; and I do not see any reason to change my views on it. But I wish to say here that I have received support in this historical conjecture of mine about the *Socratic Problem*, from a Platonic scholar of the eminence of Richard Robinson ; support which is the more significant as Robinson castigates me severely (and perhaps justly) for the tone of my attack on Plato. Nobody who reads his review of my book (*Philosophical Review*, **60,** 1951) can accuse him of undue partiality for me ; and Professor Levinson quotes him approvingly (p. 20) for speaking of my ' rage to blame ' Plato. But although Professor Levinson (in a footnote on p. 20) refers to Richard Robinson as ' mingling praise and blame in his extensive review of the *Open Society* ', and although (in another footnote, on p. 61) he rightly refers to Robinson as an authority about ' the growth of Plato's logic from its Socratic beginnings through its middle period', Professor Levinson never tells his readers that Robinson agrees not only with my main accusations against Plato, but also, more especially, with my conjectural solution of the *Socratic Problem*. (Incidentally, Robinson also agrees that my quotation mentioned here in point (5) is correct ; see below.)

Since Robinson, as we have heard, ' mingles praise and

blame ', some of his readers (anxious to find confirmation for their ' rage to blame ' me) may have overlooked the praise contained in the surprising last sentence of the following forceful passage from his review (p. 494) :

'Dr. Popper holds that Plato perverted the teaching of Socrates . . . To him Plato is a very harmful force in politics but Socrates a very beneficial one. Socrates died for the right to talk freely to the young ; but in the *Republic* Plato makes him take up an attitude of condescension and distrust towards them. Socrates died for truth and free speech ; but in the *Republic* " Socrates " advocates lying. Socrates was intellectually modest ; but in the *Republic* he is a dogmatist. Socrates was an individualist ; but in the *Republic* he is a radical collectivist. And so on.

' What is Dr. Popper's evidence for the views of the real Socrates ? It is drawn exclusively from Plato himself, from the early dialogues, and primarily from the *Apology*. Thus the angel of light with whom he contrasts the demon Plato is known to us only from the demon's own account ! Is this absurd ?

' It is not absurd, in my opinion, but entirely correct.'

This passage shows that at least one scholar, admitted by Professor Levinson to be an authority on Plato, has found that my view on the *Socratic Problem* is not absurd.

But even if my conjectural solution of the *Socratic Problem* should be mistaken, there is plenty of evidence left for the existence of humanitarian tendencies in this period.

Concerning the speech of Hippias, to be found in Plato's *Protagoras*, 337e (see above p. 70 ; Professor Levinson seems for once not to object to my translation ; see his p. 144), Professor Levinson writes (p. 147) : ' We must begin by assuming that Plato is here reflecting faithfully a well-known sentiment of Hippias.' So far Professor Levinson and I agree. But we disagree completely about the relevance of Hippias' speech. On this I have now even stronger views than those I expressed in the text of this volume. (Incidentally, I don't think I ever asserted that there was evidence that Hippias was an opponent of slavery ; what I said of him was that ' this spirit was bound up with the Athenian movement against slavery ' ; thus Professor Levinson's elaborate argument that I am not justified ' in including him [Hippias] among the opponents of slavery ' is pointless.)

I now see Hippias' speech as a manifesto—the first perhaps—of a humanitarian faith which inspired the ideas of the Enlightenment and the French Revolution : that all men are brothers, and that it is conventional, man-made, law and custom which divide them and which are the source of much avoidable unhappiness ; so that it is not impossible for men to make things better by a change in the laws—by legal reform. These ideas also inspired Kant. And Schiller speaks of conventional law as ' the fashion ' which sternly (' *streng* ')—Beethoven says ' insolently ' (' *frech* ')— divides mankind.

As to slavery, my main contention is that the *Republic* contains evidence of the existence of tendencies in Athens which may be described as opposition to slavery. Thus the ' Socrates ' of the *Republic* (563b) says, in a speech satirizing Athenian democracy (I quoted it in chapter 4, ii, p. 43E = p. 44A ; but I am here using Shorey's translation) : ' And the climax of popular liberty . . . is attained in such a city when the purchased slaves, male and female, are no less free than the owners who paid for them.'

Shorey has a number of cross-references to this passage (see footnote below) ; but the passage speaks for itself. Levinson says of this passage elsewhere (p. 176) : ' Let us contribute the just-quoted passage to help fill the modest inventory of Plato's social sins ', and on the next page he refers to it when he speaks of ' Another instance of Platonic *hauteur* '. But this is no answer to my contention that, taken together with a second passage from the *Republic* quoted in my text (p. 43E = p. 44A), this first passage supplies evidence of an anti-slavery movement. The second passage (which follows in Plato immediately after an elaboration of the first, here quoted at the end of the preceding paragraph) reads in Shorey's translation (*Republic* 563d ; the previous passage was *Republic* 563b) : ' And do you know that the sum total of all these items . . . is that they render the souls of the citizens so sensitive that they chafe at the slightest suggestion of servitude [I translated ' slavery '] and will not endure it ? '

How does Professor Levinson deal with this evidence ? First, by separating the two passages : the first he does not discuss until p. 176, long after he has smashed to bits (on p. 153) my alleged evidence concerning an anti-slavery movement. The second he dismisses on p. 153 as a grotesque mistranslation of mine ; for he writes there : ' Yet it is all a mistake ; though Plato uses the word *douleia* (slavery or servitude), it bears *only a figurative allusion* [my italics] to slavery in the usual sense.'

This may sound plausible when the passage is divorced from its immediate predecessor (only mentioned by Professor Levinson more than twenty pages later, where he explains it by Plato's *hauteur*) ; but in its context—in connection with Plato's complaint about the licentious behaviour of slaves (and even of animals)—there can be no doubt whatever that, in addition to the meaning which Professor Levinson correctly ascribes to the passage, the passage also bears a second meaning which takes ' *douleia* ' quite literally ; for it says, and it means, that the free democratic citizens cannot stand slavery in any form—not only do they not submit themselves to any suggestion of servitude (not even to laws, as Plato goes on to say), but they have become so tender-hearted that they cannot bear ' even the slightest suggestion of servitude '—such as the slavery of ' purchased slaves, male or female '.

Professor Levinson (p. 153, after discussing Plato's second passage) asks : ' in the light of the evidence . . . what, then, can fairly be said to remain standing in Popper's case . . . ? The simplest answer is " Nothing," if words are taken in anything like their literal sense.' Yet his own case rests upon taking ' *douleia* ', in a context which clearly refers to slavery, not in its literal sense but as ' only a figurative allusion ', as he himself has put it a few lines earlier.[1]

And yet, he says of the grotesque ' mistake ' I made in translating ' *douleia* ' literally : ' This misreading has borne fruit in the

---

[1] Added in 1965. That the word ' *douleia* ' in the passage in question (*Republic* 563d) bears this literal meaning (*in addition* to the figurative meaning which Professor Levinson correctly attributes to it) is confirmed by Shorey, the great Platonist and open enemy of democracy, whom Professor Levinson considers an authority on Plato's text. (I can often agree with Shorey's interpretation of Plato because he rarely tries to humanize or liberalize Plato's text.) For in a footnote which Shorey attaches to the word ' servitude ' (*douleia*) in his translation of *Republic* 563d, he refers to two parallel passages : *Gorgias* 491e, and *Laws* 890a. The first of these reads in W. R. M. Lamb's translation (Loeb Edition) : ' For how can a man be happy if he is a slave to anybody at all ? ' Here the phrase ' to be a slave ' has, like the one in the *Republic*, not only the figurative meaning ' to submit oneself' but also the literal meaning ; indeed, the whole point is the merging of the two meanings. The passage from the *Laws* 890a (an elaborate attack on certain Sophists of the Great Generation) reads in Bury's translation (Loeb Edition) as follows : ' these teachers [who corrupt the young men] attract them towards the life . . . " according to nature " which consists in being master over the rest, in reality [*alētheia*], instead of being a slave to others, according to legal convention.' Plato clearly alludes here among others to those Sophists (p. 70E = p. 70A and note 13 to chapter 5) who taught that men cannot be slaves ' by nature ' or ' in truth ', but only ' by legal convention ' (by legal fiction). Thus Shorey connects the crucial passage of the *Republic* by this reference at least indirectly to the great classical discussion of the *theory of slavery* (' slavery ' in the literal sense).

preface to Sherwood Anderson's play *Barefoot in Athens* . . .
where the unsuspecting playwright, following Popper ' (Professor
Levinson asserts on p. 24 that ' the Andersonian version of Plato
plainly bespeaks a close and docile reading of Popper ', but he
gives no evidence for this strange accusation) ' passes on to his
readers in turn the allusion, and declares flatly . . . as on Plato's
own authority, that the Athenians . . . " advocate[d] the manu-
mission of all slaves " . . .'

Now this remark of Maxwell (*not* Sherwood) Anderson's may
well be an exaggeration.   But where have I said anything similar
to this ?   And what is the worth of a case if, in its defence, the
defender has to exaggerate the views of his opponent, or blacken
them by associating them with the (alleged) guilt of some ' docile '
reader ?   (See also the Index to this volume, under 'Slavery'.)

(3′) My contention that Plato encouraged his rulers to use
ruthless and lawless violence, though it is combatted by Professor
Levinson, is nowhere really denied by him, as will be seen from his
discussion of the   kill-and-banish ' passage of the *Statesman* mentioned in this *Addendum* towards the end of section A.   All he
denies is that a number of other passages in the *Republic*—the
canvas-cleaning passages—are similar, as both Shorey and I
think.   Apart from this, he tries to derive comfort and moral
support from some of our modern violent practices—a comfort
which, I fear, will be diminished if he re-reads the passage of the
Statesman together with its commencement, quoted by me, but
first omitted by Professor Levinson, and later dismissed as
irrelevant.

(4′) As to Plato's racialism, and his injunction to his rulers to
use lies and deceit for the benefit of the state, I wish to remind my
readers, before entering into any discussion with Professor Levinson, of Kant's saying (see p. 139E = p. 137A) that though ' *truthfulness is the best policy* ' might be questionable, ' *truthfulness is better
than policy* ' is beyond dispute.

Professor Levinson writes (p. 434, referring to my pp. 138 ff. E
= pp. 136 ff. A, and especially to pp. 150E = pp. 148A) very fairly :
' First of all, we must agree that the use of lies in certain circumstances is *advocated* [my italics] in the *Republic* for purposes of
government . . .' This, after all, is my main point.   No
attempt to play it down or to diminish its significance—and no
counter-attack on my alleged exaggerations—should be allowed
to obscure this admission.

Professor Levinson also admits, in the same place, that ' there can be no doubt that some use of the persuasive art of speech would be required to make the auxiliaries " blame chance and not the rulers " when they are told [see my p. 150E = p. 148A] that the fall of the lot has determined their marriages, whereas really these are engineered by the rulers for eugenic reasons '.

This was my second main point.

Professor Levinson continues (pp. 434 f. ; my italics) : ' In this instance we have the only sanctioning by Plato of an outright practical lie,[1] to be told, to be sure, for benevolent reasons (and only for such purposes does Plato sanction the telling), but a lie and nothing more. We, like Popper, find this policy distasteful. This lie, then, *and any others like it* which Plato's *rather general permission* might justify, constitute such basis as exists for Popper's charge that Plato proposes to use " lying propaganda " in his city.'

Is this not enough ? Let us assume that I was wrong in my other points (which, of course, I deny), does not all this at least excuse my suspicion that Plato would not have scrupled to make some further use of his ' rather general permission ' of ' the the use of lies '—especially in view of the fact that he actually ' *advocated* ' the ' use of lies ' as Professor Levinson has it ?

Moreover, the lying is here used in connection with ' eugenics ', or more precisely, with *the breeding of the master race*— the race of the guardians.

In defending Plato against my accusation that he was a racialist Professor Levinson tries to compare him favourably with some ' notorious ' modern totalitarian racialists whose names I have tried to keep out of my book. (And I shall continue to do so.) He says of these (p. 541 ; my italics) that their ' breeding schedule ' ' was primarily intended to *preserve the purity of the master race*, an aim which we have been at some pains to show Plato did not share.'

Did he not ? Was my quotation from one of the main eugenic discussions of the *Republic* (460c) perhaps a mistranslation? I wrote (pp. 51E = p. 52A) ; I am here introducing new italics) :

' " *The race of the guardians must be kept pure* ", says Plato (in defence of infanticide) when developing the racialist argument

---

[1] It is by no means the only instance, as may be seen from my chapter 8. The passage quoted in the text to note 2, for example (*Rep.*, 389b), is a different instance from the passage (*Rep.*, 460a) which Professor Levinson has in mind. There are several other passages. See *Rep.*, 415d and especially *Tim.*, 18e, which prove that Plato finds his instruction to lie of sufficient importance to be included in the very brief summary of the *Republic*. (See also *Laws*, 663d down to 664b.)

that we breed animals with great care while neglecting our own race, an argument which has been repeated ever since.'

Is my translation wrong ? Or my assertion that this has been, ever since Plato, the main argument of racialists and breeders of the master race ? Or are the guardians not the masters of Plato's best city ?

As to my translation, Shorey puts it a little differently ; I shall quote from his translation (the italics are mine) also the preceding sentence (referring to infanticide) : '. . . the offspring of the inferior, and any of those of the other sort who are born defective, they [the rulers] will properly dispose of in secret, so that no one will know what has become of them. " That is the condition," he said, " *of preserving the purity of the guardian's breed.*" '

It will be seen that Shorey's last sentence is slightly weaker than mine. But the difference is trifling, and does not affect my thesis. And at any rate, I stick to my translation. ' At all events the breed of the guardians must be preserved pure ' or ' If at all events [as we agree] the purity of the breed of the guardians must be preserved ' would be a translation which, using some of Shorey's words, brings out precisely the same meaning as my translation in the body of the book (pp. 51E = p. 52A) and here repeated.

I cannot see, therefore, what the difference is between Professor Levinson's formulation of that ' notorious . . . breeding schedule ' of the totalitarians, and Plato's formulation of his own breeding aims. Whatever minor difference there may be is irrelevant to the central question.

As to the problem whether Plato allowed—very exceptionally —a mingling of his races (which would be the consequence of promoting a member of the lower race), opinions may differ. I still believe that what I said is true. But I cannot see that it would make any difference if exceptions were permitted. (Even those modern totalitarians to whom Professor Levinson alludes permitted exceptions.)

(5') I have been repeatedly and severely attacked for quoting —or rather misquoting—a passage from the *Laws* which I have taken as one of the two mottos of *The Spell of Plato* (the other and contrasting passage is from Pericles' funeral oration). These mottos were printed by my American publishers on the jacket of the American edition ; the English editions have no such advertisement. As is usual with jackets, I was not consulted by the publishers about them. (But I certainly have no objection to my

American publishers' choice : why should they not print my mottos—or anything else I wrote in the book—on their jackets ?)

My translation and interpretation of this passage has been pronounced to be correct by Richard Robinson, as mentioned above ; but others went so far as to ask me whether I had not consciously tried to hide its identity, in order to make it impossible for my readers to check the text ! And this although I have taken more trouble, I think, than most authors to make it possible for my readers to check any passage quoted or referred to. Thus I have a reference to my mottos at the beginning of my notes— although it is somewhat unusual to make references to one's mottos.

The main accusation against me for using this passage is that I do not say, or do not emphasize sufficiently, that it refers to military matters. But here I have testimony in my favour from Professor Levinson himself who writes (p. 531, footnote ; my italics) :

' Popper, in citing this passage in his text, p. 102 [= p. 103E] *duly emphasizes* its reference to military matters.'

Thus this charge is answered. However, Professor Levinson continues : ' . . . but [Popper] protests simultaneously that Plato means the same " militarist principles " to be adhered to in peace as well as in war, and that they are to be applied to every area of peaceful existence rather than simply to the program of military training. He then quotes the passage with perverse mistranslations which tend to obscure its military reference . . .' and so on.

Now the first charge here is that I ' protest simultaneously ' that Plato means these militarist principles to be adhered to in peace as well as in war. Indeed I have said so—quoting Plato : *it is Plato who says so.* Should I have suppressed it ? Plato says, in Bury's translation of which Professor Levinson approves (though I prefer mine : I ask my readers whether there is any difference of *meaning* between them, as distinct from one of clarity ; see p. 103E = p. 102A) : ' . . . nor should anyone, whether at work or in play, grow habituated in mind to acting alone and on his own initiative, but he should *live always* both in war *and peace*, with his eyes fixed constantly on his commander . . .' (*Laws*, Loeb Library, vol. ii, p. 477 ; my italics).

And later (p. 479) :

' This task of ruling, and of being ruled by, others must be practised *in peace* from earliest childhood . . .'

As to mistranslation, I can only say that there is practically no difference between my translation and Bury's—except that I have broken up Plato's two very long sentences which, as they stand, are not quite easy to follow. Professor Levinson says (p. 531) that I have ' made great and illegitimate use ' of this passage ; and he continues : ' His journalistic misapplication of a selection from it on the dust cover ' [the publishers' advertisement ; see above] ' and on the title page of Part I of his book will be dissected in our note, where we also print the passage in full.'

The dissection of my ' journalistic misapplication ' in this note consists, apart from some alleged ' corrections ' of my translation which I do not accept, mainly of the same charge—that I have printed the passage on the jacket and in other important places. For Professor Levinson writes (p. 532 ; italics mine) :

' This small unfairness is entirely eclipsed, however, by what Popper has done with the passage elsewhere. On the title page of Part I of his book, and also on the dust jacket ' [who is unfair to whom ?] ' *he prints* a carefully chosen selection from it, and beside it prints, as its very antithesis, a sentence drawn from Pericles' funeral oration. . . . *This is to print in parallel a political ideal and a proposed military regulation ;* yet Popper has not only failed to apprise the reader of this selection of its military reference, but employing the same mistranslations, has deleted absolutely all those parts of the passage which would reveal the fact.'

My answer to this is very simple. (*a*) The mistranslations are non-existent. (*b*) I have tried to show at length that the passage, in spite of its military reference, formulates, like the Pericles passage (which incidentally also has some, though less, military reference), *a political ideal*—that is, Plato's political ideal.

I have seen no valid reason to change my belief that I am right in holding that this passage—like so many similar passages in the *Laws*—formulates Plato's political ideal. But whether this belief of mine is true or not, I have certainly given strong reasons for it (reasons which Professor Levinson fails to undermine). And since I have done so, and since Professor Levinson does not at all question the fact that I believe that I have done so, it constitutes neither a ' small unfairness ' nor a great one if I try to present the passage as what I believe it to be : Plato's own description of his political ideal—of his totalitarian and militaristic ideal state.

As to my mistranslations, I shall confine myself to the one which Professor Levinson finds important enough to discuss in his text (as distinct from his footnote). He writes, on p. 533 :

'A further objection concerns Popper's use of the word
" leader." Plato uses " *archōn* ", the same word he employs for
officials of the state and for military commanders ; it is clearly the
latter, or the directors of the athletic contests, whom he has here
in mind.'

Clearly, there is no case for me to asnwer. (Should I have
perhaps translated ' director ' ?) Anybody who consults a Greek
dictionary can ascertain that ' *archōn* ', in its most basic meaning,
is properly and precisely rendered by the English word ' *leader* '
(or the Latin ' *dux* ' or the Italian ' *il duce* '). The word is
described, by Liddell and Scott, as a participle of the verb ' *archō* '
whose fundamental meaning, according to these authorities, is
' to be first ', either ' in point of Time ', or ' in point of Place or
Station '. In this second sense the first meanings given are : ' *to
lead, rule, govern, command, be leader or commander* '. Accordingly we
find, under *archōn*, ' *a ruler, commander, captain* ; also, with respect
to Athens, *the chief magistrates at Athens,* nine in number.' This
should suffice to show that ' leader ' is not a mistranslation, provided it fits the text. That it does can be seen from Bury's own
version in which, it will be remembered, the passage is rendered
as follows : ' but he should live always, both in war and peace,
with his eyes fixed constantly on his *commander* and *following his
lead* '. In fact, ' *leader* ' fits the text only too well : it is the
horrifying fittingness of the word which has produced Professor
Levinson's protest. Since he is unable to see Plato as an advocate
of totalitarian leadership, he feels that it must be my ' perverse
mistranslations ' (p. 531) which are to be blamed for the horrifying
associations which this passage evokes.

But I assert that it is Plato's text, and Plato's thought, which
is horrifying. I am, as is Professor Levinson, shocked by the
' leader ', and all that this term connotes. Yet these connotations
must not be played down if we wish to understand the appalling
implications of the Platonic ideal state. These I set out to bring
home, as well as I could.

It is perfectly true that in my comments I have stressed the fact
that, although the passage refers to military expeditions, Plato
leaves no doubt that its principles are to apply to the whole life of
his soldier-citizens. It is no answer to say that a Greek citizen
was, and had to be, a soldier ; for this is true of Pericles and the
time of his funeral oration (for soldiers fallen in battle) at least as
much as of Plato and the time of his *Laws*.

This is the point which my mottos were meant to bring out as

clearly as possible.   This made it necessary to cut out one clause
from this unwieldy passage, thereby omitting (as indicated by the
insertion of dots) some of those references to military matters
which would have obscured my main point : I mean the fact that
the passage has a general application, *to war and to peace*, and that
many Platonists have misread it, and missed its point, because of
its length and obscure formulation, and because of their anxiety
to idealize Plato.   This is how the case stands.   Yet I am accused
in this context by Professor Levinson (p. 532) of using ' tactics '
which ' make it necessary to check in merciless detail every one of
Popper's citations from the Platonic text ', in order to ' reveal how
far from the path of objectivity and fairness Popper has been swept '.

Faced with these accusations and allegations, and with sus-
picions cast upon me, I can only try to defend myself.   But I am
conscious of the principle that no man ought to be judge in his
own cause.   It is for this reason that I wish here to quote what
Richard Robinson says (on p. 491 of *The Philosophical Review*, **60**)
about this Platonic passage, and about my translation of it.   It
should be remembered that Robinson is ' mingling praise with
blame ' in his review of my book, and that part of the blame
consists in the assertion that my translations of Plato are biased.
Yet he writes :

' Biased though they are, they should certainly not be dis-
regarded.   They draw attention to real and important features
of Plato's thought that are usually overlooked.   In particular,
Dr. Popper's show piece, the horrible passage from *Laws* 942
about never acting on one's own, is correctly translated.   (It
might be urged that Plato intended this to apply only to the
military life of his citizens, and it is true that the passage begins as
a prescription for army discipline ; but by the end Plato is clearly
wishing to extend it to all life ; cf. " the anarchy must be removed
from all the life of all the men " [*Laws*, 942d 1].).

I feel that I should add nothing to Robinson's statement.

To sum up.   I cannot possibly attempt to answer even a
fraction of the charges Professor Levinson has brought against me.
I have tried to answer only a few of them, bearing in mind, as well
as I could, that more important than the problem of who is unfair
to whom is the question whether or not my assertions about Plato
have been refuted.   I have tried to give reasons for my belief that
they have not been refuted.   But I repeat that no man ought to
be judge in his own cause : I must leave it to my readers to decide.

Yet I do not wish to end this long discussion without re-affirming my conviction of Plato's overwhelming intellectual achievement. My opinion that he was the greatest of all philosophers has not changed. Even his moral and political philosophy is, as an intellectual achievement, without parallel, though I find it morally repulsive, and indeed horrifying. As to his physical cosmology, I have changed my mind between the first and second edition (more precisely, between the first English edition and the first American edition) of this book ; and I have tried to give reasons why I now think that he is the founder of *the geometrical theory of the world* ; a theory whose importance has continuously increased down the ages. His literary powers I should think it presumptuous to praise. What my critics have shown is, I believe, that Plato's greatness makes it all the more important to fight his moral and political philosophy, and to warn those who may fall under his magic spell.

IV (1965)

In note 31 to Chapter 3 I mentioned a number of works which seemed to me to anticipate my views of Plato's politics. Since writing this note I have read Diana Spearman's great attack, of 1939, on appeasers and dictators, *Modern Dictatorship*. Her chapter, ' The Theory of Autocracy ', contains one of the deepest and most penetrating, and at the same time one of the briefest analyses of Plato's political theory that I have seen.

INDEX OF PLATONIC PASSAGES

Indices of Subjects and of Authors will be found at the end of each volume

This Index has been compiled upon the suggestion of Mr. Richard Robinson, made in *The Philosophical Review*, 60, 1951, p. 503. Numbers in brackets refer to Platonic passages. Numbers outside brackets refer to pages of vol. I of the present book ; those following brackets refer to pages where the passages in brackets are quoted or discussed.

INDEX OF NAMES

Crossman, R. H. S., 87, 130 f., 133, 139, 169, 216, 246 f., 267, 270, 304, 313, 315.
Cyrus, the Younger, 226, 305.

Dalziel, Margaret, x.
Damon, 229 f.
Daniel (Prophet), 272.
Darwin, Charles, 314, 317.
Davies, J. L., 247, 258, 271, 313.
Democritus, 12, 185 f., 206, 233, 276, 278 f., 294, 299, 320.
Demos, 311.
Dickens, C., 100 f., 258, 268.
Diels, H., 204, 206 f., 213, 230, 233, 235, 254, 259, 273, 279, 294, 299–301, 303, 319, 321.
Dio, 136, 154, 200, 282, 316 f.
Diogenes, the Cynic, 241, 278 f., 282.
Diogenes Laertius, 241, 279.
Dionysius (the Elder), 18, 43, 283, 297, 304, 311.
Dionysius (the Younger), 44, 136, 283, 303, 316.
Dropides, 208, 282.
Dudley, D. R., 277.
Duemmler, F., 277.
Durkheim, E., 175.

Eastman, M., 210, 284.
Eddington, A. S., 237.
Eisler, R., 204, 211, 227, 233, 242, 254, 256, 272, 282, 321.
Empedocles, 208 f., 214, 217 f.
Engels, F., 220.
England, E. B., 104, 216, 222 f., 259.
Epictetus, 279.
Estabrooks, G. H., 317.
Euclid, 249, 251, 267, 319 f., 322.
Euphacus, 268.
Eurastus, 268.
Euripides, 70, 95, 185, 236, 259, 278 f., 299.
Euthyphro, 197, 315.
Ewer, T. K., x.
Ewing, A. C., 246.

Farrington, B., 217.
Fichte, J. G., 247, 280.
Field, G. C., 88, 208, 210, 214 f., 236, 247, 260, 273, 277, 281, 307, 311, 313.
Fite, W., 217, 313.
Fowler, H., 326, 328.
Frederick II of Prussia, 276, 304.
Freud, S., 295, 313.

Friedlein, G., 320
Fritz, Kurt von, 277.

Galileo, G., 319.
Gard, Roger Martin du, 157, 164, 284.
Glaucon, 97–9, 116–18, 150 f., 166, 228, 241, 254, 258, 262 f., 272, 313, 315.
Gobineau, Count J. A., 9, 203.
Gombrich, E. H., x, 253.
Gomperz, T., 88, 187, 214, 224, 228, 236, 246, 257, 259, 276, 299, 301 f., 304 f.
Gorgias, 70, 114, 152, 185, 261, 276, 278.
Green, T. H., 260.
Grenfell, B. P., and Hunt, A. S., 229.
Grote, G., 80, 88, 204, 208, 211, 216, 226, 242, 246 f., 255, 268, 273, 275, 297, 303, 305, 315, 330.

Hastie, W., 247.
Hayek, F. A. von, x, 207 f., 285 f., 315.
Heath, T., 249, 251 f.
Hegel, F., 10, 17, 40, 107, 121, 144, 161, 203, 207, 221, 232, 238 f., 246 f., 297, 314, 325.
Hegemann, W., 298, 304.
Heraclides, 136, 316.
Heraclitus, 10–21, 24, 28, 38 f., 42, 55 f., 60, 73, 80, 83, 124, 148, 172 f., 189, 203–9, 214, 216, 232 f., 294 f., 301, 312 f.
Herder, J. G., 232, 247, 293.
Hermias, 268.
Hermocrates, 311.
Hermodorus, 13.
Herodotus, 95, 173, 185, 222, 233, 255, 294, 299.
Hesiod, 11 f., 15, 37 f., 55, 153, 188, 204, 209, 211, 218 f., 228, 235, 254, 271, 295.
Hippias, 70, 95, 233, 236, 278, 294, 333.
Hippodamus, 173, 211, 294 f.
Hobbes, T., 118, 142, 315.
Homer, 11, 204, 226, 228 f., 280, 295, 312, 327.
Hume, D., 230, 261.
Hunt, A. S., see Grenfell, B. P.
Husserl, E., 216.
Huxley, A., 121.

Inge, W. R., 316.

INDEX OF SUBJECTS

Italicized page-numbers indicate that the reference is of special importance. The letter ' t ', which stands for ' term', placed after a page number, indicates that the meaning of the term in question is discussed. The letter ' n ' stands for ' note'.

221, 227, 228, 258, 267–9, 328 f.; Socrates on, 129–30, 133 ; state control of, 103, 111, 130–1 ; totalitarian, 54, 103.

egoism, 100, 101, 104 (see also collectivism ; utilitarianism, collectivist).

Egypt, 224, 231, 275.

elections, general, 124–5 (see also paradox, of democracy ; of sovereignty).

ends and means, 161, 286–7, ch. 9, n. 6.

engineering, 68, 163 ; social, see social engineering.

Enlightenment, the, 333 f.

equalitarianism, 69, 70, 95, ch. 6(IV, 235, ch. 5, n. 6, 284, ch. 9, n. 2 ; in Greece, 46, 69, 70, 95, *186*, 236, 261, 278, 299 (see also slavery, Athenian movement for abolition of) ; Plato's standard objection to and Rousseau's reply, 256–7 ; ch. 6, n. 20 ; Kant's, 256.

equality : arithmetical and geometrical, 248, 250, 262 ; before the law, 89, 96, 254, 255.

Eros, 211, 218.

escapism, 238, 314.

essence, 29, 31 (see also definition, methodological essentialism) ; Plato, 28–30, 74, 75, 200 ; Socrates, 29–30.

ethics, morals, morality, equalitarian, humanitarian and Christian, *65*, 66, 73, *235*, ch. 5, n. 6, 257, 263 ; totalitarian collectivist and tribalist, 101–3, 107–8, 112–13, 139, 256, 258, 325, 331, 339 f. ; and æsthetics, *65*, *165*, 292 ; and politics, 113, 139, 260 ; and religion, see religion ; 'scientific', 237, ch. 5, n. 18 ; see also dualism of facts and decisions ; naturalism ; positivism ; relativism ; utilitarianism ; ends and means ; pain and pleasure.

evolutionism, 40 (cp. 314 ; see also progressivism) ; of Hegel, 314.

experiment : social, *162*, 163, 167 (see also social engineering ; social science).

explanation : causal, 211t.

faith in reason, 185.

fame and fate, Heraclitean and Hegelian philosophy of, 17t.

fire, Heraclitus' theory of, *14*, 15, 73, 206–7, ch. 2, n. 7, 212.

flux, Heraclitus' theory of, 12, *189*, *204*–7, ch. 2, n. 2, 208, 211, 214, 217, 300, 301, 314.

forms, see ideas.

freedom : limitations of, 110–11, 247, 131 (see also paradox of freedom) ; of thought and speech, Plato against, 267, 268, 270, 275 (see also state, state censorship ; education).

French Revolution, the, 17, 203, 208, 294, 334.

funeral oration of Pericles, 186, 255, ch. 6, n. 16.

futurism : æsthetic, 230.

geometrical theory of the world, 248–253, 320, 343.

geometry, Plato's, 248–53, ch. 6, n. 9, 267, 319–20 ; *vs.* arithmetic, 248.

'Glauconic edict', the, 150t, 151.

God (see monotheism) ; Antisthenes on, 276, 278 ; Plato on, 213, 276 ; will of, and historicism, 8, 24.

Golden Age, 11, 19, 21, 25, 43, 204, 209, 210, 218.

'golden rule', Kant's, 102, 256.

good, the, 237–8 ; Plato's idea of, 145–6, ch. 8(IV), 217, 274–5, ch. 8, n. 32.

Gorgias, 116.

government, 124 (see also state) ; Plato on, 222, 261.

Great Generation, the, 70, 185t–189, 194, 196, 199, 278, 299, 332.

great men, genius, 17, 231 (cp. page vii).

Great Year or Great Cycle, 19, 206t, 207, 208–19, ch. 3, n. 6, 219, 220.

Greeks, 171–2, 294, 341.

happiness : Plato on, 74, 169, 240.

harmony, 108, 197, 313.

'hauteur', Platonic, 334.

Heaven on earth, 165.

hedonism, see utilitarianism.

Hegel, influenced by Heraclitus, 17, 203.

Hegel's influence, 238, 297.

Heraclitus, 12, 189 ; cosmology, 12–13, 204–5 ; influence, 12, 203 (see also Hegel) ; natural philosophy, 14, 60, 206, ch. 2, n. 7.